Sexual Solipsism

Rae Langton here draws together her ground-breaking work on pornography and objectification, and shows how both involve a kind of solipsism, a failure to treat women as fully human. She argues that pornography is a speech act that subordinates and silences women, and that, given certain liberal principles, women have rights against it. She explores the traditional Kantian idea that there is something wrong with treating a person as a thing, and highlights an additional epistemological dimension to objectification: it is through a kind of self-fulfilling projection of beliefs about women as subordinate that women are treated as things. These controversial essays will be stimulating reading for anyone interested in feminism's dialogue with moral and political philosophy

Rae Langton is Professor of Philosophy at the Massachusetts Institute of Technology

Sexual Solipsism

Philosophical Essays on Pornography and Objectification

Rae Langton

OXFORD
UNIVERSITY PRESS

OXFORD

UNIVERSITY PRESS

Great Clarendon Street, Oxford OX2 6DP

Oxford University Press is a department of the University of Oxford.
It furthers the University's objective of excellence in research, scholarship,
and education by publishing worldwide in

Oxford New York

Auckland Cape Town Dar es Salaam Hong Kong Karachi
Kuala Lumpur Madrid Melbourne Mexico City Nairobi
New Delhi Shanghai Taipei Toronto

With offices in

Argentina Austria Brazil Chile Czech Republic France Greece
Guatemala Hungary Italy Japan Poland Portugal Singapore
South Korea Switzerland Thailand Turkey Ukraine Vietnam

Oxford is a registered trade mark of Oxford University Press
in the UK and in certain other countries

Published in the United States
by Oxford University Press Inc., New York

© Rae Langton 2009

The moral rights of the author have been asserted
Database right Oxford University Press (maker)

First published 2009

British Library Cataloguing in Publication Data
Data available

Library of Congress Cataloging in Publication Data
Data available

Typeset by Laserwords Private Limited, Chennai, India
Printed in Great Britain
on acid-free paper by
CPI Antony Rowe, Chippenham, Wiltshire

ISBN 978-0-19-924706-6 (Hbk.)
ISBN 978-0-19-955145-3 (Pbk.)

10 9 8 7 6 5 4 3 2 1

Acknowledgements

When I arrived at graduate school in Princeton, many years ago, I had no thought of working on political philosophy, or moral philosophy, or feminist philosophy. My sights were set on metaphysics, and the history of philosophy. I had come from the University of Sydney, which then had two philosophy departments, who were still at war with each other about the nature of the subject, along an old continental vs. analytic battle-line. I spent time in each, and gained the impression from both sides that feminists did not engage with analytic philosophy, and analytic philosophers did not engage with feminism. I'm grateful to each department, one for stirring an interest in existentialism, the other for helping me become a better philosopher, and sparking my enthusiasm for metaphysics and the history of philosophy. It was only at Princeton, though, that the startling thought first occurred that I might have something to discover—might even have something to say—as a feminist *and* a philosopher. It is not, perhaps, the most likely venue for such a revelation, but what made it possible at that time were four teachers, to whom I am much indebted.

Will Kymlicka, then a visitor, opened my eyes to political philosophy, and feminism's contribution to it. Michael Smith, in a seminar on philosophy of law, provided occasion for me to vent my indignation about the double-thinking of Ronald Dworkin, and helped me channel it into a more respectable form. These two encouraged me in practical ways to convey my thoughts to a wider audience, despite my initial incredulity at the prospect. Through their seminars, I was introduced to the work of Catharine MacKinnon, which shattered my relative complacency. Susan Brison, also a visitor, was actively writing about the pornography issue from a feminist perspective, and gave much-appreciated encouragement. Sally Haslanger brought tremendous energy and commitment to the challenges of living and thinking as a feminist philosopher; she continues to be an inspiration, to me and to so many others lucky enough to know her.

For the years thereafter I owe thanks to the friendly and collegial philosophical communities in Australia, first at Monash University, then at the Research School of Social Sciences at the ANU in Canberra, where the virtues of curiosity, good humour, encouragement, and incisive criticism were all routinely manifested. Special thanks are due to Michael Smith, Lloyd Humberstone, John Bigelow, Karen Green, Jeanette Kennett, and Philip Pettit. The Women in Philosophy association provided opportunities for fruitful interaction with other feminist philosophers. Among philosophers of law, I have had, at an early and formative stage, particularly helpful exchanges with Frederick Schauer, Wojciech Sadurski, and Elizabeth Gaze. For helpful conversations at the University of Delhi I want to thank Nirmalangshu Mukherji and Veena Das. For conversations that helped me think more carefully about objectification, thanks are due to colleagues at Sheffield University, especially Jennifer Saul and Leif Wenar; and, at Edinburgh University, especially Peter Kail. I'm grateful to Jennifer Hornsby and Caroline West, with whom I found so much in common that I was able to collaborate with them on two papers in this volume. I was glad of the Society for Women in Philosophy in the UK, for helping provide a community where one was not in a small minority. And I have so much to be grateful for in my new philosophical home at MIT: not only my colleagues, but also our graduate students, whose intelligence and engagement have not yet ceased to amaze me. Another treasure is the Boston area Workshop on Gender and Philosophy (which meets at MIT), where I've had the good fortune to benefit from searching comments, diverse perspectives, and warm intellectual companionship.

I have had the privilege of presenting this work at Philosophy programs too numerous to mention here, in Australia, New Zealand, the UK, Switzerland, India, Canada, and the USA, and have benefited from discussion at all of them. For enabling me to engage with an audience beyond philosophy, I want to thank the Law Schools at Columbia University, the University of Texas at Austin, the University of California at Berkeley, Victoria University B.C., the University of Sydney, the Australian National University, and the University of Melbourne; the Kennedy School at Harvard University, the Department of Social Anthropology at the University of Delhi, the Politics Departments at Oxford University, Harvard University, and Princeton University.

The intellectual influences on the papers here are evident: the groundbreaking work of Catharine MacKinnon on pornography, with its political and epistemological dimensions; the political philosophy of Ronald Dworkin; the moral philosophy of Kant, and of recent interpreters of Kant, especially Christine Korsgaard and Barbara Herman; recent work on social construction, especially by Sally Haslanger; ideas about 'treating people as things' in philosophers as different as P. F. Strawson and Martha Nussbaum; ideas about 'direction of fit' in Elizabeth Anscombe and Lloyd Humberstone. To all these theorists and more I owe a great debt.

In writing 'Speech Acts and Unspeakable Acts', I received helpful comments from Susan Brison, Mark Hannam, Sally Haslanger, Jennifer Hornsby, Lloyd Humberstone, Philip Pettit, Sarah Richmond, Frederick Schauer, Michael Smith, Natalie Stoljar, and the Editors of *Philosophy and Public Affairs*. For helpful advice on 'Whose Right? Ronald Dworkin, Women and Pornographers' I thank Susan Brison, Gilbert Harman, Sally Haslanger, Will Kymlicka, Mark van Roojen, Michael Smith, Scott Sehon, Natalie Stoljar, and the Editors of *Philosophy and Public Affairs*. For feedback about ideas in 'Dangerous Confusion? Response to Dworkin' and 'Equality and Moralism: Response to Dworkin' I thank Michael Smith, Monima Chadha and Peter Singer. For feedback about ideas in 'Pornography's Authority? Reply to Green', I am grateful to those present at a Getty seminar on 'Censorship and Silencing' in 1995, especially Leslie Green, Judith Butler, and Robert Post; and in addition Lloyd Humberstone and Sally Haslanger. For helpful comments on 'Scorekeeping in a Pornographic Language Game' I thank an audience at the Australian National University, and in addition Philip Pettit and David Lewis. For comments on 'Duty and Desolation' I thank audiences at Monash University, the University of Delhi, the Australian National University; and Philip Pettit, Michael Smith, Margaret Wilson, and Christine Korsgaard. Ideas in 'Projection and Objectification' were presented in my inaugural lecture as Professor of Moral Philosophy in 2002 at the University of Edinburgh, and I am grateful to my audience there. In writing 'Feminism in Epistemology: Exclusion and Objectification' I received helpful suggestions from Jennifer Saul, Christopher Hookway, and Leif Wenar. Ideas in that paper were first aired at a 'Women in Philosophy' conference on 'Feminism and Reason' at the Australasian Association of Philosophy Conference, 1992. Karen Green, Sally Haslanger, Jennifer Hornsby, Lloyd Humberstone, and Natalie Stoljar all gave useful comments on that earlier formulation. 'Speaker's Freedom and Maker's Knowledge' benefited from interchange with audiences at the University of Edinburgh; Oxford University; the Safra Center for Ethics at the Kennedy School, Harvard; Princeton; and the Law School at the

University of Victoria, B.C. I am grateful to a Monash conference audience for comments on 'Sexual Solipsism', special thanks being due to Marcia Baron, Jeanette Kennett, Sally Haslanger, Catriona Mackenzie, and Michael Smith. In writing 'Love and Solipsism' I received helpful comments from Roger Lamb.

For time to write new material and put the book together, I am grateful for funding from the Arts and Humanities Research Board (as it used to be called); and for the exchange agreement between MIT and Balliol College, Oxford. I'm thankful for the opportunities available, at these final stages of writing, as a visitor at the Centre for the Study of Social Justice, Oxford; and the Centre for Ethics and Philosophy of Law, Oxford.

Finally, thanks of a different order to Richard Holton, whose help has combined the philosophical and personal in ways for which I cannot begin to find adequate words; and since I cannot, I ought not.

Note on the Essays

Three of the essays have been written for this volume. The others have been published in some form elsewhere, and I am grateful to the copyright holders and my co-authors for permission to include them. ('Freedom of Illocution? Response to Daniel Jacobson' is co-authored with Jennifer Hornsby; 'Scorekeeping in a Pornographic Language Game' is co-authored with Caroline West). Many of them have been revised, chiefly with a view to shortening them, and reducing overlap. Some, including 'Speech Acts and Unspeakable Acts', 'Whose Right?', 'Duty and Desolation', and 'Sexual Solipsism', have been left pretty much as first published. In making changes, the hope—possibly futile—has been to balance two conflicting desiderata: avoidance of repetition, and retention of an essay's independent intelligibility.

1. 'Speech Acts and Unspeakable Acts'

Almost unchanged from 'Speech Acts and Unspeakable Acts', *Philosophy and Public Affairs* 22 (1993), 305–30. Reprinted with permission.

Reprinted wholly or partly in Tom Campbell and Wojciech Sadurski, eds., *Freedom of Communication in Australia*, Dartmouth Applied Legal Philosophy Series (Dartmouth: Dartmouth University Press, 1994); Susan Dwyer, ed., *The Problem of Pornography* (Belmont, Ca: Wadsworth, 1995); Diane Michelfelder Wilcox, ed., *Applied Ethics in American Society* (Fort Worth, TX: Harcourt Brace, 1997); Stephen Satris, ed., *Taking Sides: Clashing Views on Controversial Moral Issues* (Guilford, Ct: McGraw-Hill, 2000).

2. 'Dangerous Confusion? Response to Ronald Dworkin'

Revised extract from 'Pornography: A Liberal's Unfinished Business', *Canadian Journal of Law and Jurisprudence,* Special Issue on Legal Theory (1999), ed., Wilfrid Waluchow, 109–33.

Reprinted with permission.

3. 'Freedom of Illocution? Response to Daniel Jacobson', with Jennifer Hornsby

Revised and shortened version of 'Free Speech and Illocution', with Hornsby, *Legal Theory* 4 (1998), 21–37.

Copyright © 1998 Cambridge University Press. Reprinted with permission.

4. 'Pornography's Authority? Response to Leslie Green'

Revised and shortened version of 'Subordination, Silence and Pornography's Authority', *Censorship and Silencing,* ed., R. Post (Los Angeles, Ca: Getty Research Institute, 1998), 261–83.

Permission to reprint a revised version of "Subordination, Silence, and Pornography's Authority" by Rae Langton, originally published in Censorship and Silencing: Practices of Cultural Regulation, ed. Robert C. Post, granted by the Getty Research Institute, Los Angeles, CA. © 1998 Getty Research Institute.

5. 'Pornography's Divine Command? Response to Judith Butler'

Previously unpublished.

6. 'Whose Right? Ronald Dworkin, Women, and Pornographers'

Unchanged from 'Whose Right? Ronald Dworkin, Women, and Pornographers', *Philosophy and Public Affairs* 19 (1990), 311–59. Reprinted with permission.

Reprinted wholly or partly in eds., Patrick Grim, Gary Mar, and Peter Williams, *The Philosopher's Annual XIII* (Atascadero, Ca.: Ridgeview,

1992), the voted 'ten best' articles in the philosophical literature of 1990; Susan Dwyer, ed., *The Problem of Pornography* (Belmont, Ca.: Wadsworth, 1995); K. Weisberg, ed., *Feminist Legal Theory* (Philadelphia, PA: Temple University Press, 1996).

7. 'Equality and Moralism: Response to Ronald Dworkin'

Revised extract from 'Pornography: A Liberal's Unfinished Business', *Canadian Journal of Law and Jurisprudence,* Special Issue on Legal Theory (1999), ed., Wilfrid Waluchow, 109–33.

Reprinted with permission.

8. 'Scorekeeping in a Pornographic Language Game', with Caroline West

Almost unchanged from 'Scorekeeping in a Pornographic Language Game' with West, *Australasian Journal of Philosophy* 77 (1999), 303–19.

Reprinted with permission. http://www.informaworld.com

9. 'Duty and Desolation'

Almost unchanged from 'Duty and Desolation', *Philosophy* 67 (1992), 481–505.

Original reprinted wholly or partly as 'Maria von Herbert's Challenge to Kant' in Peter Singer, ed., *Oxford Reader: Ethics* (Oxford: Oxford University Press, 1994); Christina Hoff Sommers and Fred Sommers, eds., *Vice and Virtue in Everyday Life* (Fort Worth, Tx: Harcourt Brace, 1996); James Sterba, ed., *Ethics: Classical Texts in Feminist and Multicultural Perspectives* (Oxford: Oxford University Press, 1999).

I make use of translations by Arnulf Zweig with his kind permission and that of the University of Chicago Press. See Zweig, *Kant: Philosophical Correspondence 1759–99* (Chicago: University of Chicago Press, 1967). © 1967 by The University of Chicago.

10. 'Autonomy–Denial in Objectification'

Written especially for this volume, but a shorter version of it appeared as Part 3 of 'Feminism in Philosophy', *The Oxford Handbook of Contemporary Philosophy*, eds., Frank Jackson and Michael Smith (Oxford: Oxford University Press 2005), 231–57.

11. 'Projection and Objectification'

Almost unchanged from 'Projection and Objectification', in *The Future for Philosophy*, ed., Brian Leiter (Oxford: Oxford University Press, 2004).

12. 'Feminism in Epistemology: Exclusion and Objectification'

Slightly revised version of 'Feminism in Epistemology: Exclusion and Objectification', *Cambridge Companion to Feminism in Philosophy*, eds., Jennifer Hornsby and Miranda Fricker (Cambridge: Cambridge University Press, 2000), 127–45.

Copyright © 2000 Cambridge University Press. Reprinted with permission.

13. 'Speaker's Freedom and Maker's Knowledge'

Previously unpublished.

14. 'Sexual Solipsism'

Slightly revised version of 'Sexual Solipsism', *Philosophical Topics* 23 (1995), Special Issue: Feminist Perspectives on Language, Knowledge and Reality, ed., Sally Haslanger, 181–219.

15. 'Love and Solipsism'

Revised and shortened version of 'Love and Solipsism', in *Love Analyzed,* ed., Roger Lamb (Boulder, Co.: Westview Press, 1997), 123–52.

Reprinted with permission.

Every effort has been made to contact the original publishers of the essays. If you notice any errors or omissions in the information given please contact Oxford University Press who will be pleased to rectify these at the earliest opportunity.

Contents

Introduction

Solipsism

In a busy street, men and women walk their ways, rugged up in their coats and hats against the winter chill. Above in a stove-heated room, someone glances meditatively at them, and wonders if they are things, machines in disguise. 'Do I see any more than hats and coats which could conceal automatons?' Perception cannot tell him they are people, since he has not yet found grounds to trust it. So thinks the hero of the journey towards knowledge described in René Descartes' *Meditations*.[1] He must, for the sake of knowledge, refuse to treat people as people. He must make solipsism his home, at least for the moment.

Another philosopher saw things differently. For Immanuel Kant, the refusal to treat people as people is the path, not to knowledge, but to moral failure. Solipsism is not a brave epistemological rite of passage, but a moral desert at our doorstep. We should never treat someone as an object, an automaton, a tool, but treat humanity in oneself and others always as a person, not as a thing.[2]

Feminist thinkers have likewise made solipsism more than a problem in epistemology. They have in mind a solipsism of a less global, more local variety than that of Descartes's meditator. 'What peculiarly signalizes the situation of woman', said Simone de Beauvoir,

is that she—a free and autonomous being like all human creatures—nevertheless finds herself living in a world where men . . . propose to stabilize her as an object.

---

[1] René Descartes, *Meditations on First Philosophy* (1641), trans. John Cottingham (Cambridge: Cambridge University Press, 1986), 32.

[2] Immanuel Kant, *Groundwork of the Metaphysics of Morals* (1785), trans. Mary Gregor (Cambridge: Cambridge University Press, 1997).

This bears on the situation of woman, and of man. In the company of a creature stabilized 'as an object', she said, 'man remains alone'. Sexual oppression is solipsism made real, the philosopher's word made flesh. It is a solipsism less global and more tempting than that of the meditator; she thought it was, for many, 'a more attractive experience than an authentic relatio nship with a human being'.[3]

A distinctive way of treating someone 'as an object' is to be found in pornography, so recent feminists have added, saying that in pornography 'the human becomes thing'. The ambiguity of that striking phrase conveys the thought that through pornography human beings—women—are treated as things, and also that things—pornographic artifacts—are treated as human beings. The phrase comes from Catharine MacKinnon:

> as the human becomes thing and the mutual becomes one-sided and the given becomes stolen and sold, objectification comes to define femininity, and one-sidedness comes to define mutuality, and force comes to define consent as pictures and words become the forms of possession and use through which women are actually possessed and used.[4]

Notice that the concerns of de Beauvoir and MacKinnon are practical: the treatment of certain people as things is a matter of doing, a matter of 'possession' and 'use'. The solipsism Descartes wrote about is, by contrast, a matter of attitude, a suspension of belief supposedly without practical significance, since the task of the meditator 'does not involve action'.[5] These ideas are different enough that it might seem strained to juxtapose them, and give both the name 'solipsism'—it might seem strained to link the epistemological solitude of the meditator for whom people are automatons, with the solitariness of an oppressor for whom women are stabilized as objects, or as images for sexual use. But I shall be arguing in the essays that follow that there is a link between the epistemological and the moral; and the juxtaposition, will not, I hope, seem odd in the end.

The essays here range in mode from the argumentative to the exploratory, and they range across time from present law to letters long past. There is some unity in this miscellany: all address the topic of objectification, in pornography or elsewhere, and all are philosophical, driven by the

---

[3] Simone de Beauvoir, *The Second Sex*, trans. H. M. Parshley (1949) (London: Pan, 1988), 29, 286.
[4] Catharine MacKinnon, *Only Words* (Cambridge, Mass.: Harvard University Press, 1993), 25–6.
[5] Descartes, *Meditations*, 22.

aim of understanding a subject that is, to my mind, both important and recalcitrant. Questions from far afield have seemed surprisingly relevant: questions about how speech may be an act, and what this means for the idea of silence; questions about what can be learned from fiction; questions about projection and wishful thinking. There are dangers in casting so wide a net, most obviously the danger of taking on too much, and doing justice to nothing. It is painful to be aware of leaving depths ignored, questions unaddressed that others take to be central, even compulsory. For example, I do nothing to address the complexities posed by the kind of pornography created for gay and lesbian consumers. The feminist concern about pornography has not primarily been a concern about that kind of material, but it is possible that even here there could be eroticization of dominance and heirarchy in ways that help recreate gender roles within gay and lesbian relationships. And my attention is focused primarily on debate about pornography as it has progressed in the western cultures with which I am particularly familiar.[6] There are many important questions about pornography and objectification that I do not address here; but the questions I do address pose plenty of challenges of their own.

The book divides into two halves. The first eight essays develop arguments about pornography, and are intended to be more or less direct contributions to debate in political philosophy. The seven later essays take up a broader understanding of objectification, bringing in some wider concerns from epistemology and moral philosophy.

Pornography

On the feminist view I defend and develop here, pornography subordinates women: it is, as MacKinnon puts it, 'a practice of sexual politics, an institution of gender inequality'.[7] And it silences women: 'pornography

---

[6] See Drucilla Cornell, ed., *Feminism and Pornography* (Oxford: Oxford University Press, 2000) for a collection which admirably achieves greater breadth of perspective on both of these fronts. Nellie Wieland amends a definition of pornography drafted by MacKinnon, in a way which restricts attention to material made for consumption by heterosexual men, and I am sympathetic to this. See 'Linguistic Authority and Convention in a Speech Act Analysis of Pornography', *Australasian Journal of Philosophy* 85 (2007), 435–56, 441.

[7] MacKinnon, *Feminism Unmodified* (Cambridge, Mass.: Harvard University Press, 1987), 148.

and its protection have deprived women of speech, especially speech against sexual abuse'.[8] The argument against pornography is therefore based both on considerations of equality, and, surprisingly, of free speech itself. These claims that pornography subordinates and silences have provoked skepticism from philosophers and from courts. They have also provoked skepticism from certain feminists, and I do not mean to suggest a monolithic feminist orthodoxy on the matter.[9] The reasons for skepticism have been, in part, philosophical.

Much depends, of course, on what one takes pornography to be, and on this feminist view, it is 'the graphic sexually explicit subordination of women in pictures or words that also includes women dehumanized as sexual objects, things, or commodities'—in the words of the definition drafted by MacKinnon and Andrea Dworkin.[10] What makes the approach distinctive is also what provokes accusations of philosophical confusion: the focus on pornography's relation to women, and on pornography as a certain sort of *act*, 'an act against women'[11]—a speech act, if pornography is speech. Grasping pornography's role, says MacKinnon, 'requires understanding it more in active than in passive terms, as constructing and performative'.[12]

This latter feature recalls J. L. Austin, who famously said that speech is a matter of *doing*, not simply a matter of representing the world a certain way. He said philosophers were wrong to focus on the content and the effects of words, while ignoring the act performed in saying them, wrong to neglect what he called the 'illocutionary' dimension to speech. The

---

[8] MacKinnon, *Only Words*, 9.

[9] For a range of dissenting feminist views see e.g. Nadine Strossen, *Defending Pornography: Free Speech, Sex, and the Fight for Women's Rights* (New York: Scribner, 1995); L. Duggan, N. Hunter, and C. Vance, 'False Promises: Feminist Anti-pornography Legislation', in *Caught Looking: Feminism, Pornography, and Censorship*, ed., Feminist Anti-Censorship Taskforce (Seattle: The Real Comet Press, 1986); Varda Burstyn, ed., *Women Against Censorship* (Vancouver: Douglas and McIntyre, 1985); Judith Butler, *Excitable Speech: A Politics of the Performative* (New York and London: Routledge, 1987); Drucilla Cornell, ed., *Feminism and Pornography*.

[10] In more detail: 'the graphic sexually explicit subordination of women in pictures or words that also includes women dehumanized as sexual objects, things, or commodities; enjoying pain or humiliation or rape; being tied up, cut up, mutilated, bruised, or physically hurt; in postures of sexual submission or servility or display; reduced to body parts, penetrated by objects or animals, or presented in scenarios of degradation, injury, torture; shown as filthy or inferior; bleeding, bruised, or hurt in a context which makes these conditions sexual.' See MacKinnon, 'Francis Biddle's Sister', 176, in *Feminism Unmodified,* cf. *Only Words*, 121, n. 32.

[11] MacKinnon, *Only Words*, 11.   [12] Ibid., 27.

important question is not just what you mean by your words, but what you *do* with your words.[13]

That insight has implications here, on an assumption that pornographic pictures and words are speech.[14] The mistake Austin identified is the mistake of those who look at what pornography says, and are blind to what it does. Attending to illocution allows us to make sense of the claims about subordination and silence, as I argue in 'Speech Acts and Unspeakable Acts'. If pornography is an authoritative speech act that ranks women as inferior, legitimates discrimination against women, and deprives women of powers and rights, then it subordinates women. And if pornography stops women from doing things with words, it silences women. A woman's testimony against sexual abuse may be silenced, if pornography makes abuse look like sex. A woman's attempt to refuse sex may also be silenced, if 'no' does not count as a refusal for a hearer in the grip of rape myths legitimated by pornography. This kind of silencing I describe as 'illocutionary disablement'. So speech act theory helps one see how pornography might be an act of subordination; and how it might silence, if it thwarts the speech acts of women.

These conclusions have proved to be controversial, and as I began to engage with objections, I began to get a sense of two different visions of free speech, both at odds with what I was wanting to argue. On one picture, free speech is easy to have. It is a matter of saying the words you want, when you want. Free speech gets hard to have mainly when the state starts breathing down your neck, with its threats and orders; but in a democratic society like the one we live in, the state does not breathe down your neck. Censorship is nowhere. So free speech is easy to have. On another picture, free speech is hard to have. Nothing you say is really free. Whatever you try to say is silenced before you even begin. Whatever you say is constrained. Culture, discourse, perhaps language itself, all breathe down your neck with their threats and orders, and they never go away. You are a prisoner in an invisible cage, invisibly gagged, allowed to say

---

[13] J. L. Austin, *How to Do Things with Words* (Oxford: Oxford University Press, 1962).

[14] That assumption could be questioned: for alternative views see e.g. Frederick Schauer, *Free Speech: A Philosophical Enquiry* (Cambridge: Cambridge University Press, 1982); Ishani Maitra and Mary Kate McGowan, 'Limits of Free Speech: Pornography and the Question of Coverage', *Legal Theory* 13 (2007), 41–68; Melinda Vadas, 'The Manufacture-for-use of Pornography and Women's Inequality', *Journal of Political Philosophy* 13 (2005), 174–93.

one thing, prevented from saying others. Censorship is everywhere. So free speech is hard to have.

The pictures are cartoons of course, but one occasionally finds the first picture in the background of certain liberal objections to feminist argument about pornography, and the second in the background of certain postmodern objections. The two pictures are two sides of a coin which, however tossed, are likely to turn up the same result for a debate about pornography and women's silence. If censorship is nowhere, women are not silenced at all. So women are not silenced by pornography. If censorship is everywhere, then women are silenced—but so is everyone, all the time. If censorship is everywhere, there is no point making distinctions, no point saying that some people are silenced, some are not; some are silenced at some times, not at others; some are silenced here, but not there, some in a bad way, some in an innocent way. If censorship is everywhere, it might as well be nowhere. And the coin will, however tossed, turn up the same result for a debate about pornography and women's subordination. The state is not breathing down women's necks, so women are not subordinated. Or else, women are indeed subordinated, imprisoned in an invisible cage—but so is everyone, all the time. There is nothing special about women, or about pornography.

In the next four essays I consider some philosophical objections, explicit or implicit, to the strategy of argument in 'Speech Acts and Unspeakable Acts'. The first three critics come from a broadly liberal perspective. Ronald Dworkin objects, on grounds of political principle, to MacKinnon's claim that pornography silences. Daniel Jacobson objects, on political and speech-act-theoretic grounds, to my interpretation of the claim that pornography silences. Leslie Green objects, on political grounds, to my interpretation of the claim that pornography subordinates. The fourth, from a postmodern perspective, is Judith Butler. She objects to my interpretation of the claims about subordination and silence on political grounds, in ways that draw on her distinctive views about language.[15] I make no attempt to be comprehensive: some objections by these critics receive little attention; and

---

[15] My responses in most cases draw on lengthier pieces published elsewhere, duly noted towards the beginning of each essay. The preceding description of the 'two pictures' itself draws on the introductory section of Langton, 'Subordination, Silence and Pornography's Authority', in *Censorship and Silencing: Practices of Cultural Regulation*, ed., Robert Post (Los Angeles, Cal.: Getty Research Institute, 1998), 261–83.

some significant critics regrettably receive no attention at all.[16] Common themes do emerge in the objections I consider, though.

The main question about whether pornography subordinates has been about whether it is relevantly authoritative. This question is posed by Green: he argues that even if pornography were authoritative, women would not be in the jurisdiction of that authority. It is also posed by Butler: she reads the claim about subordination as a kind of 'divine command' theory of pornography. The main question about whether pornography silences has been about whether illocutionary disablement is indeed a notion of silencing—and, if it is, whether it is a silencing that matters to freedom of speech. This question is posed, in different ways, by most parties. Dworkin and Jacobson concede that pornography silences women, but argue, for different reasons, that it is not the sort of silencing that matters to freedom of speech, and that attempts to say otherwise are confused. Butler adds that the silencing of speech is not only ubiquitous, but something to celebrate, since it makes it possible to subversively read oppressive speech 'against itself'.

My responses to these critics develop the initial argument, taking issue along the way with the assumptions of these two background pictures. Contrary to Dworkin and Jacobson, the silencing argument does not rest on a confusion, whether of political principle, or of speech act theory. With the help of my co-author Jennifer Hornsby, I say more about why the notion of speech in 'free speech' should include illocution. I look more closely at the notion of authority and its jurisdiction, and argue that women would, on Green's premises, be in the domain of pornography's authority. In responding to Green and Butler, I consider the involvement of authoritative speech acts in social construction. As MacKinnon puts it, 'authoritatively *saying* someone is inferior is largely how structures of status and differential treatment are demarcated and actualized'.[17] This involves some peculiarities of *direction of fit*. Usually when speakers say something,

---

[16] Significant criticisms to which I have not yet responded include Nancy Bauer, 'How To Do Things With Pornography', in *Reading Cavell*, eds., Sanford Shieh and Alice Crary (New York, NY: Routledge, 2006); Alexander Bird, 'Illocutionary Silencing', *Pacific Philosophical Quarterly* 83 (2002), 1–15; Mary Kate McGowan, 'Conversational Exercitives and the Force of Pornography', *Philosophy and Public Affairs* 31 (2003), 155–89; Wojciech Sadurski, 'On "Seeing Speech Through an Equality Lens": A Critique of Egalitarian Arguments for Suppression of Hate Speech and Pornography', *Oxford Journal of Legal Studies* 16 (1996), 713–23; Jennifer Saul, 'Pornography, Speech Acts and Context', *Proceedings of the Aristotelian Society* (2006), 229–48; Wieland, 'Linguistic Authority'.

[17] MacKinnon, *Only Words,* 31.

they aim for their speech to fit the world: they aim for their speech to match up to how the world independently is. However, when speakers with authority say something, the world can come to fit what they say. Instead of the words conforming to the world, the world conforms to the words. Authoritatively saying so can sometimes help to make things so, and this is one way that speech acts can be involved in social construction.

This brings us to a further question. If pornography is supposed to be a kind of authoritative 'saying', there is a difficulty: one might query whether, authoritative or not, pornography even *says* that women are inferior, for it rarely says so explicitly, and in any case much of it is fiction. In 'Scorekeeping in a Pornographic Language Game' I address this question, with the help of my co-author Caroline West. We conclude that pornography may still say such things, even if it does not say so explicitly, and even if it is fiction. Lies about the real world may be told through fiction, and fiction may likewise embody illocutions of real-world permission. It is a familiar thought that racist propaganda may be fictional, and yet be a slander, a permission to discriminate, and an incitement to hatred. The same can apply to pornography, and our paper spells out some of the pragmatic features of language use that make this possible.

The grounds for thinking pornography subordinates and silences women are, I conclude, philosophically plausible. Does this mean pornography should be restricted, whether through censorship, or civil actionability? My arguments remove some barriers to that conclusion, and to that extent support this feminist case, though there is inevitably a gap between philosophical and legal conclusions. What will, I hope, become obvious, however, is that this is no narrow partisan issue, but one that liberals need to take seriously: the feminist arguments against pornography are grounded in principles at the heart of liberalism, principles of equality, and of free speech itself.

This is at odds with a certain orthodox opinion, since liberal political philosophy is supposed to adopt a permissive stance towards pornography. Among liberals, Dworkin has been at the vanguard, providing a classic defence of a right to pornography, and forceful criticism of feminist counter-argument.[18] His defence of a right to pornography fails, as I point out in

---

[18] Ronald Dworkin, 'Do We Have a Right to Pornography?', *Oxford Journal of Legal Studies* 1 (1981), 177–212; reprinted in *A Matter of Principle* (Cambridge, Mass.: Harvard University Press, 1985), 335–72;

'Whose Right? Ronald Dworkin, Women, and Pornographers'. Indeed his philosophy provides resources to vindicate the feminist argument: women have a right *against* pornography. In Dworkin's own terms, there is an argument of principle to be made against permitting pornography. The reason is that preferences for pornography depend on prejudiced views about the inferior worth of women; they are therefore the sorts of preferences ('external' preferences) that establish a right against a policy of permitting pornography. By the lights of Dworkin's own philosophy, this right looks as robust as a right against racial discrimination. Moreover there is a separate argument of policy to be made on women's behalf. Suppose a government, aiming to promote social equality, proposes a policy of restricting pornography. Such a policy, whatever its merits, would violate no one's right to free speech. The reason is that the policy aims for equality, and its rationale does not depend on moral prejudice. By the lights of Dworkin's own philosophy, this policy looks as robust as a comparable policy of racial reverse discrimination. Nor is there anything in Dworkin's more recent writings to counter feminist argument against pornography, construed in either of these two ways, as I explain in 'Equality and Moralism'. We have here, then, a liberal vindication of feminist argument, whose conclusion liberals can reject only on pain of rejecting its liberal premises.

It is often thought that feminist argument about pornography must simply be argument about pornography's harmful effects on women; whereupon hands are thrown up, heads shaken, shoulders shrugged, and the whole debate enmired in the supposed dubiety of empirical evidence. I myself do not find the evidence especially dubious, nor apparently did the US courts when Judge Frank Easterbrook agreed that pornography 'tends to perpetuate subordination', which 'in turn leads to affront and lower pay at work, insult and injury at home, battery and rape on the streets.'[19] However, a feature of the arguments developed in these eight essays is that they focus attention on something other than pornography's

also Dworkin, 'Liberty and Pornography', *The New York Review of Books*, 15 August 1991, 12–15; published as 'Two Concepts of Liberty' in *Isaiah Berlin: A Celebration*, eds., Edna and Avishai Margalit (Chicago: University of Chicago Press, 1991), 100–9; his review of MacKinnon's *Only Words* appeared as 'Women and Pornography', in *The New York Review of Books*, 21 October 1993, 36, 37, 40–2.

[19] American Booksellers Inc. v. Hudnut, 771 F2d 329 (7th Cir. 1985).

effects. An argument that pornography subordinates hinges on whether it is authoritative; an argument that women have rights against pornography hinges on why consumers want it. That is not to say empirical questions are irrelevant: questions about authority, and of consumers' preferences, are empirical ones after all; but they are not simply questions about the evidence of harm.

Objectification

The idea that women are subordinated and silenced is in part the idea that women are somehow treated as more thing-like, less human; so a central theme in feminist work on pornography is that of objectification. That idea is present in the definition of pornography as the 'sexually explicit subordination of women . . . that also includes women *dehumanized* as sexual objects, things or commodities'. The silencing claim is also linked with a claim about objectification: 'Pornography makes women into objects', says MacKinnon. 'Objects do not speak'.[20] What is objectification, then? The seven remaining essays address this broader question, maintaining a focus on sexual objectification, and often connecting it back to the issue of pornography.

The answer I propose is that objectification has both moral and epistemological dimensions. The moral dimension finds a familiar antecedent in the thought of Immanuel Kant, the first philosopher to place on center stage the wrongness treating someone as a mere means, a thing to be used. Kant said we should 'treat humanity . . . always . . . as an end, and never merely as a means'.[21] To objectify is 'to make into, or present as, an object', according to the dictionary, and the Kantian idea, suitably unpacked, might suggest what it is to treat a person this way.[22]

I begin with a correspondence that brings the Kantian way of thinking alive. In 1781 Kant received a letter from a young Austrian woman, Maria von Herbert: 'Great Kant', she wrote, 'as a believer calls to his God, I call

---

[20] MacKinnon, *Feminism Unmodified*, 182. Note too the title of MacKinnon's more recent book, *Are Women Human? And Other International Dialogues* (Cambridge, Mass.: Belnap Press, 2006).

[21] Kant, *Groundwork of the Metaphysics of Morals*, 4: 429. (Translation slightly adapted.)

[22] *Oxford English Dictionary* (Oxford: Clarendon Press, 1933).

to you for help, for comfort, or for counsel to prepare me for death'.[23] What follows is a story of friendship and secrecy, love and despair. It is also a story of life as a rational agent in a sexual marketplace, and of the battle between two standpoints, the strategic and the human. These letters and their story form the topic of 'Duty and Desolation'. They illustrate what it can mean to treat someone as an object, and offer a challenge to Kant that is at once personal and philosophical.

The epistemological dimension to objectification is less familiar than the Kantian, and perhaps harder to pin down. But the dictionary also tells us that to objectify can be 'to express in an external or concrete form' or 'to render objective'. Here the idea is not, primarily, that of treating *someone* as an *object*, when she is not, but treating *something* as *objective*, when it is not. This conveys the idea of projection, harking back to an older epistemological usage of 'objectification'. For this sense the dictionary offers as a sample reference the nineteenth-century philosopher William Hamilton. Writing on the phenomenology of consciousness, he said that 'consciousness . . . projects, as it were, [a] subjective phenomenon from itself,—views it at a distance,—in a word, objectifies it'. We can add that in our own time, J. L. Mackie famously argued, in his skeptical work on ethics, that we 'objectify' value, by which he meant that moral properties are mere projections. A salient philosophical antecedent here is not in Kant's account of how we (mistakenly) treat persons as objects, but in the work of David Hume: he thought that we (mistakenly) treat many merely subjective properties—color, causality, even identity—as objective, given the projective propensity of the human mind to 'spread itself on external objects'.[24]

This 'Humean', epistemological idea about the mistake of projection might appear at first sight to have no bearing on the 'Kantian' moral idea about the mistake of treating people as things. However, they come together in the feminist understanding of objectification; that, at any rate, is what I aim to bring out in these essays.

---

[23] Letter to Kant from Maria von Herbert, 1791, trans. Arnulf Zweig, *Kant: Philosophical Correspondence 1759–1799* (Chicago: University of Chicago Press, 1967).

[24] William Hamilton, *Lectures on Metaphysics and Logic,* eds., H. L. Mansel and J. Veitch, vol. ii (Edinburgh and London: Blackwood, 1859), 432; J. L. Mackie on 'The Objectification of Value' in *Ethics: Inventing Right and Wrong* (Harmondsworth: Penguin, 1990), ch. 1; David Hume, *A Treatise of Human Nature,* ed., L. A. Selby-Bigge, revised P. H. Nidditch (Oxford: Clarendon Press, 1978), 167. A different genealogy might consider later developments of the idea of objectification by Marx, the Frankfurt School, and psycho-analytic film theory, but that is beyond the scope of these essays.

Both ideas are evident in MacKinnon's account of objectification. Sexual objectification is partly a matter of the 'possession' and 'use' of women, she says; and it is at the same time 'an elaborate projective system'.[25] Feminists share with Hume an interest in how the mind spreads itself on the world—but with a special interest in how the pornographic mind spreads itself on the world of women. Equally important to feminist thinking is the impact of this projection, and here the interest goes well beyond its Humean antecedent. For Hume, a propensity to project causal connections onto the world is not something that makes causal connections real. For Hume, the projection is just an illusion. But a propensity to project properties onto women might help make those properties real, in circumstances where, as MacKinnon puts it, 'the world actually arranges itself to affirm what the powerful want to see'.[26] Projection of sexual submissiveness, for example, might help make women sexually submissive. Treating some property as objective may have the result, sometimes, that the property comes into objective existence. So feminists are interested in objectification as a kind of projection that is not merely, not wholly, an epistemological mistake.

We can see now how objectification in the epistemological sense might hook up with objectification in the moral sense. Projecting sexual submissiveness onto women, in such a way that women become objectively submissive, might also be a way of making women more thing-like. Objectification brings moral and epistemological ideas together, since it is partly through projection that women are treated as objects, denied autonomy. Putting the idea bluntly: when object-hood is projected onto women, women not only seem more object-like, but are made to become more object-like.

---

[25] MacKinnon, *Toward a Feminist Theory of the State* (Cambridge, Mass.: Harvard University Press, 1989) 140–1. Note that in 'Not a Moral Issue' (*Feminism Unmodified*, 146–62) MacKinnon denies that objectification in pornography is a 'moral' issue, meaning that the feminist argument is not about community standards, or private sexual mores, or the transgression of taboos; but it is clearly an issue of morality more broadly understood (as are many issues in which the law takes an interest).

[26] MacKinnon, *Feminism Unmodified*, 164. This contribution to invisibility is a topic of Langton, 'Projection and Objectification', this volume. It is a large topic, discussed by many writers, but see for example Sally Haslanger, 'Ontology and Social Construction', *Philosophical Topics* 23 (1995), 95–125; Mary Kate McGowan, 'On Pornography: MacKinnon, Speech Acts, and "False" Construction', *Hypatia* 20 (2005) 23–49.

Notice how direction of fit is assuming importance here too. We noted earlier some peculiarities about speech acts and their direction of fit—how even when someone's authoritative saying aims to fit the world, it can nonetheless help to make the world come to fit itself. The same thought extends to states of mind. The question whether *saying* so can sometimes make things so, is matched by a question whether *thinking* so can sometimes make things so. We ordinarily assume that speech and thought are in the business of fitting the world, and we tend to ignore anomalies of fit. But it is the anomalies that are likely to be of interest here. Yes, belief is supposed to fit the world: but if we are interested in objectification, we may be interested in how belief wishfully comes to fit desire; and if we are interested in how attitudes have impact, we might be interested in how the world comes to fit belief.

Two important studies of objectification bring out the two dimensions. The moral dimension of objectification, which I am calling 'Kantian', is taken up by Martha Nussbaum in her classic study; in MacKinnon's terms, she takes up the idea of 'possession' and 'use'. The epistemological dimension of objectification, which I am calling 'Humean', is taken up by Sally Haslanger, in an equally illuminating essay; in MacKinnon's terms, she takes up the idea of an 'elaborate projective system'. Both studies provide inspiration and reference points for the later essays collected here.[27]

The moral side to objectification is the topic of 'Autonomy-denial in Objectification', where Nussbaum's proposal is the starting point. Building on Kant and on recent feminist work, Nussbaum suggests that, at its heart, objectification is a matter of treating someone as an instrument, and denying autonomy. She gives considerable content to the notion of 'object', in that idea of 'treating as an object': a paradigm object is tool-like, lacking in autonomy and subjectivity, inert, fungible, replaceable, a possession. I argue that Nussbaum's account of 'treating as an object' should be augmented, both on the 'object' side, and the 'treating' side, of that idea. An important feature of object-hood is that of *silence*, if 'objects do not speak', as MacKinnon puts it. And the notion of 'treating' especially needs attention. Is 'treating' a matter of *viewing* someone in a certain way? Perhaps it is, say, regarding them as lacking in autonomy. Or is 'treating' a matter of

[27] Martha Nussbaum, 'Objectification', *Philosophy and Public Affairs* 24 (1995), 249–91; Sally Haslanger, 'On Being Objective and Being Objectified' in *A Mind of One's Own*, eds., Louise Antony and Charlotte Witt (Boulder Co.: Westview Press, 1993), 85–125.

doing something to someone? Perhaps it is, say, violating their autonomy. If we make space for different ways of 'treating', we can allow for many sorts of 'autonomy-denial'—failing to attribute autonomy, violating autonomy, stifling autonomy—and in the process bring out possible connections between autonomy-denying attitudes, and acts.

This expansion is not just an exercise in taxonomy, but can help resolve some polemical stand-offs in debate about pornography. Suppose one party, for instance, says that the film *Deep Throat* affirms women's sexual autonomy, that it is the voice of the new liberated woman. Suppose another says it objectifies women, and denies women's autonomy. *Both* can be right. Making space for different kinds of treatment allows us to see that affirming someone's autonomy can sometimes be a way of denying their autonomy. This has an air of paradox, but makes good sense once we are alert to the ways in which a false attribution of autonomy can be the enemy of autonomy. An affirmation that someone is acting autonomously, when they are not, will assist and hide the violation of autonomy. *Deep Throat* affirmed the autonomy of its star Linda Marchiano—the appearance of choice, willingness and enthusiasm was crucial for the film's success. But at the same time, it denied her autonomy, since (according to her testimony) it took rape, threats, and beatings to make her do it. The appearance of choice—the attribution of autonomy—was crucial to the destruction of choice—the violation of autonomy.

Looking next at the epistemological side of objectification, I turn to Hume's metaphor of the mind 'spreading itself on external objects'. In 'Projection in Objectification' I distinguish a number of projective mechanisms for the generation of desire-driven belief, each discernible in Hume, and each with a role to play in sexual objectification. They all involve anomalies with respect to direction of fit. Instead of belief fitting the world, belief fits desire; instead of belief fitting the world, the world fits belief. These projective mechanisms help objectification, and they help to hide it too.

Central to objectification's moral aspect is autonomy-denial. Central to objectification's epistemological aspect is a double anomaly, projection and its real or apparent fulfillment—roughly, a *wishful thinking so*, which *helps to make it so*. Putting these together, we have the idea that objectification is an act or process that denies autonomy, through projection and its real or apparent fulfillment.

Is this epistemological aspect necessary to objectification, on this pro-posal? Consider a classic example of an objectifier, in the traditional moral sense of that term: a slave owner, say, or a rapist, who knows exactly what he is doing, and in whose autonomy-denying treatment no role is played by projection or its self-fulfillment. Is such behaviour objectifying? The answer would be 'yes' on Nussbaum's account. But if we make projection a *necessary* component of objectification, the answer looks like 'no', and we seem to have travelled far from the notion's Kantian roots. My view is that a dogmatic response here is probably best avoided. Objectification may be a cluster concept, as Nussbaum suggests, one which applies when enough of the cluster is in play, and which lacks a simple rule for its application. Viewed in these terms, my proposal is to augment the cluster: to add the idea of desire-driven projection, and its real or apparent fulfillment, and place it close to the cluster's core. Actions might still count as objectifying in the absence of the epistemological dimension, if the rest of the cluster is sufficiently in play.[28] But projection and its associated masking do belong there somewhere, if we are to do justice to the notion which is important to feminist analysis.

If objectification has an epistemological aspect, it becomes relevant to broader concerns in epistemology, including the controversial enterprise known as a feminist 'critique of reason'. That's the topic of 'Feminism in Epistemology: Exclusion and Objectification', where I review some of the grounds for thinking that, when it comes to knowledge, women get left out, and women get hurt. I look at how an epistemological norm of objectivity, or rather of *assumed* objectivity, might be understood to hurt women, by helping and hiding objectification, in a way that Haslanger describes.

What is pornography's epistemological role here? The answer suggested in these essays goes something like this. Pornography has a two-fold contribution, relating to desire and to belief. Pornography has a role as *shaper of desire*. It may, for example, shape sexual desires that are commodifying or violent. Such desires may in turn be a source of desire-driven projective

---

[28] An alternative to the cluster concept approach would be to think in terms of a family of different concepts of objectification (objectification according to Kant, according to Haslanger, etc.), which diverge in their extensions, but bear intelligible and overlapping relations to each other. A related conceptual question is whether to take 'objectification' as necessarily pejorative, or allow that in some contexts it can be be a good thing, as argued by Nussbaum, 'Objectification' and Leslie Green 'Pornographies', *Journal of Political Philosophy* 8 (2000), 27–52. This is partly a terminological issue, but I tend to assume a pejorative usage.

belief. Pornography has a second role as *provider of evidence for belief*. It may, for example, directly support belief that women are inferior, or submissive, or enjoy rape. (Compare here the earlier idea of pornography as 'authoritative saying' that ranks a group as inferior, and legitimates discrimination). Connected with this is its role as *suppressor of counter-evidence for belief*. Pornography may, for example, silence the testimony of women who would offer evidence against it. (Compare here the earlier idea of pornography as creator of illocutionary disablement.) If pornography also works in a partly self-fulfilling way, it has a role as *shaper of women*. This brings together the desire–related and belief–related roles, and allows pornography to be an indirect, as well as a direct, provider of evidence for belief. Desire that women be a certain way (because pornography has made that desirable), plus belief that women are that way (because pornography has made that credible) yield actions that shape women, and thereby create further evidence that women are indeed as pornography says they are.[29]

The epistemological conception of objectification has a surprising and little–noted consequence. While pornography may be partly a source of lies about women, as feminists argue, it is also, partly, a source of truths, and thus of *knowledge*. When pornography self-fulfillingly says something about women, that can be a justified true belief. It has affinities to 'maker's knowledge', the kind of knowledge God was supposed to have of his creatures, and that we are supposed to have of our actions. In 'Speaker's Freedom and Maker's Knowledge' I look at the implications of this for arguments about pornography that take their inspiration from J. S. Mill. And I conclude that the 'maker's knowledge' involved in pornography is at once knowledge, and harm.

It may seem strange to focus on the epistemological aspect of objectifica-tion, when, if these claims are true, it is surely their moral aspect that matters most. If women suffer sexual violence, are silenced, are made to conform to pornography's script, then women are made more thing-like—and isn't *that* the most important issue? Yes, it is; but we don't have here a case of either/or. The epistemological aspect is philosophically subtle, and to that extent deserves some attention in its own right; but the main reason for our

---

[29] The desire–related role is implicitly a topic of 'Scorekeeping in a Pornographic Language Game' and 'Projection in Objectification'. The belief–related role is implicitly a topic of, in addition to these two, 'Speech Acts and Unspeakable Acts', 'Exclusion and Objectification'.

attention is its connection with how women are treated as things. Because of its epistemological dimension, objectification can be hard to see, and all the harder to combat.

Pornography is sometimes considered, more straightforwardly, as an artifact that gets sexually used in place of a human being—as Anthony Burgess once put it, 'a pornographic book . . . is, in a sense, a substitute for a sexual partner'.[30] For some users, the substitute might even be viewed as an improvement on the reality:

I don't see how any male who likes porn can think actual sex is better, at least if it involves all the crap that comes with having a real live female in your life.[31]

Pornography here fulfils de Beauvoir's nightmare: woman is stabilized 'as an object' through pornography, man 'remains alone', in an isolation 'more attractive . . . than an authentic relationship with a human being'.[32] And this brings us back to the solipsism with which we began.

Think back to the world of Descartes's meditator, which is one kind of solipsistic world. Solipsism is false, but he believes it true: surrounded by people, but thinking and acting as if he is alone, he *treats those people as things*, as automatons. Imagine now the opposite. Solipsism is true, but he believes it false: surrounded by things, he *treats those things as people*. That would be another kind of solipsistic world. Both of these global solipsisms have local counterparts, captured in that double-meaning remark from MacKinnon that in pornography use, 'the human becomes thing': things (pornographic artifacts) are treated as people, and at the same time people (women) are treated as things.[33]

Now it presumably matters, morally, when people are treated as things, at least beyond the confines of the philosopher's stove-heated room. But it doesn't matter, as a rule, when things are treated as people. There is nothing wrong with animating things, singing lullabies to a doll, thrashing a car that won't start, snarling 'There, that'll teach you!' while knotting

---

[30] Anthony Burgess, 'What is Pornography?', in *Perspectives on Pornography,* ed., Douglas A. Hughes (New York: St. Martin's, 1970), 4–8, quoted in Joel Feinberg, *Offense to Others: The Moral Limits of the Criminal Law* (Oxford: Oxford University Press, 1985), 130.

[31] Contributor to an on-line discussion of pornography, cited by Pamela Paul, *Pornified: How Pornography is Transforming Our Lives, Our Relationships, Our Families* (New York: Henry Holt, 2005), 39. She cites TalkAboutSupport.com, 29 January, 2004.

[32] De Beauvoir, *The Second Sex*, 29, 286.

[33] The use of pornography involves 'sex between people and things, human beings and pieces of paper, real men and unreal women', MacKinnon, *Only Words*, 109–10.

a disobedient towel to its slippery rail.[34] If treating people as things, and treating things as people, can both be described as solipsisms, doesn't it seem to be the first, not the second, that matters morally? Is MacKinnon equivocating, conflating a guilty solipsism with an innocent? In 'Sexual Solipsism', I argue this is no conflation, but a substantive claim about how one leads to the other in pornography, so that somehow, when these objects are treated as women, women are treated as objects. The idea of a connection between these two solipsisms is unique, as far as I know, to feminist discussion of pornography. One aim of this essay is to explore what the connection might be, whether causal, or constitutive, or both.

'Sexual Solipsism' also brings the Kantian dimension of objectification to bear on pornography, looking at Kant's own reflections on sexual ethics. Kant is pessimistic about sexual love, and thinks it tends inevitably to the solipsistic. Sexual love, he says,

is *an appetite for another human being*...Human love is good will, affection, promoting the happiness of others and finding joy in their happiness. But it is clear that when a person loves another purely from sexual desire, none of these factors enter into love. Far from there being any concern for the happiness of the loved one, the lover, in order to satisfy his desire, may even plunge the loved one into the depths of misery. Sexual love makes of the loved person an object of appetite; as soon as that appetite has been stilled, the person is cast aside as one casts away a lemon that has been sucked dry.[35]

That pessimism is not quite the whole picture. Elsewhere, including in the letters to Maria von Herbert, Kant describes sexual love in terms of friendship, and friendship in terms that eloquently suggest escape from solipsism. The person without a friend is like the Cartesian meditator, who must 'shut himself up in himself', and be 'completely alone with his thoughts, as in a prison'; friendship is a release from this into 'an intimate union of love and respect'.[36]

What are we to make of that pessimism, though: how is sexual love supposed to make of the loved person 'an object of appetite'? The alleged

---

[34] The last two examples: from BBC comedy *Fawlty Towers*, 'Gourmet Night'; and from Rosalind Hursthouse's 'Arational Actions', *Journal of Philosophy* 88: 2, 1991, 57–68.

[35] Kant, *Lectures on Ethics*, (1775–1780) trans. Louis Infield, (London: Methuen, 1930), 163.

[36] *Doctrine of Virtue*, (1797) trans. Mary Gregor (New York: Harper and Row, 1964), 144, *Lectures on Ethics*, 202.

problem might be that sexual love is sometimes *reductive*: it takes a person as its object not *qua* person, but *qua* body. That is how Barbara Herman suggests we read Kant. Alternatively, the problem might be that sexual love is sometimes *invasive*: it takes a person as its object *qua* person, not *qua* body—but *qua* person to be possessed. That is how Christine Korsgaard suggests we read Kant. These two interpretations are addressed in 'Sexual Solipsism' and its companion piece, 'Love and Solipsism', providing spring-boards for a wider exploration that surveys the 'objective' attitudes described by P. F. Strawson, a kind of sadism described by Roger Scruton, and a solipsistic love described by Marcel Proust, driven by an invasive 'thirst for a life'.

Afterthoughts and Aspirations

Times have changed since some of these essays on pornography and objectification were written. Back then, the pornographer was cast by liberals as a member of a persecuted minority, needing protection from the tyranny of a supposed moralistic majority. Ronald Dworkin wanted to save the pornographer from embarrassment, and make sure he got a brown paper bag to disguise his purchases. Liberals found it hard to imagine how pornography might be harmful. Dworkin wondered idly whether pornography might be like breakfast television, in distracting people from useful work, and having a deleterious effect on the economy—in which case a harm-based argument against it might, he thought, be justified.[37] Notwithstanding the disagreements between liberals and feminists, there was also back then a broad consensus on some issues: for example, pornography should be subject to zoning laws; and children should neither be used in pornography, nor should they consume it.

Now, with the growth of the internet, pornography has become almost mainstream. Policies for which there was, and officially is, consensus, have gradually been eroded with the new ubiquity of pornography. Material is increasingly violent and non-consensual. There is more child pornography.[38] Back then, the question was whether some people could

---

[37] Dworkin, 'Do We Have a Right to Pornography', 358, 354.

[38] Ubiquity: pornographic sites are visited three times more often than the search engines Google, Yahoo! and MSN Search combined, according to a 2004 study ('Porn More Popular than Search',

have the option of having pornography. Now we are in the world of pornography, unless we opt out. Pornography invades every web-accessing household that has not the will and the resources to block it.

Back then, all parties were agreed that children shouldn't be porn stars. The US Constitution does not protect child pornography, made with real children. But we have had to learn, since Ashcroft, that it does protect 'virtual' child pornography, created either by morphing non-explicit images of children into sexually explicit images; or by animation; or by making adult actors appear like children.[39] So children shouldn't be porn stars—unless they are morphed porn stars.

Back then, liberals agreed that children shouldn't be porn customers. Now most children who use the Internet will come into contact with pornography at some point, and many become habitual users. Whereas in the past, childhood encounters with pornography were a matter of discovering a pile of magazines in the back of a relative's closet, it is now a matter of a mouse-click, perhaps curious, perhaps accidental, while doing homework, or visiting a school-friend; a click which takes the user through an ever-proliferating jungle of sites.[40]

The commercial pornography industry could take some responsibility here, but it does not, and legal efforts to make it take responsibility

InternetWeek.com, June 4, 2004); according to comScore, an Internet traffic-measuring service, 70% of eighteen to twenty-four-year-old men visit a pornographic site in a typical month; John Schwartz, 'Leisure Pursuits of Today's Young Man', *New York Times*, 29 March, 2004. On peer-to-peer networks, 73% of movie searches were for pornography, while 24% of image searches were for child pornography; Frank Coggrave, 'Bugwatch: the Perils of Peer-to-Peer', VNU Business Publications, 31 March, 2004. Violent content: in one study 25% of pornographic magazines, 27% of pornographic videos, and 42% of depictions in Usenet groups on the internet; Michael Barron and Michael S. Kimmel, 'Sexual Violence in Three Pornographic Media: Toward a Sociological Explanation', *Journal of Sex Research* 37 (2000). Child pornography: cases handled by the FBI increased twenty-three fold between 1996 and 2004; David B. Caruso, 'Internet Fuels Child Porn Trafficking', Associated Press, 15 January, 2005. British Telecom, a UK internet service provider, blocked 20,000 searches per day for child pornography, when it introduced filtering technology in 2004; Nicole Martin, 'BT Blocks 20,000 Attempts a Day to Access Child Porn', *Daily Telegraph* (London), July 21, 2004. These references are cited by Pamela Paul, *Pornified* 15, 60, 58, 190, 196. Paul's book is an excellent and accessible recent study of the growth and effects of pornography on ordinary people in the USA, drawing on remarkably frank interviews, a Harris poll she commissioned, and a range of empirical literature.

    [39] Ashcroft v. Free Speech Coalition, 535 US 234 (2002).

    [40] A study by the London School of Economics found that 68% of teenagers who regularly use the internet said they had seen pornography on the internet, 20% saying 'many times'. Sonia Livingston and Magdalena Bober, 'UK Children Go On-Line: Final Report of Key Project Findings', London School of Economics, April 2005 http://www.children-go-online.net/

have not fared well. US Federal legislation requiring pornography sites to restrict access to minors, via the supply of credit card numbers, was struck down as unconstitutional.[41] US State legislation attempting to regulate internet access of pornography by minors has been found constitutionally 'overbroad' and in conflict with the First Amendment. One Californian court said state funded libraries could provide unfettered access to minors, since the government has 'no constitutional duty' to protect minors from harmful materials available over the internet.[42] The effects of extensive exposure to pornography are being felt by many, including the most vulnerable.[43]

In the essays included here, I have not advanced a simple harm argument against pornography, but that is not because I think it implausible. It is, I think, very plausible; but as a philosopher I am looking, here, at how more complex questions about equality, silencing, and knowledge bear on the issue. There is good evidence about pornography's harmful effects: that pornography affects a variety of its consumers' attitudes—factual beliefs, normative beliefs, and desires. It changes male consumers' factual beliefs about what women and girls are likely to want, and about the statistical normality of certain sexual behaviour, such as group sex and rape. It changes normative beliefs about the value of women, and the acceptability of rape. And it changes desires, so that they are more likely to want sexual experiences they did not want before, and want to act differently, and more violently, than they did before.[44]

---

[41] The US Federal 'Child Online Protection Act' 1988 was found unconstitutional.

[42] Kathleen R. v. City of Livermore, 87 Cal. App. 4th 684 (Ct. App. 2001).

[43] Two examples: a videotaped gang rape, in Orange County in 2002, of an unconscious 16-year-old girl, by three teenage boys, involving assault with a pool cue and other objects; a witness for their defense explained that such 'positions' were popular in pornography; Paul, *Pornified*, 182–3 (see her chapter 6 for further reports). A 2002 survey in France found that nearly half of French children had seen an adults-only sex film by the time they were 11. Claude Rozier, who headed the survey, said 'Hardcore porn has become the principal vehicle for quite young children's understanding of everything to do with love and sexuality, sometimes their only point of reference.' French psychologists believe pornography normalizes gang-rape for some adolescents, including eight who gang-raped a 15-year-old classmate in Lyons. Public prosecutor Robert Esch said 'It's quite extraordinary. Clearly, in their minds, it's as if what happened was some kind of virtual game. They seem to have no idea of the gravity of the acts they are accused of.' Jon Henley, 'Pornography forms French children's views on sex', *Guardian*, 25 May, 2002.

[44] Edward Donnerstein, Daniel Linz, and Steven Penrod, *The Question of Pornography: Research Findings and Policy Implications* (New York: Free Press; London: Collier Macmillan, 1987); Paul, *Pornified*, cites many studies, including a classic study by J. Bryant and D. Zillman, which (using tamer materials, and in a public context, therefore without reinforcement of masturbation) found these kinds

Where to go from here, then? We are in a troubling situation, where the evidence about pornography's effects is stronger than it has ever been, at the same time that pornography is achieving ever greater social acceptance. We could shrug; or we could look for something better. Let me conclude with some ill-assorted aspirations, first for politics, and then for life more generally.

At the level of politics, we could hope for a renewed alliance between liberals and feminists who care, to a certain extent, about the same things: equality, autonomy, freedom to speak, freedom from violence. Although I often focus, in these essays, on disagreements, in fact, as just noted, there used to be agreement between feminists and liberals. We agreed that people should not be confronted with pornography, and that zoning laws, at least, were appropriate. All parties agreed about restrictions on child pornography, and about the exposure of children to pornography. And many liberals agreed with feminists that certain extremely violent and sadistic forms of pornography should be restricted. Bernard Williams, in the context of his broadly liberal report, said that 'films, even those shown to adults only, should continue to be censored', especially films which

... reinforce or sell the idea that it can be highly pleasurable to inflict injury, pain or humiliation (often in a sexual context) on others.[45]

Much of this common ground between liberals and feminists continues to exist in principle, but has been left behind in practice. One might hope for renewed collaborative efforts—on the specific issues of zoning and its internet counterparts, child pornography, access to pornography by

---

of effects on factual and normative beliefs, in J. Bryant and D. Zillman, 'Pornography and Sexual Callousness, and the Trivialization of Rape', *Journal of Communication* 32 (December 1982), 10–21. In more recent years several meta-analyses of existing studies have emerged, confirming that pornography has such effects; they are reviewed in Neil M. Malamuth, Tamara Addison and Mary Koss, 'Pornography and sexual aggression: Are there reliable effects and can we understand them?', *Annual Review of Sex Research* 11 (2000), 26–91.

[45] Williams Report: Home Office, *Report of the Committee on Obscenity and Film Censorship*. Cmnd. 7772 (London: Her Majesty's Stationery Office, 1979), 145. In similar vein the UK government is currently considering legislation that would restrict 'extreme pornography', including pornography that eroticizes extremely violent and life-threatening behaviour; Criminal Justice and Immigration Bill, House of Commons, Session 2007–8, vol. i P. 5 http://services.parliament.uk/bills/2007–08/criminaljusticeandimmigration.html, consulted 26 March 2008.

children, and extreme pornography—aiming to put this shared common ground back into practice. One could hope for much more than this; but one should hope at least for this.

Discussion of pornography has been dominated by political debate about legislation and censorship, but this should not blind us to other questions that are closer to home. How should one live? That ancient Socratic question is being offered a particular answer by an industry that makes billions of dollars through a product that creates exploitation and abuse in its production; and creates dependency, desensitization, and worse in its consumption. Pornography can create a sexual solipsism, both within its immediate context of use and beyond. Heavy consumers of pornography can end up effectively treating women as pornography. One heavy user said of sex with his wife, 'All the while I was thinking either about porn or trying to make her say things she didn't want to say. I was really just using her—she was like a masturbatory accessory'. Another woman felt effectively alone, during sex with her husband.

I obviously knew where his body was, but where was his mind? He would sort of be there at first, but then I didn't know where he went. . . . At a certain point I realized I was just a tool. I could have been anything or anybody. I felt so lonely, even when he was in the room.[46]

At first, an encounter with pornography is a way of imagining being with a woman. Later, an encounter with a woman becomes a way of imagining being with pornography. This kind of sexual solipsism falls far short of the sexual violence that has been the focus of political debate. But, whether or not it should be counted as harm for the purposes of a political argument, it is surely relevant to questions that an individual might have about his, or her, own life. Why choose to have one's imagination and relationships invaded, and made to march to an alien drum? MacKinnon famously said that pornography is 'not a moral issue'.[47] She had an important point: feminist argument about pornography is not 'moralism', in the legal sense

---

[46] This and the previous quotation are from interviews done by Pamela Paul, *Pornified*, 232–3, in her seventh chapter, which focuses on compulsive users.

[47] See her eponymous essay in *Feminism Unmodified*. For a moral argument quite independent of either 'moralism' or political debate about free speech, see Susan Dwyer, 'Enter Here—At Your Own Risk: The Moral Dangers of Cyberporn', in Robert Cavalier, ed., *The Impact of the Internet on Our Moral Lives* (Albany: SUNY Press, 2005), 69–94.

of that term. It is a political argument. But pornography *is* a moral issue, as well as a political one. That might not matter to legislators; but it should matter to those who have some stake in finding an answer to that ancient question about how to live—which I hope (and here is my last aspiration) includes us all.

1

Speech Acts and Unspeakable Acts

Pornography is speech. So the courts declared in judging it protected by the First Amendment. Pornography is a kind of act. So Catharine MacKinnon declared in arguing for laws against it. Put these together and we have: pornography is a kind of speech act. In what follows I take this suggestion seriously.[1]

If pornography is speech, what does it say? If pornography is a kind of act, what does it do? Judge Frank Easterbrook, accepting the premises of antipornography legislation, gave an answer. Pornography is speech that depicts subordination. In the words of the feminist ordinance passed in Indianapolis, pornography depicts women

dehumanized as sexual objects, things or commodities; enjoying pain or humiliation or rape; being tied up, cut up, mutilated, bruised, or physically hurt; in postures of sexual submission or servility or display; reduced to body parts, penetrated by objects or animals, or presented in scenarios of degradation, injury, torture; shown as filthy or inferior; bleeding, bruised or hurt in a context which makes these conditions sexual.[2]

Pornography is a kind of act that has certain effects. Depictions of subordination, said Easterbrook, 'tend to perpetuate subordination. The

[1] This essay first appeared in *Philosophy and Public Affairs* 22 (1993), 293–330. For the declaration see e.g., Catharine MacKinnon, 'Linda's Life and Andrea's Work', *Feminism Unmodified* (Cambridge, Mass.: Harvard University Press, 1987), 130. Pornography, as defined by MacKinnon, and as discussed in this paper, is not the same as obscenity. See MacKinnon, 'Not a Moral Issue', ibid.; and Frank Michelman, 'Conceptions of Democracy in American Constitutional Argument: The Case of Pornography Regulation', *Tennessee Law Review* 56 (1989): 294 n.8. MacKinnon drafted an ordinance that was passed in Indianapolis in 1984, but was then challenged and defeated. See American Booksellers, Inc. v. Hudnut, 598 F. Supp. 1327 (S. D. Ind. 1984). The ordinance made trafficking in pornography civilly actionable, rather than simply prohibiting it. I do not address this admittedly important feature of the legislation here.

[2] MacKinnon, 'Francis Biddle's Sister', *Feminism Unmodified*, 176.

subordinate status of women in turn leads to affront and lower pay at work, insult and injury at home, battery and rape on the streets'. His conclusion was that the ordinance was unconstitutional: for, he said, 'this simply demonstrates the power of pornography as speech.'[3]

Pornography, on this view, depicts subordination and causes it. A closer look at the words of the ordinance shows us that MacKinnon is saying something more. Before describing what pornography depicts, the ordinance begins: 'We define pornography as the graphic sexually explicit subordination of women in pictures or words'. Besides depicting and causing subordination, as Easterbrook allowed, pornography *is*, in and of itself, a form of subordination.[4]

This latter aspect of the legislation provoked the ire of judges and philosophers alike. In proposing that pornography actually is subordination, the drafters of the ordinance were tricksters, guilty of 'a certain sleight of hand', said Judge Barker, in the district court.[5] They were guilty of conceptual confusion, and their claim was 'philosophically indefensible', said William Parent in the *Journal of Philosophy*.[6] It is all very well to talk about what pornography depicts; and it is all very well to talk about the effects it has on the lives of women. It is all very well to say, with Easterbrook, that pornography depicts subordination and causes it. Such claims may be unnerving, and they may be empirically false, but they are not, at least, incoherent. MacKinnon wants to say something more: she

[3] American Booksellers, Inc. v. Hudnut, 771 F. 2d 329 (7th Cir. 1985).

[4] Easterbrook's omission has been commented upon by Melinda Vadas in 'A First Look at the Pornography/Civil Rights Ordinance: Could Pornography Be the Subordination of Women?', *Journal of Philosophy* 84 (1987), 487–511. Vadas is interested, as I am, in saving the 'subordinating' claim from charges of conceptual confusion, and she develops an interesting analysis which differs from that offered here. She says that some predicates can apply to a representational depiction because they apply to the scene depicted. 'Subordinates' is such a predicate, in her view, so pornographic depictions of subordination can themselves subordinate. My view is that the link is not as close as she sees it: an utterance's depicting subordination is neither necessary nor sufficient for its having the force of subordination. The reasons for this will emerge shortly.

[5] Hudnut, 598 F. Supp. 1316 (1984).

[6] W. A. Parent, 'A Second Look at Pornography and the Subordination of Women', *Journal of Philosophy* 87 (1990), 205–11. Parent's article is a response to Vadas's. He argues, by means of the following remarkable non sequitur, for the different conclusion that pornography is morally evil (p. 211). 'Evil' means 'depraved'. 'To deprave' means 'to debase'. 'To debase' means 'to bring into contempt'. Pornography brings women into contempt, ergo pornography is evil. What actually follows from Parent's lexicographical premises is of course that *women* are evil. Women are brought into contempt (by pornography), therefore debased, therefore depraved, therefore evil.

wants to attend not simply to the content of pornographic speech, nor simply to its effects, but to the actions constituted by it.

What she says may strike a chord of recognition among those who recall an older, more tranquil debate in the philosophy of language, and a philosopher who took as his starting point the slogan that 'to say something is to *do* something'. In *How to Do Things with Words*, J. L. Austin complained of a 'constant tendency in philosophy' to overlook something of great importance: a tendency to consider the content of a linguistic utterance, and its effects on hearers, but to overlook the action constituted by it.[7] Austin encouraged philosophers to shift their gazes away from statements considered in isolation, sentences that describe, truly or falsely, some state of affairs, and look instead at 'the issuing of an utterance in a speech situation'.[8] Words, he said, were used to perform all kinds of actions—warning, promising, marrying, and the like—that philosophy had blithely ignored.

To say something is usually to do a number of different things. An example (from Austin):[9] Two men stand beside a woman. The first man turns to the second, and says 'Shoot her.' The second man looks shocked, then raises a gun and shoots the woman. You witness the scene and describe it later. The first man said to the second, 'Shoot her', meaning by 'shoot' to shoot with a gun, and referring by 'her' to the woman nearby. That description roughly captures the content of what was said: it captures what Austin called the *locutionary* act. To perform a locutionary act is to utter a sentence that has a particular meaning, as traditionally conceived.[10] However, there is more to what you witnessed, so you describe the scene again. *By* saying 'shoot her', the first man *shocked* the second; by saying 'shoot her', the first man *persuaded* the second to shoot the woman. That description captures some of the effects of what was said: it captures what Austin called the *perlocutionary* act. But if you stop there you will still have left something out. You will have ignored what the first man did in saying what he said. So you go on. *In* saying 'shoot her', the first man *urged* the second to shoot the woman. That description captures the action constituted by the utterance itself: it captures what Austin

---

[7] J. L. Austin, *How to Do Things with Words* (Oxford: Oxford University Press, 1962).
[8] Ibid., 139.   [9] Ibid., 101 (my version is a slight elaboration).   [10] Ibid., 109.

called the *illocutionary* act. The actions listed earlier—warning, promising, marrying—are illocutionary acts. Austin's complaint was that this latter dimension to speech was often ignored, that there was 'a tendency in philosophy to elide [illocutions] in favour of the other two'.[11]

Pornography is not always done with words. Yet Easterbrook's description exemplifies the tendency of which Austin complained. Pornography depicts subordination and causes it. That—in Austin's terms—is to describe its locutionary and perlocutionary dimensions. What is missing is a description of the actions constituted by pornographic utterances: in Austin's terms, pornography's *illocutionary* force. MacKinnon supplies such a description when she says that pornography is an act of subordination.

Like Austin, MacKinnon wants to undermine the dichotomy between word and action. 'Which is saying "kill" to a trained guard dog, a word or an act?' she asks, in a passage that echoes Austin's example.[12] MacKinnon has accordingly been interpreted as saying that pornography is unprotected conduct rather than protected speech,[13] and one might imagine that Austin's approach gives this idea some support. If pornography is a kind of act, and action is conduct, then, one might think, pornography is unprotected by the First Amendment. But that interpretation of MacKinnon is wrong. 'To state the obvious', she says, 'I do not argue that pornography is "conduct" in the First Amendment doctrinal sense'.[14] In any case Austin's approach would give it no support, for it does not help us to distinguish conduct from speech. If there is a line that divides speech from conduct in the law, it does not divide speech from action in Austin's philosophy. On his view, *all* speech acts are actions. To say that pornography is a kind of act is not to say that pornography is conduct, and nothing that I say will turn on that claim. The important point is that actions, whether speech or conduct, can be protected or unprotected by law.[15] Whether they are protected should

---

[11] Ibid, 103.   [12] MacKinnon, 'Not a Moral Issue', *Feminism Unmodified*, 156.

[13] For example by Barker, 598 F. Supp. 1316, 1330 (1984).

[14] 'Francis Biddle's Sister', *Feminism Unmodified*, 300 n.155.

[15] Expressive conduct is protected; speech of various kinds—libel, for instance—is unprotected. See Laurence Tribe, *American Constitutional Law*, 2nd edn. (Mineola, N.Y.: Foundation Press, 1988), ch. 12. Tribe also comments: 'The trouble with the distinction between speech and conduct is that it has less determinate content than is sometimes supposed. . . . It is . . . not surprising that the Supreme Court has never articulated a basis for its distinction; it could not do so, with the result that any particular course of conduct may be hung almost randomly on the "speech" peg or the "conduct" peg as one sees fit' (p. 827). Speech act theory gives some grounds for being dubious about the distinction, but that is not the point of what I have to say.

depend, in general, on the effects they have, and the actions they are. On MacKinnon's view pornography is speech, not conduct, but it is speech that should be left unprotected for the same kinds of reasons that other actions are sometimes left unprotected: because of the effects they have, and because of the actions they are.

Austin and MacKinnon are emerging as close, if unlikely, cousins. In this essay I exploit the work of the former to illuminate and defend the latter. I shall be concerned with two central claims. First is the claim already encountered, that pornography *subordinates* women. If Austin is right, the accusations of trickery and conceptual confusion leveled at this claim may be misguided. Second is the claim that pornography *silences* women.[16] This idea is sometimes offered in reply to the traditional 'free speech' defense of pornography. 'The free speech of men silences the free speech of women. It is the same social goal, just other *people*', says MacKinnon, arguing that feminist antipornography legislation is motivated by the very values enshrined in the First Amendment.[17] This claim too has been regarded as problematic: its detractors describe it as 'dangerous confusion', while even sympathizers have reservations, conceding that the silence in question is 'figurative', 'metaphorical'.[18] Drawing on Austin, we can show that the silence is not metaphorical, but literal, and that the second feminist claim is as defensible as the first.

The claim that pornography subordinates women, however interpreted, is a claim that pornography determines women's inferior civil status. Viewed thus, the ordinance poses an apparent conflict between liberty and equality: the liberty of men to produce and consume pornography, and the rights of women to equal civil status. That is how the case was viewed by the courts. It posed a conflict between the right to free speech guaranteed by the First Amendment, and the right to equality guaranteed by

[16] This idea is developed by MacKinnon and others in many places, but see, e.g., MacKinnon, 'The Sexual Politics of the First Amendment', *Feminism Unmodified*, 209.

[17] MacKinnon, 'Not a Moral Issue', ibid., 156. (I don't think much hinges here on MacKinnon's talk of free speech being a social goal, rather than a right.)

[18] Defending censorship in the name of liberty is 'a dangerous confusion'; the idea that pornography silences is 'confusion'; see Ronald Dworkin, 'Two Concepts of Liberty', in *Isaiah Berlin: A Celebration*, ed., Edna and Avishai Margalit (London: Hogarth Press, 1991), 103, 108. The claim that pornography silences is 'somewhat figurative', and 'metaphorical', according to Frank Michelman, 'Conceptions of Democracy', 294 n.8. (This figurativeness is not a handicap to the silencing argument in his view, however.) Dworkin's argument is criticized in more detail by Jennifer Hornsby, 'Disempowered Speech', *Philosophical Topics* 23 (1995), 127–47; and Langton, 'Dangerous Confusion?', this volume.

the Fourteenth Amendment. The claim that pornography silences women expresses a different conflict, one within liberty itself. Viewed thus, the ordinance poses an apparent conflict between the liberty of men to produce and consume pornography, and the liberty of women to speak.

One eminent liberal theorist is on record as saying that only an argument based on this second claim could have any prospect of success. It is only by developing the argument that pornography silences women that one could 'hope to justify censorship within the constitutional scheme that assigns a preeminent place to free speech', says Ronald Dworkin in a recent essay.[19] His conclusion there is that the 'silencing' argument is unsuccessful. Dworkin is mistaken in his assumption, as there are other ways of arguing for censorship. Indeed Dworkin's own theory provides an excellent resource for supplying such arguments, as I have shown elsewhere.[20] I think he is also mistaken in his conclusion, and although this paper does not address his argument directly, the final section will go some way towards showing why.

My paper divides into two parts, addressing the two ideas one at a time. Once we consider pornographic images and texts as speech acts, we are in a position to apply to them Austin's distinctions between locutionary, illocutionary, and perlocutionary acts. We can make good sense of some central feminist claims when we focus on the illocutionary aspect of pornographic speech. In the first section I develop and defend the claim about subordinating. In the second section I develop and defend the claim about silencing, drawing again on Austin. The relationship between speech and power is a large and daunting topic, but without getting into deep theoretical water we can begin with the following simple observation. The ability to perform speech acts of certain kinds can be a mark of political power. To put the point crudely: powerful people can generally do more, say more, and have their speech count for more than can the powerless. If you are powerful, there are more things you can do with your words.

---

[19] Dworkin, 'Two Concepts', 108.

[20] In 'Whose Right?', this volume. There I develop two independent arguments from a Dworkinian theoretical perspective for the conclusion that pornography ought to be censored. The first is an argument of principle: the fact that preferences of pornographers are by Dworkin's standards external preferences shows that women would have rights against a permissive policy. The second is an argument of policy: a prohibitive policy might have social equality as its goal, and pornographers would then have no rights against it.

This bears on the question about silence. If you are powerful, you sometimes have the ability to silence the speech of the powerless. One way might be to stop the powerless from speaking at all. Gag them, threaten them, condemn them to solitary confinement. But there is another, less dramatic but equally effective, way. Let them speak. Let them say whatever they like to whomever they like, but stop that speech from counting as an *action*. More precisely, stop it from counting as the action it was intended to be. That is the kind of silencing I will consider, and it is a kind of silencing about which Austin had something to say, without commenting on its political significance. Some speech acts are *unspeakable* for women in some contexts: although the appropriate words can be uttered, those utterances fail to count as the actions they were intended to be. If it can be shown that pornography contributes to this kind of silencing, then we will have a new way of understanding the second feminist claim.

My task, then, is partly diagnostic and partly polemical. Some of what I have to say will be as tentative and exploratory as Austin's own suggestions were. Some will not. Readers may find glaring sins of omission. Speech other than pornography may subordinate and silence women, and this raises important questions that are beyond the present project. But I will develop an analysis of the claims about subordinating and silencing that, if correct, will vindicate an argument that has been dismissed as philosophically incoherent. Whatever grounds one might have for doubting MacKinnon's conclusions, philosophical indefensibility is not among them. Understanding how pornographic utterances are speech acts will help to vindicate the claim about subordination. Understanding how some potential speech acts can be made unspeakable for women will help to vindicate the claim about silencing. If the argument makes the first claim plausible, pornography poses a conflict between liberty and equality. If it makes the second plausible, pornography poses a conflict between liberty and liberty: in particular between the free speech of men and that of women.

If pornography does pose these conflicts, how then should it be treated by the law? On MacKinnon's view, speech that subordinates and silences women is speech that should not be protected by law. Those who share MacKinnon's view may find in my arguments direct support for censorship. However, some may see a gap between conclusions about the defensibility of these feminist claims and conclusions about the need for censorship.

There may well be such a gap, and if there is, it is one that I do little to bridge here with independent argument. The reader must rest content with a more modest result: the twin feminist claims are certainly coherent, and, granting some not entirely implausible empirical assumptions, they may well be true.

1. 'Pornography Subordinates'

Speech Acts

Before considering whether pornographic speech acts may subordinate, we will first look at speech acts in closer detail, and then ask whether in principle speech acts may subordinate.

Austin's chief concern was with illocutionary speech acts, and much labor in *How to Do Things with Words* is devoted to discovering what is distinctive about them. An illocutionary act is the action performed simply *in* saying something. A perlocutionary act is the action performed *by* saying something. A perlocutionary act is an utterance considered in terms of its consequences, such as the effects it has on its hearers. Austin took pains to distinguish illocutions from perlocutions, and he thought that the phrases 'in saying' and 'by saying' were typical—though by no means infallible—markers of the two. 'In saying "I do" I was marrying; by saying "I do" I greatly distressed my mother.' Saying 'I do' in the right context counts as—constitutes—marrying: that is the illocutionary act performed. It does not count as distressing my mother, even if it has that effect: that is the perlocutionary act performed.

The illocutionary act bears certain relations to the other two. It can be thought of as a *use* of the locution to perform an action. In the earlier example, the first man used the locution 'shoot her' to *urge* the second to shoot, whereas he might have used the very same locution to perform a different action: to *order* the second, or to *advise* perhaps. An illocutionary act may have a particular perlocutionary effect as its goal. When the first man urged the second to shoot, he may have aimed to *persuade* the second to shoot.

Austin's belief that there is something distinctive about illocutionary acts seems right. What we have here are utterances whose force is something more than the semantic content of the sentence uttered—the locution—and something other than the effects achieved by the utterance—the perlocution. What is responsible for this important third dimension? Austin's answer was that an utterance has illocutionary force of a certain kind when it satisfies certain felicity conditions. These are typically set by conventions, written or unwritten, and typically require that the speaker is intending to do something with his words. Speech acts are a subset of actions in general, so there will always be some description under which a speech act is intentionally performed, and not mere noise and motion of lips.[21] The intention to perform an illocution of a particular kind often has an important role to play in determining what illocution is performed. Whether in saying 'I do' the speaker is marrying depends on the felicity conditions of marriage, which require that the speaker intends to marry, and that the utterance takes place in the course of a particular conventional procedure, with appropriate participants (adult heterosexual couple, unmarried, plus priest or registrar). The speaker will also need to secure 'uptake': that is to say, the hearer must recognize that an illocution of a certain kind is being performed. So, at any rate, the typical cases run.

However, speech acts are heir to all the ills that actions in general are heir to.[22] What we do, and what we aim to do, are not always the same. Speech acts can be unhappy, can misfire. Sometimes one performs an illocution one does not intend to perform. The first man, of the earlier example, may have ordered the second to shoot the woman, even if he did not intend to order, but merely, say, to advise. 'Coming from him, I took it as an order', the second might have said.[23] This is because the intention to perform an

---

[21] See Jennifer Hornsby, 'Philosophers and Feminists on Language Use', *Cogito* 2 (Autumn 1988), 13–15. For a similar approach to some of the questions addressed in this article, see Hornsby's excellent piece, 'Illocution and Its Significance', forthcoming in *Foundations of Speech Act Theory: Philosophical and Linguistic Perspectives*, ed., S. L. Tsohatzidis (London and New York: Routledge, 1994). Hornsby develops a sophisticated and somewhat different account of illocutions, and uses it to explain how women can be silenced. She too considers the examples of refusal and giving testimony considered later in this article.

[22] Austin, *How to Do Things with Words*, 105.

[23] See ibid., 76. (The ordering discussed in this passage is contrasted with requesting, rather than advising, as I have it.) This interpretation conflicts with some views about speech-act theory, but not, I think, with Austin's. See for example ibid., 114 n.1., where the ordering versus advising example appears. What the example has in common with those Austin labeled misfires is that there is a gap between the intended and the actual illocution.

illocution of a certain kind is not always a necessary felicity condition for that illocution. Here the context determines the uptake secured, which in turn determines the illocution performed. Moreover, sometimes one fails to perform an illocution one intends to perform. A misfire would occur, for instance, if the marriage ceremony was not completed, if the celebrant turned out to be an actor in priestly garb, or (Austin's example) if the prospective spouse was a monkey.[24] This is because the intention to perform an illocution of a certain kind is not the only felicity condition for that illocution. These kinds of unhappiness will occupy our attention in the final section.

Subordinating Speech Acts

We turn now to the second preliminary task: the question of whether speech acts can, in principle, subordinate. Austin placed his theory of speech and action firmly in the arena of social activity, and there is a political dimension to this arena. People manage to do all kinds of things with words. Besides advising, warning, and marrying one another, people also manage to hurt and oppress one another. A child may chant that 'sticks and stones may break my bones, but names will never hurt'. Names do hurt, though. That is just why she chants. And that is why the law regards some speech as injury. Words can break bones. 'Shoot her!' might break a few, as a perlocutionary act at any rate. ('By saying "shoot her" he caused her skull to be fractured'.) Speech can do more than break bones. It can determine civil status, as Easterbrook agreed, interpreting the idea in perlocutionary terms: by depicting subordination, pornographers perpetuate subordination.

When MacKinnon says that speech can subordinate, she means something more: that pornography can have the illocutionary force of subordination, and not simply have subordination as its locutionary content, or as its perlocutionary effect: *in* depicting subordination, pornographers subordinate. This is the alleged 'sleight of hand'.[25]

We need to evaluate this charge. Can a speech act be an illocutionary act of subordination? The answer, I think, is yes. Consider this utterance: 'Blacks are not permitted to vote.' Imagine that it is uttered by a legislator in Pretoria in the context of enacting legislation that underpins

---

[24] See ibid., 24.   [25] Judge Barker's accusation, see 598 F. Supp. 1316 (1984).

apartheid. It is a locutionary act: by 'Blacks' it refers to blacks. It is a perlocutionary act: it will have the effect, among others, that blacks stay away from polling booths. But it is, first and foremost, an illocutionary act: it makes it the case that blacks are not permitted to vote. It—plausibly—subordinates blacks. So does this utterance: 'Whites only.'[26] It too is a locutionary act: by "Whites" it refers to whites. It has some important perlocutionary effects: it keeps blacks away from white areas, ensures that only whites go there, and perpetuates racism. It is—one might say—a perlocutionary act of subordination. But it is also an illocutionary act: it orders blacks away, welcomes whites, permits whites to act in a discriminatory way towards blacks. It subordinates blacks.[27] If this is correct, then there is no sleight of hand, no philosophical impropriety, about the claim that a certain kind of speech can be an illocutionary act of subordination.

In virtue of what do the speech acts of apartheid subordinate? In virtue of what are they illocutionary acts of subordination? In virtue of at least the following three features, I suggest. They *rank* blacks as having inferior worth. They *legitimate* discriminatory behavior on the part of whites. And finally, they *deprive* blacks of some important powers: for example, the power to go to certain areas and the power to vote. Here I am in broad agreement with MacKinnon, who says that to subordinate someone is to put them in a position of inferiority or loss of power, or to demean or denigrate them.[28]

There are two brief caveats before I go on. First, on the notion of legitimating: the illocutionary act of legitimating something is to be distinguished from the perlocutionary act of making people believe that something is legitimate. Certainly one effect of legitimating something is that people believe it is legitimate. But they believe it is legitimate because it has been legitimated, not vice versa. People believe discriminatory behavior to be legitimate because it has indeed been made legitimate in that particular

---

[26] MacKinnon uses this example to make the point that words can be 'an integral act in a system of segregation, which is a system of force' (MacKinnon, 'On Collaboration', *Feminism Unmodified*, 202).

[27] Here I depart from Vadas ('A First Look'), for it is not in virtue of depicting subordination that the 'whites only' sign subordinates, if it does. That utterance does not depict subordination, any more than 'I do' depicts a marriage. So something can subordinate without depicting subordination. The converse is also true. Something can depict subordination without subordinating (a documentary, for example). Some examples of this will be considered shortly.

[28] MacKinnon, 'Francis Biddle's Sister', 176.

arena of activity (though there may still be some perspective outside that arena from which one can say that discriminatory behavior is never truly legitimate).[29] Second, I do not suggest that all acts of ranking, legitimating, or depriving of powers are acts of subordination. Someone may rank an athlete as the fastest, legitimate beer drinking on campus, or deprive a driver of his license. These may be illocutionary acts that rank, legitimate, or deprive people of powers, yet they are not acts of subordination. But, unlike these, the speech acts of apartheid are acts of subordination: they *unfairly* rank blacks as having inferior worth; they legitimate *discriminatory* behavior on the part of whites; and they *unjustly* deprive them of some important powers.

Speech acts of this kind belong to an important class of illocutions discussed by Austin towards the end of his work. Some illocutions involve the authoritative delivery of a finding about some matters of fact or value. Actions of ranking, valuing, and placing are illocutions of this kind, labeled *verdictive* by Austin. For example: An umpire calls 'Fault' at a tennis match. He expresses his opinion. He describes the world as he sees it. But he does much more than that: he gives his verdict. A bystander says 'Fault'. He expresses his opinion. He describes the world as he sees it. What he says has just the same content as what the umpire says: they perform the same locutionary act. But the bystander's utterance makes no difference to the score. The umpire's does. A government's action of ranking members of a certain race as inferior to others can be compared to the speech of the umpire, rather than the bystander. The authoritative role of the speaker imbues the utterance with a force that would be absent were it made by someone who did not occupy that role.

Close relatives of verdictives are illocutions that confer powers and rights on people, or deprive people of powers and rights. Actions of

---

[29] Compare an example borrowed from David Lewis. A master says to a slave: 'It is now permissible to cross the white line.' In saying that, the master makes a certain move, performs a certain illocutionary act: he makes it legitimate for the slave to cross the white line. The boundaries of what is legitimate and what is not change immediately. The beliefs of the slave as to what is legitimate will also change—that is to speak of the action's effects, its perlocutionary dimension. Here too there may also be some perspective from which we might say that it was never truly illegitimate for the slave to cross the line, but that would be to move outside the bounds of the language game in question. See Lewis, 'Scorekeeping in a Language Game', *Philosophical Papers*, vol. 1 (Oxford: Oxford University Press, 1983), 233–49.

ordering, permitting, prohibiting, authorizing, enacting law, and dismissing an employee are illocutions of this kind, labelled *exercitive* by Austin.[30] The speech acts of apartheid that legitimate discriminatory behavior and unjustly deprive blacks of certain rights have an exercitive force that would be absent if they were made by speakers who did not have the appropriate authority.

It is in virtue of these particular verdictive and exercitive dimensions, then, that the speech acts of apartheid subordinate. This already tells us something important about any claim that a certain kind of speech subordinates. For the crucial feature of verdictive and exercitive illocutions is their sensitivity to the speaker's authority, and we can accordingly group them together under the label *authoritative* illocutions: actions whose felicity conditions require that the speaker occupy a position of authority in a relevant domain. Sometimes that authority is officially recognized. That is true of the utterances of the legislator enacting the laws of apartheid, and it is true of the umpire giving a verdict on a fault. But the principle that illocutionary force can vary with the authority of the speaker is more general. A slave may say to his master, 'Is there anything to eat?' and the utterance may have the force of an entreaty. The master may say to the slave, 'Is there anything to eat?' and the utterance may have the exercitive force of an order. And the domains of authority can vary in size and scope. The domain of the legislator's authority is vast—the entire population of a nation, present and future. There are smaller domains. A parent who prohibits a child from venturing barefoot into the snow has authority in the local domain of the family. A patient who prohibits a doctor from administering life-saving medication has authority in the very local domain of his own life, his own body. In all these cases the action performed depends on the authority of the speaker in the relevant domain. Subordinating speech acts are authoritative speech acts, so if we are ever to count some class of speech acts as subordinating speech, the speakers in question must have authority. This is something to bear in mind in what follows.

[30] Austin's discussion of verdictives and exercitives is in lecture 11, especially sections 1 and 2, 152–6. The description I give of exercitives is used by him for what is strictly a proper subset of that class (p. 155).

Pornography

MacKinnon thinks that pornography in particular subordinates. The courts sometimes view this claim as a description of pornography's content. 'Those words and pictures which *depict women in sexually subordinate roles* are banned by the Ordinance', said Judge Barker in the district court, giving this as grounds for the Indianapolis Ordinance's unconstitutionality.[31] Barker is mistaken: the ordinance does not ban material simply by virtue of its content, for at this locutionary level there is nothing particularly distinctive about pornography. Not all sexually explicit depictions of subordination are pornography, as MacKinnon herself points out.[32] Utterances whose locutions depict subordination do not always subordinate. Locutions that depict subordination could in principle be used to perform speech acts that are a far cry from pornography: documentaries, for example, or police reports, or government studies, or books that protest against sexual violence, or perhaps even legal definitions of pornography. It all depends, as Austin might have said, on the *use* to which the locution is put. If we are to find what is distinctive about pornography, it seems that we must look elsewhere.

The perlocutionary aspect of pornographic utterances has rightly attracted much attention. This, as we saw, is how Easterbrook interpreted MacKinnon's claim when he said that pornography 'perpetuates' subordination. At the perlocutionary level, pornographic speech can be variously described. Some hearers are entertained and sexually aroused by it. At this level a difference between pornography and documentaries that depict subordination does emerge. Although similar locutions may be used in both cases, different effects are achieved in the hearers: sexual arousal in the one case, indignation, perhaps, in the other. Pornography does more than arouse. Some of its hearers are distressed by it, as was made evident at the 1983 Minneapolis hearings. Some, it seems, have their attitudes and behavior altered by it in ways that ultimately hurt women: they can become more likely to view women as inferior, more disposed to accept rape myths (for example, that women enjoy rape), more likely to view rape victims as deserving of their treatment, and more likely to say that they

---

[31] 598 F. Supp. 1316 (1984), my italics.   [32] MacKinnon, 'Francis Biddle's Sister', 176.

themselves would rape if they could get away with it.[33] This in turn means that some women are hurt by it. In Easterbrook's words, pornography perpetuates the cycle of 'insult and injury at home, battery and rape on the streets'.

The claim that pornography harms women is not yet the perlocutionary claim conceded by the court that pornography perpetuates women's subordination. Plenty of people are harmed by cigarettes, but they are not thereby subordinated. A link between harm and subordination is made, though, when we shift our perspective on the asymmetric pattern of sexual violence and view it afresh, not simply as harm or as crime, but as an aspect of women's subordinate status.[34] To view it otherwise would be to obscure its systematically discriminatory nature, and to obscure the fact that the perpetrators are nearly always members of one class of citizens, the victims nearly always members of another. This shift in perspective is an important feature of feminist political analysis, and it affects how we are to characterize pornography in perlocutionary (and, we shall see shortly, illocutionary) terms. If pornography has sexual violence as its effect and sexual violence is an aspect of women's subordination, then pornography is a *perlocutionary* act

[33] So I interpret the available evidence. See Edward Donnerstein, Daniel Linz, and Steven Penrod, *The Question of Pornography: Research Findings and Policy Implications* (New York: Free Press; London: Collier Macmillan, 1987), to which the reader is referred for details of some relevant studies. Under the influence of violent pornography, viewers 'come to cognitively associate sexuality with violence, to endorse the idea that women want to be raped, and to trivialize the injuries suffered by a rape victim. As a result of these attitudinal changes, men may be more willing to abuse women physically (indeed the laboratory aggression measures suggest such an outcome)' (p. 20). Of material that is violent and sexually arousing, though less sexually explicit (probably R-rated in the USA): 'Men who were exposed to the large doses of filmed violence against women judged the victim of a violent assault and rape to be significantly less injured, and evaluated her as generally less worthy than did the control group of subjects who saw no films' (p. 128). Of material that is sexually explicit but 'dehumanizing' rather than violent: 'subjects exposed to the dehumanizing material were more likely to report that they might commit a rape if assured that no one would know and they would not be punished', i.e., more likely than control subjects and subjects exposed to merely erotic material (p. 78). Moreover 'male subjects still had a propensity to trivialize rape 3 weeks after exposure to nonviolent [dehumanizing] pornography' (p. 77). The authors observe that evidence regarding the latter material is mixed, and hypothesize that the effects depend on concentrated dosage of dehumanizing scenes and relatively long exposure. See also *Public Hearings on Ordinances to Add Pornography as Discrimination Against Women*, Committee on Government Operations, City Council, Minneapolis, Minn. (Dec. 12–13, 1983). The transcript of the hearings was published as *Pornography and Sexual Violence: Evidence of the Links* (London: Everywoman, 1988), and mentions a study in which viewers exposed to pornography perceived half as many rapes in a film as other viewers did, suggesting a decreased ability to perceive rape as rape (p. 21) See also Edward Meese (Chair), *Report of the Attorney General's Commission on Pornography* (Washington, D.C.: United States Government Printing Office, 1986).

[34] MacKinnon argues for this change of perspective in 'Francis Biddle's Sister' and elsewhere.

of subordination. That is how we reach the claim conceded by Easterbrook: pornography perpetuates women's subordination.

However, the claim that pornography subordinates women is an illocutionary claim that goes beyond these locutionary and perlocutionary dimensions, and it is related to other illocutionary claims that feminists have made about pornography. Pornography is said to *rank* women as sex objects, 'defined on the basis of [their] looks . . . [their] availability for sexual pleasure'.[35] Pornography represents degrading and abusive sexual behavior 'in such a way as to *endorse* the degradation'.[36] MacKinnon has a striking list of illocutionary verbs: 'Pornography sexualizes rape, battery, sexual harassment . . . and child sexual abuse; it . . . *celebrates, promotes, authorizes* and *legitimates* them'.[37] These descriptions bear on the claim that pornography subordinates. Recall that we found three features in virtue of which the speech acts of apartheid were plausibly described as illocutionary acts of subordination. They rank certain people as inferior; they legitimate discriminatory behavior towards them; and they deprive them of powers and rights. The feminist claims we have just considered ascribe to pornography the first two of the three features. Pornography is, first, verdictive speech that ranks women as sex objects, and, second, exercitive speech that legitimates sexual violence. Since sexual violence is not simply harm, not simply crime, but discriminatory behavior, pornography subordinates because it legitimates this behavior. (Now we see how the feminist shift of perspective on violence affects our characterization of pornography at the illocutionary level as well.) For these two reasons, then, pornography is an *illocutionary* act of subordination. That, at any rate, is the claim.

However, there is disagreement—to put it mildly—about the correct ascription of pornography's illocutionary force. And this raises some questions. How, in general, do we discover what illocutionary force an utterance has? And what do we do in the face of disagreement? These are difficult questions, whose difficulty Austin acknowledged and sought—with limited

---

[35] MacKinnon, 'Francis Biddle's Sister', 173.

[36] Helen E. Longino, 'Pornography, Oppression and Freedom: A Closer Look', in *Take Back the Night: Women on Pornography*, ed., Laura Lederer (New York: William Morrow, 1980), 29. (Longino has the entire phrase in italics.)

[37] MacKinnon, 'Francis Biddle's Sister', 171, emphasis mine. I do not italicize 'sexualizes' because I think it may be a perlocutionary rather than an illocutionary verb, meaning something like 'makes viewers find the thought of rape, etc., sexually arousing'. But perhaps it is an illocutionary verb meaning something like 'legitimates rape, etc., in describing it as if it were normal sex'.

success—to alleviate. Disagreements about the ascription of illocutionary force can be hard to settle, the utterances in question needing to have 'a construction put upon them by judges'.[38]

In situations of disagreement, the disputed illocution usually falls short of the paradigm case for the given illocution. In the paradigm case, one knows just what the felicity conditions for the given illocution are, and one knows that they are all satisfied. She said 'I do' in the presence of priest and groom, the ceremony was uninterrupted, she intended to marry, etc., so in saying 'I do', she must have been marrying. Moreover, in the paradigm case, one knows that appropriate uptake is secured: all present took the parties to have been marrying. And one knows about the perlocutionary effects: the later beliefs of others that the parties were married, the mother's distress, the grandmother's joy, and so forth. But when a speech act falls short of the paradigm, though not far short, there may be dispute as to what illocutionary act was performed. Suppose the marriage ceremony is interrupted at the very end by the priest's sudden heart attack. Not quite all the felicity conditions for marriage are satisfied, and doubtless the event is infelicitous in our usual sense of that term, but it may be near enough, perhaps, to count as a marriage nonetheless. Or suppose it is not known for certain that the priest's qualifications meet the required standard, for he is a refugee whose papers are missing. Not all the felicity conditions for marriage are known to be satisfied, but near enough, perhaps, to count as a marriage nonetheless. The first case presents a problem of vague boundaries: we know that not all conditions have been satisfied, but perhaps it is close enough. The second presents a problem of ignorance: we do not know that all conditions have been satisfied, but again, perhaps it is close enough. In both cases, what we have resembles but falls short of the paradigm, and we have to ask ourselves, how close is close enough? Here there is scope for argument.

One may argue in different ways. First, one may argue that, vagueness or ignorance notwithstanding, *some* felicity conditions—important ones—are satisfied, and that is good enough. 'Shoot her' might count as an order, even if it failed exactly to match the paradigm—e.g., if it was intended merely as advice, but was spoken by someone in authority, in an appropriate context. Second, one may argue that *uptake* appropriate for the claimed illocution

---

[38] Austin, *How to Do Things with Words*, 114.

has been secured. 'Coming from him, I took it as an order', as the hearer may have said. Its being taken as an order may be a reason for thinking it was an order. Third, one may argue that a speech act's effects are best *explained* by supposing that it has a certain illocutionary force. Part of the explanation for my arriving at your party is that you performed a certain illocutionary act: you invited me. Part of the explanation for my taking the glass is that you performed another illocutionary act: you offered it to me. Part of the explanation for whites' discriminatory behavior is that such behavior has been legitimated by law. Part of the explanation for blacks keeping away from certain areas is that they have been ordered away. In such cases the illocutionary acts explain the perlocutionary effects.

All three ways of arguing are fallible, and they come in an ascending order of fallibility. The first, which says that at any rate *some* important felicity conditions have been satisfied, is tolerably secure. It is certainly a part of our practice of ascribing illocutions in everyday life, where the problems of vagueness and ignorance do not halt us in our tracks. 'In ordinary life', as Austin says, 'a certain laxness . . . is permitted'.[39] The second is more fallible: securing appropriate uptake may not be sufficient for the illocution in question. The third is also fallible, since there may be other possible explanations for the known effects: I may have come to your party uninvited. However, each of the three, or some combination of them, may be useful, depending on the evidence we have.

We are now in a position to consider the disputed question: does pornography subordinate? Since there is a dispute, it may be that pornography fails to match exactly the illocutionary paradigm. I have not tried to say exactly what the paradigm for subordination is, but I have suggested that the speech acts of apartheid offer a clear example. They have verdictive and exercitive force: they rank a class of people, legitimate discrimination against them, and deprive them of rights and powers. Their felicity conditions include the condition that the speakers occupy a position of authority. They are speech acts that achieve a certain uptake: they are taken to be verdictive and exercitive acts (though not all hearers will take them to be subordinating acts). They are illocutions that have a pattern of perlocutionary effects on the beliefs and behavior of the population:

---

[39] Austin, *How to Do Things with Words*, 37. Austin is speaking in particular here about failures to satisfy completely the procedural felicity conditions for an illocution.

whites believe blacks to be inferior, believe discrimination against them to be legitimate, and believe them to have fewer rights; whites discriminate against blacks, and blacks stay away from polling booths. Such speech acts are clearly acts of subordination.

Pornography falls short of this devastating paradigm in a number of important respects, but it may nonetheless be subordination. There is scope for argument in all three of the ways I discussed above. I begin with the third. We might find *explanations* for pornography's perlocutionary effects in terms of its illocutionary force. If the earlier claims are right, then pornography has a certain pattern of perlocutionary effects. It can affect attitudes and behavior, making its hearers more likely to view women as inferior, more disposed to accept rape myths, more likely to view rape victims as deserving of their treatment, and more likely to say that they themselves would rape if they could get away with it. Part of the explanation for this pattern might be that pornography has a particular illocutionary force: it ranks women as sex objects, and legitimates that kind of behavior. If pornography has the perlocutionary effects MacKinnon claims, then there is some reason for thinking it has the illocutionary force she and other feminist writers have ascribed to it.

This conclusion is reached by inference to the best explanation, and it is fallible. The hypothesis that you invited me to your party may best explain my arrival, but there are other possible explanations. Similarly, the hypothesis that pornography ranks women and legitimates certain attitudes and behavior may well explain the presence of these attitudes and behavior, but there are other possible explanations. The feminist claim would be strengthened if there were other ways to argue for the conclusion that pornography subordinates.

Let us consider the second way of arguing. What *uptake* does pornography secure in its hearers? What act do its hearers take it to be? The answer is mixed. Some hearers take it to be entertainment, escapist storytelling. Other hearers take it to be subordination. They take pornography to be something that ranks them, judges them, denigrates them, and legitimates ways of behaving that hurt women. Here we find vivid disagreement among the hearers as to just what the speech act is. Austin said that in such cases utterances are liable to have 'a construction put upon them by judges', but who is in a position to judge? We might say that those women who take pornography to be subordination are in a better position to judge, that they can tell better than some other hearers what ranks them, what demeans and denigrates them, and what seems to legitimate ways of acting that are violent. But unless we privilege one group of hearers in this way, our result with this way of arguing will be inconclusive, though it may give some support to the claim that pornography subordinates.

We come now to the first way of arguing. The task of discovering whether some important *felicity conditions* are met looks more hopeful, for at least we know one felicity condition for subordination, and could in principle know whether pornography satisfies it. Since verdictives and exercitives are both *authoritative* illocutions, we know that the ability to perform them depends on the speaker's authority. The umpire, and not the bystander, can call a fault. The government, and not the private citizen, can enact law that ranks and legitimates. The authority in question need not be as formally recognized as in those cases, but it needs to be there. This means that in order to answer the question, 'Does pornography subordinate?' one must first answer another: 'Do its speakers have authority?' If they do, then a crucial felicity condition is satisfied: pornographers' speech acts may be illocutions that authoritatively rank women, legitimate violence, and thus subordinate.

This question is, I think, at the heart of the controversy. If you believe that pornographic utterances are made by a powerless minority, a fringe group especially vulnerable to moralistic persecution, then you will answer negatively. Not so if you believe, with MacKinnon, that pornography's voice is the voice of the ruling power. Liberal debate about pornography has typically been premised on the former belief, and part of MacKinnon's task is to persuade us that it is false. Just as the speech of the umpire is authoritative within a certain domain—the game of tennis—so pornographic speech is authoritative within a certain domain—the game of sex. The authors of pornographic speech are not mere bystanders to the game; they are speakers whose verdict counts. Pornography tells its hearers what women are worth: it ranks women as things, as objects, as prey. Pornography tells its hearers which moves are appropriate and permissible: if it tells them that certain moves are appropriate because women want to be raped, it legitimates violence. If pornography is authoritative speech it may subordinate.

Does pornographic speech have the authority required to substantiate MacKinnon's claim? Is this crucial felicity condition satisfied? These are not really questions to be settled from the philosopher's armchair. To answer them one needs to know about the role pornographers occupy as authoritative speakers about the facts, or supposed facts, of sex. What is important here is not whether the speech of pornographers is universally held in high esteem: it is not—hence the common assumption among liberals that in defending pornographers they are defending the underdog. What is important is whether it is authoritative in the domain that counts—the domain of speech about sex—and whether it is authoritative for the hearers that count: people, men, boys, who in addition to wanting 'entertainment', want to discover the right way to do things, want to know which moves in the sexual game are legitimate. What is important is whether it is authoritative for those hearers who—one way or another—do seem to learn that violence is sexy and coercion legitimate: the fifty percent of boys who 'think it is okay for a man to force a woman if he is sexually aroused by her', the fifteen percent of male college undergraduates who say they have raped a woman on a date, the eighty-six percent who say that they enjoy the conquest part of sex, the twelve percent who rank faces of women displaying pain and fear to be more sexually attractive than faces showing pleasure.[40] In this domain, and for

---

[40] 'More than half the boys...thought that it was okay for a male to force (that is, rape) a female if he was sexually aroused by her', Robin Warshaw, *I Never Called it Rape* (New York: Harper and Rowe, 1988), 120, citing research by Jacqueline D. Goodchilds, Gail Zellman, Paula B. Johnson, and Roseann Giarusso, 'Adolescents and their Perceptions of Sexual Interactions', in A. W. Burgess, ed., *Rape and Sexual Assault*, vol. ii (New York: Garland Publishing Company, 1988). Warshaw is commenting on the proportion of boys who thought it was 'okay' to 'force sex' when 'she gets him sexually excited' (51%), 'she has led him on' (54%), or 'she is going to have sex with him and changes her mind' (54%). Warshaw describes studies which 'showed 15 percent of the male respondents reporting having raped a date', p. 14, citing work by Barry R. Burkhart and Annette L. Stanton, 'Sexual Aggression in Acquaintance Relationships', in *Violence in Intimate Relationships*, ed., Gordon Russell, Spectrum Press, 1985; eighty-six percent of male undergraduates surveyed said they enjoyed 'the conquest part of sex', in research done by Virginia Greendlinger and Donn Byrne, 'Coercive Sexual Fantasies of College Men as Predictors of Self-Reported Likelihood to Rape and Overt Sexual Aggression', *Journal of Sex Research* 23 (1987), 1–11; and a proportion of men 'rated the faces of women displaying emotional distress to be more sexually attractive than the faces showing pleasure', Warshaw giving the proportion as 30 percent (*I Never Called it Rape*, 97) and citing Alfred B. Heilbrun Jr. and Maura P. Loftus, 'The Role of Sadism and Peer Pressure in the Sexual Aggression of Male College Students', *Journal of Sex Research* 22 (1986), 320–32. However the 30 percent figure (cited by Warshaw, and by me in previous versions of the present essay) is, it seems, a relativized one, and in absolute terms 'only 12%' ranked distress as more sexually attractive than happiness. For this correction I am indebted to Alan Soble, 'Bad Apples: Feminist Politics and Feminist Scholarship', *Philosophy of the Social Sciences* 29 (1999), 354–88 at 376. The studies drawn from Warshaw are discussed by Naomi Wolf, in *The Beauty Myth* (London: Vintage, 1991), which is where I first came across them.

these hearers, it may be that pornography has all the authority of a monopoly.[41]

I have tried to show that pornography may subordinate, even if it falls short of the illocutionary paradigm. We earlier distinguished two ways in which actions may fall short. There may be vague boundaries in a situation where we know that not all conditions are satisfied and wonder whether what we have is close enough. There can be ignorance, where we do not know whether all conditions are satisfied. It may be that pornography falls short in both ways. We have the problem of ignorance: we are not certain that pornography is authoritative, and hence not certain whether it satisfies a crucial felicity condition for subordination. But supposing the problem of ignorance were remedied and pornography was known to satisfy this condition, the problem of vague boundaries might still remain. We might know that pornography satisfied many, but not all, the usual conditions for subordination. One typical feature of actions of ranking and legitimating, for example, is that the speakers *intend* to rank and legitimate. I have not argued that pornography satisfies that condition. But if pornography conforms closely enough to the paradigm in other respects, it may subordinate nonetheless.

The claim that pornography subordinates has good philosophical credentials: it is not trickery, or 'sleight of hand'; it is by no means 'philosophically indefensible'. Moreover, considerations about explanation, uptake, and the felicity conditions for subordination give us reasons—though not conclusive ones—for thinking that the claim may be true. Pornography's effects may be best explained by supposing that it has the illocutionary force of subordination. An important group of pornography's hearers—even if not its intended hearers—take it to be subordination. And if the empirical premise about pornography's authority turns out to be true, then pornography satisfies a crucial felicity condition for subordination.

What we have not yet considered, however, is whether speech that subordinates should be restricted by law. As we noted at the outset, it does not immediately follow from the claim that pornography subordinates women that censorship is the best answer. What follows is that there is a conflict between liberty and equality, just as the courts declared. One

---

[41] For a good discussion of the effect of this monopoly on the fantasy lives of these hearers and women as well, see Wolf, *The Beauty Myth*, esp. 162–8.

possible response to this conflict might be to fight for equality in ways compatible with respecting the liberty of pornographers. What I have said leaves open that possibility. If pornography subordinates women, then it is not in virtue of its content but of its authority that it does so. It need not have that authority. There are imaginable circumstances where material just like pornography in other respects would have no authority, and in such circumstances such speech would not subordinate. MacKinnon's claim is that those circumstances are not ours, though one can hope that someday they will be.

This way of understanding the subordination claim thus has implications for policy. There may be ways of undermining pornography's authority that fall short of outright censorship, ways that would eventually relegate pornographers to the status of mere bystanders to the game, whose speech does not count. Perhaps pornographic speech could be fought with more speech: the speech of education to counter pornography's falsehoods, where women tell the world what women are really like,[42] or with the speech of competition to counter pornography's monopoly, where women themselves become authors of erotica that is arousing and explicit but does not subordinate.[43]

All this may be possible if women can indeed fight speech with more speech. But if pornography not only subordinates but *silences* women, it is not easy to see how there can be any such fight. At this point the second feminist claim demands our attention. Whether women can fight speech with more speech depends on whether, and to what extent, women can speak.

2. 'Pornography Silences'

Silenced Speech Acts

If speech is action, then silence is failure to act. If pornography silences women, then it prevents women from doing things with their words.

[42] In the final chapter of *The Question of Pornography*, Edward Donnerstein advocates education to counteract pornography's harmful effects.

[43] This is advocated by the Women Against Censorship group, who, as *amici curiae*, protested against the MacKinnon ordinance; see also *Pleasure and Danger: Exploring Female Sexuality*, ed., Carole Vance (London: Routledge and Kegan Paul, 1984); and the collection *Sex Exposed: Sexuality and the Pornography Debate*, eds., Lynne Segal and Mary MacIntosh (New Brunswick, N.J.: Rutgers University Press, 1993).

Before considering whether pornography silences women, I will look at how speech acts, in general, may be silenced, and then ask whether in principle speech acts can silence.

The ability to perform speech acts can be a measure of political power. Those who are able to use the utterance 'Blacks are not permitted to vote' with the illocutionary force of prohibition are, as we saw, the ones with authority. Conversely, one mark of powerlessness is an inability to perform speech acts that one might otherwise like to perform. Corresponding to Austin's three-fold distinction, we can distinguish three kinds of silence, for there are three kinds of acts one may fail to perform. All three have their political significance, I think, but my chief interest will be in the third.

At the first and most basic level, members of a powerless group may be silent because they are intimidated, or because they believe that no one will listen. They do not protest at all, because they think that protest is futile. They do not vote at all, because they fear the guns. In such cases no words are uttered at all. In Austin's terms, speakers fail to perform even a *locutionary* act.

Sometimes, however, people will speak, but what they say will fail to achieve the effects that they intend: such speakers fail to perform their intended perlocutionary act. Silencing of this second kind, which we can call *perlocutionary frustration*, is a common enough fact of life: one argues, but no one is persuaded; one invites, but nobody attends the party; one votes, hoping to oust the government, but one is outnumbered. Such frustration can have a political dimension when the effects achieved depend on the speaker's membership in a particular social class.

But there is a third kind of silencing that happens when one speaks, one utters words, and fails not simply to achieve the effect one aims at, but fails to perform the very action one intends. Here speech misfires, and the act is unhappy in the way that Austin described: although the appropriate words are uttered, with the appropriate intention, the speaker fails to perform the intended illocutionary act. Silencing of this third kind we can call *illocutionary disablement*, and it is that to which we now turn our attention.[44]

---

[44] Habermas too is interested in the connection between the social power of speakers and the opportunities those speakers have to select and employ speech acts. But the constraints on speech acts that interest him (e.g., economic, psychological) are different from the structural constraints that interest me here. Insofar as illocutionary acts are identified by Habermas with *communicative* speech acts, which are to be found in the utopian 'ideal speech situation', his version of speech-act theory would in

In the previous section we considered how certain illocutions include among their felicity conditions the requirement that the speaker have authority in a relevant domain. Having authority can thus enable a speaker to perform illocutionary acts not otherwise available. Illocutionary disablement presents us with the other side of the same phenomenon: not having authority in the relevant domain can disable a speaker from performing illocutionary acts. That is why the ability to perform illocutionary acts can be viewed as a measure of authority, a measure of political power. Think again about the master and the slave. The master can order the slave or advise him. The master can grant or deny the slave permission to act in certain ways. The slave cannot grant or deny his master permission. He cannot order his master, though he may entreat him. The asymmetry of the power balance is reflected in the asymmetry of their abilities to perform certain illocutionary acts. Attempts by the slave to order or forbid will always be unhappy in Austin's sense. Such acts are unspeakable for the slave. Something has silenced his speech, not in the sense of rendering his spoken words inaudible or written marks illegible, but in the sense of depriving those sounds and marks of illocutionary force: of preventing those utterances from counting as the actions they were intended to be.

Example (1): *Warning.*   This example is from Donald Davidson.

Imagine this: the actor is acting a scene in which there is supposed to be a fire. . . . It is his role to imitate as persuasively as he can a man who is trying to warn others of a fire. 'Fire!' he screams. And perhaps he adds, at the behest of the author, 'I mean it! Look at the smoke!' etc. And now a real fire breaks out, and the actor tries vainly to warn the real audience. 'Fire!' he screams. 'I mean it! Look at the smoke!' etc.[45]

___

fact make the analysis I give here impossible. See Jürgen Habermas, *The Theory of Communicative Action* (Boston: Beacon Press, 1984), esp. vol. 1, 288–91. I am interested in precisely those illocutions that he leaves aside, those that are made against a backdrop of social inequality and sometimes help to bring that inequality about.

[45] Donald Davidson, 'Communication and Convention' in *Inquiries into Truth and Interpretation* (Oxford: Oxford University Press, 1984), 269. Davidson does not, of course, take this example to illustrate the power of convention, as I do. On the contrary, he infers from this example that convention can do far less than it is commonly supposed to do; in particular, convention could never succeed in making an utterance count as an assertion. I am not sure that I have any quarrel with the latter, but I am interested here in a different question: whether conventions of a different kind, those of theatre, can sometimes be sufficient to block an utterance's having the intended illocutionary force.

The actor says words that are appropriate for the action he wants to perform. He gets the locutionary act exactly right. He intends to warn; if appropriate intention is among warning's felicity conditions, then that is a condition he satisfies. But he does not warn. Uptake is not secured. Something about the role he occupies prevents his utterance from counting as a warning. Something, perhaps, about the conventions of theatre constrains the speech acts he can make. The same words said with the same intentions by an audience member would count as a warning. The actor, though, has been silenced. The act of warning has been made unspeakable for him.

Example (2): Marriage.   To say 'I do' is, given the right circumstances, to marry, given that the felicity conditions of marriage are satisfied. Suppose now that both parties intending to marry are male. They sincerely intend to marry. The speaker uses the right locution. The priest is no mere actor. The ceremony is performed by the book. The speaker satisfies all the felicity conditions but one. Something about who he is, and who his partner is, prevents him from satisfying one crucial felicity condition. The act of marrying misfires. The felicity conditions of marriage are such that two male participants cannot succeed. The act of marriage is not speakable for homosexual couples. The power to marry, an important power available to other citizens, is not available to them.

Example (3): Voting.   A white South African makes marks on a piece of paper in a polling booth. A black South African makes marks that look just the same, and in similar conditions. Their intentions, we can imagine, are just the same. But the former has succeeded in doing something significant. He has voted. The latter has not. Something about who he is prevents him from satisfying a crucial felicity condition. South African law prevents his utterance from counting as a vote: voting is not speakable for him. He too lacks an important political power available to other citizens.

Example (4): Divorce.   To utter the words '*mutallaqa, mutallaqa, mutallaqa*' (literally 'divorced, divorced, divorced') is to perform the illocutionary act of divorce in a country where Islamic law is in force, provided certain felicity conditions are met. Pronounced by a husband to his wife, it is an act of divorce. Not so if it is pronounced by the wife to her husband. No matter how hard she tries, a woman cannot succeed in divorcing her spouse by making that or any relevantly similar utterance. Divorce of that kind is an act that is unspeakable for women.[46]

Silencing Speech Acts

We have just considered briefly some ways in which speech can be silenced: simple silence, where nothing is said at all; perlocutionary frustration, where a speaker says words, succeeds in performing the intended illocution, but fails to achieve the intended effect; and the special silence of illocutionary disablement, singled out and illustrated in the above examples. The next task is to address the question of whether and how speech can actively silence. This question has been addressed by many other writers, and there are all kinds of subtle ways that speech can silence that I shall not consider. But we will see that each of the three kinds of silence to which I drew attention in the last section can be brought about by speech. This means we can usefully distinguish three kinds of silencing speech, in line with Austin's categories. My chief interest is in the question of whether speech can bring about the third silence of illocutionary disablement; and my way in to this question will be to consider, by way of contrast, the two kinds of silencing speech that differ.

Some speech is silencing speech by virtue of being an order or a threat. Suppose a judge, faced with a heckling crowd, says, 'Silence in the court'. His illocution is an order, and it aims to achieve a certain effect, namely silence in the court. That is the perlocutionary goal of the judge's utterance, as Austin would have put it. The ensuing silence of the would-be hecklers is real, and it is simple silence: no sounds are made at all, not even a locutionary act is performed. The same is true of the silence that is a response to a threat. Some speech, however, silences not by preventing a speaker from uttering words, but by preventing a speaker from achieving their intended effect. The perlocutionary goal of the man who said 'shoot her' might have been frustrated had the woman said 'Don't!' and the second man heeded her, and disobeyed the first man. Her action might have silenced the first man by frustrating the effect he intended.

---

[46] As far as *talak* divorce is concerned, 'a woman [has] no power of divorce'; see Honorable Moulvi Mahomed Yusoof Khan Bahadur, *Mahomedan Law*, vol. 3 (Calcutta: Thacker, Spink and Co., 1898), 47. However, there are some qualifications. The husband may delegate the right of *talaq* to his wife; see Keith Hodkinson, *Muslim Family Law* (London: Croom Helm, 1984), 222. Although *talaq* is the commonest kind of divorce, there are other means of achieving divorce, some of which are available to women in certain special circumstances (ibid., 219–306).

Neither of these is the silence of illocutionary disablement. The woman would not make the first man's illocution unspeakable. He has already spoken. She would not prevent him from ordering, but she prevents him from being obeyed. Nor does the judge make the heckler's intended illocution literally unspeakable when he says 'silence'. Someone courageous enough or foolhardy enough could speak up anyway. He would then be disobeying the judge, and may well be punished for it, but he would have succeeded in performing his intended action nonetheless. Contrast this with the previous examples. A black who makes marks on the ballot paper does not *disobediently vote*; he does not vote. A homosexual who says 'I do' does not *disobediently marry*; he does not marry. These actions, unlike the order, unlike the heckling, really have been made unspeakable.

Is it possible for speech to silence in this latter way? Is it possible to silence someone, not by ordering or threatening them into simple silence, not by frustrating their perlocutionary goals, but by making their speech acts unspeakable? This is a question about the role speech may play in disabling speakers, preventing them from satisfying the felicity conditions for some illocutions they might want to perform. So far we have noted the phenomenon of illocutionary disablement, but not yet asked how it comes about. Austin offers little explicit guidance here, but there is an implicit answer.

Felicity conditions, he says, are fixed by conventions. In examples (2)–(4) they are formal laws spelling out the conditions that must be met for marriage, voting, and divorce. Felicity conditions are not always (not even usually) spelled out in laws though, and for promising, warning, urging, protesting, and so forth, it will not always be clear just what the felicity conditions are, what the conventions are, or whether there are really conventions at all. Suppose we go with Austin and use 'convention' as a loose label for whatever sets felicity conditions. How do these come into being? When we consider some of Austin's paradigm cases, we see that one way that conventions are brought into being, one way that felicity conditions are set, is indeed by means of other speech acts. These are *'words that set conditions'* in MacKinnon's phrase.[47] In examples (2)–(4), laws are *enacted* that set felicity conditions for marriage, voting, and divorce. Some illocutionary

---

[47] MacKinnon, *Feminism Unmodified*, 228, my italics. She is referring here to the words of legal enactments, but it is not quite—or rather, not just—*felicity* conditions she has in mind.

acts fix the range and scope of other illocutionary acts. Some speech acts build a space, as it were, for other speech acts, making it possible for some people to marry, vote, and divorce. Some speech acts, in contrast, set limits to that space, making it impossible for other people to marry, vote, divorce. Some speech determines the kind of speech there can be. This shows that it is indeed possible to silence someone, not just by ordering or threatening them into simple silence, not just by frustrating their perlocutionary goals, but by making their speech acts unspeakable. It is possible to use speech to disable speakers, and possible to prevent them from satisfying the felicity conditions for some illocutions they might want to perform.

Felicity conditions for illocutions in general are rarely spelled out in the words of legal enactments. What then of the conventions that set conditions for other illocutions, warning, protesting, urging, and the rest? If it is hard to say just what the conditions are, it will be harder still to say what sets them. But again, the answer may be that, by analogy with the legal cases, they can be set by what is said, this time by informal practices of speech and communication that gradually establish precedents and informal rules about what counts as, for example, a warning. As in the legal examples, felicity conditions can be set by words. The space for potential speech acts can be built by speakers, as can the limits on that space, the constraints responsible for the silence of illocutionary disablement. Let us at least take this as our working hypothesis.

Pornography

We have seen how speech can be silenced, and we have seen how speech can silence. MacKinnon's claim is that pornographic speech, in particular, silences the speech of women. It is time now to address that claim. But I approach it indirectly, with some more examples.

Example (5): Refusal.   Consider the utterance 'no'. We all know how to do things with this word. We use it, typically, to disagree, to refuse, or to prohibit. In sexual contexts a woman sometimes uses it to refuse sex, to prohibit further sexual advances. However, in sexual contexts something odd happens. Sometimes a woman tries to use the 'no' locution to refuse sex, and it does not work. It does not work for the twenty percent of undergraduate women who report that they have been date raped. It does not work for the twenty-five percent of final-year schoolgirls who report that they have been sexually forced.[48] Saying 'no' sometimes doesn't work, but there are two ways in which it can fail to work. Sometimes the woman's hearer recognizes the action she performs: i.e., he recognizes that she is refusing. Uptake is secured. In saying 'no', she really does refuse. By saying 'no', she intends to prevent her hearer from continuing his advances. But the hearer goes ahead and forces sex on the woman. She prohibits, but he fails to obey. She fails to achieve the goal of her refusal. Her refusal is frustrated. 'Perlocutionary frustration' is too meek and academic a label for what is simple rape.

Sometimes, though, there is the different phenomenon of illocutionary disablement. Sometimes 'no', when spoken by a woman, does not *count* as the act of refusal. The hearer fails to recognize the utterance as a refusal; uptake is not secured. In saying 'no' she may well intend to refuse. By saying 'no' she intends to prevent sex, but she is far from doing as she intends. Since illocutionary force depends, in part, on uptake being secured, the woman fails to refuse. She is in the position of the actor in Davidson's story, silenced as surely as the actor is silenced. He shouts 'Fire!' He performs the appropriate locutionary act. He means what he says. He intends to warn. He tries to warn. But what he says misfires. Something about him, something about the role he occupies, prevents him from warning the audience. She says 'no'. She performs the appropriate locutionary act. She means what she says. She intends to refuse. She tries to refuse. But what she says misfires. Something about her, something about the role she occupies, prevents her from voicing refusal. Refusal—in that context—has become unspeakable for her. In this case refusal is not simply frustrated but disabled.

Example (6): *Protest.* The following appeared in a mail-order catalog advertising 'adult reading', flanked by such titles as *426. Forbidden Sexual Fantasies* and *428. Orgy: An Erotic Experience.*

---

[48] The first statistic comes from a study of students at the University of South Dakota. There are comparable and worse figures for other universities: St. Cloud State University (twenty-nine percent of the women students reported having been raped), Auburn University (twenty-five percent reported having been raped at least once), and Brown University (sixteen percent reported having been date raped), cited in Wolf, *The Beauty Myth*, 166, 167. The second statistic comes from J. Caputi, *The Age of Sex Crime* (London: The Women's Press, Ltd., 1987), 119.

No. 427 ORDEAL: an autobiography by Linda Lovelace. With M. McGrady. The star of *Deep Throat* tells the shocking story of her enslavement in the pornographic underworld, a nightmarish ordeal of savage violence and unspeakable perversion, of thrill seeking celebrities and sadistic criminals. For Sale to Adults Over 21 Only.

Ordeal is a book that has been much cited by feminists who oppose pornography.[49] The testimony of Linda Lovelace, or Linda Marchiano, to use her real name, features in evidence about pornography presented at the 1983 Minneapolis hearings.[50] In the book Marchiano tells the story of her involvement with the making of the film *Deep Throat*, describing how she was beaten, hypnotized, and tortured in order to perform her starring role. Austin once commented that one can perform the illocutionary act of protest a number of different ways: one can shout words in protest; one can hurl a tomato in protest.[51] One can also write a book in protest. *Ordeal* is an act of protest, a resounding denunciation of the industry in which Marchiano says she was forced to perform. One can see why it was used in the antipornography hearings. As a locutionary act *Ordeal* depicts the subordination of a woman: it depicts a woman 'in scenarios of degradation, injury and torture'. But it does not invite fantasy and arousal. It invites indignation. It does not 'endorse the degradation'; it does not 'celebrate, promote, authorize and legitimate' the sexual violence. It does not have pornography's illocutionary force.

Why then is *Ordeal* in a mail-order catalog for adult reading? The answer is simple. It is there because it is pornography after all: here, in this context, for these intended hearers, the uptake secured is bound to be that of pornography. Marchiano says the words appropriate for an act of protest. She uses the right locutions, words that graphically depict her own subordination. She intends to protest. But her speech misfires. Something about who she is, something about the role she occupies, prevents her from satisfying protest's felicity conditions, at least here. Though the threats and gags are gone, there is silence of another kind. She too is in the plight of Davidson's actor. Warning was unspeakable for him. Protest is unspeakable

[49] Linda Lovelace, with Mike McGrady, *Ordeal* (Secaucus, N.J.: Citadel Press, 1980).
[50] See *Hearings.*   [51] Austin, *How to Do Things with Words*, p. 118.

for her.[52] What he tries to say comes out as 'merely acted'. What she tries to say comes out as pornography. Her protest has been disabled.

MacKinnon claims that pornography silences the speech of women. But how? We noted that one way that speech can silence is in virtue of being an order or a threat that induces simple silence in its hearers. That is the first kind of silencing. MacKinnon cites cases where pornography itself is used to threaten: children coerced into pornography are blackmailed into silence by pornographers who threaten to show the pornography to their parents and teachers. Pornographic depictions of their subordination are used to threaten and thereby perpetuate that same subordination.[53] The silence here is simple: the children say nothing because they are afraid.

Pornography may silence in the second way: by preventing women, not from speaking, but from achieving the effects they want to achieve. If, as was argued above, pornography legitimates sexual violence, then it follows that one of pornography's effects may be to prevent a woman's refusal of sex from achieving its intended purpose. If pornography legitimates rape, then it may silence refusal by frustrating its perlocutionary goal. For many cases of rape, and probably all that reach the courts, match the first pattern described in (5) above: the woman whose hearer recognized that she refused, and persisted in spite of it, or perhaps because of it; the woman whose hearer recognized the prohibition and disobeyed. If pornography legitimates rape of this kind, it does so by sexualizing the use of force in response to refusal that is recognized as refusal. Such pornography eroticizes refusal itself, presenting the overpowering of a woman's will as exciting. Someone learning the rules of the sexual game from that kind of pornography would recognize a woman's refusal and disobey it. This would be one way in which pornography frustrates the goals of women's speech.

But we have seen that there is the possibility of a different kind of silence: the silence not just of frustration but of illocutionary disablement,

---

[52] *Ordeal* has not misfired *tout court*; in many contexts it has succeeded as an illocutionary act of protest. A similar sexually explicit depiction of subordination that aims to be protest rather than pornography is Andrea Dworkin's *Mercy* (London: Secker and Warburg, 1990), and it may provoke similar paradoxes. Harriet Gilbert argues that Dworkin's *Mercy* and Sade's *Justine* have much in common, and that the former could arguably count as pornography by the ordinance definition, showing, in her view, the futility of attempts at legal definition ('So Long as It's Not Sex and Violence', in *Sex Exposed*).

[53] MacKinnon, 'Francis Biddle's Sister', 180, citing evidence from the Minneapolis hearings.

manifested by the would-be warnings, marriages, votes, and divorces of examples (1)–(4). And this silencing is manifested in examples (5) and (6): the illocutionary disablement of the second rape victim, whose attempted refusal is not even recognized as a refusal; the disablement of an author whose attempted protest is not recognized as protest. These misfires betray the presence of structural constraints on women's speech. If Austin is right, the explanation for the unhappiness here is that the felicity conditions for refusal, for protest, are not being met. Something is robbing the speech of its intended force. Whatever the conventions governing sexual interactions may be, they can mean that intending to refuse, intending to protest, is not enough. The rules fixing possible moves in the language games of sex are such that saying 'no' can fail to count as making a refusal move, and telling the story of one's own subordination can fail to count as a move of protest. These are illocutions whose felicity conditions, it seems, cannot be satisfied by women, at least in these contexts.

What, if anything, has pornography to do with this third kind of silence, this disablement of women's speech that can make rape so hard to prevent and hard to protest about? If the felicity conditions for such illocutions constrain women in these contexts, we need to ask how those conditions came into being. This question was asked about the conditions that constrain illocutions of marriage, divorce, and the like, and the answer was that they were set by the speech of the legislator. How then are these other felicity conditions set? We know that felicity conditions for illocutions in general can be set by other speech acts. MacKinnon's claim that pornography silences women can be interpreted in just this way. *The felicity conditions for women's speech acts are set by the speech acts of pornography.* The words of the pornographer, like the words of the legislator, are 'words that set conditions'. They are words that constrain, that make certain actions—refusal, protest—unspeakable for women in some contexts. This is speech that determines the kind of speech there can be.

Let us see how this might apply to the second refusal in (5). Pornography might legitimate rape, and thus silence refusal, by doing something other than eroticizing refusal itself. It may simply leave no space for the refusal move in its depictions of sex. In pornography of this kind there would be all kinds of locutions the women depicted could use to make the consent move. 'Yes' is one such locution. 'No' is just another. Here the refusal move is not itself eroticized as in the pornography considered earlier: it is absent altogether. Consent is the *only* thing a woman can do with her words in this game. Someone learning the rules of the game from this kind of pornography might not even recognize an attempted refusal. 'Coming from her, I took it as consent', he might say.[54] Refusal would be made unspeakable for a woman in that context.

How common is silencing of this kind and the rape that accompanies it? It is hard to tell because so tiny a fraction of rapes are reported and these would be least reported of all. But the study that found that one in four final-year schoolgirls had been sexually forced also found that one in seven boys of the same age reported having refused to take no for an answer. One reading of this is that the boys in question recognized the refusal and persisted in spite of it. Naomi Wolf's comment suggests something further: that

boys rape and girls get raped *as a normal course of events*. The boys may even be unaware that what they are doing is wrong; violent sexual imagery may well have raised a generation of young men who can rape women without even knowing it.[55]

If young men can rape without knowing it, then women sometimes fail to secure uptake for their attempted refusals. This is the silence, not simply of frustration, but of disablement.

Refusal, here, is a kind of prohibition, and it is an exercitive illocution, in Austin's terms. To satisfy its felicity conditions, the speaker must have authority in a relevant domain. A government that prohibits has authority over a large domain; a parent who prohibits has authority within the smaller domain of the family; a patient who prohibits treatment has authority within the local domain of his own life, his own body. A woman who prohibits sexual advances also has authority within the local domain of her own life, her own body. If she cannot prohibit, cannot refuse, the authority is absent. If she is disabled from speaking refusal, it is a sign

---

[54] This paraphrases Austin's example, in *How to Do Things with Words*, 76. These different motivations for rape were described by an anonymous and articulate young rapist interviewed on the Australian Broadcasting Commission's documentary 'Without Consent' (1992), who said that rapes are committed for the thrill of overpowering a woman's will; the gang rapes he had taken part in for the sake of mateship and male camaraderie were not rapes at all, on his view, despite the women's lack of consent. His idea seemed to be that it was only rape if the woman's lack of consent was essential to the rapist's experience.

[55] Wolf, *Beauty Myth*, 167. 'Refusing to take no for an answer' might be ambiguous between failing to recognize a woman's refusal and failing to obey it. The study of Toronto schoolchildren is discussed in Caputi, *The Age of Sex Crime*.

that her body is, in a sense, not her own. If pornography prevents her from refusing, then pornography destroys her authority as it twists her words.

Part of the concern about whether pornography silences women is a concern that pornography may prevent women from fighting speech with more speech. In considering the feminist ordinance, the courts had to consider whether pornographic speech 'operates self-entrenchingly, disabling its natural enemies—its victims—from countering it with effective speech of their own'.[56] 'Effective' is ambiguous. One way your speech can be effective is when you can perform just the illocutionary acts you want to perform: when you intend to warn, marry, or refuse, you really do warn, marry, or refuse. Another way your speech can be effective is when you perform just the perlocutionary acts you want to perform: you warn, aiming to alert your hearers; you refuse, aiming to prevent unwanted sex; and you fulfill your goals. Both kinds of effective speaking are important, and both are needed to counter the speech of pornography.

The story about *Ordeal* in (5) is anecdotal, but it illustrates the way that pornography can operate self-entrenchingly. Marchiano tries to protest, but she only succeeds in making more pornography. The pornographers know how to do things with her words: stories of 'savage violence' and 'enslavement in the pornographic underworld' are simply pornography to readers for whom violence has been legitimated as sex. And there is ironic truth in what the pornographers say: the violence is indeed 'unspeakable' for Marchiano, for they have made it so. If you are a woman using sexually explicit speech, describing in some detail the savage sexual violence you have suffered, and especially if you are already a famous pornography star, what you say simply counts as pornography. It is an effective way to silence, not simply by depriving speech of its intended illocutionary force, but by replacing it with a force that is its antithesis.

The story is not, I think, an isolated anecdote. If MacKinnon is right, it has something in common with a phenomenon that is widespread and pernicious, a phenomenon that deserves more attention than I give it here: namely, the analogous disablement encountered by women who give testimony in court about rape and about sexual harassment, and whose testimony, and descriptions of their experience, achieve the uptake

---

[56] See Michelman, 'Conceptions of Democracy', 299.

appropriate to a description of normal sex.[57] If pornography legitimates violence as sex, then it can silence the intended actions of those who want to testify about violence. This too is an aspect of its self-entrenching character.

If pornography sets up the rules in the language games of sex—if pornography is speech that determines the kind of speech there can be—then it is exercitive speech in Austin's sense, for it is in the class of speech that confers and removes rights and powers. We saw that the claim that pornography subordinates requires the premise that pornography is authoritative speech, otherwise it could not rank and legitimate. We can now see that the claim that pornography silences requires the same premise: pornographic speech must be authoritative if it is to engender the silence of illocutionary disablement.

The claim that pornography silences women, like the claim about subordination, has been taken to be philosophically problematic. It is at best 'metaphorical', and at worst a 'dangerous confusion'. I have tried to show that it is neither.

The claim that pornography silences is one that can be taken literally. One might object that the silencing I have described is not literal silencing because pornography does not—except in rare circumstances when it is used to threaten—literally prevent women from uttering words.[58] It does not—in Austin's terms—usually prevent women from performing locutionary acts. But to think that way is to exhibit just the tendency of which Austin complained, to be preoccupied with the content of what is said, at the expense of the action performed. One way of being silent is to make no noise. Another way of being silent—literally silent—is to perform no speech act. On Austin's view, locutions on their own are nothing. Locutions are there to be used. Words are tools. Words are for doing things with. There is little point in giving someone tools if they cannot do things with them. And there is little point in allowing women words if we cannot do things with them. That, at any rate, is not free speech.

The claim is not metaphor; it is not confusion either. Dworkin says that it is a confusion to suppose that pornography silences women, because it

---

[57] It is estimated that only one in ten rapes are reported to the police and far fewer make it to court. See MacKinnon, *Feminism Unmodified*, 110–15.

[58] Michelman says this in 'Conceptions of Democracy', 296 n. 13.

is a confusion to 'characterize certain ideas as silencing ideas'.[59] Dworkin misconstrues the argument. The feminist claim is not that ideas are silencing ideas, but that acts can be silencing acts. That, as we have seen, is no confusion. People do all kinds of thing with words: besides advising, warning, and hurting one another, they also silence one another. They silence by preventing speakers from doing things with words. They can silence simply, by ordering or by threatening; they can silence by frustrating a speaker's perlocutionary acts; they can silence by disabling a speaker's illocutionary acts. We have seen that pornography can silence in all three ways.

The silencing claim is not really about ideas at all, but about people and what they do. It is not uncommon, in discussions about free speech, to cast ideas as the heroes of the story. Free speech is a good thing, because it provides a free marketplace for ideas where the best and truest ideas can win out in the end.[60] To say that some speech silences is to describe a kind of shopping problem: some ideas that could be on the market are not. Censorship may or may not be needed as a means of improving the marketplace, a little local regulation to improve things overall. Perhaps some ideas must be censored so that others can find space on the shelves.[61] Here again we have the tendency of which Austin complained: a focus on content, while ignoring the speech act performed. The claim that pornography silences women is not about ideas, but about people. Free speech is a good thing because it *enables people to act*, enables people to do things with words: argue, protest, question, answer. Speech that silences is bad, not just because it restricts the ideas available on the shelves, but because it constrains people's actions. It is true that women have problems developing and expressing new ideas about themselves, about sexuality, about life, when pornography has a market monopoly. The marketplace is certainly missing out on some valuable ideas. But that is not the point. The point is that a woman's liberty to speak the *actions* she wants to speak has been curtailed: her liberty to protest against pornography and rape, to refuse sex when she wants to, to argue about violence in court, or to celebrate and promote new ways of thinking about sexuality. The point

[59] Dworkin, 'Two Concepts', 108.

[60] 'The best test of truth is the power of the thought to get itself accepted in the competition of the market', said Justice Holmes in Abrams, quoted in Tribe, *Constitutional Law*, 686.

[61] This is—roughly—Dworkin's version of Frank Michelman's argument, 'Two Concepts', 108.

is that women cannot *do things* with words, even when we think we know how.

3. Concluding Remarks

Our exploration has taken us through some rocky terrain. In the first section we addressed the first feminist claim, that pornography subordinates, but in order to do so, we had first to ask how speech can be action, and then to ask whether, in principle, speech can subordinate. The answer was that speech can subordinate when it has a certain verdictive and exercitive force: when it unfairly ranks members of a social group as inferior, when it legitimates discriminatory behavior towards them, and when it unjustly deprives them of some important powers. The speech acts of pornography may subordinate, it was argued, because they may fulfill the first and second of these functions: they may rank women as sex objects, and legitimate discriminatory behavior towards them. Whether pornography subordinates depends on whether it is authoritative.

In the second section we addressed the second feminist claim, that pornography silences; and in order to do so, we had first to ask how speech acts can be silenced, and whether speech can silence. The answer was that speech can indeed silence, and in a number of ways. The speech acts of pornography may silence if they prevent women from speaking certain actions, frustrating their intended perlocutionary acts and disabling their intended illocutionary acts. I drew special attention to the speech acts of refusal and protest. Whether pornography silences depends, again, on whether it is authoritative. If pornography disables women's speech, then it deprives women of an important power. We thus come full circle, for this is the third aspect of subordination, unattended to in Section 1. To subordinate is to rank, to legitimate discrimination, to unfairly deprive of a power; to silence is to deprive of a power. So there is a link between the subordination claim and the silencing claim: one way of subordinating is to silence, to deprive someone of certain liberties that are available to others—the opportunity, for example, freely to speak.

The claims that pornography subordinates and silences women make perfect sense; they are not sleight of hand, not philosophically indefensible, not confused. Moreover, if pornographic speech is indeed authoritative, the claims may well be true. The premise about pornography's authority is an empirical one. If you think it is false, you will disagree with the conclusion about the truth of the claims, but not, I hope, with the conclusion about their coherence.

If pornography subordinates women, it presents a conflict between pornographers' right to liberty and women's right to equality. If pornography silences women, it presents a conflict within liberty itself, between pornographers' right to speak and women's. If pornography silences women, women will have difficulty fighting subordinating speech with speech of their own. Does this give us reason for thinking that MacKinnon may be right, not only in the two claims considered, but in her view that pornography should be restricted by law? Perhaps. Or perhaps we need independent argument to bridge the gap. Such an argument is beyond my project here, but it may not be too hard to find. For an influential liberal view has it that it is wrong for a government to allow private citizens to violate the liberty of other citizens by preventing them from saying what they wish. That liberal view has been eloquently expressed by Ronald Dworkin, among others.[62] If that is correct, it may be wrong to permit some speakers to silence others by preventing them from speaking the actions they wish to speak. Women wish to be able to speak some important actions: to be able to refuse, to protest, or to give testimony. The speech of pornographers may prevent them from doing so. If it does, then it may be wrong for a government to allow pornographers to speak.

[62] Ibid., 108. Dworkin's actual words are 'violate the negative liberty'. He wants to say that if pornography silences (which he doubts), it does so by depriving women of a positive liberty rather than a negative liberty: it 'denies them the right to be their own masters', 106, and prevents them from contributing to the process through which ideas battle for public favor. It should be evident from what I have said that, on the contrary, pornography silences by depriving women of the *negative* liberty to perform some important speech acts.

2

Dangerous Confusion? Response to Ronald Dworkin

Old wars about pornography and censorship have 'new armies' in radical feminists, Dworkin once remarked, defending the renewed relevance of his classic liberal defense of free speech in 'Do we Have a Right to Pornography?' Dworkin was right about the new battles, but wrong about his argument, which on the new battle-ground not only failed to justify the permissive conclusion he desired, but, as I have argued, helped to justify the prohibitive conclusion he despised. More recently Dworkin has paid feminism the compliment of attacking directly the arguments of her 'armies', or of one soldier at any rate, singling out the work of Catharine MacKinnon. His critique, developed in 'Liberty and Pornography', and 'Women and Pornography', goes beyond anything in his classic paper, explicitly addressing two feminist arguments: that pornography conflicts with a commitment to equality for women; and that pornography silences women. His argument about equality deserves attention, which I shall give it elsewhere; here our topic is his critique of the silencing argument.[1]

According to Ronald Dworkin, the feminist claim that pornography silences women is 'dangerously confused', and he singles out the work

---

[1] This response to Ronald Dworkin is a revised extract from 'Pornography: A Liberal's Unfinished Business', *Canadian Journal of Law and Jurisprudence* 12 (1999), 109–33, which also addresses Dworkin's response to feminist 'egalitarian' argument. The latter part is included as 'Equality and Moralism' in this volume. For the relevant works by Dworkin see: 'Do We Have a Right to Pornography?', *Oxford Journal of Legal Studies* 1 (1981), 177–212, reprinted in *A Matter of Principle* (Cambridge, Mass.: Harvard University Press, 1977); the remark about 'new armies' is on p. 1 of that volume. 'Liberty and Pornography', *The New York Review of Books*, 15 August 1991, 12–15 (page citations are to this version); published as 'Two Concepts of Liberty' in *Isaiah Berlin: A Celebration*, eds., Edna and Avishai Margalit (Chicago: University of Chicago Press, 1991), 100–9. Dworkin's review of MacKinnon's *Only Words* appeared as 'Women and Pornography', in *The New York Review of Books*, 21 October 1993, 36, 37, 40–2. I argue that Dworkin's own premises justify the feminist conclusion in 'Whose Right? Ronald Dworkin, Women, and Pornography', this volume.

of Catharine MacKinnon in two articles, 'Liberty and Pornography', and 'Women and Pornography', published subsequent to his classic defence of a right to pornography. Dworkin's argument against MacKinnon would, if successful, refute the idea of silencing as illocutionary disablement. But I shall show here that it does not succeed: that Dworkin's argument itself rests on a confusion, and one that may better deserve the title 'dangerous'.

The feminist claim that pornography silences women is, according to Dworkin, a claim that pornography deprives women of a *negative* liberty to speak, putting the point in terms borrowed from Isaiah Berlin.[2] It presents a conflict within the negative liberty of free speech itself. He thinks it is a significant argument, for when confronted with conflicting negative liberties, the government may indeed have to balance them, restricting one negative liberty in order to protect another. Confronted with heckling speech that drowns out other speakers the government may restrict the negative liberty of the heckler. On the feminist argument, pornography acts like the heckler.[3] By changing her audience's perceptions of her character, needs, desires, perhaps her own sense of what she is, pornography prevents a woman from being understood by her audience, and perhaps prevents her from speaking at all. Pornography prevents women from expressing their own ideas; and since we want free speech in order to have a society where no idea is barred from entry, we must censor some ideas in order to make room for others. This is Dworkin's understanding of the feminist argument that pornography silences women. He rejects the argument, attempting to show that, appearances notwithstanding, it is in fact an argument about—in Berlin's terms—a mere positive liberty.

In response to Dworkin, I shall be setting aside the question about positive and negative liberty, saying briefly why, in the context of Dworkin's political philosophy, that question is ultimately irrelevant. Instead I shall be spelling out the implications of Dworkin's argument for the idea that pornography might silence women by bringing about illocutionary disablement. I shall argue that Dworkin implicitly relies on an overly

[2] In 'Liberty and Pornography'.

[3] For an important development of the idea that pornography silences women in a way that is relevantly like a heckler, and that state intervention might well support free speech values, see Owen Fiss, 'Freedom and Feminism', *Georgetown Law Review* 80 (1992), 2041–62; and especially *The Irony of Free Speech* (Cambridge, Mass.: Harvard University Press, 1996).

narrow conception of free speech as, roughly, freedom of locutionary acts; and that he misinterprets the feminist silencing claim, taking it to be demanding a very broad kind of perlocutionary freedom. The notion of speech as illocution, and correspondingly of silence as illocutionary disablement, therefore remains unaddressed.

In 'Women and Pornography' Dworkin considers the example of sexual refusal. Pornography, he says, conditions men to 'misunderstand' what women say:

It conditions them to think, for example—as some stupid judges have instructed juries in rape trials—that when a woman says no she sometimes means yes.[4]

Dworkin here seems to accept, for the sake of argument, the premise that pornography silences in the sense that, by conditioning men's beliefs and expectations, pornography affects some men's capacity to adequately recognize a woman's intended sexual refusal. However this, he says, is not the kind of silencing that the law should prevent. Freedom of speech does not include 'a guarantee of a sympathetic or even competent understanding of what one says'. Feminists say otherwise, but their argument

is premised on an unacceptable proposition: that the right to free speech includes a right to circumstances that encourage one to speak, and a right that others grasp and respect what one means to say. These are obviously not rights that any society can recognize or enforce. Creationists, flat-earthers, and bigots, for example, are ridiculed... That ridicule undoubtedly dampens the enthusiasm many of them have for speaking out and limits the attention others pay to what they say.

The 'silencing' argument supposes that everyone—the bigot and the creationist as well as the social reformer—has a right to whatever respectful attention on the part of others is necessary to encourage him to speak his mind and to guarantee that he will be correctly understood.[5]

This is an implicit rejection of the understanding of silence as illocutionary disablement. If one claims that a woman's speech is disabled when she fails to achieve 'uptake', fails to achieve the hearer's *recognition* of what she is intending to do, then one claims (merely) that she fails to gain a 'sympathetic' or 'competent' hearer. One claims (merely) that she is 'misunderstood'. And Dworkin's argument is that free speech provides no guarantee of understanding and sympathy on the part of hearers.

---

[4] 'Women and Pornography', 38.   [5] Ibid., 38, 40.

Dworkin's argument, thus interpreted, fails to appreciate the different kinds of understanding that are relevant in thinking about speech and free speech: the minimal understanding required for uptake, and thus for *illocutionary* success; and the substantial understanding which is sympathy and respectful attention, aimed for as a further consequence of one's speech, and thus for *perlocutionary* success. His failure perhaps stems from a conception of speech as 'only words': a conception of speech as mere locution.[6] On this conception, if someone is free to utter words, they are free to speak. Dworkin is right to suppose that the feminist argument wants something more than this, something more than 'only words'; but, failing to distinguish an illocutionary something from a perlocutionary something, he is wrong in identifying what this 'something more' amounts to. The feminist argument supposes that the 'speech' in 'free speech' includes illocution, indeed something more than locution. But the argument does not have to suppose that free speech includes more than illocution: it does not have to suppose that free speech includes the perlocutionary features characteristic of a positive liberty, as Dworkin describes it—respect, a sympathetic hearing, and the like.[7]

Whether a feminist inclusion of illocution in free speech really amounts to making free speech a positive liberty, as Dworkin effectively alleges, is a question we can leave aside, for it is in the end—notwithstanding Dworkin's solemn pronouncements on the matter—a red herring.[8] It would be significant only on an assumption of negative liberty absolutism, i.e. an assumption that negative liberty must trump all else, including positive liberty. But negative liberty absolutism is not to be found in

---

[6] This is argued by Hornsby in 'Speech Acts and Pornography', *Women's Philosophy Review* 10 (1993), 38–45, reprinted in Susan Dwyer, ed., *The Problem of Pornography* (Belmont, CA: Wadsworth, 1995); 'Disempowered Speech', *Philosophical Topics* 23 (1995); and by Hornsby and Langton in 'Free Speech and Illocution', *Legal Theory* 4 (1998), 21–37. The conception of free speech as a matter of locution only is explicit in Daniel Jacobson, 'Freedom of Speech Acts? A Response to Langton', *Philosophy and Public Affairs* 24 (1995), 64–79.

[7] There may be an argument, with roots in Mill, to say that free speech requires even more, that it requires attentive, 'listening' audiences: see Hornsby and Langton, 'Free Speech and Illocution', 34, and 'Freedom of Illocution', this volume. See also David Braddon-Mitchell and Caroline West, 'What is Free Speech?', *The Journal of Political Philosophy* 12 (2004), 437–60.

[8] I do not here resolve whether illocutionary freedom would be a positive or negative liberty. Dworkin himself proves unable to clearly distinguish positive and negative liberty in his paper devoted to the topic (a paper whose attribution of 'confusion' to feminists rests on our supposed 'conflation' of the two). I assume in 'Speech Acts and Unspeakable Acts' that it is a negative liberty, by Dworkin's lights (see final footnote). For some different possibilities, and further argument, see Langton, 'Pornography: A Liberal's Unfinished Business', 125–30; and Hornsby and Langton, 'Free Speech and Illocution'.

Dworkin's broader philosophy, where, absent the exigencies of a *Festschrift* in honour of Isaiah Berlin, he finds no need to force his arguments into this alien framework. The strange thing about 'Liberty and Pornography' is that Dworkin here affirms principles from Berlin which his own political philosophy *denies*—most notably, the sovereignty of liberty over equality, and the independence of liberty from equality.[9] Moreover, negative liberty absolutism is not even to be found in Berlin's philosophy. Traffic laws violate negative liberty, and that loss is permissibly traded for convenience and safety, according to both Dworkin and Berlin. Workplace regulation violates negative liberty, and that loss is permissibly traded for economic equality. If censorship were to violate pornographer's negative liberty, it is not obvious why that loss could not likewise be permissibly traded for a gain in positive liberty for women, if it were indeed women's positive liberty at stake. Since neither Dworkin nor Berlin are negative liberty absolutists, contrary to the rhetoric of 'Liberty and Pornography', the question of negative and positive liberty can be left aside. The important point is that—positive or negative liberty—freedom of speech should be understood to include freedom of illocution.

Dworkin's failure to appreciate what is at stake here is especially plain when we consider his analogies. So let us consider the *silenced* parties whose silence Dworkin finds comparable—the woman who says no, and the person who says that the earth is flat; and then the *silencing* parties whose actions of silencing Dworkin finds comparable—the pornographer, and the 'stupid' judge. Take, first of all, the woman and the flat-earther. The comparison perplexes. A woman's inability to be understood, when she says 'no' to sex, is like the flat-earther's inability to achieve respectful attention. A woman's inability to act, to perform the illocution of refusal, is like the flat-earther's inability to gain sympathy for his ideas. The woman is like the flat-earther, in having her 'ideas misunderstood'. Her 'ideas', like his, are 'being given little consideration'. This comparison is remarkable for its perspective on sexual violence: a woman's capacity to refuse sex is supposed

---

[9] A conflict between equality and liberty could be 'resolved simply on the ground that liberty must be sovereign', 'Liberty and Pornography', 14. Elsewhere he says if there were a conflict between equality and liberty, liberty would *lose*, 'What is Equality? Part 3: The Place of Liberty', *Iowa Law Review* 73 (1987), 9. Dworkin apparently endorses Berlin's famous claim that 'Everything is what it is: liberty is liberty, not equality or fairness or justice or culture, or human happiness or a quiet conscience', 'Liberty and Pornography', 15; elsewhere, e.g. in 'Do We Have a Right?', he affirms the dependence of liberty on equality.

to be as optional, in the law's eyes, as a flat-earther's capacity to achieve respectful attention—notwithstanding the difference these capacities make to human life, and notwithstanding the fact that the law presupposes the former capacity, but nowhere presupposes the latter. The law presupposes that women have a capacity to perform illocutions of refusal, when the law defines rape as a crime; the capacity for refusal and consent is exactly the capacity which allows the difference between rape and consensual sex.

The comparison is also remarkable for its insistence that speech is expression of ideas, that speech is a matter of saying words, a matter of mere locution. That insistence here reaches ludicrous depths. 'No' is the expression of an idea, that may or may not be understood. 'The earth is flat' is the expression of an idea, that may or may not be understood. Both, in fact, are speech acts: the first, an intended illocution of *refusal*, whose perlocutionary aim is to prevent unwanted sex; the second, an intended illocution of *assertion*, whose perlocutionary aim is, perhaps, to gain 'respectful attention' from the hearer, and to persuade the hearer that the earth is flat.

When we become alert to the nature of the two speech acts, we see that the confusion in Dworkin's comparison is not just moral but philosophical. Dworkin, thus understood, confuses perlocutionary failure with illocutionary failure. What is missing in the case of silenced refusal is this: recognition on the hearer's part that the speaker is intending to refuse. What is missing in the case of the silenced flat-earther is this: respectful attention on the hearer's part. The woman who is silenced in the way Dworkin describes fails to perform her intended illocution, which is *refusal*. The flat-earther who is silenced in the way Dworkin describes does not fail to perform his intended illocution, which is *assertion*. In the situation envisaged by Dworkin, the flat-earther is recognized to be intending to assert, and is moreover recognized to be intending to assert that the earth is flat. But he does fail to achieve his perlocutionary goal of achieving respectful attention. If there is a failure of understanding on the part of hearers, it is not a failure to understand that he is intending to assert, or even to understand what he is asserting. It is precisely *because* his intended illocution has been recognized by hearers that he fails to find a sympathetic hearing. It is because he is understood that he fails to achieve respectful attention. His failure at the perlocutionary level is explained by his *success* at the illocutionary level. His action is understood: he achieves uptake. But he fails to achieve his perlocutionary goals. Not so for the woman who says no. She is silenced at the illocutionary level. It is true that in one sense she still has her words: she has freedom of what Austin called locution. But a proper understanding of free speech will include more than 'only words', if it includes freedom of illocution.

Now let us think about Dworkin's comparison of the silencing parties. Pornography, says Dworkin, is like the judge who instructs a jury in a rape trial, 'When a woman says no, she sometimes means yes'. Pornography is like the 'stupid' judge. When the judge says those words, he may be more than stupid: he may, as Dworkin perhaps envisages, create an expectation in the jury, that the woman did not mean no when she said no. He may affect what the woman can do with her words, in court, and in so doing, silence her more effectively than any heckler could. Dworkin might agree that such words by judges should not be sanctioned. But if such words, when said by judges, should not be sanctioned, then perhaps such words, when said by pornographers, should not be sanctioned either. A permissive argument about pornography will need to tell us how the two examples are different. Since Dworkin tells us only that they are alike, his permissive conclusion comes as a surprise.

The example is a reminder of a famous case in British law in which some men were told of a particular woman: when she says no, she means yes.[10] Mr. Morgan invited three drinking companions to come home with him and have sex with his wife. He told them not to be surprised if she struggled against them, since that was what turned her on; she would say no, and mean yes. When they acted on that invitation, she said no, and meant no. At the trial, the men said (falsely) they believed she meant yes. Suppose their testimony had been true, to this extent: when she said no, the men did not take her to be refusing. Suppose Mr. Morgan's words had really undermined the potential for uptake which would have allowed her words to be recognized as refusal. That was not so: the friends knew, in fact, that she refused. But suppose it had been so. There has rightly been much interest in this hypothetical question, but I am interested in an aspect orthogonal to the main discussion.[11]

---

[10] Director of Public Prosecutions v. Morgan [1976] AC 182 (House of Lords, 1975).

[11] See, for example, E. M. Curley, 'Excusing Rape', *Philosophy and Public Affairs* 5 (1976); M. T. Thornton, 'Rape and Mens Rea', in Kai Nielsen and Steven C. Patten, eds., New Essays in Ethics

What would Dworkin then say about Mr. Morgan's lie? It would be a lie that disabled Mrs. Morgan's refusal, in a way that is analogous to the disablement engendered by pornography, on the argument here proposed. In the case of pornography, the process may be more indirect, more gradual, more cumulative. But that is not Dworkin's stated reason for rejecting the feminist argument. He says that if pornography silences women by leading men to think that when a woman says no, she means yes, that silence is no business of the law, no business of political argument. So what is Dworkin's advice to Mrs. Morgan, when she hopes for redress for her husband's lie? Perhaps he will say that the lie is no business of the law: the law does not guarantee that those who hear her attempted refusal will have a 'competent understanding' of what she says. Perhaps he will say she is unreasonable to hope that the law cares about whether her hearers 'grasp' what she 'means to say'. Perhaps he will say she is unreasonable to hope for help in removing the obstacle to 'competent understanding'—the obstacle which is Mr. Morgan's lie. Perhaps he will say she is like the flat-earther, who complains that his ideas have failed to gain respectful attention; or that the freedom she hopes for is a mere positive liberty; or that the lie expresses an idea, and an idea is as powerful as the audience allows it to be, and that any unhappy effects depend on 'mental mediation'.[12] Perhaps he will say she should fight speech with more speech, that she should fight the lie with the truth; and then offer sympathy when she says she did her best.

A person silenced by a heckler is free to make sounds, say words, but he is not free to do things with his words—not free to do the illocutionary things he might wish to do. Dworkin is right to say that, on the feminist argument, pornography is relevantly like the heckler. And he allows that the person silenced by the heckler can hope for legal redress. If the person silenced by the heckler can hope for legal help to enable him to escape—to enable him not just to say his words, but do things with his words—there is no obvious reason why women cannot, in principle, hope for the same. That hope for women's speech is not over-demanding. It is not a hope that women's speech should be effective in a perlocutionary sense, as Dworkin mistakenly thought: it is not a hope that women's speech should actually

and Public Policy, *Canadian Journal of Philosophy*, suppl. vol. 8 (1982); C. L. Ten, *Crime, Guilt and Punishment* (Oxford: Oxford University Press, 1987), 104–5.

[12] This is paraphrased from Easterbrook's judgement about pornography in Hudnut, quoted approvingly by Dworkin in 'Liberty and Pornography', 15.

persuade others, or provoke sympathy, or generate respect, though these may well be desired perlocutionary goals of speech. What is hoped for is a certain capacity to perform communicative illocutions, especially those of sexual communication. This illocutionary potential requires from hearers only a minimal receptivity, a capacity for uptake, a capacity to recognize the kind of thing a speaker may be trying to do with her words. The hope is modest: for example, successful refusal is no guarantee against rape, if it is illocutionary success we are speaking of. It is no guarantee that a refusal will be honoured, only that it will be recognized for the act it is intended to be. But illocutionary success, for these speech acts, is perhaps a minimum to hope for. Illocutionary success at least gives a speaker a fighting chance. To think this way is, admittedly, to think that free speech is more than a matter of words mouthed against a heckler's din. But free speech is not, after all, freedom to speak only words, if speech itself is not only words.

3

Freedom of Illocution? Response to Daniel Jacobson

(CO-AUTHORED WITH JENNIFER HORNSBY)

What one ought to mean by 'speech', in the context of discussions of free speech, is whatever it is that a correct justification of the right to free speech justifies one in protecting. What one ought to mean, it may be argued, includes illocution, in the sense of J. L. Austin. Some feminist writers, accepting that free speech includes free illocution, have been led to take the notion of silencing seriously in discussions of free speech.[1]

We say that people are silenced when they are prevented from doing certain illocutionary things with words. People who utter words but fail to perform the illocution they intend may be silenced. The silenced person encounters illocutionary disablement: her speech misfires; what she does is 'unhappy'.[2] The silenced person is deprived of illocutionary potential; she does not have it in her power to do with language what she might want to.[3] Our understanding of silencing has implications for a feminist claim about pornography. Catharine MacKinnon has claimed that the free speech of men silences the free speech of women.[4] One way

---

[1] This essay is a revised and shortened version of Jennifer Hornsby and Rae Langton, 'Free Speech and Illocution', *Legal Theory* 4 (1998), 21–37. See J. L. Austin, *How to Do Things with Words* (Oxford: Oxford University Press, 1962). Catharine MacKinnon, Rae Langton, and Jennifer Hornsby are among those who have developed the 'silencing' argument, see footnotes 2–4 below. Ishani Maitra develops the idea of silencing as 'communicative disablement', on Gricean rather than Austinian lines, in 'Silencing Speech', forthcoming.

[2] This way of putting the point is in Rae Langton's 'Speech Acts and Unspeakable Acts', this volume.

[3] This way of putting the point is in Jennifer Hornsby's 'Speech Acts and Pornography', *Women's Philosophical Review* Nov. 1993, 38–45, reprinted with a 'Postscript' in *The Problem of Pornography,* ed., Susan Dwyer (Belmont, Ca.:Wadsworth, 1995), 220–32. See also Hornsby, 'Disempowered Speech', in *Philosophical Topics* 23 (1995), 127–47

[4] See Catharine MacKinnon, 'Francis Biddle's Sister', in *Feminism Unmodified* (Cambridge, Mass.: Harvard University Press, 1987), and *Only Words* (Cambridge, Mass.: Harvard University Press, 1993).

to understand this is as telling us that pornography has interfered with women's freedom of speech. Given certain empirical assumptions about the effects of the pornography's production and consumption, pornography has prevented women from doing certain illocutionary things with words. On this way of thinking, there might be a free speech argument against pornography.

This way of thinking has been criticized.[5] The stumbling block has not been the empirical assumptions (although these need, of course to be evaluated), but the very idea that free speech includes illocution. It has been doubted that 'speech' could mean anything more than locution (again in the sense of Austin). Daniel Jacobson has held that the free speech argument against pornography fails, because free speech is 'freedom of locutionary acts', not freedom of illocutionary acts. Ronald Dworkin shares the same opinion, although in his case it works as an implicit assumption.[6] And Jacobson tells us that, even if free speech could include illocution, the argument against pornography would still fail: 'the claim that pornography . . . contributes to illocutionary disablement rests on a confusion', he says. Worse still, the argument would have the absurd and disturbing consequence that clear cases of rape would not after all count as rape.[7] We shall address the challenges about confusion and absurdity in due course; our main aim, though, is to show that illocution serves better than locution to give the sense of 'speech' in 'free speech'.

1. Illocution

Catharine MacKinnon's claim about silence has its place in a more general view about speech—about how to think about it, and what the

---

[5] Daniel Jacobson, 'Freedom of Speech Acts? A Response to Langton', *Philosophy and Public Affairs* 24 (1995), 64–79. Our full response is in 'Free Speech and Illocution'. Jacobson has a further response, 'Speech and Action: Replies to Hornsby and Langton', *Legal Theory* 7 (2001), 179–201, which we don't address here, though it has informed the revision of this edited version, to forestall some minor misunderstandings.

[6] Ronald Dworkin, 'Liberty and Pornography', *The New York Review of Books*, 15 Aug. 1991, 12–15; published as 'Two Concepts of Liberty' in *Isaiah Berlin: A Celebration*, eds., Edna and Avishai Margalit (Chicago: University of Chicago Press, 1991), 100–9; and 'Women and Pornography', in *The New York Review of Books*, 21 October 1993, 36–7, 40–2. The assumption was exposed in Hornsby, 'Speech Acts and Pornography'.

[7] Jacobson, 'Freedom of Speech Acts?', 71, 76.

point of it is. MacKinnon says that speech is more than mere words, hence the (ironic) title of her work, *Only Words*. MacKinnon has something in common with those philosophers who think that speech is best understood in the context of an account of speech acts. Speech is not a matter simply of the making of meaningful noises, but, as Austin put it, of doing things with words: hence the title of his *How to Do Things with Words*.[8] Thinking of speech as a sort of action suggests a different perspective on the point of protecting it. And it also suggests a different perspective on the question of silence. If speech is action, then silence is not simply a matter of failure to make a sound; it is failure to to do something one might want to do with words.

There are countless things people do with their words. But following Austin, one may distinguish three broad kinds of things, three sorts of speech act. (1) There is the saying of words that have a certain meaning, or content: that is the *locutionary* act. (Austin's example: one man says to another, 'Shoot her', meaning by 'shoot' to shoot with a gun, referring by 'her' to a nearby woman.) (2) There is the saying of certain words such that, *in* saying those words, one performs an action: that is the *illocutionary* act. (In saying 'Shoot her', one man ordered another to shoot.) (3) There is the saying of certain words, such that *by* saying those words, certain other things are done: that is the *perlocutionary* act. (By saying 'Shoot her', one man persuaded another to shoot.)[9] Illocutionary speech acts are done when the saying of relevant words satisfies certain success conditions: felicity conditions, as Austin called them. For some illocutionary speech acts, the conditions are formal and conventional. These are the speech acts on which Austin concentrated early on in *How to Do Things with Words*: he confined his attention to such acts as christening ships and getting married, where particular forms of words are tailored to the carrying out of some institutionalized procedure. The conditions for carrying out these acts relate to the procedure: for instance, 'I do' is only an act of marrying if the speaker intends to marry, the celebrant is authorized, those present recognize the person to be marrying, and so on. But there are other illocutionary speech acts whose conditions are not bound up with particular procedures, and which require only the institution of language

---

[8] J. L. Austin, *How to Do Things with Words*.

[9] Some have doubted whether the distinction between illocutionary and perlocutionary acts can be adequately made out; for response, see Langton and Hornsby, 'Free Speech and Illocution', 24.

use itself. Their conditions will include a hearer's recognition of the speaker's intention to perform the illocution in question. By involving the hearer as well as the speaker, illocutionary acts reveal language as communicative.

How is it that uttering words can be doing some illocutionary thing? Well, a background condition which makes this possible is what Hornsby calls 'reciprocity'.[10] Reciprocity between speakers provides for someone's making of some noises being not merely her expression of a meaningful thought (which is a locutionary act) but also, for instance, her stating something (which is an illocutionary act). People who share a language have the capacity not simply to understand one another's words, but also to grasp what illocutionary acts others might be trying to make. Normally when a speaker tells someone something, for instance, the hearer takes herself to have been told something—she knows what the speaker was up to. This is 'uptake' in Austin's sense. Uptake consists in the speaker's being taken to be performing the very illocutionary act which, in being so taken, she (the speaker) is performing. Language use then relies on a mutual capacity for uptake, which involves a minimal receptiveness on the part of language users in the role of hearers. This minimal receptiveness doesn't mean that a hearer will agree with what a speaker is saying: but it does mean that a hearer has a capacity to grasp what communicative act a speaker might be intending to perform. When reciprocity is present, the speaker's utterance works as she means it to. Its working so appears to depend on nothing more than speaker and hearer being parties of a normal linguistic exchange, in which a speaker's attempt to communicate is successful. A speaker tries to do an illocutionary thing; a hearer's recognizing that the speaker is trying to do that thing is then sufficient for the speaker's actually doing it.

If silence is failure to act, as MacKinnon has suggested, then perhaps it is a failure to perform an illocutionary act. Let us think about some examples. A man tries to marry, in saying 'I do', and later discovers with horror that the 'priest' was an actor in costume: so he failed to marry. An actor in a play has a role in which he shouts (to the amusement of the audience) 'Fire! I mean it! Look at the smoke!'; and a real fire breaks out, and in real

---

[10] Hornsby, 'Illocution and its Significance', in *Foundations of Speech Act Theory*, ed., S. L. Tsohatsidis (London: Routledge, 1984). This provides a fuller account of the speech act theoretical material relevant here.

desperation he shouts (to the amusement of the audience), 'Fire! I mean it! Look at the smoke!': but, actor that he is, he fails to warn.[11]

In these cases the speech has misfired: it has gone wrong in a way that manifests illocutionary disablement. The acts are unspeakable for the speakers. There is a failure at the illocutionary level: a failure to marry, or to warn. These speech acts go wrong because the speakers somehow fail to satisfy the felicity conditions for the speech acts they want to perform. When MacKinnon says that pornography silences women, she means that pornography prevents women from doing certain things with their words. She may have in mind the different ways women's speech acts can go wrong in sexual contexts.

One way might be this. A woman says 'No' to a man, when she is trying to refuse sex; she uses the right locution for an act of refusal, but somehow her speech act goes wrong. The woman says 'No' and the man does not recognize what she is trying to do with her words. She says 'No', intends to refuse, but there is no uptake in her hearer. She fails to perform the illocutionary act of refusal. She is like the actor in the story, who says 'Fire!', intending genuinely to warn, using the right locution for warning, but who fails to warn. Her speech has misfired.

On Austin's account, speech acts are enabled and constrained by their felicity conditions. MacKinnon says there can be 'words that set conditions': some kinds of speech can set the conditions for other kinds of speech, making some speech acts possible for some, and impossible for others. Speech acts of legal enactments, for example, can make speech acts of divorce possible for men, and not women. MacKinnon thinks pornography can be 'words that set conditions'.[12]

Pornographic speech acts help create a communicative climate in which the felicity conditions for some of women's speech are not met. Pornography is part of the explanation for why speech acts go wrong for some women, when, for example, they try to refuse. Pornography can make certain speech acts unspeakable for women.

---

[11] These examples are discussed in Langton, 'Speech Acts and Unspeakable Acts', where the argument of this and the following part is given in more detail. The example of the actor who shouts 'Fire' is from D. Davidson, 'Communication and Convention' (1982) in *Inquiries into Truth and Interpretation* (Oxford: Oxford University Press, 1984), 269, though he used it for a different purpose.

[12] See MacKinnon, *Only Words*, 63–8.

What conditions might constrain women's speech, and might be affected by pornography? We have seen that conditions for performing an illocution typically include a hearer's recognition of a speaker's intention to perform an illocution, and that such recognition requires reciprocity to be at work. When reciprocity is at work, a speaker tries to perform an illocution, a hearer recognizes that she is trying to perform that illocution, and that is sufficient for her performing it. In the case of refusal, a speaker says 'No', intending to refuse, a hearer recognizes that the speaker is intending to refuse, and so the speaker does refuse. The refusal may or may not be respected, but at least it is recognized for what it is. When reciprocity fails the speaker, though, what she attempts to do, she isn't recognized as attempting to do, thus cannot be understood as having done, and therefore, given how illocution works, simply cannot do. When reciprocity fails the speaker, she is silenced.

If pornography creates the climate for women's speech (or for a specific area of women's speech), then one way it might do so is by undermining reciprocity: by undermining the capacity of hearers to grasp the illocutions that women are trying to perform. Perhaps it does so by building an expectation that when a woman says 'No' she does not intend to refuse. Hearers with this expectation will not recognize the intention when it is there, and then the hearer's part of the illocutionary deal—the uptake—is absent. In this way pornography might contribute to illocutionary disablement.

2. The Allegation of Confusion

Jacobson thinks that the claim that pornography contributes to illocutionary disablement 'rests on a confusion' about speech act theory. He concentrates on one example—the case of sexual refusal—and argues that pornography, even on the feminist hypothesis, does not silence in the sense that Langton intended. Jacobson allows, for sake of argument, that pornography might contribute to situations where a woman's 'No' is not recognized as a refusal, and that rapes might occur as a result. But he denies that in such a situation a woman encounters illocutionary disablement. According to Jacobson, the woman in this example fails only to achieve a perlocutionary result she aims at: her speech does not have the intended further consequences of a refusal. To think otherwise, Jacobson says, would both misunderstand speech act theory, and have an absurd result—namely, that the woman in the situation described is *not raped*.

We shall show that a woman is disabled at the illocutionary level in the case described; and that if pornography contributes to this disablement, then it can be said to silence women. We also show that this does not have the alleged absurd result.

Langton's argument was made against the backdrop of Austin's classic account of speech act theory, as Jacobson is aware. Austin suggests—as Jacobson points out—that an illocutionary act must secure uptake. Austin says 'I cannot be said to have warned an audience unless it hears what I say and takes what I say in a certain sense'.[13] Likewise, then, for a speaker to perform an illocutionary act of refusal, it is necessary that the hearer take the speaker to be refusing. So the woman whose 'No' is not taken to be a refusal does not perform the *illocutionary* act of refusal. The argument about refusal, then, rests only on Austinian premises. Jacobson's allegation of confusion is actually quite puzzling: Austin supposes that uptake is necessary, is quoted as saying so, and is applauded as a 'heavyweight of speech–act theory';[14] Langton supposes that uptake is necessary, and is said to be confused.[15] What is fair for the gander one might hope is fair for the goose.

Jacobson himself, though, disagrees with the Austinian premise. To think that uptake is a necessary condition for the performing of a particular illocution is 'to hold the performance of an illocutionary act hostage to the perversity of one's audience'.[16] But evidently when illocution is thought of in Austinian terms, this is no objection; Austinian illocutions, for which uptake is required, are indeed, in one relevant sense, 'hostage to one's audience': linguistic communication presupposes reciprocity, but reciprocity may be missing because of one's *audience's* states of mind. Of course there are, as Jacobson says, 'delicate' issues about speech act theory here. There are writers who have ignored Austin's emphasis on uptake. And there are writers who have thought that it is a mistake to include uptake in conditions for illocutionary act performances: Strawson is an

---

[13] J. L. Austin, *How to Do Things with Words*, 115, quoted by Jacobson in 'Freedom of Speech Acts', 72.

[14] Jacobson, 'Freedom of Speech Acts', 72, 73.   [15] Ibid., 76.

[16] Ibid., 74. Alexander Bird also develops the objection that neither illocution generally, nor refusal in particular, require uptake, in 'Illocutionary Silencing', *Pacific Philosophical Quarterly* 83 (2002), 1–15.

example. But Jacobson for his part tells us that he does not rely upon his sympathies with Strawson.[17] He thinks that he has no need to rely upon these, because he thinks that he has an actual counterexample to the claim that uptake should be treated as necessary.

Suppose Bill, in the grips of some paranoid fantasy, thinks Sally has only sent him an invitation to her wedding in order to gloat—that she does not really want him to attend. Bill, we must imagine, does not conclude this from his cold reception at her other parties, but only because his dosage has been too precipitously reduced. We should say that Sally has invited Bill, despite the fact that he misconstrues her act.[18]

Jacobson wants to say that uptake has not been secured in this case, and that Austin would therefore have to deem the attempted invitation a misfire. But it is not: Sally *does* invite Bill. So uptake is not a necessary condition of illocutions, contrary to Austin.

Jacobson's is a nice story, but it does not prove his point. There is a difference between inviting someone to your wedding and wanting him to attend, and there is a corresponding difference between someone's believing that he is invited to a wedding and his believing that his attendance there is wanted. Sally may well invite Uncle Harry, who will only get drunk and loudly reminisce about the war, because she feels she has to invite him. So she intends to invite him, she sends the invitation, he recognizes that she intends to invite him, uptake is achieved, and she does invite him—even if Uncle Harry also (rightly) believes she does not want him there. Her invitation does not misfire. Bill, likewise, can recognize that Sally intends to invite him even if he (wrongly) believes she does not want him there. One may agree with Jacobson's intuitions about this case (Sally does invite), while continuing to see the point in Austin's own view that uptake is a necessary condition for illocution. Jacobson's example is ineffective, then.

Jacobson thinks the example demonstrates a need for a novel account of illocutionary acts. We would have to go beyond our present task if we were to discuss the merits of the account which he proposes. Our point should be clear already. The speech act theory in which we have worked, unlike

---

[17] In P. F. Strawson, 'Intention and Convention in Speech Acts', *Philosophical Review* 73 (1964), 439–60, it is said that the aim, not the achievement, of securing uptake is essential to the illocutionary act.

[18] Jacobson, 'Freedom of Speech Acts', 76.

Jacobson's, has recognizably Austinian origins. On an Austinian account, it is at the illocutionary level that something goes wrong when a hearer fails to recognize which thing (like refusing) a speaker intends to do with her words. We have explained how what goes wrong can be characterized as a kind of silence. If the publication, dissemination, and consumption of pornography brings it about that things do go relevantly wrong with a significant area of women's illocutionary acts, then pornography silences women.

What then of Jacobson's attempt at adducing an absurd conclusion? The charge is swiftly made:

The strange and troubling consequence of the argument from illocutionary disablement, however, is that *Langton cannot call this rape.*[19]

Apparently Jacobson thinks that, so long as there is no illocutionary act of refusal, a necessary condition for rape is not satisfied. But how could that be? Certainly on Langton's view, the state of mind of a hearer impinges upon the question of whether there was an illocutionary act of refusal. But that does not mean that the state of mind of a hearer impinges upon any question about the content of a speaker's intentions. The fact that the woman performed no illocutionary act of refusal could then have no tendency to show that she was someone who gave her consent. Equally the fact, if it were one, that the man took the woman to perform an illocutionary act of consent could have no tendency to show that the woman consented. This seems obvious. If a speaker's illocutionary acts depend on the fulfillment of her intentions, and such fulfillment is uptake on the part of the hearer, then of course no view of the speaker's states of mind can be based solely upon what illocutionary acts she performed. Equally evidently, no view of the speaker's states of mind can be based upon how the hearer takes her speech. Jacobson conflates a condition necessary for refusal with a condition sufficient for consent: seeing that Langton regards the man's taking the woman to refuse as necessary for the illocutionary act of refusal, he then supposes that Langton must regard the man's taking the woman to consent as sufficient for consent. It is Jacobson's conflation, and not any premise of Langton's, which gives the absurdity.[20]

---

[19] Jacobson, 'Freedom of Speech Acts', 77; the italics are Jacobson's.

[20] An alternative diagnosis might be that Jacobson extended to the case of consent a possible implicit suggestion of Langton's that uptake appropriate for pornography could be sufficient for making

3. Freedom of Illocution

We turn now to the question of whether free speech includes freedom of illocution. Austin introduced illocution because he wanted us to think of language use not merely as the production of meaningful sounds, but as the doing of various things with words. Taking illocutionary things to be things done with words, we see how someone might, through no fault of her own, be unable to do some of the things that can be done with words. If these things—illocutionary acts—count as 'speech' in the free speech sense, then such a person—a silenced person—is impeded in the actualization of the very capacity whose exercise a right to free speech is supposed to protect. Thus our account of silencing will have repercussions for debates about free speech.

But there is a different view. The capacity to speak may be conceived as something that a person can exercise on an occasion unless she is then physically obstructed: someone raised in the use of a language, who has the usual human cognitive resources and vocal apparatus simply can speak. On this view, the freedom to speak is something which a speaker in isolation can be conceived as having in isolation: you do not need an audience to make meaningful sounds. On this view, pornographers could not interfere with the speech of women except by literally gagging them all. On this view, freedom of speech is freedom of locution only. And this is Jacobson's view. Jacobson thinks that the feminist argument connecting pornography with silencing cannot proceed from the value of freedom of speech, but must stem from a strange and unwarranted commitment to freedom of illocution.

Jacobson tells us that Mill is on his side:

Free speech, as glossed by Mill, is roughly the freedom of locutionary acts. . . . what about freedom of illocutionary acts?. . . . freedom of expression is not the freedom of illocutionary acts. Illocutionary silencing is beyond the pale of what even

---

something pornography. This extension would be a misunderstanding; for more details, see Hornsby and Langton, 'Free Speech and Illocution', 31 n. 29. Alexander Bird, Nancy Bauer, and Nellie Wieland each develop in different ways the challenge that the silencing argument reduces the *mens rea* of rapists, though only Wieland puts it in quite these terms. See Bird, 'Illocutionary Silencing'; Bauer, 'How To Do Things With Pornography', in *Reading Cavell*, eds., Sanford Shieh and Alice Crary (New York: Routledge, 2006), 68–97; Wieland, 'Linguistic Authority and Convention in a Speech Act Analysis of Pornography', *Australasian Journal of Philosophy* 85 (2007), 435–56.

arch-defenders of free speech have tried to protect. No one has or should seek a First Amendment right to be able to knight, to exonerate, and to canonize.[21]

We shall have to say something about the suggestion that the argument is committed to advocating a right to any old illocution—to knight, to exonerate, or to canonize.[22] In speaking of this, we can start to make clear the extent to which our own view is in fact in harmony with Mill's. That will put us in a good position to show that Jacobson's attribution of his own view to Mill is erroneous.

It is surprising to find the claim of a right to do any old illocutionary thing being attributed to the silencing argument, given that it was also argued in 'Speech Acts and Unspeakable Acts' that pornographic speech acts may be illocutionary acts of subordination. If there were a commitment to freedom of illocutionary acts *tout court*, then that argument would have defended pornography, rather than questioned a license to publish it. The silencing argument did not assume that there is a free speech right to any illocution anyone might want to perform. What it assumed was only that the capacity to perform the illocution of refusal is an important capacity. Faced with a conflict between freedoms to speak—faced, for example, with a conflict between subordinating with words and refusing with words—perhaps one should judge that refusal matters more.

Jacobson's list of sample illocutionary acts focuses on the kinds of acts on which Austin concentrated in order to illustrate his idea of performativeness—acts where particular forms of words are tailored to the carrying out of some procedure. Evidently, arguments for the protection of such illocutionary acts will involve one in questions about the institutions of which the procedures are a part. Questions about the honours system and about sainthood, for example, would arise when acts of knighting and canonization were defended. But such questions evidently have little bearing on questions about free speech generally, so that someone who wants to defend a general view of free speech as free illocution will not have Jacobson's narrow focus. Someone interested in free speech will have a conception of illocutionary acts that extends beyond those acts whose conditions are bound up with specific institutions; it will extend to all of

---

[21] 'Freedom of Speech Acts?', 71, 72, 76.

[22] Note that Maitra's proposal about silencing as 'communicative disablement' is developed in part to avoid perceived difficulties about freedom of 'any old' illocution, and about the illocutionary/perlocutionary distinction: Maitra, 'Silencing Speech'.

those acts which Austin came to say are illocutionary—acts which reveal language as communicative. Certainly this includes the institutional acts upon which Jacobson focuses and about which special questions arise; but it includes a great deal more besides—refusing is just one example of what else it includes.

Now there is nothing here with which Mill would disagree. Mill defended a free market of ideas. He argued that a general license to speak is conducive toward the spread of truth. But the spread of truth is something that does not even come into the picture if we confine ourselves to the locutionary acts of speakers, to their makings of meaningful sounds. As Mill put it himself:

[T]ruth has no chance but in proportion as every side of it, every opinion which embodies even a fraction of the truth, not only finds advocates, but is so advocated as to be listened to.[23]

Illocution in fact demands less of audiences than Mill indicates here. Illocution demands only minimal receptiveness on the part of audiences, whereas Mill is saying that realization of the good that free speech can bring requires attentive, 'listening' audiences.[24] If one were to demand even less than illocution demands—if one asked only that speakers should be able to come out with meaningful noises—then obviously one would not be in a position to claim for free speech the sort of value that Mill thinks attaches to it.

Still, Jacobson claims textual support for his idea that Mill believed free speech is free locution. He tells us that Mill allowed the prohibition of illocutionary acts, citing the following passage:

Opinions lose their immunity when the circumstances in which they are expressed are such as to constitute their expression a positive instigation to some mischievous act. An opinion that the corn dealers are starvers of the poor... may justly incur punishment when delivered orally to an excited mob assembled before the house of a corn dealer.[25]

But in drawing the line at instigating riots, Mill did not draw the line at locution. Mill never denies anyone a right (for instance) to say and be

---

[23] J. S. Mill, *On Liberty* (1859), ch. 3, *On Liberty and Other Writings*, ed., Stefan Collini (Cambridge: Cambridge University Press, 1989), 53.

[24] For further argument about a Millian account of free speech, and what it requires of hearer's understanding, see David Braddon-Mitchell and Caroline West, 'What is Free Speech?', *The Journal of Political Philosophy* 12 (2004), 437–60.

[25] Mill, *On Liberty*, 53–4.

taken as saying, that the corn dealers are starvers of the poor: he never denies a right to illocution. If he had, then that would have fitted ill with his concern that people should be able to speak their opinions to one another, and to tell one another things—to do illocutionary things, that is. In circumstances in which a riot would ensue from expressing one's opinion to others, however, 'immunity' to express it is 'lost'.

A locutionary conception of speech is not what one needs unless one thinks that all of the value of free speech resides in people's ability to make noises that are recognizable as speech. The value of free speech surely resides in fact in people's ability to be recognized as doing what they mean to be doing in making noises—to be communicating. Caring about free speech is a matter of caring about people's powers of doing things with words, including illocutionary, communicative things. And this seems to be true whatever detailed account is offered of why free speech is valuable.

4

Pornography's Authority?
Response to Leslie Green

Subordinating speech is authoritative speech. There is a great difference between 'Blacks are not permitted to vote', said by a reporter in apartheid South Africa, and 'Blacks are not permitted to vote', said by a legislator enacting apartheid law. The legislator, unlike the reporter, does something that ranks a class of people as inferior, deprives them of powers and rights, and legitimates discrimination against them. Of course, one does not always need the authority of the legislature in order to perform speech acts that rank, deprive of powers and rights, and alter facts about permissibility, whether or not in ways that subordinate. Performing such speech acts is a routine enough matter for parents, teachers, and academic professors, done in ways that, let us hope, are not usually subordinating. But here too, the ability to perform such speech acts depends in part on the speaker's authority. If pornography is to be subordinating speech, and subordinating speech is a kind of ranking, depriving of powers, and legitimating, then pornography must be authoritative, or so I have argued.[1]

Leslie Green says that pornography does not subordinate because it is not authoritative in the right way; more precisely, it is not authoritative for the relevant people. His argument raises two interesting questions: one is about whether and how authoritative 'saying so' can make it so; the other is about the jurisdiction of authority. Even if pornography were to

---

[1] This essay is a revised and shortened version of Langton, 'Subordination, Silence and Pornography's Authority', 261–83, in *Censorship and Silencing: Practices of Cultural Regulation*, ed., Robert Post (Los Angeles, Cal.: Getty Research Institute, 1998), 261–83. I argued that pornography must be authoritative in Rae Langton, 'Speech Acts and Unspeakable Acts', this volume; drawing on J. L. Austin, *How to Do Things with Words* (Oxford: Oxford University Press, 1962).

have authority, women would not, he thinks, be within its jurisdiction, so pornography would not subordinate women. In response to the first question, I want to explore further the connection between authoritative speech and social construction; and in response to the second, I want to argue that women would be in the jurisdiction of pornography's authority, even in the situation he envisages.[2]

Alternative responses are possible. For example, someone might be tempted to answer that pornography does not, after all, need the special kind of authority I ascribed to it, in order to subordinate. Mary Kate McGowan says pornography could be interpreted as altering facts about permissibility in a manner very different to that of an authoritative legislator, and more similar to the way that ordinary, modestly authoritative speakers alter facts about permissibility within everyday conversations. Nellie Wieland says that pornography could be interpreted as altering the conventions governing speech acts of sexual refusal in ways that are continuous with the ordinary convention-altering activities of ordinary speakers.[3]

For present purposes however, let us go on with the antecedently plausible thought that authority is an important felicity condition for subordinating speech acts. An umpire, but not a bystander, can call a fault; a jury, but not a bystander, can acquit; a government, but not a private citizen, can disenfranchise. This understanding is in harmony with MacKinnon, who says, in a passage also quoted by Green,

Together with all its material supports, authoritatively *saying* someone is inferior is largely how structures of status and differential treatment are demarcated and actualized. Words and images are how people are placed in hierarchies, how social stratification is made to seem inevitable and right, how feelings of inferiority and

---

[2] Leslie Green, 'Pornographizing, Subordinating, Silencing', in *Censorship and Silencing: Practices of Cultural Regulation*, ed., Robert Post (Los Angeles, Cal.: Getty Research Institute, 1998), 285–311. Judith Butler and Nancy Bauer also object that pornography lacks appropriate authority; Butler, *Excitable Speech: A Politics of the Performative* (New York and London: Routledge, 1997); Bauer, 'How To Do Things With Pornography', in *Reading Cavell*, eds., Sanford Shieh and Alice Crary (New York: Routledge, 2006), 68–97.

[3] Mary Kate McGowan, 'Conversational Exercitives and the Force of Pornography', *Philosophy and Public Affairs* 31 (2003), 155–89; Nellie Wieland, 'Linguistic Authority and Convention in a Speech Act Analysis of Pornography', *Australasian Journal of Philosophy* 85 (2007), 435–56. I'm sorry not to do better justice to these proposals here. As I understand it, McGowan endorses her interpretation, but Wieland ultimately rejects hers, on the grounds that it undermines the *mens rea* of rapists. McGowan's proposal has some features in common with Langton and West, 'Scorekeeping in a Pornographic Language Game', this volume.

superiority are engendered, and how indifference to violence against those on the bottom is rationalized and normalized.[4]

What follows, if the speech act analysis of pornography succeeds? One thing is that, as Green observes, we have here an argument that differs from a traditional causal argument. Pornography may have harmful effects; it may, in Austin's terms, be a harmful 'perlocutionary' act. But it is also, in itself, subordination: in Austin's terms, an 'illocutionary' act of subordination.[5] Does anything more dramatic follow? Green seems to think so:

> if saying simply is doing, there is no need to worry about the contingent causal connection [with harm] and the problematic evidence for it. The evidence for the harm is the evidence for the saying.[6]

We should be so lucky. I, for one, never suggested anything as easy as this. If the analysis succeeds we do face two different claims about pornography: a claim about its perlocutionary effects, and a claim about its illocutionary force. But Green goes too far if he interprets the claim that pornography is an illocutionary act of subordination as a claim about what is necessarily the case, which therefore requires no additional evidence.

Causal questions are not the only questions that involve contingent connections and evidence: illocutionary questions may do so as well, and the question of authority is such a question. Whether some particular speaker has authority is a contingent matter. While it is not a contingent matter that, for example, the umpire has authority over the tennis score, it is a contingent matter whether *that man* is the umpire. In order to determine what illocution was performed one needs to know not only that *he said 'Fault'*, but also that *he is the umpire*. So one needs not only 'evidence for the saying', as Green puts it, but also evidence for the authority of the speaker. In the case of the umpire, evidence for the authority comes as easily as evidence for the saying. (There he is, sitting in his high chair by the net, in his uniform.) Likewise in the case of the speech acts of apartheid. But one can imagine cases in which the authority of an alleged umpire, an alleged legislator, is in dispute. And in the case of pornography, evidence for the authority is more controversial than evidence for the saying. So the question about pornography's authority

[4] Catharine MacKinnon, *Only Words* (Cambridge, Mass.: Harvard University Press, 1993), 31.

[5] J. L. Austin, *How to Do Things with Words*.   [6] Green, 'Pornographizing', p. 291.

does involve evidence, and contingent connections: if pornography had no authority, then it would not subordinate, any more than that man could call a fault, if he were not the umpire. It is a contingent, context-dependent matter whether pornography has authority, and hence whether it subordinates, and it cannot, I think, wholly be answered from the philosopher's armchair.[7]

In arguing that pornography is not subordinating speech, and raising the question of its jurisdiction, Green introduces two useful tools: a different example of possibly subordinating speech; and a suggested analysis of authority, drawing upon his own work elsewhere and that of Joseph Raz.[8] Green proposes a candidate case of a speaker 'authoritatively saying someone is inferior' and possibly subordinating them. The Roman Catholic Church says that homosexuality is an 'intrinsic moral evil'. What the Church says is not 'only words', but an authoritative illocution. Does it subordinate? And if so, whom does it subordinate? We are asked to consider two men, in a situation where Catholics are a minority, and there is a liberal constitution. Mick, a gay Catholic, is within the domain of the Church's authority, accepting its jurisdiction. Mick's neighbour Max is gay and Jewish, and does not accept the Church's jurisdiction. Green asks,

Is Max subordinated by the words of the Roman Church? Does he have an objective disorder because the Church says he does?[9]

Green's implication is that Mick, the Catholic, is 'subordinated', and has an 'objective disorder' because of the Church's say-so; and that it is another question whether the same applies to Max. Green ultimately wants to say that Mick is subordinated, but Max is not. He goes on to argue that when it comes to the jurisdiction of pornography, women are more like Max than Mick.

---

[7] This way of thinking assumes a non-stipulative usage for 'pornography', following Green's usage of an 'ordinary concept' of pornography, though my discussion has an implicit restriction to the kind of pornography for which a case might be made that it subordinates and silences women. If instead one says with Catharine MacKinnon that as a matter of definition pornography subordinates, it will no longer be a contingent matter whether 'pornography' subordinates; but the question about illocutionary force will return as a contingent empirical one again, in the form of the question '*is* there any pornography, so defined?' MacKinnon, 'Frances Biddle's Sister', *Feminism Unmodified* (Cambridge, Mass.: Harvard University Press, 1987).

[8] Leslie Green, *The Authority of the State* (Oxford: Oxford University Press, 1989); Joseph Raz, *The Morality of Freedom* (Oxford: Oxford University Press, 1986).

[9] Green, 'Pornographizing', 264.

We have two different issues here. The first concerns the constructive power of authoritative speech: can saying so make it so, when the Church says that someone is subordinate, and has 'an objective disorder'? The second concerns the jurisdiction of authoritative speech: can the Church's words subordinate Max even though he does not accept its jurisdiction? We'll look at these in turn.

1. The Constructive Power of Authoritative Speech

Green implies that Mick, the Catholic, is 'subordinated', and 'has an objective disorder', because of the Church's say-so; he then devotes his attention to the comparative status of Max. Is he right about Mick, though? It may indeed be plausible to suppose that Mick is subordinated because of the Church's say-so; but it is implausible to suppose he has 'an objective disorder', because of the Church's say so. Just as well: for if Mick had 'an objective disorder', the Church would, on the face of it, be *right* in saying he had. There is a limit to how far saying so can make it so, even when the sayings are authoritative; there are limits to what illocutions can do when they 'construct' social reality.

For some illocutions, authoritatively saying so *can* instantly make it so: 'You're fired' uttered by the authoritative employer instantly makes it the case that you are fired. Such illocutions belong to a class Austin described as *exercitive*. Contrast this with the words of the umpire who says, 'Out'. This belongs to a class Austin described as *verdictive*. The umpire's verdict alters the score of the game. But does he bring it about that the ball *is* outside the white line? No, or a photograph could not show that the umpire had made a mistake. To be sure, the umpire brings something about: the ball *counts* as outside the line for the purposes of the score (which would not hold if a bystander were to say 'Out'). But it is the player, not the umpire, who brings it about that the ball *is* outside the white line—and she brings it about, not by saying something, but by hitting something.

A verdictive is an authoritative judgement that something *is* so. An exercitive is an authoritative decision 'that something *is to be so*'.[10] Both

---

[10] Austin's discussion of verdictives and exercitives occurs, with some of these examples, on pp. 152–6 of *How to Do Things with Words*. The idea of direction of fit is widely used in discussions

kinds of illocution require authority, but there is a difference in their direction of fit. A verdictive aims to fit the world; an exercitive aims for the world to fit the words. A verdictive purports to map a reality. ('The ball is out.') An exercitive purports to create a reality. ('You're out, fired!') Actions of ranking and grading are verdictive. The Church speaks verdictively, when it says that homosexuals have inferior status, and that homosexuality is an objective disorder.

If verdictives 'aim to fit the world', does this mean that they do not after all 'construct reality', and are not really involved in subordination? By no means. Consider these remarks from MacKinnon about word-to-world direction of fit, when it comes to the speech of those in power or authority.

Having power means, among other things, that when someone says, 'this is how it is' it is taken as being that way . . . [The] beliefs of the powerful become [proven], in part because the world actually arranges itself to affirm what the powerful want to see.[11]

She takes this description to apply to the workings of pornography, but it applies to much else besides. When someone authoritatively says, 'this is how it is', that can be a verdictive judgement that something is so, and it is then 'taken as being that way': verdictives construct part of reality, in making something *count* as thus and so. If the ball is called 'Out' by the umpire, it is 'taken as being' out, *counts* as out: the score adjusts itself to fit the umpire's words. There is something interesting here: for in this latter respect a verdictive has, so to speak, an exercitive dimension. Its direction of fit is a complex matter. The verdict 'Out' has a word-to-fit-world direction of fit, aiming to conform to a truth about the location of the ball; but it also has, in part, a world-to-fit-word direction of fit, aiming for part of the world, the score, to conform to the verdict.[12]

There is a second way in which verdictives, while aiming to reflect the world, may actively construct it. MacKinnon suggests that when the

---

of propositional attitudes of belief and desire, but for some applications to speech acts see J. R. Searle, *Expression and Meaning* (Cambridge: Cambridge University Press, 1979), and Lloyd Humberstone, 'Direction of Fit', *Mind* 101 (1992), 59–83.

[11] MacKinnon, *Feminism Unmodified,* 164. I have substituted 'proven' here for MacKinnon's own word 'proof'.

[12] Mary Kate McGowan examines the role of verdictives in social construction, in 'On Pornography: MacKinnon, Speech Acts, and "False" Construction', *Hypatia* 20 (2005), 23–49.

powerful say 'this is how it is', what is said can *become true*, at least in part, 'because the world actually arranges itself to affirm' what the powerful say. This second kind of 'construction' has to do with the causal effects of verdictive speech. Acts of ranking can sometimes be self-fulfilling, not just with respect to what a person *counts* as being, but what she becomes in response to the ranking. Suppose a child is authoritatively ranked as having a lower than average intelligence, and is believed by her teachers to have a lower than average intelligence. The child can, to a certain degree, really come to have a lower than average intelligence, or in any case one which is lower than she would otherwise have. When you are ranked as worse, you are treated as worse, and then really become worse.[13]

This causal self-fulfilling aspect of some verdictives is to be distinguished from the simple self-fulfilling aspect of the exercitive illocution—the self-fulfilling 'You're fired' which instantly makes it the case that you are fired. The verdictives of the Pygmalion studies—'Anna is not clever'—are not instantly self-fulfilling, though with time and the classroom neglect of Anna which they justify, they may become true. As a verdictive, the act of ranking Anna's intelligence purports to conform to reality, claims to hold up a mirror to the world. In its exercitive aspect, it constructs a part of the social world, what Anna's intelligence *counts* as being, though not, yet, what Anna's intelligence really is. But now what Anna's intelligence counts as being begins to have an effect on what Anna's intelligence really *is*, for people's lives and abilities are sensitive to rankings in a way that balls and lines on a court are not.[14]

So it seems there are two ways in which verdictive saying so can sometimes make it so, two ways in which verdictive speech can 'construct' reality.[15] The first is by making it *count* as so: 'When the powerful say "this is how it is", it is *taken to be* that way.' The second is by sometimes making

---

[13] See Robert Rosenthal and Lenore Jakobson, *Pygmalion in the Classroom* (New York: Holt, Rinehart, and Winston, 1968).

[14] This aspect of social construction has received considerable attention; see e.g. Ian Hacking, 'The Looping Effects of Human Kinds', in *Causal Cognition: A Multidisciplinary Approach*, eds., D. Sperber, D. Premack, and A. J. Premack (Oxford: Clarendon Press, 1994); Sally Haslanger, 'Ontology and Social Construction', *Philosophical Topics* 23 (1995), 95–125; Mary Kate McGowan, 'On Pornography', 23–49; Marilyn Frye, *The Politics of Reality: Essays in Feminist Theory* (Freedom, Cal.: The Crossing Press, 1983).

[15] These two ways are taken up again in Langton, 'Pornography's Divine Command: Reply to Judith Butler', this volume.

it, in part, really so; 'When the powerful say 'this is how it is', *the world arranges itself to affirm*' what the powerful say.[16]

What does this mean for Mick? Just as the umpire's verdict has an exercitive dimension in the way it alters one social part of the world—the score of the game—so the Church's verdict has an exercitive dimension in the way it alters one social part of the world—the status of gays. The Church authoritatively says Mick has inferior status, and has an objective disorder: so he counts as having inferior status, and having an objective disorder. When it comes to social status, what you have is what you socially count as having. He does have inferior status; the Church's saying so makes that so, the Church does subordinate Mick.[17] But when it comes to an objective disorder, what you have is not just what you count as having. He does not have an objective disorder; the Church's saying so does not make that so. In addition, there will be the causal effects of that verdictive speech: Mick's counting socially as inferior or subordinate is likely to have concrete effects on his self-conception, his job prospects, and relationships, so that he ends up with considerably more to contend with than simply being counted as inferior.

These conclusions about verdictives and social standing should apply equally to pornographic speech and what it does to women—but only on the assumption, contested by Green, that women are in the domain of pornography's authority.

2. Authority and its Jurisdiction

We begin by asking whether Max is subordinated, as Mick is. Green argues that Max is *not* subordinated, despite the fact that the Church's verdicts are, as claims about natural law, addressed to him also. Max is insulated from the Church's verdicts, not only because he himself rejects the Church's

---

[16] This means verdictives can disguise their constructive power. See e.g. Langton, 'Projection and Objectification', this volume; Sally Haslanger, 'On Being Objective and Being Objectified,' in *A Mind of One's Own,* eds., Louise Antony and Charlotte Witt (Boulder Co.: Westview Press, 1993), 85–125; McGowan, 'On Pornography'.

[17] Subordination in the sense of inferiority does not seem quite the same as subordination in the sense of subservience. The subordination of gays, on Green's account, seems to involve the former but not the latter; the subordination of women through pornography seems to involve both. I shan't speculate here about the relevance of this difference.

jurisdiction, but also because his country has a liberal constitution, the Church is in a minority, and its speech is merely tolerated, not endorsed, by the broader society. These factors mean, according to Green, that Max is not within the jurisdiction of the Church's authority. If, on the other hand, 'the Church were established and its dictates widely accepted as binding standards of behaviour', then the Church would have *de facto* authority over Max, and he too, like Mick, would be subordinated, notwithstanding his personal rejection of its jurisdiction.

Green and I are in agreement here that 'whether speech has the power to subordinate is not simply a function of what is said but on the whole social context in which it occurs'.[18] His example shows convincingly how speakers whose authority is less than, and different to, that of the state may none the less subordinate. But his conclusion about the jurisdiction of authority is based on a particular analysis of *de facto* authority and its conditions, and this in turn grounds his later conclusions about pornography. It is, I think, mistaken.

According to Green, the first necessary condition for the Church's *de facto* authority over someone like Max who does not himself accept the Church's authority is a widespread 'perceived legitimacy': 'the norms prescribed by the Church must be generally accepted as setting binding standards of behaviour'. I shall call this a condition of *general perceived legitimacy*. The second necessary condition is that of a kind of 'efficacy':

the Church's norms must be generally efficacious. . . . there must be . . . significant contact between Max and those who do endorse the Catholic view: they must, for example, have the power to hire or fire him, to control his education, to affect his civil rights, etc. and they must sometimes actually exercise their power.[19]

I shall call this a condition of *general efficacy*. Is Green right about these two being necessary conditions for the Church to have authority over Max?[20]

Surely not. First, suppose that the norms prescribed by the Church were not 'generally accepted', but that the Church is a powerful minority, whose members accept its voice as authoritative, while non-members are substantially in the power of the members: suppose, in other words, that

---

[18] Green, 'Pornographizing', 294.   [19] Green, 'Pornographizing', p. 294.

[20] I confess I have reservations about the efficacy condition that go beyond anything argued here. I doubt that efficacy of any kind is necessary for an illocutionary act of subordination, though it may be necessary for perlocutionary subordinating *effects*, on working conditions, sexual violence and the like. But I shall leave this concern aside.

general efficacy is satisfied, though general perceived legitimacy is not. The minority, being powerful, have the power to hire and fire Max, control his civil rights, and sometimes exercise that power. In these conditions, I suggest, Max would indeed be subordinated. What surely matters is that those with power over Max take the voice of the Church to be authoritative, not that *everyone* does. This suggests that contrary to Green, general perceived legitimacy is not a necessary condition of the Church having the authority needed to subordinate Max.

Furthermore, Max would be subordinated if there were merely *local* analogues of both of Green's two general conditions. Suppose there is local version of Green's first condition: call it *local perceived legitimacy*. Suppose that the norms prescribed by the Church are locally accepted in the community of which Max is a member. And suppose there is a local version of Green's second condition: call it *local efficacy*. Suppose there is significant contact between Max and those in his community who endorse the Catholic view, so that locally they have the power to hire or fire him, control his education, affect his civil rights, and they sometimes exercise it. Suppose that in some places beyond Max's local community, the norms prescribed by the Church are not accepted as binding, and that if he lived there, he would be outside the authority of the Church. Where he is, he is subordinated—though if he lived elsewhere, perhaps he would not be. The absence of *general* perceived legitimacy and *general* efficacy of the Church's norms does not undermine the fact that Max is subordinated, there and then. Demanding the general conditions comes close to demanding that no gays are subordinated unless all are.

Let's think about how this bears on the argument about pornography. According to Green, women are not directly within the jurisdiction of pornography's authority. 'The first chain of command is . . . the authority of pornographers . . . over men and boys'.[21] So women are to be compared, not with Mick, of his example, but with Max, the outsider to Catholicism. This means that the conditions under which women could be subordinated by pornography are like the conditions under which Max would be subordinated, according to Green's analysis: namely, when the two necessary conditions of general perceived legitimacy and general efficacy are in force.

---

[21] Green, 'Pornographizing', 295.

But then it is implausible to think that pornography subordinates women, he says, because the two conditions of general perceived legitimacy and general efficacy are not fulfilled. After all, pornography 'must compete with other putative social authorities as well, including the state, the family, and Churches'. In a liberal society the state merely tolerates the speech of pornographers, does not endorse it, and denounces sexual violence. 'In a society which endorses freedom of expression pornography is private, non-authoritative speech'.[22] These competing authoritative voices contradict the voice of pornography, and this undermines the perceived legitimacy of pornography, and its efficacy.

One could remark on the swiftness with which Green casts women as the outsiders to the illocutions of pornography. (Perhaps there are women who, so to speak, accept pornography's jurisdiction in the way that Mick accepts that of the Church: are they most subordinated of all?)[23] One could remark on Green's denial of a general perceived legitimacy of pornography, and his assumption that the voice of the courts unequivocally contradicts the voice of pornography, rather than all too often echoing it. ('Women who say no do not always mean no. It is not just a question of saying no', says judge to jury.)[24] One could remark on Green's sanguine belief that 'the broader society condemns [rape] and regularly prosecutes it'—when rape is the most under-reported crime of any, because women know that the broader society also condemns rape victims, and regularly torments them in the courts. One could remark on Green's denial of general efficacy, his assumption that there is no 'significant contact' between women and men who accept pornography's authority—his assumption that most women are *never* in the power of men who consume pornography, men who have power in women's workplaces, homes, and sexual relationships, and who sometimes exercise that power. I shall not argue that Green's two conditions of general perceived legitimacy and general efficacy are in fact satisfied, though I believe it could well be argued. For as I have shown, these two are not after all necessary conditions for subordination.

[22] Green, 'Pornographizing', 298.

[23] See Pamela Paul, *Pornified: How Pornography is Transforming Our Lives, Our Relationships, Our Families* (NY: Henry Holt, 2005), chs. 4 and 5 for some examples.

[24] Judge David Wild in 1982, as discussed by Hornsby in 'Speech Acts and Pornography', *Women's Philosophy Review* 10 (1993), 38–45, reprinted in *The Problem of Pornography*, ed., Sue Dwyer (Belmont, Ca.: Wadsworth, 1995).

We saw that Max would be subordinated if there were merely *local* analogues of Green's two general conditions, and the case is likewise for women. Suppose that the norms prescribed by pornography are locally accepted as setting standards of behaviour in the community of which a woman is a member, although she does not accept them. Suppose, in other words, that the condition of local perceived legitimacy is satisfied. And suppose there is a local version of Green's second general condition. Suppose there is significant contact between the woman and those in her community who accept the norms of pornography, so that locally they have the power to hire or fire her, control her education, affect her civil rights, and they sometimes exercise that power. Suppose, in other words, that local efficacy is satisfied. It is not true that 'in these circumstances, pornography has the character... of a private view',[25] notwithstanding the presence of competing norms elsewhere. Perhaps she could escape that local community by moving elsewhere—but that, again, supposes requisite knowledge, inclinations, and material resources, an especially questionable assumption given many women's poverty and material dependency on men. And again, the possibility of escape does not alter the fact that such a woman, where she is, in that context, *is subordinated*—for the reasons Max would be subordinated, under conditions of local perceived legitimacy and local efficacy. To demand otherwise comes close to demanding that no women are subordinated by pornography unless all are. So pornography does subordinate some women, even if one grants Green's questionable assumptions about the absent conditions of general perceived legitimacy and efficacy. Then the question is not whether, but how many women are subordinated: and then, how many women does it take before it begins to matter?

3. A Surprise Ending

At the end of Green's paper, he raises an interesting thought. He points out that pornography is not bought and sold with the intentions typically involved in speech. Pornography is intended to produce sexual arousal; it is, as MacKinnon puts it, 'masturbation material'.[26] The ordinary notion

---

[25] Green, 'Pornographizing', 296.   [26] Ibid., 304, MacKinnon, *Only Words*, 17.

of pornography is, he says, a functional notion. He expresses doubt that pornography is communicative speech at all, and wonders

whether it even makes sense to extend the speech act analogy into this realm, and to theorize about the force of 'pornographic utterances' in general.[27]

To raise this doubt, he thinks, is to raise a doubt about the entire enterprise of bringing speech act theory to bear on the issues of pornography, silence and subordination.

My arguments were indeed premised on the assumption that pornography is speech, as the courts declared. It is disputable that pornography is speech, and it has been disputed.[28] But notice this. If pornography is *not* speech, then *free speech* does not protect pornography, if anything does.[29] Either pornography is not speech, in which case a free speech principle does not protect it; or pornography is speech, in which case speech act theory can help understand it. And notice this too. Whether pornography is speech, or whether pornography is non-speech, speech act theory can help us understand how women may be *silenced*. It can help understand how women may be *silenced by pornography,* since here it is without question women's speech that is at issue. Someone may be silenced by something that is speech, or by something that is not speech. A heckler may silence a would-be speaker by shouting abusive words—or by blowing a whistle. One person may silence another by gently but ominously tapping a stick. One radio station may jam another by broadcasting, not words, but a competing melody. (I draw here on childhood memories of jammed reception of the BBC World Service, when living in Kashmir, not far from a border with the USSR.) Women's potential speech acts may be restricted and thwarted by pornography, whether or not pornography is itself speech. It would not then be true to say that pornography is speech that silences. It would still be true to say that pornography silences.[30]

---

[27] Green, 'Pornographizing', 304.

[28] For example, by Fred Schauer and Jennifer Hornsby; Schauer, *Free Speech: A Philosophical Enquiry* (Cambridge: Cambridge University Press), 1982; Hornsby, 'Speech Acts and Pornography'. See also McGowan and Ishani Maitra, 'Limits of Free Speech: Pornography and the Question of Coverage', *Legal Theory* 13 (2007), 41−68; Melinda Vadas, 'The Manufacture-for-use of Pornography and Women's Inequality,' *Journal of Political Philosophy* 13 (2005), 174−93.

[29] See Hornsby 'Speech Acts and Pornography'; and Hornsby and Langton, 'Free Speech and Illocution', *Legal Theory* 4 (1998), pp. 21-37.

[30] Green criticizes the silencing argument as well, in 'Pornographizing'; for response, see Langton, 'Subordination, Silence and Pornography's Authority', 273−7.

But now consider. If pornography is not even speech, as Green suggests in his conclusion, and if pornography does sometimes silence women (and it really is women's *speech* that is silenced), then a free speech argument *against* pornography looks stronger than ever. Well—it is nice to find agreement in surprising places.

5

Pornography's Divine Command?
Response to Judith Butler

In *Excitable Speech*, Judith Butler paints a kind of 'divine command' theory of pornography, which she goes on to reject, given the lack of a suitable divinity. On this view, pornography 'is a subject who speaks, and in speaking, brings about what it names'; pornography's authority is analogous to the 'divine'. Like the God of Genesis, who said 'Let there be light', and there was instantly light, so pornography is supposed to say 'let women be subordinate' and women are instantly subordinate. Butler herself has done more than most theorists to emphasize the role of 'performativity' in the social construction of gender, but she whole-heartedly rejects this particular application of speech act theory, which she attributes to MacKinnon and to me. I argued that pornography may be (in J. L. Austin's terms) an 'illocutionary' speech act of subordination if it has a certain authority. Butler denies the authority, and concludes that pornography does not subordinate women.[1]

The claim that pornography silences women fares no better. I argued that pornography may silence women if it is a source of 'illocutionary disablement'. A woman might encounter such silencing if she says 'no', trying to refuse sex, but finds that the 'no' fails to be recognized as a refusal.

---

[1] This response to Judith Butler is previously unpublished. See Butler, *Excitable Speech: A Politics of the Performative* (New York and London: Routledge, 1997), 69. My argument appears in 'Speech Acts and Unspeakable Acts', this volume, drawing on J. L. Austin, *How to Do Things with Words* (Oxford: Oxford University Press, 1962). Butler discusses in similar vein Mari Matsuda's work on hate speech in e.g. 'Public Response to Racist Speech', in Matsuda, Charles R. Lawrence III, Richard Delgado, and Kimberlè Williams Crenshaw, *Words that Wound: Critical Race Theory, Assaultive Speech and the First Amendment* (Boulder, Co.: Westview Press, 1993), 17–51. While the word 'divine' is hers, the reference to Genesis is my elaboration. For some of Butler's earlier work on gender and performativity, see e.g. *Gender Trouble* (New York: Routledge, 1999), and *Bodies that Matter* (New York: Routledge, 1993).

Butler allows that pornography may silence women in just this way; but it is not a way that matters. There is nothing special about the silencing of people's speech, given its inescapability. We are all silenced, all the time; there is nothing special about pornography. The silencing argument assumes and glorifies the intentions of a speaking subject. Such assumptions, she says, embody out-dated and politically dubious views about intention. We should not glory in the power of speakers to do what they mean with their words. Instead, we should glory in the failure of speakers to do what they mean with their words, when hearers twist their speech in acts of textual political subversion.

In sum, the claims that pornography subordinates and silences rely, according to Butler, on implausible assumptions about pornography's god-like authority, by which pornography's saying so is supposed to make it so; and implausible assumptions about the role of intention in speech generally. Butler is mistaken, though. The claims do not require assumptions anything like as strong as the ones she identifies, and one needs no *deus ex machina* to make them work.

1. Does Pornography Subordinate Women?

MacKinnon's argument that pornography subordinates assumes that 'pornography operates as an imperative' which has a quasi-divine 'power to realize that which it dictates', according to Butler.[2] On her interpretation, pornography is like an order: treat women as subordinate! This is how she reads MacKinnon's account of how pornography 'constructs' women:

Pornography makes the world a pornographic place through its making and use, establishing what women are said to exist as, are seen as, are treated as, constructing the social reality of what a woman is in terms of what can be done to her.[3]

Butler argues that on the contrary, pornography 'fails to wield the power to construct the social reality of what a woman is', given that its authority 'is decidedly less than divine'. Furthermore its norms and imperatives are fantastical, presented as impossible to fulfill, offering an 'allegory of

---

[2] Butler, *Excitable Speech*, 65.
[3] MacKinnon, *Only Words* (Cambridge, Mass: Harvard University Press, 1993), 25.

masculine willfulness and feminine submission...which repeatedly and anxiously rehearses its own unrealizability, [depicting] impossible and uninhabitable positions'.[4]

In responding to these objections, I'll look at the role of self-fulfilling speech in social construction, as applied to pornography, and then at the issue of pornography's authority and norms.[5]

A first question is whether pornography indeed 'operates as an imperative'. One does occasionally find this thought in MacKinnon, as when she compares pornographic speech to the utterance of the word 'kill' to a trained guard dog.[6] But there are alternative ways of thinking about it. The idea of an imperative played no part in my interpretation of the claim that pornography subordinates, according to which pornography authoritatively *ranks* women as inferior, *deprives* women of certain powers and rights, and *legitimates* discriminatory behaviour towards women. Perhaps, on MacKinnon's account, pornography need not be any kind of command, divine or otherwise.

Butler links this idea of an imperative with the idea of a self-fulfilling speech act. Pornography's 'imperative' is supposed to have 'the power to realize that which it dictates', it has a 'self-fulfilling capacity', being 'an institution with the performative power to bring about that which it depicts'. Here in the idea of self-fulfillment we have something that is indeed central to MacKinnon's understanding of subordination and social construction. But this is not, or not exactly, the idea of an imperative. All the same, the notion of an imperative may give us a useful route into thinking about different ways in which a speech act can be self-fulfilling.

Consider these three different ways to order someone to shut the door. (Imagine a parent addressing a child, with escalating levels of ire.)

(1) Please shut the door.

[4] Butler, *Excitable Speech*, 68–9.

[5] For a fuller discussion of the issues about speech acts and social construction, see Langton, 'Subordination, Silence and Pornography's Authority', in *Censorship and Silencing: Practices of Cultural Regulation*, ed., Robert Post (New York: Getty Research Institute, 1998), 261–83. A revised and shortened version, 'Pornography's Authority: Reply to Leslie Green', is in this volume. See Mary Kate McGowan's work for subtle development of the idea of an 'exercitive' dimension to many ordinary speech acts, and in pornography, e.g. in 'Conversational Exercitives and the Force of Pornography', *Philosophy and Public Affairs* 31 (2003), 155–89.

[6] MacKinnon, 'Not A Moral Issue', *Feminism Unmodified*, 156. MacKinnon's main point with this example is, I think, to illustrate how certain speech can be more than 'only words', in a way that puts it beyond legal protection.

(2) You have to shut the door.

(3) By the time I count to ten, that door will be *shut*. One, two, three . . .

Assuming they are authoritative, all three of these instantly change normative facts about what is permissible and required: the hearer has to shut the door. Assuming they are effective, and the hearer is obedient, all three of them causally change physical facts about the door: it will be shut. Which, if any, are self-fulfilling? Not (1), since it isn't apt for truth. What about (2)? In authoritatively saying that someone has to shut the door, I make it true that they have to shut the door.[7] So we could say that (2) is self-fulfilling in what Austin called an 'illocutionary' way. What of (3)? By saying 'The door will be shut . . .', and being obeyed, I make it true that the door will be shut. So we could say that (3) is self-fulfilling in a causal—in Austin's terms, 'perlocutionary'—way.

These brief reflections about imperatives give us reason to distinguish two ways a speech act might be self-fulfilling. The first is a constitutive, or illocutionary, way, where saying so, given the presence of appropriate felicity conditions, is enough to make it so. The second is a causal, or perlocutionary, way, where saying so, given the presence of appropriate felicity conditions, *and* given the production of an appropriate effect, is enough to make it so. I want to think now about how these two kinds of self-fulfillment might extend to other aspects of the idea of subordination.

Pornography subordinates, I said, if (among other things) it ranks women as inferior. An act of ranking is, in Austin's terms, a 'verdictive' illocution. It makes an authoritative claim about how the world is—it aims to fit the world. 'Guilty', said by a jury, is verdictive. An important contrast would be with an illocution that is 'exercitive', which says how the world is to be—it aims for the world to fit it. 'Sentence: twenty years' would be exercitive. Exercitives are often self-fulfilling, in an illocutionary way: the judge saying 'Sentence: twenty years' instantly makes it true that the sentence *is* twenty years. By contrast, verdictives are not obviously self-fulfilling in an illocutionary way. 'Guilty', said by the jury, does not make it the case that the accused *is* guilty: though, as we'll see in a moment, it

---

[7] I here follow David Lewis's amendment of Austin's account: see 'Scorekeeping in a Language Game', *Philosophical Papers* vol. i (New York: Oxford University Press, 1983), 233–49 at 247–8.

does it make it true that the accused socially *counts* as guilty for the purposes of the court.[8]

Is pornography, on MacKinnon's understanding, like a jury delivering a verdict on women? Or like a judge pronouncing sentence on women? One can imagine both ideas being plausibly developed in unpacking the concept of subordination; but in focusing on the idea of ranking, I have myself emphasized the verdictive idea. To oversimplify, pornography says 'Inferior', as the jury says 'Guilty'.[9]

Note that illocutions of ranking can in turn be connected with illocutions of *legitimation* of certain behaviour—legitimation being, as I argued, a further aspect of the idea of subordination. As MacKinnon says,

Together with all its material supports, authoritatively *saying* someone is inferior is largely how structures of status and differential treatment are demarcated and actualized.[10]

Authoritatively ranking women as inferior is how structures of 'status' get to be 'actualized', in part because of the acts of ranking in themselves, and in part because the acts of ranking legitimate 'differential treatment', which in turn reinforces that ranking.

In supposing that pornography is like the jury, we are supposing that it in a certain way aims to fit the world, just like the jury's verdict. 'This is how women are: inferior', is comparable to 'this is how the accused is: guilty'. And you might think, at this point, that self-fulfillment doesn't really come into it after all, since the jury's saying he is guilty doesn't make it true that is he *is* guilty.

---

[8] Austin's discussion of exercitives and verdictives occurs, with these examples, in *How to Do Things with Words*, 152–56. The distinction is a topic of Langton, 'Speech Acts and Unspeakable Acts', 'Pornography's Authority: Response to Leslie Green,' this volume, and 'Objective and Unconditioned Value', *Philosophical Review* 116 (2007), 157–85.

[9] The ideas about verdictives that follow are developed in Langton, 'Pornography's Authority', this volume. For an illuminating account of the involvement of verdictives in social construction, which shares features of the present proposal, see McGowan, 'On Pornography: MacKinnon, Speech Acts, and "False" Construction', *Hypatia* 20 (2005), 23–49. McGowan develops the idea of an 'erroneous verdictive', comparing pornography's ranking of women with a 'bad call' made by an umpire, which has a complex direction of fit: it aims to fit the world; but the world comes to fit it, in two ways. It enacts facts about what the world 'counts' as being, as with an exercitive; this in turn (unlike the situation with the umpire) produces effects on the actual world.

[10] MacKinnon, *Only Words*, 31.

But there are complexities here. As MacKinnon says,

Having power means, among other things, that when someone says, 'this is how it is' it is taken as being that way . . . [The] beliefs of the powerful become [proven], in part because the world actually arranges itself to affirm what the powerful want to see.[11]

When someone in authority says, 'this is how it is' it is 'taken as being' that way—and here we have one first sense in which verdictives *are* after all self-fulfilling. If the accused receives the verdict 'guilty', he is 'taken as being' guilty: he *counts* as guilty for the purposes of the court. Part of the world—his social status—does indeed adjust itself to fit the jury's words. In this respect a verdictive can have an illocutionary, or constitutive, self-fulfilling aspect.

By analogy if women are ranked as inferior, they count socially as inferior. Since social status does in fact depend on what you count as in the eyes of your peers, the ranking in fact alters women's status for the worse. This has implications for Butler's critique. Authoritatively saying that someone exists 'as' thus-and-so can, in the right circumstances, construct the social reality of what someone 'is'—contrary to Butler's suggestion that MacKinnon makes a kind of grammatical mistake in supposing that what pornography depicts women *as* can have implications for what a woman *is*.[12]

There is a second side to the question whether verdictives can be self-fulfilling. Going back to MacKinnon: when the powerful say 'this is how it is', something else happens too: 'the world actually arranges itself to affirm what the powerful want to see'—and by implication, to what the powerful *say*. We have here, I think, the idea that verdictives can also have a self-fulfilling aspect that is perlocutionary, or causal.

Now it must be admitted that verdictives are not usually self-fulfilling in a causal way. A jury's verdict of 'Guilty' does not have the effect that the accused person becomes guilty. An umpire's saying the ball is 'Out' will not *cause* the ball to be outside the line. My deeming a student's essay to

---

[11] MacKinnon, *Feminism Unmodified*, 164. I substitute 'proven' here for MacKinnon's own word 'proof'. MacKinnon is talking here of both the speech and the beliefs of those in power or authority, but for present purposes we focus on speech, and overlook a potentially significant distinction between power and authority.

[12] 'But if the 'as' is read as an assertion of a likeness, it is not for that reason the assertion of a metaphorical collapse into identity. Through what means does the 'as' turn into an 'is'?', Butler, *Excitable Speech*, 68.

be worth an A will not change its nature, and make it better than it would have been had I given it a B.

But there is a difference, when it comes to verdictives about people. The properties of human beings are responsive to rankings in ways that properties of tennis balls and essays are not. My ranking of an essay as intelligent will not causally alter the essay; but my ranking of the essay's writer as intelligent may well causally alter the writer, to the extent that, over time, she becomes intelligent, or more intelligent than she was. My authoritative ranking of an essay as good might make it count as good; my authoritative ranking of a student might make her not only count as good, but become good, or at any rate better. Such effects of ranking behaviour on people are widely established.[13] And the phenomenon is likely to be helped along by the above-mentioned fact that an illocution of ranking can also be an illocution of legitimating certain sorts of treatment towards the person ranked, which treatment in turn produces its distinctive effects. If pornography ranks women as inferior, that may not only make women count socially as inferior, but make women actually become inferior, as they adapt to their social role.

In sum then, verdictives in certain contexts can have two different contributions to social construction: they can, self-fulfillingly, make something count as so, in a constitutive, illocutionary way; and they can, self-fulfillingly, make something really become so, in a causal, perlocutionary way. In light of all this it should be obvious, I hope, that pornography may have, as Butler puts it, 'a self-fulfilling capacity' and be 'an institution with the performative power to bring about that which it depicts'; and that it may have all this, and be all this, without need for divine miracles.

The claim that pornography subordinates does, as I interpret it, depend on a claim that it has authority.[14] I took this claim to be an empirical

---

[13] For example, the 'Pygmalion' studies on the effects of expectation of intelligence on school children. Robert Rosenthal and Lenore Jakobson, *Pygmalion in the Classroom* (New York: Holt, Rinehart and Winston, 1968). Causal verdictive self-fulfillment probably comes under the rubric of what Sally Haslanger calls 'discursive construction', involving properties someone acquires because of what is attributed to them, see Haslanger, 'Ontology and Social Construction', *Philosophical Topics* 23 (1995), 95–125. See also Haslanger, 'On Being Objective and Being Objectified', in *A Mind of One's Own*, eds., Louise Antony and Charlotte Witt (Boulder Co.: Westview Press, 1993), 85–125 and Ian Hacking, 'The Looping Effects of Human Kinds', in *Causal Cognition: A Multidisciplinary Approach*, eds., D. Sperber, D. Premack, and A. J. Premack (Oxford: Clarendon Press, 1994).

[14] For a more detailed discussion of the authority issue, see Langton, 'Pornography's Authority', this volume. Nancy Bauer objects to the premise about pornography's authority in 'How To Do Things

one, and I supplied what I took to be evidence for it. Butler rejects the claim, but supplies no evidence to support her rejection. And in a further piece of a priori theorizing, she claims that pornography 'presents its norms as impossible to realize'. What are her reasons for thinking pornography presents its norms as impossible to realize? One, it seems, is that pornography is explicitly fictional, explicitly fantasy; another, it seems, is that pornography is open to deconstructive readings by feminist theorists. Neither of these are sufficient grounds for thinking pornography typic-ally—let alone always and everywhere—presents its norms as impossible to realize. And is it really a matter to be judged a priori? If pornography presents its norms as impossible to realize, one would expect the normative beliefs of those exposed to pornography to be unchanged by it. But that is not so, by and large.

When we look to the world, we find evidence that bears on both of Butler's claims about pornography's authority, and about its norms. Briefly, there is evidence that consumers' normative beliefs *are* measurably altered following exposure to pornography: they are more likely to view women as inferior, more likely to accept rape myths (that women enjoy rape, do not mean to refuse when they say no); more likely to think rape a less serious offense; more likely to think rape victims deserving of their treatment, more likely to say that they themselves would rape if they could get away with it.[15] These perlocutionary effects on normative beliefs are poorly

---

With Pornography', in *Reading Cavell*, eds., Sanford Shieh and Alice Crary (New York, NY: Routledge, 2006), 68–97. For an important argument that pornography does not need any special authority in order to subordinate, see the work of Mary Kate McGowan, in e.g. 'Conversational Exercitives and the Force of Pornography'. McGowan there articulates the idea of exercitives which enact permissibility facts throughout ordinary, not especially authoritative, conversations. Nellie Wieland's re-interpretation of the silencing claim strengthens it by showing how it might use convention-setting moves familiar to ordinary speakers who are not especially authoritative, in 'Linguistic Authority and Convention in a Speech Act Analysis of Pornography', *Australasian Journal of Philosophy* 85 (2007), 435–56. A detailed critique of Butler's interpretation of the speech-act-theoretic approach to pornography is given by Lisa Schwartzman, 'Hate Speech, Illocution, and Social Context: A Critique of Judith Butler', *Journal of Social Philosophy* 33 (2002), 421–41.

[15] Edward Donnerstein, Daniel Linz, and Steven Penrod, *The Question of Pornography: Research Findings and Policy Implications* (New York: Free Press; London: Collier Macmillan, 1987); J. Bryant and D. Zillman, 'Pornography, Sexual Callousness and the Trivialization of Rape', *Journal of Communication* 32 (December 1982), 10–21; Pamela Paul, *Pornified: How Pornography is Transforming Our Lives, Our Relationships, Our Families* (New York: Henry Holt, 2005).

explained by an assumption that pornography has no authority; they are better explained by an assumption that pornography does have authority, in a certain domain. The effects are poorly explained by an assumption that pornography presents its norms as impossible; they are better explained by supposing that pornography presents its norms as possible; and that pornography has legitimated these normative beliefs.

How this may be, given the avowedly fictional nature of much pornography, is an interesting question; but it poses no deep mysteries. After all, even fans of Conan Doyle's Sherlock Holmes stories may have their descriptive and normative beliefs affected. The stories make real world factual claims about the geography of London; they also, perhaps, make real world normative claims about the value of extraordinary powers of detection. Many kinds of speech—racist propaganda, ordinary advertising, edifying parables—manage to make good use of fictions to alter both descriptive and normative beliefs.[16]

Among Butler's reasons for doubting that pornography has authority is the thought that pornographic speech can be refigured, turned against itself, denied authority through rebellious acts of parody by those who would otherwise be injured by it. She thinks, in short, that pornography can itself be silenced. Pornography thus silenced is deprived of authority, and prevented from subordinating. To better assess this sanguine hope, we need to consider more carefully now her arguments about silencing, whether by or of pornography.

2. Does Pornography Silence Women?

According to Butler, the argument that pornography silences women assumes an outdated normative picture of speech acts, according to which agents do, or can, or ought to, realize their intentions through their illocutionary speech acts. She thinks this picture is mistaken in at least two ways: in its assumption that silencing is avoidable, and its assumption that

---

[16] How pornography can subordinate even if it is fiction is one theme of Langton and Caroline West, 'Scorekeeping in a Pornographic Language Game', this volume.

silencing is undesirable. The idea that silence involves a certain sort of 'deformation' assumes that speech has a 'proper form'; it assumes that there is such a thing as healthy speech:

If pornography performs a deformation of speech, what is presumed to be the proper form of speech?...Langton writes that 'the ability to perform speech acts can be a measure of political power' and of 'authority' and 'one mark of powerlessness is an inability to perform speech acts that one might otherwise like to perform'. In having a speech act silenced, one cannot effectively use the performative. When the 'no' is taken as 'yes', the capacity to make use of the speech act is undermined. But what might guarantee a communicative situation in which no one's speech disables or silences another's speech in this way?[17]

Butler considers here the example of silenced sexual refusal, apparently accepting for sake of argument that a woman's illocutionary act of refusal is indeed sometimes disabled. Does such disablement matter? Apparently it would matter only if one could demand, in general, a *guarantee* of a 'communicative situation in which no one's speech disables or silences' the speech of another. Since such silencings are everywhere, and inescapable, there is nothing special about the silencing engendered by pornography.

The 'objection to the silencing effects of...pornography' assumes, according to Butler, 'the ability...to actualize one's intention through the act of speech'. One might be tempted to respond that surely we do have this ability, since we do sometimes manage to do the things we mean to do with our words, and a good thing too. Women do sometimes say 'no' to sex and are recognized to be refusing. Is Butler questioning this? Apparently yes, although this is blurred by an overstatement that follows:

The problem is...that, from a theoretical point of view, it makes no sense to assume that intentions are *always* properly materialized in utterances, and utterances materialized in deeds.[18]

Here she seems to attribute an assumption of, not simply an ability to 'actualize one's intentions in speech', but an ability to *always* do so.

The hope for something better than silencing rests on a false and outmoded picture of language and agency, according to Butler:

The effort to guarantee a kind of efficacious speaking in which intentions materialize in the deeds they have 'in mind', and interpretations are controlled in advance

---

[17] Butler, *Excitable Speech*, 86.   [18] Ibid., 92, emphasis added.

by intention itself, constitutes a wishful effort to return to a sovereign picture of language that is no longer true, and that might never have been true, one that, for political reasons, one might rejoice over not being true.[19]

To think that illocutionary silencing of sexual refusal is a 'deformation' of a woman's speech, a mark of women's 'powerlessness', is to assume a picture of language that is a mirage. According to this picture, there is, can be, or ought to be, 'efficacious speaking', where that is understood as the ability to perform the illocutionary act you intend to perform. But no such control is possible, since speech is endlessly unruly, endlessly 'misfiring', to put Butler's point in Austin's terms.

No such control is desirable either, and here we come to Butler's second criticism of the silencing argument. We should 'rejoice' that this outmoded picture of is not true:[20]

[The] incommensurability between intention and utterance (not saying what one means), utterance and action (not doing what one says) and intention and action (not doing what one meant) . . . [produces] the possibility for a politically consequential renegotiation of language that exploits the undetermined character of these relations.[21]

Instead of pining for a lost world where intentions are, or can be, or ought to be, realized in action, we should rejoice in the loss, and rejoice in the means we accordingly have for 'a politically consequential renegotiation of language'. We can 'appropriate' racist hate speech; or, adopting a stance of worldly irony, read pornographic texts against themselves. Silencing is thus not only inevitable, but liberatory. A feminist interpretation of pornography will create a subversive reading of it, which effectively silences the pornographers, undermines their authority, and shows that the text 'is not under sovereign control'.[22]

Does the silencing argument depend, as Butler claims, on a mistaken picture of language and agency? Well, she cannot really think it assumes that, as she puts it, 'intentions *are always* properly materialized in utterances', when, in identifying the phenomenon of illocutionary disablement, it assumes (following Austin) that they are not. Does the silencing argument

---

[19] Butler, *Excitable Speech*, 93.   [20] Ibid.
[21] Ibid., 92. She puts this point as a rhetorical question; but she clearly intends (if anyone can be said to 'intend') an affirmative answer.
[22] Ibid., 68–9.

then assume that intentions *can*, or *ought* to be, 'always properly materialized in utterances'—does it assume that agents could in principle always perform whatever illocutions they intend, and that they ought to be able to do so? No. But it does admittedly make some assumptions about what is possible and desirable, when it comes to the role of intentions in speech.

The argument that pornography silences women assumes, minimally, this. There are certain illocutionary acts that women can in principle perform, and perform intentionally. Significant among these are speech acts of sexual refusal. Being able to perform these speech acts is indeed desirable. If women sometimes encounter illocutionary disablement when attempting to perform such illocutions, that is undesirable, and a mark of women's politically subordinate status. If pornography engenders silencing of this sort, that silencing is a politically significant one. These relatively modest assumptions are of course compatible with Butler's rejection of the idea that intentions always are, or can be, or should be, 'materialized in utterances' as Butler puts it. Yes, of course speakers might fail to perform the illocutions they intend. Yes, of course it might sometimes be a good thing that they fail. Suppose someone intends to incite racial hatred: it could well be a good thing for their intention to fail, whether through state censorship of their speech, or (Butler's optimistic hope) through appropriation or deconstruction of their speech by parties who would otherwise be injured by it. There is nothing here to undermine the modest assumptions of the silencing argument.

What of the fact, if it is one, that in some privileged contexts, the pornographers can themselves be silenced: that pornography can be 'read' in a way that deconstructs its authority? Butler connects this idea of deconstruction with that of appropriation, an idea that does indeed raise important issues about how groups can fight hostile speech. When epithets are appropriated and valorized, that quite possibly undermines the power of racists to what they were intending to do with their words: it possibly silences some people, and in a good way. When the gay community embraces the epithet 'queer' in its self-christening of a 'Queer Nation', that perhaps undermines the ability of homophobes to use 'queer' as an epithet.[23] I must confess that I am not convinced, however, that

---

[23] For more on the appropriation issue, see Schwartzman, 'Hate Speech, Illocution, and Social Context'; Jennifer Hornsby, 'Disempowered Speech', *Philosophical Topics* 23 (1995), 127–47; Frederick

a subversive feminist reading of pornography would be comparable to appropriation of this kind; I am not convinced that such a reading would have the political significance Butler attributes to it. However, let us assume, for the sake of argument, that she is right, and that creative readings of pornographic texts 'against themselves' are important political acts, that effectively silence the pornographers, and somehow appropriate pornography to a feminist cause.

Would that contradict the argument that pornography silences women? No. The silencing argument is perfectly compatible with the possibility of subversive deconstruction. Whether speech subordinates is, as I said, very much a context-dependent matter.[24] If there are privileged contexts where pornography is deconstructed in the way Butler advocates, that hardly shows that in other contexts pornography is silenced. And frankly, it is not easy to see how subversive readings by theorists will help the women who live in pornography's shadow. It is not easy to see how such readings are supposed to reveal to pornography's usual consumers, and their partners, the 'unrealizability', the self-defeatingness, of pornography's norms. How does a reading of pornography 'against itself' help those women who are abused and exploited in its making? How does it affect those men who want their sex lives, and their partners, to resemble ever more closely what pornography offers them?[25] Butler finds hyperbolic MacKinnon's claims about the world-altering power of words; but they pale, surely, beside Butler's own hopes for deconstruction.[26]

In conclusion, then, Butler has exaggerated the assumptions of the arguments that pornography subordinates and silences women. The arguments do not after all rest on an implausible attribution to pornographic speech of a quasi-divine authority; nor does the silencing argument rest

---

Schauer, 'The Ontology of Censorship', in *Censorship and Silencing*, ed., Robert Post (Los Angeles, Cal.: Getty Research Institute, 1998); Randall Kennedy, *Nigger: The Strange Career of a Troublesome Word* (New York: Pantheon Books, 2002).

[24] e.g. in section I, sub-sections on 'Speech Acts' and 'Subordinating Speech'. According to Jennifer Saul, this context-dependence of pornography undermines the feminist argument, see Saul, 'Pornography, Speech Acts and Context', *Proceedings of the Aristotelian Society* (2006), 229–48. For a response to Saul, see Claudia Bianchi, 'Indexicals, Speech Acts and Pornography', *Analysis* (forthcoming).

[25] As documented in e.g. Pamela Paul, *Pornified*, chs. 5 and 7.

[26] For more extended criticism addressing this theme and developing others, see Martha Nussbaum, 'The Professor of Parody', *New Republic* 220 (February 1999), 37–45; and Lisa H. Schwartzman, 'Hate Speech, Illocution, and Social Context'.

upon implausible views about language and agency. The illocutionary ways in which pornography is implicated in the subordinating 'social construction' of women, are in some ways less exciting—but correspondingly less mysterious—than Butler takes them to be; which is probably all to the good.

6

Whose Right? Ronald Dworkin, Women, and Pornographers

Amidst the heated and often acrimonious controversies about pornography and government policy, the answer to one question at least has always seemed obvious. Should liberal theorists be in favor of permitting pornography? As champions of our basic liberties, and as champions especially of free speech, liberals have found it easy to answer this question with a simple 'yes'. They are of course accustomed to viewing their opponents in this debate as conservatives, who want pornography prohibited because it is immoral; liberals view moralistic motives of this kind with deep (and doubtless justified) suspicion. But there are other voices in the debate, too, voices arguing that we have reason to be concerned about pornography, not because it is morally suspect, but because we care about equality and the rights of women. This aspect of the debate between liberals and their opponents can begin to look like an argument about liberty and equality—freedom of speech versus women's rights—and so, apparently, it has been regarded by the courts.[1]

Ronald Dworkin is one liberal theorist who has defended a right to pornography, addressing the topic in 'Do We Have a Right to Pornography?'[2] He is, in addition, a liberal who thinks that there can be no real conflict between liberty and equality.[3] Given that the pornography issue can be seen as apparently posing just such a conflict, it is natural to wonder whether Dworkin is right. In this article I put to Dworkin the question raised at

---

[1] This essay first appeared in *Philosophy and Public Affairs* 19 (1990), 311–59. 'Courts'—see American Booksellers, Inc. v. Hudnut, 598 F. Supp. 1327 (S.D. Ind. 1984) (hereafter Hudnut).

[2] Ronald Dworkin, 'Do We Have a Right to Pornography?' *Oxford Journal of Legal Studies* 1 (1981): 177–212; reprinted in *A Matter of Principle* (Cambridge, Mass.: Harvard University Press, 1985), 335–72. Page references are to the reprint in *A Matter of Principle*.

[3] Dworkin, 'What Is Equality? Part 3: The Place of Liberty', *Iowa Law Review* 73 (1987), 9.

the outset: Should liberals, or should Dworkin, at any rate, be in favor of permitting pornography? In the light of Dworkin's general theoretical commitments, the answer is not as obvious as it might appear.

In commenting elsewhere on the topical relevance of the argument he presented in 'Do We Have a Right to Pornography?' Dworkin remarks that the controversy it deals with is one that has been given 'fresh shape and importance' by recent history. 'Old wars over pornography and censorship have new armies', he writes, 'in radical feminists and the Moral Majority'.[4] The recent history here alluded to presumably includes the controversy over a feminist antipornography ordinance that was passed in 1984 by the Indianapolis City Council, was swiftly challenged, and was judged by the district court to be unconstitutional.[5]

One modest aim of this essay is to show that, whatever success Dworkin's argument may have against the armies of the Moral Majority, it does not even begin to address the approach he labels 'radical feminist'. A second and more substantial aim is to show that the latter 'feminist' argument is not only consistent with Dworkin's liberalism, but is, so far as I can tell, demanded by it. My strategy here will be to work entirely within the Dworkinian theoretical system, and to show how that system yields a conclusion about pornography that is radically at odds with Dworkin's own, as expressed in his article on this topic. I argue that Dworkin's principle of equal concern and respect requires a policy about pornography that conflicts with commonly held liberal views about the subject, and that coincides instead with the restrictive or prohibitive policy favored by his feminist foes. In the course of my argument I restrict my attention to pornography of a certain kind, and I make use of certain empirical claims that Dworkin does not consider. But, granted these not overly controversial claims, Dworkin's theoretical commitments appear to supply ample resources for the justification of a prohibitive strategy. Dworkin, of course, agrees that some empirical premises would be sufficient to support a prohibitive argument. If, for example, there were conclusive evidence linking pornography to violence, one could justify a prohibitive strategy on the basis of a simple harm principle. However, the prohibitive arguments advanced in this article do not require empirical premises as

---

[4] Dworkin, *A Matter of Principle*, 1.

[5] See Hudnut; see also 771 F.2d 323 (7th Cir. 1985), affirmed 106 S.Ct. 1172 (1986).

strong as this, nor do they rely on a simple harm principle. They rely instead on the notion of equality that forms the linchpin of Dworkinian liberal theory.

Section 1 of this essay sets out Dworkin's theoretical framework as it appears in *Taking Rights Seriously*[6] and, in particular, as it appears in 'What Rights Do We Have?'[7] In Section 2 I examine the way Dworkin applies this framework in a civil rights context in the essay 'Reverse Discrimination'.[8] In Section 3 I turn to the issue of pornography, considering Dworkin's own treatment of the subject in 'Do We Have a Right to Pornography?' Section 4 draws together the two issues of civil rights and pornography, presenting a feminist case against pornography, largely as it was argued by those who supported the above-mentioned ordinance—in particular, by Catherine MacKinnon.[9] Armed with some insights from this latter perspective on the pornography question, I return in Section 5 to the Dworkinian theoretical framework, showing that the civil rights approach that Dworkin uses in 'Reverse Discrimination' is an appropriate approach for pornography. I construct two independent arguments, modeled closely on Dworkin's own, for the conclusion that pornography should be prohibited. In Dworkinian terms, the first is an argument of principle, the second an argument of policy. Each argument is, I believe, as strong as its model in 'Reverse Discrimination'; and the conjunction of the two appears to constitute a powerful argument for a prohibitive policy. It should, however, be evident from what I have said that I am not advocating a particular legal strategy in this essay. I am not arguing that prohibition is an appropriate response to some kinds of pornography, still less that it is the best response. On such matters I remain agnostic for the present purposes, content to argue that, whatever its merits, a prohibitive strategy can apparently be justified by Dworkinian liberal theory.

Suppose I am right: what then? The question of what to conclude from this happy if unexpected marriage of Dworkinian theory and radical

---

[6] Dworkin, *Taking Rights Seriously* (Cambridge, Mass.: Harvard University Press, 1977).

[7] Dworkin, 'What Rights Do We Have?' in *Taking Rights Seriously*, 266–78.

[8] Dworkin, 'Reverse Discrimination', in *Taking Rights Seriously*, 223–39.

[9] Catharine MacKinnon, *Feminism Unmodified* (Cambridge, Mass.: Harvard University Press 1987), especially 'Francis Biddle's Sister: Pornography, Civil Rights and Speech', 163–97. Note that MacKinnon's argument is different to the 'Dworkinian' argument in favor of prohibition which I advance, although the two arguments share some common premises and have similar conclusions. I take it that if my argument succeeds, it might offer support for MacKinnon's conclusion; but if my argument fails, it does not undermine hers.

feminism would still be a matter for open debate, and in the final section of the essay (Section 6) I briefly explore some of the possibilities. Does the result represent a liberal vindication of a certain feminist argument? Or does it represent a kind of reductio of Dworkin's brand of liberalism? Either response is possible. But if we want to accept Dworkin's general theory, we must also accept the radical feminist conclusion about pornography; and if we want to reject that conclusion, we must also reject Dworkin's theory, or some part thereof. What we cannot do, if I am right, is hold on to the Dworkinian theory, and maintain at the same time a traditionally liberal stance toward pornography. An apparent corollary of the result about pornography is that Dworkin's theory seems incapable of defending a right to certain other kinds of constitutionally protected speech; indeed, it can apparently be used to construct strong arguments for their prohibition. I discuss this possibility toward the end of the article, leaving the implications of the result open, once again, to the reader's interpretation.

1. Theoretical Framework

In 'What Rights Do We Have?' Dworkin sets out some basic elements of his political theory, and the role that rights have to play in that theory. Since I need to draw on these views in some detail later on, I will take the opportunity to summarize some aspects that will become relevant.

Dworkin takes as his starting point certain 'postulates of political morality' that are central, he says, to a liberal conception of equality.[10] They can be summed up in the slogan 'Government must treat those whom it governs with equal concern and respect'. To treat citizens with concern is to treat them as creatures capable of suffering and frustration; to treat citizens with respect is to treat them as human beings capable of forming their own intelligent views about how their lives should be lived, and of acting on those views.[11]

This notion of equality, which Dworkin takes to be a straightforward explication of the common notion we all have, turns out, on closer

---

[10] Dworkin, 'What Rights Do We Have?', 272.

[11] Ibid., 272–73. (The slogan slightly paraphrases Dworkin's description of the equality principle in this passage.)

inspection, to be rather complex. First of all, the right of citizens to be treated with equal concern by no means commits the state to the *equal treatment* of its citizens, if by that is meant that each citizen is entitled to the same distribution of goods and opportunities as everyone else. The right to equality is simply a right to treatment *as an equal*: the right to have one's interests treated as fully and as sympathetically as the interests of anyone else. Second, the Dworkinian notion of equality appears to have a principle of *neutrality* at its heart: to treat people with equal respect is to treat each citizen's view of the good life with equal respect. While the principle of equal concern dictates that the government 'must not distribute goods or opportunities unequally on the ground that some citizens are entitled to more because they are worthy of more concern', the principle of equal respect dictates that the government 'must not constrain liberty on the ground that one citizen's conception of the good life of one group is nobler or superior to another's'.[12] So Dworkin's principle of equality is double-pronged: a government subscribing to it will, first, treat its citizens as persons equally worthy of concern, and, second, treat them as persons whose conceptions of the good life are equally worthy of respect.[13]

Dworkin goes on to distinguish two kinds of political argument: arguments of principle and arguments of policy. Arguments of principle invoke the notion of a *right* that is central to Dworkin's theory. Arguments of policy, on the other hand, do not involve rights: they are *goal*-based arguments, which attempt to justify a particular course of action by showing that it will achieve a state of affairs in which the community as a whole will be better off. Arguments of policy come in two varieties, depending on the character of the goal to be achieved. Utilitarian arguments of policy typically have as their end the maximal satisfaction of citizens' preferences. Ideal arguments of policy have a different end: they are not concerned with the preferences of citizens, but attempt instead to arrange things so that the community will be 'in some way closer to an ideal community.'[14]

Arguments of policy are vulnerable in a way that arguments of principle are not. While arguments of principle are rights-based, and therefore embody the conception of equality that Dworkin takes as foundational,

---

[12] Ibid., 273.   [13] Ibid., 273, 275.   [14] Ibid., 274.

arguments of policy, by contrast, do not always yield conclusions that are consistent with that conception; and where there is conflict, it is the 'equal concern and respect' principle that must triumph. In other words, the conception of equality that Dworkin takes as his starting point is one that places constraints on any argument of policy. Where the argument of policy is ideal in character, urging us to constrain liberty in order to pursue a goal that many citizens do not in fact want, the 'neutrality' aspect of the notion of equality comes into play: a government that is committed to treating its citizens with equal concern and respect is thereby committed to treating competing accounts of the good life with equal respect; it cannot do this and claim that a particular form of life is 'inherently more valuable' than another.[15] Dworkin's example of an argument of policy that might be defeated in this way is one supporting the goal of achieving a culturally sophisticated community, in a situation in which nobody in fact wants such sophistication.[16] If citizens value the pushpin way of life, it might be wrong to force poetry on them.

Where the argument of policy is utilitarian in character, the notion of equality places constraints upon it in a rather more sophisticated way. After all, utilitarian arguments give every appearance of being thoroughly egalitarian; this was a feature evident in the original Benthamite idea that each man is to count for one and no one for more than one. Dworkin notes that this egalitarian appearance is what gives utilitarianism its appeal. But he goes on to explain the way in which such an appearance is sometimes misleading: utilitarian arguments themselves may yield conclusions that conflict with principles of equal concern and respect. Consider, he says, the goal of utilitarian argument. The goal is simply the maximal satisfaction of citizens' preferences, taking into account both the number and the intensity of the preferences to be considered. Such a goal fails to take into account the status of citizens' preferences: it fails to attend to the important distinction between the preference of a citizen for his own enjoyment of goods and opportunities and the preference of a citizen for the assignment of goods and opportunities to others.[17]

This distinction between personal and external preferences is one that is crucial to the development of Dworkin's theory of rights. One simple way to see that theory (at least in the essays we are considering here) is

---

[15] Dworkin, 'What Rights Do We Have?', 274.   [16] Ibid.   [17] Ibid., 275.

as a response to the inadequacies of unrestricted utilitarianism when it is confronted with the demands of a liberal principle of equality.[18] In brief: utilitarianism tells us to maximize the satisfaction of preferences; but if we do that without first disqualifying the preferences of any citizen for the assignment of goods and opportunities to citizens other than himself, the calculations may be distorted, a form of 'double counting' may result, and the final outcome may be one that does not treat each citizen with equal concern and respect.[19] Rights are a useful theoretical means of preventing this unwelcome result; rights are a means of protecting individuals from the external preferences of other individuals.

What counts as an external preference? And how do such preferences disrupt the otherwise egalitarian character of utilitarian arguments? We can, says Dworkin, distinguish two ways in which the preferences of a citizen can be external, ways that correspond to the twin aspects of the equality principle. The citizen may, first, prefer that another citizen be assigned fewer goods and opportunities than others because he thinks that that *person* is simply worth less concern than others.[20] Consider, for example, a group of citizens who believe that blacks are simply worth less concern than whites, and whose preferences manifest this prejudice. They prefer, say, that the preferences of blacks be worth half those of whites in the utilitarian calculus. If such racist preferences are taken into account, says Dworkin, the utilitarian calculus will be distorted, and blacks will suffer unjustly as a result.

Alternatively, and here we have the second kind of preference, a citizen may prefer that another citizen be assigned fewer goods and opportunities than others because he believes the person's *conception of the good life* to be worthy of less respect than the conceptions of others. Dworkin gives as examples of this second variety the moralistic preferences of people

---

[18] My concern in this essay is almost exclusively with Dworkin's theory as it appears in *Taking Rights Seriously* and *A Matter of Principle*. Since then Dworkin's views have undergone some changes (e.g., in 'What Is Equality?'), but these are not, I think, changes that substantially affect the points I want to make here. It seems to me that both Dworkin's arguments in 'Reverse Discrimination' and the 'Dworkinian' antipornography arguments presented in this article are compatible with the equality of resources scheme presented by Dworkin in his later work.

[19] For brevity's sake I am omitting further discussion of the 'double counting' aspect of Dworkin's theory, a feature that has attracted a good deal of critical attention in its own right.

[20] Again, for the sake of brevity I am omitting Dworkin's discussion of altruistic external preferences, which have their origins in views that another citizen is worth more (rather than less) concern than others.

who disapprove of various practices (such as homosexuality, pornography, Communist party adherence) and prefer that no one in society pursue such practices. If such preferences are taken into account, the individuals in question (homosexuals, pornographers, communists) will suffer, not simply because in the competing demands for scarce resources some preferences must lose out, and they happen to be the unlucky ones. They suffer, rather, because their own views about how to live their lives are thought to be deserving of less respect.[21]

It is often difficult in practice, says Dworkin, to distinguish personal from external preferences. Democratic institutions usually do not have the resources to discriminate between them; and it is because of these pragmatic difficulties that the concept of a right comes into play. 'The concept of an individual political right . . . is a response to the philosophical defects of a utilitarianism that counts external preferences and the practical impossibility of a utilitarianism that does not. It allows us to enjoy the institutions of political democracy, which enforce overall or unrefined utilitarianism, and yet protect the fundamental right of citizens to equal concern and respect by prohibiting decisions that seem, antecedently, likely to have been reached by virtue of the external components of the preferences democracy reveals.'[22] This characterization of rights provides a means of arguing for a further central Dworkinian thesis: namely, that rights to particular liberties—freedom of speech, religion, and so on—are derivable from the fundamental right to equality. A policy that constrains a particular liberty in the interests of utility may be shown to be probably based upon an argument utilizing external preferences; equality demands that such preferences be discounted; and in such cases the threatened citizen has a right to that liberty which will trump the opposing argument of utility. This approach contrasts sharply with a commonly held view that liberalism requires a right to liberty itself amongst its basic theoretical underpinnings. It is also an approach that attempts to answer the challenge that the right to liberty and the right to equality are often in conflict. Far from being antagonistic, says Dworkin, the one would not exist but for the other.

---

[21] Dworkin, 'What Rights Do We Have?', 276.   [22] Ibid., 277.

2. Dworkin on Civil Rights

In 'Reverse Discrimination' Dworkin applies his general principles to a particular civil rights issue, in this instance, racial discrimination. He addresses the question: Must laws and practices, if they are to be consistent with the principle of equal concern and respect, always be 'color-blind?' Is discrimination on the basis of race—that is, taking race into account in making decisions about the distribution of goods and opportunities—always unjust?

He considers two cases, the first focusing on the issue of racial segregation, the second on that of an affirmative action program. In the former, a black man, Sweatt, was denied admission to the Law School at the University of Texas on the grounds that the school was for whites only. In the latter, a white, DeFunis, was denied admission to the Law School at the University of Washington on the grounds that his grades and test scores were too low; however, the school had an affirmative action policy that granted admission to certain minority candidates with similar scores and grades. Both Sweatt and DeFunis argued that their rights to equal protection of the law under the Fourteenth Amendment had been violated. Each found, or might have found, the policy to which he objected deeply insulting.[23] In terms of these cases, the question just raised amounts to: Do Sweatt and DeFunis stand or fall together?

Dworkin's analysis of the issues aims to show that the two cases do indeed differ in very significant ways. The practice of segregation, as it appears in Sweatt, does conflict with the principle of equal concern and respect, and is therefore (given that this is the principle behind the Fourteenth Amendment) unconstitutional. Such a policy is inherently insulting, and there is a powerful rights-based argument—that is, an argument of principle—to be mounted against it. On the other hand, the practice of affirmative action, as it appears in DeFunis, does not conflict with the equality principle, is not inherently insulting, and indeed there is a powerful argument of policy to be presented in its favor. Since my

---

[23] Dworkin, 'Reverse Discrimination', 231.

own argument in Section 5 will draw on some general structural features of these two arguments, it will be worth looking at them in a little more detail.

Let us begin with Sweatt. What kind of argument might be used to justify the discriminatory practice of the University of Texas? According to Dworkin, it would be an argument of policy, and a utilitarian one at that.[24] It might take the following form: Segregation of the Law School benefits society as a whole, and any resulting disadvantage to blacks is simply the unfortunate price that must be paid for the overall gain. There are—it might be argued—many ways in which society benefits from the practice: the economy needs white lawyers and needs no black lawyers; black lawyers would only be a liability to any corporation that hired them; alumni gifts to the school would plummet if blacks were admitted; the school's white students prefer the company of their own kind.

Such claims may have had considerable plausibility at the time, and may indeed point to the conclusion that segregation of the Law School offered a means of satisfying more citizens' preferences than any alternative. But what kind of preferences do we have here? Dworkin replies that the utilitarian argument relies crucially on the *external* preferences of its citizens, that is, preferences that members of a certain group be assigned fewer opportunities because those people are worth less concern. We have already seen that such preferences must be disqualified if justice is to prevail. But are the preferences in question really external? On the face of it, many of those mentioned above appear to be personal. For example, a preference for the kind of company one keeps is not explicitly a preference for the assignment of goods or opportunities to others, nor does it, at first blush, seem to commit one to any views about the *worth* of other people.

At this point Dworkin has a more detailed discussion of what is to count as an external preference in a situation in which prejudice abounds, that is, a situation in which beliefs about the inferior worth of another class of citizens are strong and pervasive. In such circumstances, says Dworkin, we have to take special care. It is not enough to ask: Are the preferences explicitly for a certain allocation of goods or opportunities to an individual or group other than themselves? One must also ask a further question: If the prejudice did not exist, would the preferences justifying the policy

---

[24] Ibid., 230–4.

exist? If it can be shown that the preferences in question exist only as a result of the racist views of those who have them, then such preferences must be counted as external. The thought here seems to be that there is an important connection between certain beliefs and desires and that this connection has implications for political theory. The equality principle demands that preferences that depend on certain beliefs (beliefs about the inferior worth of some other people, for instance) should not be counted.

Dworkin thinks that in cases of widespread prejudice, it will often be impossible to answer this counterfactual question. When preferences are affected by prejudice it is often the case that 'personal and external preferences are so inextricably tied together, and so mutually dependent, that no practical test for measuring preferences will be able to discriminate the personal and external elements in any individual's overall preference. . . . In any community in which prejudice against a particular minority is strong, then the personal preferences upon which a utilitarian argument must fix will be saturated with that prejudice; it follows that in such a community, no utilitarian argument purporting to justify a disadvantage to that minority can be fair'.[25] In such situations one must regard the relevant personal preferences as effectively corrupted by prejudice, and count them as external. Associational preferences for the company of whites offer an example of this kind of preference, in Dworkin's view. Such preferences manifest, however indirectly, 'contempt for blacks as a group'.[26] And since the utilitarian argument of policy in favor of Texas's practice of segregation must rely critically on preferences of this kind, it is in conflict with the principle of equal concern and respect, and unconstitutional. In opposition to such an argument, we can raise an argument of principle: Sweatt has a right to treatment as an equal, and he therefore has rights protecting him from the influence of the external preferences of others, in this case, rights against the University of Texas and its policy of segregation.

The pattern of argument Dworkin uses here for identifying Sweatt's rights is very similar to the pattern he uses to identify rights in other contexts. One notes first of all that there is an apparent utilitarian argument for a particular policy, and that this policy appears to disadvantage some person or group. One investigates the preferences exploited by the utilitarian argument and discovers that a crucial set of them are, according to some

---

[25] Ibid., 236–7.   [26] Ibid., 236.

criterion, external preferences. One concludes, finally, that the individual or group has rights against the policy. However, there is something a little different in Dworkin's application of this general pattern in the civil rights context of Sweatt, and it amounts, I suggest, to a certain shifting of the burden of proof.

Consider, first of all, the notion of an *external preference* that Dworkin invokes in his analysis of Sweatt. It is important to see that he has extended rather dramatically the notion of an external preference that we saw at work in 'What Rights Do We Have?' I noted in Section I that preferences are external if they explicitly concern the allocation of resources to another citizen, whether because that citizen is thought to be worthy of less concern, or because his conception of the good life is thought to be worthy of less respect. But that notion alone seems too weak to supply the resources necessary for dealing with certain special cases of prejudice. An associational preference of white law students for company of their own kind is *not* explicitly a preference for the allocation of fewer opportunities to others, but seems rather a personal preference. In order to take such cases into account, Dworkin has elaborated the notion of an external preference here in ways that we can summarize, in a rough-and-ready fashion, as follows. Preferences are to be counted as external if they satisfy any of the following three conditions. (Conditions [2] and [3] come into play when prejudice against the group in question is strong and pervasive.)

(1) The preferences concern the allocation of resources to another citizen, *simpliciter.*[27]
(2) The following counterfactual holds: Were the prejudice not to exist, the preferences in question would not exist.
(3) We find that the truth of the counterfactual in (2) is difficult to determine, and there is some likelihood that prejudice has affected the preferences.[28]

So, while not denying that there may be many personal components in the preferences underlying the Texas policy, given that there is widespread prejudice against blacks, our *presumption* is that the relevant preferences are affected by prejudice, therefore external, and therefore to be dismissed. It is

---

[27] e.g., Dworkin, 'What Rights Do We Have?', 275.
[28] Dworkin, 'Reverse Discrimination', 236–8. It is not entirely clear that Dworkin wants to separate these two, but it seems to me that they ought to be distinguished.

only by using this extended conception of an external preference that one can succeed in raising an argument of principle against the policy.

Consider, second, the question of whether Sweatt is *disadvantaged* by the Texas policy. There is no doubt that Sweatt *is* disadvantaged in this particular instance: he wants to enter the Law School, but he cannot, and in denying him admission the Law School is denying him opportunities that are not otherwise open to him. Although there was a black law school to which Sweatt could have gained admission, it was much inferior to the white school.[29] But how important to Dworkin's argument of principle is establishing this fact of Sweatt's disadvantage? Suppose the Sweatt case were being made against a backdrop of a so-called separate-but-equal segregatory social policy whereby blacks and whites were channeled into separate but—arguably—equally good law schools. In such a situation it would be much more difficult to establish that Sweatt was disadvantaged by the Texas policy. Dworkin mentions such a possibility in a footnote, remarking with evident approval that even in such circumstances a policy like that of Texas would be found unconstitutional: 'There is no doubt that an all-white law school would be unconstitutional today, even if an all-black law school were provided that was, in a material sense, the equal of that provided for whites.'[30]

I infer from this that Dworkin would want to raise an argument of principle in Sweatt's favor even in a 'separate-but-equal' social context, as one surely would. But if this is so, then it seems that Sweatt's right does not depend on Sweatt's being clearly disadvantaged, 'in a material sense', by the Texas policy. If one were to begin nevertheless by assuming that Sweatt *is* disadvantaged by the policy, the Law School's hypocritical cries of 'separate but equal' notwithstanding, one would in effect be placing the burden of proof in Sweatt's favor. And there is surely a great deal to be said for placing the burden of proof in this way: even if it is true that 'separate-but-equal' social policies are invariably 'equal' in name only, and in practice harm blacks, the onus should not have to be on blacks such as Sweatt to produce empirical arguments establishing that this is so. One could accept that Sweatt had prima facie cause for complaining about the policy (without supposing that this was in itself sufficient to justify the conclusion that he had been unjustly treated); and the ensuing

---

[29] Ibid., 229 n. 1.   [30] Ibid.

investigation into the nature of the preferences upon which the policy was based would reveal, assuming Dworkin's analysis is right, that this complaint was justified. The important step is the latter one. The important fact, says Dworkin, is that the policy of segregation has a certain 'objective feature',[31] a feature that is quite independent of the disadvantage the policy causes blacks such as Sweatt, and quite independent of the insult blacks feel because of it. The policy has its roots in racism: it has its justification in an argument that rests on racist (and therefore external) preferences. And *this* is the crucial factor, the 'objective feature that would disqualify the policy even if the insult [to blacks] were not felt'.[32] It is this feature that entitles us to conclude that Sweatt can mount an argument of principle against the Texas policy.

Can DeFunis mount a similar argument of principle against the University of Washington? Since rights, for Dworkin, can be identified only relative to background theoretical justifications, one can answer this question only after one has considered another. What *grounds* does the Law School have for its affirmative action policy?

According to Dworkin, the Law School might plausibly raise an ideal argument of policy in support of its affirmative action program, an argument that has equality as its goal.[33] The school might argue that regardless of people's preferences, and even if the general welfare were to deteriorate as a result, affirmative action programs in fact work to produce a more equal society, and that is what counts. This ideal argument rests on a particular empirical hypothesis: it may, as Dworkin says, be 'controversial whether a preferential admissions program will in fact promote [the goal of equality], but it cannot be said to be implausible that it will'.[34]

Bearing in mind that rights are trumps, and that arguments of principle defeat arguments of policy, we can now ask: Is it possible for DeFunis to offer an argument of principle against the practice of affirmative action in a manner analogous to that of Sweatt? The Fourteenth Amendment guarantees him a right to treatment as an equal; has that been violated?

---

[31] Dworkin, Ibid., 231.   [32] Ibid.

[33] Ibid., 232. Dworkin also thinks it might be possible to mount a utilitarian argument of policy in favor of affirmative action; since such a policy probably would not rest on external preferences, DeFunis would have no right against that policy either (p. 239).

[34] Ibid., 228.

Dworkin reminds us that the right to equal concern and respect should not be seen as the right to equal treatment per se. DeFunis has no right to admission simply on the grounds that others have been granted admission. What he does have is a right to treatment as an equal: a right to be considered as fully and sympathetically as any other applicant.[35]

Dworkin goes on to discuss various criteria by which applicants are judged, concluding, for reasons we need not go into here, that there is nothing in the notion of race itself to make it more suspect as a criterion than intelligence or industriousness. What is important is the reasoning behind such a policy, in this case, the ideal argument. This argument is a strong one, and although its empirical premise (that this course of action *will* indeed work to bring about a more equal society) may be questioned, it is not, says Dworkin, 'the business of judges, particularly in constitutional cases, to overthrow decisions of other officials because the judges disagree about the efficiency of social policies'.[36] The 'business of judges' (and presumably of legal philosophers) is to determine whether DeFunis's rights have been violated, and, says Dworkin, they have not. The ideal argument does not conflict with the notion of equal concern and respect; it does not rely on external preferences, since it does not rely on any preferences at all, 'but on the independent argument that a more equal society is a better society even if its citizens prefer inequality. That argument does not deny anyone's right to be treated as an equal himself'.[37]

The argument for affirmative action presents us with a potent combination. Notice that here again there is a certain assumption about burdens of proof, concerning, this time, the effectiveness of the proposed policy. The ideal argument makes use of an empirical hypothesis that may well be 'controversial', but this is no bar to the constitutionality of the policy relying on it. The structure of the overall argument consists essentially of the following: an ideal argument of policy, with equality as its goal, conjoined with the complete absence of any opposing rights-based argument. I will be drawing on some of the strengths of this form of Dworkinian argument in discussing the pornography question in Section 5.

---

[35] Ibid., 227.   [36] Ibid., 224.   [37] Ibid., 239.

3. Dworkin on Pornography

In 'Do We Have a Right to Pornography?' Dworkin considers a question that has attracted attention from many political theorists, from liberals at one end of the spectrum to the redoubtable 'new armies' of conservatives and feminists at the other. What might we expect Dworkin's approach to be? On the one hand, Dworkin is first and foremost a liberal theorist, and the freedom to produce and consume pornography has long been a liberal cause. But he is at the same time a writer famous for taking the principle of equality to be the starting point for sound political thinking; a writer whose sensitivity in dealing with the complex issues surrounding prejudice against an oppressed group we have already witnessed; and a writer who begins his discussion of the pornography question by drawing an analogy between laws concerning pornography and laws concerning racist speech. 'Should we be free to incite racial hatred?' he asks his readers in the opening paragraph—an interesting question and one whose implications seem worth pursuing.

Given this hopeful start, and given also that the feminist 'armies' had already begun to mass at the time of his writing,[38] we might reasonably expect that a rights-based argument *against* pornography would merit at least some brief mention in the essay. Such hopes, as it turns out, are disappointed, and Dworkin's question in the opening paragraph is not pursued in any detail. He considers, at various points throughout the essay, a vast number of ways in which pornography might more or less plausibly be construed as a harm. The sample that follows is by no means exhaustive, but I can assure my reader that there is one construal that is conspicuous by its absence, namely, that women as a group might be harmed by pornography.

Here is the quick sample. Since most people would prefer censorship, permitting pornography harms general utility by leaving the majority of preferences unsatisfied.[39] Pornography damages the cultural environment.[40] It upsets and disgusts people.[41] It limits people's ability to lead the kind of lives they would want for themselves and their children.[42] It makes sex

---

[38] As demonstrated, for example, in the classic collection of essays *Take Back the Night: Women on Pornography*, ed., Laura Lederer (New York: William Morrow, 1980), containing essays published earlier.

[39] Dworkin, 'Right to Pornography?', 335.   [40] Ibid., 337, 340.   [41] Ibid., 344–45.
[42] Ibid., 349.

seem less valuable.[43] People find discomfort in encountering blatant nudity because they detest themselves for taking an interest in the proceedings, and they are forcefully reminded of what their neighbors are like and of what their neighbors are getting away with.[44]

To be fair, Dworkin does indeed raise the issue of whether pornography ever presents a 'special danger of personal harm narrowly conceived',[45] and although he usually takes this to be a question about people's responses when directly confronted with pornography, he, along with the Williams Committee, 'concedes . . . the relevance of the question whether an increase in the amount of pornography in circulation in the community is likely to produce more violence or more sexual crimes of any particular sort. . . .'.[46] This is as close as Dworkin ever gets to considering whether or not it may be women who are, in the end, the ones hurt by the pornography industry. As a rule, when he raises the possibility of any link between pornography and harm to women of a concrete and familiar sort, he fails to take it seriously. Indeed, were it not for the evidence we already have of Dworkin's awareness of the subtle complexities surrounding questions of group oppression, the reader might be tempted to suppose that Dworkin's chief interest is to lampoon the idea. Imagining that pornography might lead to violence is like imagining that reading *Hamlet* might lead to violence.[47] Or, in another passage, he wonders whether pornography might be like 'breakfast television': both might be found to encourage absenteeism from work, and thereby have (perish the thought!) 'some special and deleterious effect on the general economy'.[48] But as he continues with such comparisons, we begin to discover that he thinks that questions about concrete harm are mere 'academic speculation';[49] the pornography issue is itself a 'relatively trivial' problem.[50] By contrast, embarrassment—that is, embarrassment on the part of the 'shy pornographer'—he describes as raising an 'interesting and important question'.[51] When it comes to the plight of the shy pornographer, Dworkin displays a touching concern; he suggests that legislators should make sure that the consumer can, should he so desire, buy an umbrella at his favorite adult bookstore, so as to disguise his secret and perhaps shameful habits.

---

[43] Ibid., 356.   [44] Ibid.   [45] Ibid., 340.   [46] Ibid., 338.
[47] Ibid., 355.   [48] Ibid., 354.   [49] Ibid., 355.   [50] Ibid., 359.
[51] Ibid., 358. Note that Dworkin uses the term *pornographer* to mean 'consumer of pornography'; I follow his usage for the purposes of this essay.

Readers may have gathered by now that Dworkin and I do not share exactly the same view about what is and what is not an important question. Embarrassment is not, all things considered, a very important question; the well-being of women is. Leaving such sympathies aside, there are of course some relevant empirical questions to be addressed here. And on certain questions of this kind Dworkin accepts the findings of the Williams Committee, namely, that there is no persuasive evidence that pornography causes violent crime.[52] On other empirical questions—for example, questions about pornography's possible role in a society in which women happen to be widely oppressed—Dworkin is comfortably silent. One wonders whether he would have been as comfortable had Sweatt's opponents cited, in support of their case, similar findings that had reached a similarly happy conclusion that there was no persuasive evidence that the practice of racial segregation causes violent crime. One does not always need conclusive evidence about crime to have cause for concern, nor is violence the only worry in situations in which there is widespread prejudice and discrimination against a particular group. In such situations, as Dworkin has already taught us, our investigation must take special care.

Readers of 'Do We Have a Right to Pornography?' may be a little puzzled at this point. Why, we may be forgiven for asking, does Dworkin consider this 'relatively trivial' issue to be worthy of serious attention, worthy in fact of a full forty-five pages of sophisticated political analysis? If we look again at the first of Dworkin's suggestions about the harm pornography brings about, we will find our answer. Most people, he says, would *prefer* censorship; if, in spite of this, we permit pornography, *general utility* will be harmed, since the majority preferences will be left unsatisfied.

This is enough to give us a fair idea of Dworkin's special interest in the question. We have the starting point for a familiar Dworkinian recipe for identifying rights, where one begins by noting that there is a good utilitarian argument for a certain policy, and that certain individuals will suffer as a result of this policy; investigates the preferences upon which the utilitarian argument is based; shows that they are external preferences; and finally concludes that the individuals concerned have rights that must

---

[52] Dworkin, 'Right to Pornography?', 338. As we will see later, this finding did not prevent the Williams Committee from making prohibitive recommendations with respect to pornography of certain kinds.

defeat the policy in question. This was Dworkin's response to Sweatt; and this is his response to pornography also.

Before offering this analysis in any detail, however, Dworkin is anxious to show the inadequacies of competing attempts to argue for the permission of pornography.[53] The Williams Committee, says Dworkin, attempted to do so by invoking a certain goal-based strategy, according to which free expression is a means to an important social end. Free expression is necessary if we are to have 'a society that is most conducive to human beings' making intelligent decisions about what the best lives for them to lead are, and then flourishing in those lives'.[54] Given the value of free expression, we should accept a presumption against any prohibition of it. Dworkin goes on to argue that a goal-based strategy of this kind, however admirable, simply does not have the resources to support an argument for permitting pornography; what one needs, instead of this argument of policy, is an argument of principle, that is, an argument that uses the concept of a right.

Dworkin's verdict on the Williams Report is not vital to our present inquiry, but it strikes me that he may have mischaracterized the difference between his own approach and that of the Williams Committee. Rather than presenting a contrast between goal-based and rights-based strategies for the defense of free expression, a more plausible analysis of the difference might be that it consists in a contrast between two rights-based strategies, Dworkin seeing a need to derive the right in question from a basic right to equality, and the Williams Committee seeing no such need. The following passage from the Williams Report can surely be read as an explicit rejection of the merely goal-based strategy that Dworkin attributes to the committee: 'The value of free expression *does not lie solely in its consequences.* ... It is rather that *there is a right to free expression* ... and weighty considerations in terms of harm have to be advanced by those who seek to curtail it'.[55]

Dworkin proceeds to show how it is possible to mount an argument of principle against a prohibitive policy. Suppose, he says, that the policy

---

[53] Home Office, *Report of the Committee on Obscenity and Film Censorship.* Cmnd. 7772 (London: Her Majesty's Stationery Office, 1979) (hereafter Williams Report). The Williams Report recommended, in brief, that some kinds of pornography (including live sex shows and child pornography) be banned, and that other kinds of pornography be permitted on a restricted basis. Dworkin's chief, but by no means exclusive, concern is with its permissive aspect.

[54] Dworkin, 'Right to Pornography?', 338.   [55] Williams Report, 56; italics mine.

of prohibiting pornography would satisfy the preferences of the majority,[56] and that the opportunities of the consumers of pornography would be curtailed as a result. Our next step, if we are interested in finding out whether pornographers might have rights against this policy, is to consider the character of the preferences upon which the policy relies, since the right to equality demands that certain preferences be disregarded. Does the prohibitive policy rely on any external preferences? Remember that external preferences can be of two broad types: one can prefer that another person receive fewer goods and opportunities because one thinks that that person is worth less concern, or, alternatively, because one thinks that that person's conception of the good life deserves less respect. The external preferences involved in the Sweatt argument were of the former variety; in the case of pornography I take it that Dworkin thinks they are of the latter. People want pornography to be prohibited chiefly because they think that it is ignoble or wrong, and that a conception of the good life that holds otherwise deserves less respect. 'Moralistic' preferences of this kind must, says Dworkin, be defeated by a corresponding 'right to moral independence', which he describes as 'the right not to suffer disadvantage in the distribution of social goods and opportunities, including disadvantage in the liberties permitted to them by the criminal law, just on the ground that their officials or fellow citizens think that their opinions about the right way for them to lead their own lives are ignoble or wrong'.[57] Insofar as the utilitarian argument hinges on moralistic preferences, the consumers of pornography have rights that trump the prohibitive policy, and our policy should be permissive.[58]

It is crucial to note that pornographers are said to have rights not because there is something special about speech per se, and pornography is speech; nor because there is something special about the private domain in which pornography is often consumed; but simply because they are vulnerable to the effects of the external preferences of others, and equality demands that such preferences be ignored. This essay provides a good

---

[56] Dworkin, 'Right to Pornography?', 335, 360.   [57] Ibid., 353.

[58] Insofar as this permissive policy would in turn constrain the ability of other people to lead the lives of their choice, we have an argument for restriction of some form. So what Dworkin ends up with, balancing these conflicting considerations, is an endorsement of the compromise solution offered by the Williams Report, i.e., that most pornography should be permitted but restricted through measures such as zoning (ibid., 358).

illustration of Dworkin's strategy of deriving traditional liberties from the principle of equality alone. It is also worth pointing out that Dworkin claims that his own strategy, as illustrated here, does justice to deeply held liberal convictions about the value of free speech in a way that competing theoretical strategies cannot hope to do.[59]

4. Pornography and Civil Rights: A Feminist Response

The purpose of this section is to review briefly a certain feminist civil rights argument about pornography, in the hope of showing how the question is transformed once it is placed in a civil rights context. Some, but by no means all, aspects of this argument will be relevant to the later argument in Section 5 of this paper, and at the beginning of that section I will outline the aspects that are. The reader should be aware that the argument reviewed in this section is one of a variety of feminist responses, many of which disagree with both the analysis and the course of action advocated by this one.[60]

In contrast to the argument discussed in Dworkin's paper on the topic, this feminist argument against pornography sets aside questions about 'morality' and focuses instead on the civil status of women. The argument has been put very forcefully by Catharine MacKinnon,[61] who has written widely on the subject, and who was involved in the drafting of the Indianapolis ordinance. In that ordinance pornography is defined as a civil

---

[59] Ibid., 352.

[60] For a range of views other than MacKinnon's, see, e.g., Gail Chester and Julienne Dickey, eds., *Feminism and Censorship: The Current Debate* (Bridport: Prism Press, 1988); Nan D. Hunter and Sylvia A. Law, 'Brief Amici Curiae of Feminist Anti-Censorship Taskforce, et al.', in American Booksellers, Inc. v. Hudnut, 771 F.2d 323 (1985); Andrea Dworkin, *Pornography: Men Possessing Women* (London: The Women's Press, 1981); Varda Burstyn, ed., *Women Against Censorship* (Vancouver: Douglas and MacIntyre, 1985); and Edward Donnerstein, Daniel Linz, and Steven Penrod, *The Question of Pornography: Research Findings and Policy Implications* (New York: Free Press; London: Collier Macmillan, 1987), chs. 7, 8.

[61] See MacKinnon, *Feminism Unmodifed*, esp. 'Francis Biddle's Sister'. There are many important aspects of MacKinnon's argument that I do not take time to consider in any detail here—for example, the claim that pornography constitutes a form of subordination (which has been considered by Melinda Vadas in 'A First Look at the Pornography/Civil Rights Ordinance: Could Pornography be the Subordination of Women?', *Journal of Philosophy* [1987], 487–511), and the claim (in answer to the champions of free speech) that pornography silences women, preventing women's exercise of free speech. These claims are addressed in 'Speech Acts and Unspeakable Acts', this volume.

rights violation:[62] 'We define pornography as the graphic sexually explicit subordination of women through pictures or words that also includes women dehumanized as sexual objects, things, or commodities; enjoying pain or humiliation or rape; being tied up, cut up, mutilated, bruised, or physically hurt; in postures of sexual submission or servility or display; reduced to body parts, penetrated by objects or animals, or presented in scenarios of degradation, injury, torture; shown as filthy or inferior; bleeding, bruised or hurt in a context which makes these conditions sexual.'[63] The ordinance distinguished pornography from erotica, taking erotica to be sexually explicit material other than that covered by the above definition. It should be emphasized that according to this argument, and in contrast to 'moralistic' arguments, there is nothing wrong whatsoever with materials that are simply sexually arousing and explicit; the focus of concern lies elsewhere.[64] Insofar as the ordinance is not concerned with explicit material per se, it departs of course from a more traditional or popular conception that simply equates pornography with the sexually explicit, a conception I take Dworkin to have been using. Pornography as defined above is a subset, though, of pornography as it is popularly conceived, and

---

[62] It should be noted that the ordinance made pornography civilly actionable, rather than a criminal offense. The definition used here is one that raises many difficult legal and philosophical questions in its own right, but I am afraid that such questions, while admittedly important, lie beyond the scope of this essay. A further question related to the definitional problems is that of the 'slippery slope', a question that rightly concerned Dworkin (and the Williams Committee) and again deserves more attention than I give it here. While the 'slippery slope' problem raises many difficulties, one should not, I take it, assume that it is insoluble; I proceed on the assumption that the problem is not so daunting that it rules out the possibility of discussion.

[63] MacKinnon, 'Francis Biddle's Sister', 176.

[64] To give the reader some idea of the kind of pornography that might be covered by the above definition, I offer the following description of a relatively soft-core example, which appeared on the cover of an issue of *Hustler*: 'The photograph is captioned "Beaver Hunters". Two white men, dressed as hunters, sit in a black Jeep. The Jeep occupies almost the whole frame of the picture. The two men carry rifles. The rifles extend above the frame of the photograph into the white space surrounding it. The men and the Jeep face into the camera. Tied onto the hood of the black Jeep is a white woman. She is tied with thick rope. She is spread-eagle. Her pubic hair and crotch are the dead center of the car hood and the photograph. Her head is turned to one side, tied down by rope that is pulled taut across her neck, extended to and wrapped several times around her wrists, tied around the rearview mirrors of the Jeep, brought back across her arms, crisscrossed under her breasts and over her thighs, drawn down and wrapped around the bumper of the Jeep, tied around her ankles. . . . The text under the photograph reads: "Western sportsmen report beaver hunting was particularly good throughout the Rocky Mountain Region during the past season. These two hunters easily bagged their limit in the high country. They told HUSTLER that they stuffed and mounted their trophy as soon as they got her home" '. (Description given in Andrea Dworkin, *Pornography: Men Possessing Women*, 25–6.)

Dworkin's remarks about the relevance of his own argument to the 'radical feminist' case[65] indicate that he views pornographers as having a right to this kind of pornography as well.

The distinctive feature of the MacKinnon argument is that it views pornography—as defined in the ordinance—as having implications for sexual equality: pornography is seen as a practice that contributes to the subordinate status of women, just as certain other practices (segregation among them) contribute to the subordinate status of blacks. The argument seeks to establish at least two things: one is that women do not, as a matter of fact, currently have equal status; and the other is that pornography does, as a matter of fact, contribute significantly to the continuing subordinate position of women.

The first claim is, I think, not very controversial, and a cursory glance at sociological facts about the distribution of income and power should be enough to confirm it. One dimension to the inequality is the economic; women earn substantially less than men, and a disproportionate number of women live in poverty.[66] A further dimension to the inequality is to be found in the scale of the sexual abuse, including but not confined to rape, that women suffer and that men, as a rule, do not.[67] The advent of feminism has brought with it a new and more acute awareness of the conditions of women, says MacKinnon. I will let her continue:

Rape, battery, sexual harassment, forced prostitution, and the sexual abuse of children emerge as common and systematic. . . . Sexual harassment of women by men is common in workplaces and educational institutions. Based on reports in one study of the federal workplace, up to 85 percent of women will experience it, many in physical forms. Between a quarter and a third of women are battered in their homes by men. Thirty-eight percent of little girls are sexually molested inside or outside the family. . . . We find that rape happens to women in all contexts,

[65] Dworkin, *A Matter of Principle*, 1.

[66] 'What women do is seen as not worth much, or what is not worth much is seen as something for women to do', comments MacKinnon about women's pay, which at the time of her writing was 59 cents to the man's dollar ('Francis Biddle's Sister', 171). According to more recent figures, women in the United States who work full time now earn 66 cents to the man's dollar and constitute more than 60 percent of adults living below the federal poverty line (Claudia Wallis, 'Onward Women!', *Time*, 4 December 1989, 85).

[67] This is not, of course, to say that it is only women who suffer sexual abuse, or to underrate the extent of the sexual violence suffered by children of both sexes, or by men in prisons. It is only to say that, as a pervasive phenomenon, sexual violence seems to be directed mainly against women.

from the family, including rape of girls and babies, to students and women in the workplace, on the streets, at home, in their own bedrooms, by men they do not know and by men they do know, by men they are married to, men they have had a social conversation with, and, least often, men they have never seen before. Overwhelmingly, rape is something that men do or attempt to do to women (44 percent of American women according to a recent study) at some point in our lives.[68]

What is different about MacKinnon's approach to facts like these is that she sees sexual violence not simply as 'crime' (as Dworkin seemed apt to do), but rather as a dimension to the inequality of the sexes, and one that calls for an explanation. These things are done to women; they are not, by and large, done to men. To call such violence simply 'crime', says MacKinnon, without remarking upon the interesting fact that the perpetrators are nearly always members of one class of citizens, and the victims members of another, would be to disguise its systematically discriminatory nature.

Turning now to the second claim, the feminist argument can be seen as offering a hypothesis about the explanation for this pattern of sexual abuse: part of the explanation lies in the fact that certain kinds of pornography help to form and propagate certain views about women and sexuality. Such pornography is said to work as a kind of propaganda, which both expresses a certain view about women and sexuality and perpetuates that view; it 'sexualizes rape, battery, sexual harassment, prostitution, and child sexual abuse; it thereby celebrates, promotes, authorizes and legitimizes them'.[69] To back up this claim, a substantial amount of empirical evidence was cited by those supporting the ordinance (in the form of both social science studies and testimony of people whose lives had been directly affected by pornography) which pointed to the conclusion that pornography influences behavior and attitudes, and does so in ways that undermine both the

---

[68] MacKinnon, 'Francis Biddle's Sister', 169. (I have taken some liberties with the order of these passages.) MacKinnon cites a formidable array of studies in support of these claims; the constraints of space dictate that I cannot reproduce all of her sources here, so I refer the reader to the notes in her work (*Feminism Unmodified*, 277–9). Joel Feinberg cites 1980 FBI Uniform Crime statistics, according to which 'a twelve-year-old girl in the United States has one chance in three of being raped in her lifetime' (*Offense to Others* [New York: Oxford University Press, 1985], 149).

[69] MacKinnon, 'Francis Biddle's Sister', 171–2.

well-being of women and sexual equality.[70] In the light of evidence of this kind, the Indianapolis City Council issued the following findings:

Pornography is a discriminatory practice based on sex which denies women equal opportunities in society. Pornography is central in creating and maintaining sex as a basis for discrimination. Pornography is a systematic practice of exploitation and subordination based on sex which differentially harms women. The bigotry and contempt it promotes, with the acts of aggression it fosters, harm women's opportunities for equality of rights in employment, education, access to and use of public accommodations, and acquisition of real property; promote rape, battery, child abuse, kidnapping and prostitution and inhibit just enforcement of laws against such acts; and contribute significantly to restricting women in particular from full exercise of citizenship and participation in public life.[71]

The case was viewed by the district court as presenting a conflict between First Amendment guarantees of free speech and the Fourteenth Amendment right to be free from sex-based discrimination.[72] The ordinance would survive constitutional scrutiny only if the state's interest in sex-based equality were 'so compelling as to be fundamental', for 'only then can it be deemed to outweigh interest of free speech'.[73] And the court concluded,

---

[70] The question of what is involved in making a causal claim of this kind is an important one. No one is claiming, of course, that there is a simple link; one can agree with Feinberg that 'pornography does not cause normal decent chaps, through a single exposure, to metamorphose into rapists' (*Offense to Others*, 153). For an interesting discussion of the notions of causality that bear on questions of this kind, see Frederick Schauer, 'Causation Theory and the Causes of Sexual Violence', *American Bar Foundation Research Journal* 4 (1987), 737–70. Questions about the empirical evidence are also important, and deserve more attention than I can give them here, but in brief: the social science studies seem to suggest that pornography, especially some kinds of violent pornography, can increase aggression against women in certain circumstances, and that it can change attitudes in the following ways. Subjects who are exposed to it can become more likely to view women as inferior, more disposed to accept 'rape myths' (e.g., that women enjoy rape), more callous about sexual violence, more likely to view rape victims as deserving of their treatment, and more likely to say that they would themselves rape if they could get away with it. The personal testimony cited at the original Minneapolis Public Hearings (with reference to an ordinance nearly identical to that passed at Indianapolis, which did not, however, become law) included, among other things, testimony of women who had been victims of 'copycat' rapes inspired by pornography. See the transcript of the 1983 Minneapolis Public Hearings, published as *Pornography and Sexual Violence: Evidence of the Links* (London: Everywoman, 1988); see also Eva Feder Kittay, 'The Greater Danger—Pornography, Social Science and Women's Rights: Reply to Brannigan and Goldenberg', *Social Epistemology* 2 (1988): 117–33; for a more comprehensive discussion of the social science evidence, see Donnerstein et al., *The Question of Pornography*.

[71] Hudnut 1320.   [72] Hudnut 1327.

[73] Hudnut 1316. The case also raised constitutional problems in connection with the 'due process' requirements of the Fifth and Fourteenth Amendments. The ordinance was judged to be vague and to

as a matter of law, that the state's interest in sex-based equality was not so compelling.[74]

It is worth noting that the empirical findings were not disputed; in fact, when the case went to the court of appeals, Judge Frank Easterbrook went so far as to say, 'We accept the premises of this legislation. Depictions of subordination tend to perpetuate subordination. The subordinate status of women in turn leads to affront and lower pay at work, insult and injury at home, battery and rape on the streets'. His conclusion, however, is that 'this simply demonstrates the power of pornography as speech'.[75]

5. A New Start

What I want to do now is take certain elements from the feminist case that was presented briefly in the preceding section and put them in the context of Dworkinian political theory. The result will be two arguments that are Dworkinian in spirit and that see the pornography issue as analogous to the issue of race discussed by Dworkin in 'Reverse Discrimination'. Both are civil rights issues; and the broad approach that Dworkin exploits in 'Reverse Discrimination' is apparently just as applicable to pornography.

In presenting these arguments I will be relying on a number of claims that Dworkin does not consider, which I draw largely from Section 4. Briefly, these are the claims: that women do not have equal status in this society; that widespread prejudice against women exists; that certain practices in this society express that prejudice and probably perpetuate that inequality, and thereby disadvantage women; and that the consumption of a certain kind of pornography is one such practice.

1. Prohibiting Pornography: An Argument of Principle

Let us begin by reminding ourselves of the general Dworkinian recipe for a good argument of principle. We saw this general recipe at work in both 'Reverse Discrimination' and 'Do We Have a Right to Pornography?': (a) Begin with what looks like a good utilitarian argument for a particular

---

establish prior restraint of speech, and would therefore have been unconstitutional on those grounds alone.

[74] Hudnut 1326.   [75] 771 F.2d 329 (7th Cir. 1985).

policy; (b) look at the individuals who appear to suffer as a result of the policy, and ask whether the policy violates the rights of those individuals; (c) inspect the preferences upon which the utilitarian argument is based, and show that they are external preferences; (d) conclude that the individuals concerned do have rights that are trumps against the policy in question. This is precisely the recipe I now propose to follow, bearing in mind that this is a civil rights argument which works on an analogy with Sweatt, and that the assumptions about burdens of proof that applied in Sweatt apply in this context as well.

a. The Utilitarian Argument.   In the two essays mentioned above, Dworkin's starting point was an apparent utilitarian argument in favor of a position that most liberals would eschew. In the case of Sweatt, the balance of preferences apparently comes out in favor of segregation; in the case of pornography, the balance of preferences apparently comes out in favor of prohibition.

Could there be a utilitarian argument for *permitting* pornography? Such an idea sounds odd, since we are accustomed to casting the debate in the language of fundamental liberties, rather than utility. But I suggest that there might be at least a germ of a utilitarian argument in the background: people want pornography, so let them have it. If one were to take up this idea and add some other speculative premises, one might construct a simple utilitarian argument in favor of permitting pornography: most people would prefer that pornography be permitted, and so our policy should be to permit pornography.

To suppose this would be to question one of Dworkin's assumptions. In 'Do We Have a Right to Pornography?' Dworkin assumed that unanalyzed preferences about pornography would come out in favor of prohibition. I am not so sure. The power of the pornography industry in sheer monetary terms[76] bears eloquent witness to the popularity of its product; and although it is difficult to gauge how much of this would count as pornography by MacKinnon's definition, it seems that pornography of the

---

[76] According to Itzin, the pornography industry in the United States currently has a $10-billion-a-year turnover, although this total almost certainly includes material that would count as erotica by the ordinance definition ('Sex and Censorship: The Political Implications', in *Feminism and Censorship*, ed., Chester and Dickey, 45). See Gordon Hawkins and Franklin E. Zimring, *Pornography in a Free Society* (Cambridge and New York: Cambridge University Press, 1988) ch. 3, for a survey of attempts to estimate the size of the general pornography market.

latter kind is a fairly widespread phenomenon, appearing in some guise on the shelves of most newsagents and video stores.[77] Given these facts, and given a general ignorance about or indifference to pornography's influence, can we be sure, as Dworkin seems to be, that a utilitarian argument would support a prohibitive policy? I do not know. I think it is at least possible that overall preferences would come out in favor of a permissive policy.

Suppose I am wrong about this empirical question. No matter. For, strange as it may sound, Dworkin himself has supplied us with a certain kind of utilitarian argument for the permission of pornography, and I would be perfectly willing to use this as a starting point. Recall that Dworkin concluded, having argued that the rights of pornographers must trump the preferences of the moralists, that pornography should be permitted; and, granted that Dworkin views his argument as relevant to the feminist case,[78] his conclusion is presumably that pornography—including violent and degrading pornography—should be permitted. What exactly was the justification for this policy of permitting pornography? It rested partly, of course, on the failure of the opposing moralistic argument, as we have seen; but it also rested on the important fact that the remaining preferences were *in favor of* the policy. Majority preferences—leaving aside those of the moralists—are in favor of permitting pornography. The justification for the permissive policy advocated by Dworkin can be seen, in other words, as resting ultimately on a *utilitarian* argument that has been laundered of moralistic antipornography preferences, the rights of the pornographers

---

[77] Even if one leaves aside, for the sake of avoiding needless controversy, that clause of the definition which counts subordinating depictions of women in postures of 'display' as pornography, it seems that some of the more straightforwardly 'violent and degrading' material may have found a niche in magazines that have wide circulation (see Feinberg, *Offense to Others*, 151, for some *Penthouse* examples, and note 64 above for one from *Hustler*). Accurate figures for pornography generally, let alone violent pornography, are hard to find. It seems that the pornography that concerns MacKinnon is prevalent, although it is almost certainly not 'the *most* prevalent [form] of pornography', as is claimed in the *Report of the Attorney General's Commission on Pornography* ([Washington, D.C.: United States Government Printing Office, 1986], 323; italics mine), even if one does include 'threatened violence' (p. 323). Certainly there has been a widespread perception that violent pornography is very much on the increase (Donnerstein et al., *The Question of Pornography*, 88). Donnerstein suggests that 'we may be more aware of the sexually violent forms of pornography because all forms of pornography are more prevalent than they once were' (ibid., 91). Feinberg cites studies according to which some time ago (before 1980) the number of violent scenes in hard-core pornography was 'as high as 20%', and in leading pornographic magazines such material constituted 'as much as 10% of the total' number of cartoons and pictorials (*Offense to Others*, 149).

[78] Dworkin, *A Matter of Principle*, 1.

serving to effect this laundering.[79] To interpret Dworkin's result this way is only to suggest that there is a sense in which an argument of principle against an unreconstructed utilitarian argument just *is* a reconstructed utilitarian argument. (I will suggest later that this particular argument is not in fact *fully* reconstructed.)

In short, there is, I suggest, an apparent utilitarian argument in favor of permitting pornography. Whether one takes the argument to be apparent at first sight, as I am inclined to do, or evident only after a careful weeding out of moralistic preferences, as Dworkin does, is immaterial for my purposes. Most people (or: most people, excluding the moralists) would prefer that pornography be permitted, so our policy should be to permit pornography.

b. The Individuals Who Suffer.   Women appear to suffer as a result of this policy. In what ways? We should be careful not to misconstrue this question. We are not asking, at this point, whether women suffer in any respect that would be sufficient to justify changing the policy, but only whether they suffer at all. The purpose of this step in the argument is only to establish a certain prima facie cause for complaint; the question of whether such complaint is justified is addressed only at a later stage of the argument. Sweatt and DeFunis both had cause for complaint in this sense: each might have felt deeply insulted by the admissions policy that excluded him; each was apparently disadvantaged by the policy; each was, arguably, denied opportunities that would not otherwise have been available to him. This was true despite the fact that the University of Washington's treatment of DeFunis was not ultimately unjust. And it would have been true even if it had been difficult to prove that the Texas admissions policy harmed Sweatt, as it might well have been had the case arisen in the context of a worked-out 'separate-but-equal' social policy. Keeping in mind, then, the modest scope of the question we are asking, we can return to it once more: In what ways does the permissive policy harm women?

---

[79] I do not know whether Dworkin would resist this description of his argument of principle as a 'laundered' argument of policy. (As will become evident later, it is in my view only partially 'laundered'; there is an important set of external preferences that it has failed to eliminate.) But surely one natural way to see Dworkin's general strategy is to interpret him as advocating that we launder utilitarian arguments (assuming that they are the relevant arguments) of external preferences by means of rights, since it is too difficult, pragmatically speaking, to launder such arguments by any other means at the disposal of democratic governments.

Beginning with what we have clearest evidence for, it is certainly the case that some women feel deeply distressed about and insulted by pornography. Dworkin would, I take it, agree that this counts as harm, since part of his argument against Williams relies on the claim that distress at the mere thought that pornography exists is indeed a kind of harm, and one that governments have a prima facie obligation to take into account.[80] Of course, the fact that a policy causes some insult and distress is not sufficient reason for thinking that there is something wrong with the policy, when that policy is otherwise justified. 'Everything depends', as Dworkin so clearly puts it in the Sweatt context, 'upon whether the feeling of insult is produced by some more objective feature that would disqualify the policy even if the insult were not felt.' If no such feature can be found, then the felt insult 'must be based on a misperception'.[81] Whether the permissive policy has an 'objective feature' of this kind is a question I will turn to in the next step of the argument.

However, to leave the harm at the level of 'insult and distress' would be to seriously misrepresent the feminist argument I am attempting to interpret. The central point of that argument is that some pornography can work as a kind of propaganda, which constitutes a threat to women's well-being, and, more generally, a threat to women's equality. If this were true, then the harm might be in the first instance something like 'harm to reputation',[82] although almost certainly not of a kind that would count as libel under current law. It would surely be a kind of harm nonetheless. One does not have to accept all the findings of the Indianapolis City Council to agree that some pornography might work in this way. Some liberal theorists seem to come close to concurring with the view that pornography of certain kinds can be like propaganda. Violent pornographic depictions of certain kinds 'reenforce macho ideology', writes Joel Feinberg, and this ideology is one that has done 'manifest harm' to women.[83] To avoid needless controversy, let me confine the discussion of harm to some aspects about which there seems to be a greater likelihood of achieving

---

[80] Dworkin, 'Right to Pornography?', 345.   [81] Dworkin, 'Reverse Discrimination', 231.

[82] Susan Brison has written convincingly on this subject in 'The Autonomy Defense of Free Speech', *Ethics* 108 (1998), 312–39.

[83] Feinberg, *Offense to Others*, 150–1. Feinberg, it should be noted, does not think that violent pornography is like libel; he thinks the macho ideology has done manifest harm to men as well; and although he thinks violent pornography 'reenforces' that ideology, he does not think it is a major cause of it (p. 153).

agreement. It is probably the case that violent and degrading pornography 'reenforces macho ideology', as Feinberg puts it, and thereby perpetuates the subordinate status of women; the resulting 'manifest harm' to women probably includes, but is not confined to, sexual abuse of various kinds (including sexual harassment and rape), harm to reputation, and loss of credibility.

It will be seen that what I have described above is something other than the conclusive evidence of crimes of violence that Dworkin appeared to demand of an antipornography argument. I have spoken of 'probable' harm, and of harm other than violence. This talk of 'probable' harm raises, of course, difficult questions about burdens of proof. Recall that we attributed to Dworkin a certain implicit principle about burdens of proof, a principle that was relevant in some important contexts, such as the civil rights context of *Sweatt*. One could accept that Sweatt had prima facie cause for complaint, even if he were bringing his case in the context of a broader 'separate-but-equal' social policy; even if, that is, it were impossible to establish conclusively that Sweatt was disadvantaged by the segregatory policy (since it would, *ex hypothesi*, have been possible for him to gain admission to a black law school that was 'in a material sense' the equal of the white school). As we saw earlier, to take such an approach would be reasonable, and would amount to a certain presumption in Sweatt's favor. Given the social circumstances, there would be a presumption that he probably is harmed by the policy, a presumption that is not yet sufficient to justify changing the policy, but rather prompts us to ask the further question about whether there is real injustice. I assume a similar burden of proof here: we are entitled to say that women are probably harmed by the permissive policy, and that although this harm is not (as far as this argument is concerned) sufficient to warrant changing the policy, it prompts us to move on to the question of whether there is real injustice.

Before we move on to consider that question, it may be worth pointing out that this assumption is not novel, and not confined to feminist arguments about pornography: the Williams Committee, although noted for its liberal recommendations, appears to have taken a similar approach, at least with respect to certain kinds of pornography. While the committee explicitly endorsed a principle that discourages the conclusion that there is a link between pornography and harm, requiring 'that the causation of harm should lie "beyond reasonable doubt" '[84] it apparently saw little need in practice to apply this strong principle in justifying some of its prohibitive recommendations. It recommended, for example, 'that films, even those shown to adults only, should continue to be censored',[85] especially those films that 'reinforce or sell the idea that it can be highly pleasurable to inflict injury, pain or humiliation (often in a sexual context) on others'.[86] It is interesting to see how the shift in burden of proof relevant to such material was expressed: 'It *may* be that this very graphically presented sadistic material serves only as a vivid object of fantasy, and does no harm at all. There is certainly no conclusive evidence to the contrary. But there is no conclusive evidence in favor of that belief either, and in this connection it seems entirely sensible to be cautious'.[87] Many would agree that caution in the face of uncertain evidence for serious risks is sensible,[88] and that in some contexts it is appropriate to use a burden of proof that is more modest than the 'beyond reasonable doubt' principle. In sum, given that a more modest burden of proof appears to have some independent plausibility for cases of the kind we are considering, and given also that there are grounds for thinking that Dworkin would endorse it in the relevantly similar context of Sweatt, I see no reason not to adopt it here—especially in view of the fact that our purpose, unlike that of the Williams Committee, is not to establish whether there is harm sufficient to justify prohibition, but only to establish whether there is some prima facie cause for complaint sufficient to motivate further inquiry.

Women apparently suffer as a result of the policy of permitting violent and degrading pornography. We can now ask: Does that policy violate women's rights?

c. Preferences.   At this point we must look more closely at the preferences upon which the utilitarian policy might be based. There are all kinds of reasons that people might have for wanting pornography to be permitted. Many people like pornography (including violent pornography), and want to be able to consume it without restriction; some people do not like it

---

[84] Williams Report, 59.   [85] Ibid., 146.   [86] Ibid., 145.

[87] Ibid. I am indebted to the discussion in Hawkins and Zimring, *Pornography in a Free Society* (pp. 128–30) for drawing this aspect of the Williams Report to my attention.

[88] One might wonder, though, why it is only *films* of such a kind that concern the committee. The members of the Williams Committee do think that film is a 'uniquely powerful instrument', deserving of special attention; see Williams Report, 145.

themselves, but are happy enough for others to enjoy it; some people are afraid of the 'slippery slope', and worry that allowing the state to prohibit pornography would raise the likelihood of government abuse of power. It seems likely that the preferences upon which the argument hinges will be of the very first kind, namely, the preferences of the consumers of pornography for pornography itself.

What kind of preferences are these? On the face of it, they all seem to be personal. How could a preference for what one reads or watches behind closed doors fail to be anything other than personal? But we must not stop here, if we are to be true to the Dworkin of 'Reverse Discrimination': there is more to the notion of an external preference than an explicit reference to the allocation of resources to another citizen. Dworkin has already endorsed a version of the view that the personal is sometimes political, or, more precisely, that apparently personal preferences can have implications for political questions about rights. We need to refer back at this point to the extended notion of an external preference discussed in Section 2. Is the situation we are considering one in which prejudice against the disadvantaged group is strong and pervasive in society? Surely that much at least is uncontroversial.

But if so, there are further questions to be asked. If the prejudice against women did not exist, would the preferences for this kind of pornography exist? This is a complicated hypothetical question, but at least one eminent liberal theorist has offered a fairly confident answer to it. This kind of violent pornography 'does not appeal at all', says Feinberg, to a male who is 'not in the grip of the macho cult. In fact these pictures, stories, and films have no other function but to express and reenforce the macho ideology. "Get your sexual kicks", they seem to say, "but make sure you get them by humiliating the woman, and showing her who's boss" '.[89] Feinberg thinks that the possession of 'macho' values is a necessary condition for the appeal of violent pornography; he also thinks that macho values embody a view about the worth of women.[90] If one were to accept his suggestion, one

---

[89] Feinberg, *Offense to Others*, 151.

[90] According to macho values, says Feinberg, men ought to be 'utterly dominant' over women, treating them as little more than 'trophies' (ibid., 150). In an earlier note I mentioned that while Feinberg thinks that violent pornography may 'reenforce macho ideology', he thinks that it is not a major cause of either the macho ideology or the violence (the latter being an effect not of the pornography but of the macho cult). Feinberg seems to think that the considerations raised here—that having 'macho values' is a prerequisite for the appeal of violent pornography—constitute evidence

would be accepting that a preference for pornography of this kind depends upon a view about the worth of women, and hence that such preferences are, by Dworkinian standards, external preferences.

What Feinberg is suggesting here sounds interestingly similar to Dworkin's description of the associational preference of a white law student. Recall that Dworkin described such a preference as 'parasitic upon external preferences . . . a white student prefers the company of other whites because he has racist social and political convictions, or because he has contempt for blacks as a group'.[91] If Feinberg is right, then what we have in the case of violent and degrading pornography is just the same kind of thing. To paraphrase Dworkin's words, an apparently personal preference for such pornography is really 'parasitic upon external preferences . . . the consumer prefers pornography of this kind because he has macho social and political convictions, or because he has contempt for women as a group'.

Feinberg's suggestion surely has some plausibility. One could, however, be somewhat more cautious. One could suppose that, while a great many such preferences depended on the possession of certain antecedent values, people were sometimes drawn to violent pornography through other motives, such as curiosity, or simple peer pressure. Such preferences might

---

against the feminist claim that pornography is one of the causes of the pattern of sexual abuse suffered by women. Although his concessions (i.e., that pornography of this kind 'reenforces' macho culture, which in turn manifests itself in abuse, and that it may in addition have some small but direct 'spillover' effects into real-world violence) would be sufficient for my argument to go through, I think it would be a mistake to infer as Feinberg has done. Tracing causal connections of this kind is undoubtedly a difficult task, but it would surely be wrong to argue with respect to, for example, racist propaganda, that it made no difference, on the grounds that readers of such material would already be racist and hence that the material would be 'merely' reinforcing existing attitudes. Such an argument would perhaps betray a rather simple view about how tastes and attitudes are formed. There is no contradiction involved in thinking that propaganda can sometimes appeal to people because they already have certain beliefs and values, or are disposed to have them; and that it can sometimes influence beliefs and values, reinforcing them in some cases, and pushing them in certain directions in others. I presume that it is precisely because expression does have this central role in forming beliefs and values that liberals think it so important. It is one thing to believe that pornography of this kind should be protected because it is expression, and expression must be protected at all costs; it is quite another to believe that it should be left alone because it is more or less causally inert, as Feinberg seems to be suggesting. Easterbrook recognized that expression is far from impotent when he concluded that the existence of pornography's pervasive effects was precisely what demonstrated 'the power of pornography as speech' (771 F.2d 329 [7th Cir. 1985]).

   One could accept that not every case of apparently violent and degrading pornography embodies a view about the worth of others, while acknowledging that a significant number do have this feature (see, e.g., Feinberg, *Offense to Others*, 144–6). It might be argued that some lesbian and homosexual pornography offers an example of apparently violent and degrading material that does not embody such a view.

   [91] Dworkin, 'Reverse Discrimination', 236.

simply be personal. While there is some likelihood that many of the relevant preferences are affected by prejudice, it is possible that what one has here is a complicated situation of the kind Dworkin describes elsewhere, in which 'personal and external preferences are so inextricably tied together, and so mutually dependent, that no practical test for measuring preferences will be able to discriminate the personal and external elements in any individual's overall preferences'.[92] Suppose that this is the case. Suppose it is difficult to disentangle personal preferences about pornography of this kind from external preferences, difficult to answer the hypothetical question about the dependence of the desire on the prejudice. What should we conclude in such circumstances? We should still, if we are following the third of Dworkin's conditions (listed in Section 2), count the preferences in question as external.

In sum, if we are to be faithful to the Dworkin of 'Reverse Discrimination', we ought, it seems, to conclude that the preferences of men for pornography of this kind are external preferences.

d. Conclusion.   Women as a group have rights against the consumers of pornography, and thereby have rights that are trumps against the policy of permitting pornography. The permissive policy has a certain 'objective feature', to use Dworkin's phrase; it relies on external preferences, that is, preferences that are dependent on views about the worth of other people. This is enough to establish that the permissive policy is in conflict with the principle of equal concern and respect, and that women accordingly have rights against it.[93]

---

[92] Ibid.

[93] One possible response to this argument that I do not address here is that the argument, if correct, shows that pornography of this kind presents an apparent conflict of rights, the rights of pornographers against moralists and the rights of women against pornographers. How one goes about resolving such conflicts is not clear, but one way might be to think about what a fully reconstructed utilitarian argument might look like, that is, one that laundered out external preferences of both varieties. On this subject one must, perforce, be somewhat speculative; but if we were to talk of preferences at all, we might begin by considering the following three varieties: (i) preferences of some women that some pornography not be permitted because they view it as deeply insulting; preferences of women for an environment in which they can pursue their goals and life plans without the threat of the discrimination and sexual abuse that pornography of this kind arguably engenders; (ii) moralistic preferences of disapprovers, who want pornography prohibited because they view it as immoral; and (iii) preferences of pornographers that pornography be permitted. There may be others, but these would surely be among the most important. Dworkin considers chiefly the second and third varieties. By Dworkin's argument, the second set count as external; I accept this for the purposes of this essay. I have argued that the preferences of the third variety are also external. This would leave the laundered utilitarian

It should be clear that this argument is rather different in kind to arguments against pornography that are based on a simple harm principle. Recall that Dworkin appeared to think that a successful antipornography argument would have to produce conclusive evidence of some grave harm, for example, evidence that pornography causes violent crime. This, I hope I have shown, is a mistake. The argument above does not need to claim that grave harm results from having a permissive policy, nor does it need to have conclusive evidence for the harm it cites. The argument focuses chiefly on the *preferences* underlying the permissive policy. To make this clear, let me sum up the argument once more, this time in the conditional mode. If there were a utilitarian argument for the policy of permitting violent and degrading pornography, women would have rights against it. Women are apparently disadvantaged by the permissive policy, and therefore have prima facie cause for complaint. Some women feel deeply distressed and insulted by it; and it is probable that the existence of such pornography reinforces and perpetuates attitudes and beliefs that undermine the well-being of women and undermine sexual equality; it probably contributes, for example, to an environment in which sexual abuse is more likely to occur. Given that women have cause to be concerned about the permissive policy, one can ask whether it violates their rights. Since it is likely that a utilitarian permissive policy would rely on the preferences of consumers for pornography of this kind, and since such preferences are external preferences, by the criteria used by Dworkin in 'Reverse Discrimination', women have rights against the permissive policy.

One possible reply to what I have attempted to do here is that it rather misconceives the role that rights are supposed to play in a Dworkinian framework. As a general rule, it might be said, we invoke rights to protect individuals from the consequences of public institutional policies of one kind or another, policies that are justified by arguments that are apparently legitimate, but in fact rest on external preferences. We do not, on this view, invoke rights in the context of individual private actions motivated by prejudice. There are certain personal situations in which the state simply should not interfere to protect those who are disadvantaged, unless the

calculus with only the first to consider. I take it that preferences of the first variety are personal, and while pornographers may have rights against the second variety, they would have no rights against the first. So a fully reconstructed utilitarian argument would, it seems, yield a restrictive conclusion.

harm suffered is very acute. The state should not, for example, intervene in a situation in which it is merely a child's self-esteem rather than her safety that is being systematically undermined by a cruel and sexist father.

There are two distinct thoughts behind a response like this, and one way of making them clear is to compare the pornography case with the one that I suggested was analogous. Remember that the above argument against pornography was modeled on Dworkin's argument regarding Sweatt; and it might be objected that while I stressed the similarities between the issues, I missed two important differences.

The first may already be evident. An important difference between the policy of institutional racial segregation like that of the University of Texas and the policy of permitting pornography is that law schools are in the *public* sphere whereas the reading of violent pornography is not. Regulating educational institutions is one thing, regulating private consumption of sexual literature quite another. A second difference might be the following. Arguments of principle are always directed against a *policy*. Institutional racial segregation clearly is a policy, and therefore offers an appropriate context in which to raise questions about rights of individuals threatened by the policy. But is 'permitting pornography' really a policy? The thought here rests on something like an acts/omissions distinction. It would perhaps be odd to say, for example, that the state had a 'policy' of permitting people to have cornflakes for breakfast, unless there had been careful deliberation, perhaps some suitable legislation, and so on. In short, the objection runs, we begin to consider rights only when individuals are suffering as a result of a genuine public policy. The practice of institutional segregation counts as a public policy; the practice of 'permitting pornography' simply does not.

What are we to make of these responses? The first objection, which invokes a public/private distinction, is one that many liberals might want to make. However, whatever its merits, it is not at all clear that Dworkin is in a position to make it. For Dworkin seems to have disavowed any public/private distinction other than that which can be derived from the equality principle. His strategy in 'Do We Have a Right to Pornography?' offered a good illustration of his method: pornographers could be defended, not because they had a fundamental right to privacy, *simpliciter*, but because they had a right to moral independence, derivable from their right to equal concern and respect. While such a right may protect pornographers from moralistic arguments of policy, it is hard to see how it could protect them from an argument of principle of the kind I have constructed. What of the second objection? We say quite naturally of certain countries or governments that they have 'permissive policies' about various activities, about drugs or public nudity, for example. Is this simply a figure of speech? Is there an important conceptual distinction between active public policies on the one hand and 'pseudo-policies' that merely permit an activity on the other—a distinction that renders arguments of principle inapplicable when we are dealing with the latter? Whatever the answer to this interesting question, my response for the purposes of this article is to leave it to one side, pausing only to express a suspicion, yet again, that Dworkin is not in a position to provide a basis for the necessary conceptual distinction.[94]

It is possible, though, to construct a second Dworkinian argument for prohibiting pornography which is immune to any such objection, for it is not a rights-based argument at all. Since I think there is nothing obviously wrong with the first argument, I take this second, independent, argument to be simply bolstering the former.

2. Prohibiting Pornography: An Argument of Policy

In constructing a Dworkinian argument of principle in favor of prohibiting pornography, I took as my model Dworkin's argument regarding Sweatt.

---

[94] This is a large issue, and one that deserves more attention than I have scope to give it here. It seems that Dworkin's 'principle of victimization', which is introduced in his more recent writings (e.g., in 'What Is Equality', 48) does in effect draw a significant distinction between acts and omissions as far as government policy is concerned. The principle 'denies that equality can be improved when someone is victimized'; someone is victimized when the community imposes a 'liberty deficit', that is, 'a loss of power, in virtue of legal constraint, to do or achieve something one would have had the power to do or achieve following a defensible distribution' (ibid.). One apparent consequence of this principle is that there is an important difference between *allowing* someone to continue in a state in which they have less power than they would in the ideal situation following a 'defensible distribution', and *forcing* such a state on someone. I lack space here to discuss this topic in more depth, but some brief comments are in order. First, the victimization principle does not seem to be derivable from the equality principle, even in the new context of equality of resources. Second, it does not seem very plausible: surely equality *can* be improved when someone is 'victimized' in Dworkin's technical sense. Suppose you have a community in which a large group of people have almost no power to do or achieve anything, and a small group have a great deal; and suppose the only possible way of increasing the power of the large group is by temporarily reducing the power of the smaller group to a level very slightly below that which they would have in the ideal situation. If it were indeed the only means possible, then surely to reject it, on the grounds that it was in conflict with the victimization principle, would be to take a course that would itself conflict, rather than harmonize, with a principle of equal concern and respect.

In constructing an argument of policy for the same conclusion, I again take my lessons from Dworkin's approach in 'Reverse Discrimination', this time looking not at Sweatt but at DeFunis.

We were presented in the analysis of DeFunis with the following powerful argumentative strategy: (a) There was an *ideal* argument of policy, with equality as its goal: the practice of affirmative action was taken to be one that would lead to a more equal, and therefore more just, society (regardless of the preferences of its citizens); and (b) there was also, crucially, an *absence* of any countervailing argument of principle. DeFunis was found to have no right against the policy in question, and given that there were no further objections, that particular affirmative action policy was held to be in harmony with the principle of equal concern and respect. In order to apply this approach to the pornography question, an argument that has both of the above features will be needed.

a. The Ideal Argument.   We begin, then, by offering an ideal argument of policy. We consider the policy of prohibiting violent pornography, and form the hypothesis that this policy would help us make progress toward an important goal, namely, a more equal, and therefore more just, society. Given that there is some evidence that pornography of this kind plays a role in perpetuating the subordinate status of women, in reinforcing 'macho ideology', it is not altogether unreasonable to suppose that to prohibit pornography would be to remove one of the many impediments to women's equal civil status.

This empirical hypothesis is of course vulnerable. Although it cannot be said to be implausible, it may be controversial. Perhaps the policy will not work in the way we hope. Perhaps it will turn out to have some bad effects, although if Dworkin were right the consequences of the policy would not be too dire; in Dworkin's view, it 'seems implausible that any important human interests are damaged by denying dirty books or films',[95] and if it seems implausible for pornography generally, it will presumably seem even more so for the subset of pornography we are considering here. It is possible, though, that the policy will backfire, and promote, say, misogyny rather than equality. However, the fact that the hypothesis is controversial should not in itself be a bar to the policy's constitutionality, if Dworkin is

---

[95] Dworkin, 'Right to Pornography?', 369–70.

right. For it is not, says Dworkin, 'the business of judges . . . to overthrow decisions of other officials because the judges disagree about the efficiency of social policies'.[96] If one is to condemn the policy as unjust, it must be for reasons other than its possible inefficiency. Let us move on to consider whether there are such reasons.

b. Absence of Any Countervailing Argument of Principle.   We must ask at this point whether there is any countervailing argument of principle that would defeat the proposed policy. Do people have a *right* to pornography? Dworkin is, as we have seen, a champion of the rights of pornographers against those who seek censorship. Can his argument provide a means of trumping this argument of policy? It seems not. First of all, Dworkin's rights-based argument was directed against a utilitarian, rather than an ideal, argument of policy. Pornography was to be prohibited, not because such a policy would promote the equality of its citizens, but because most citizens were thought to *prefer* that pornography be prohibited. Given the utilitarian starting point of Dworkin's analysis in 'Do We Have a Right to Pornography?' his approach there has little to say in response to an ideal argument of the kind being proposed here, an argument that does not consider the preferences of citizens at all. Pornographers may well have a 'right to moral independence' of the kind Dworkin describes, namely, 'the right not to suffer disadvantage in the distribution of social goods and opportunities, including disadvantage in the liberties permitted to them by the criminal law, just on the ground that their officials or fellow cit- izens think that their opinions about the right way for them to lead their own lives are ignoble or wrong'.[97] But such a right, however admirably it may protect the liberty of pornographers from moralistic arguments, will do them no good here. This prohibitive argument of policy is no more moralistic than the argument invoked in DeFunis. The policy will, admittedly, somewhat restrict the liberty of the pornographer; but this does not have to be interpreted as a denial of his treatment as an equal. Policies that constrain the liberty of the pornographer conflict with the equality principle 'only when the constraint is justified in some way that depends on the fact that others condemn his convictions or values'.[98] The policy

[96] Dworkin, 'Reverse Discrimination', 224.   [97] Dworkin, 'Right to Pornography?', 353.
[98] Ibid., 366.

we are considering here depends on no such fact. It relies rather 'on the independent argument that a more equal society is a better society even if its citizens prefer inequality'.[99]

Although it seems that Dworkin has provided no answer to the ideal argument proposed here, it would perhaps be unfair to stop at this point. All arguments of policy, whether utilitarian or ideal, are vulnerable, according to Dworkin, to arguments of principle. While Dworkin's failure to supply a defense of a right to pornography against the feminist argument outlined above suggests that his remarks about the relevance of his argument to 'recent history' were a little hasty, it should not be taken as implying that no such defense is possible. How might one go about trying to construct a rights-based argument against an ideal, rather than a utilitarian, argument?

Ideal arguments of policy can sometimes conflict with the principle of equal concern and respect. An example mentioned by Dworkin that we noted earlier is that of an argument of policy that supports the goal of achieving a culturally sophisticated community, in a situation in which no one wants such sophistication. A goal of this kind is in conflict with the 'neutrality' aspect of the equality principle: a government that is committed to treating competing accounts of the good life with equal respect cannot act on the grounds that 'cultural sophistication' is inherently more valuable than some other conception of the good life.[100]

But in the context of pornography, as in the context of affirmative action, we are dealing with a goal of a rather different kind: namely, equality itself. While one can see how a goal like cultural sophistication might be vulnerable in the way that Dworkin suggests, it is harder to see how equality itself could come into conflict with the equality principle. There is, of course, an important distinction to be aware of here. As Dworkin comments, 'part of the importance of DeFunis's case [is] that it forces us to acknowledge the distinction between equality as a policy and equality as a right, a distinction that political theory has virtually ignored'.[101] Even policies that have equality as their goal can conflict with the principle of equal concern and respect, and in such cases it will be possible to raise

[99] Dworkin, 'Reverse Discrimination', 239.
[100] Dworkin, 'What Rights Do We Have?', 274.
[101] Dworkin, 'Reverse Discrimination', 226.

an argument of principle against the policy. Dworkin has an imaginary example:

Suppose a law school were to charge a few middle class students, selected by lot, double tuition in order to increase the scholarship fund for poor students. It would be serving a desirable policy—equality of opportunity—by means that violated the right of the students selected by lot to be treated equally with other students who could also afford the increased fees.[102]

But the policy of prohibiting pornography that we are considering here does not seem to be inequitable in this procedural way; and in the absence of any further clues as to how we are to go about identifying rights in the context of ideal arguments, we need pursue this path no further. Given that the ideal argument does not depend on the fact that others condemn the pornographer's convictions and values, and given that it is not otherwise in conflict with the equality principle, we can conclude that a prohibitive policy is permissible. Ideal arguments of this kind, whether for affirmative action or for the prohibition of some kinds of pornography, apparently work hand in hand with the principle of equal concern and respect, relying as they do 'on the independent argument that a more equal society is a better society even if its citizens prefer inequality. That argument does not deny anyone's right to be treated as an equal himself'.[103]

6. Concluding Remarks

In the preceding section I advanced two 'Dworkinian' arguments in favor of prohibiting a certain kind of pornography. The first was an argument of principle that relied on the idea of equality as a right, and took the following form: To permit such pornography is to have a policy that relies crucially on external preferences; so such pornography should not be permitted. The second was an argument of policy that relied on the idea of equality as a goal, and took the following form: Prohibiting pornography of this kind would help achieve a desirable social goal, namely, equality; given that there is no countervailing rights-based argument, such pornography should be prohibited.

---

[102] Dworkin, 'Reverse Discrimination', 226.   [103] Ibid., 239.

Notice that pornography is to be prohibited, according to these two arguments, not because there is conclusive evidence that it causes violent crime, but rather because it is in conflict with equality. Conclusive evidence of a causal link to violence is not demanded, as it might be demanded by an argument that relied on a simple harm principle. It should be clear that these Dworkinian strategies have significantly altered the burden of proof, with regard to both the argument of principle and the argument of policy. With respect to the argument of principle, demanding conclusive evidence that pornography causes violent crime would be like requiring of Sweatt (in a hypothetical 'separate-but-equal' social context) that he produce conclusive evidence that the 'separate-but-equal' strategy harmed him. With respect to the argument of policy, demanding such evidence would be like requiring the University of Washington Law School to supply proof that *failure* to have an affirmative action policy brought about some grave harm, rather than simply expecting the administrators to have a reasonable empirical hypothesis about the probable social benefits of affirmative action, and to ensure that the policy violates no one's right to be treated as an equal. In sum, if Dworkin were demanding that a case against pornography produce conclusive evidence about violence, then he is requiring both a kind of harm and a degree of evidence that he would not demand in civil rights contexts like that of Sweatt and DeFunis. Now, if there *is* something special about the pornography case that requires us to apply standards of proof that are quite different to apparently similar civil rights cases, then it is surely up to Dworkin to explain what that is.

It is time now to return to the question I posed at the beginning of the essay. What are we to make of all this? What, exactly, has been achieved by demonstrating an apparent harmony between Dworkin's theory and the feminist view he opposes? Two responses are possible.

The first response is that what we have here is an interesting conclusion about pornography and liberalism. A prohibitive policy about violent and degrading pornography is not only consistent with, but apparently demanded by, liberal theory. Well, so much the worse for pornography. What has been shown is the depth of liberalism's commitment to equality; liberalism will approve whatever steps are necessary to protect the right to equality, and to achieve equality as a social goal, even when those steps seem restrictive, provided that no one's right to be treated as an equal is violated. Perhaps such a conclusion will prompt some reevaluation of the liberal agenda, that loose package of causes described by Dworkin in his article 'Liberalism'.[104] Liberals, he says, traditionally 'support racial equality and approve government intervention to secure it, through constraints on both public and private discrimination'.[105] However, he continues, 'they oppose other forms of collective regulation of individual decision: they oppose regulation of the content of political speech...and they oppose regulation of sexual literature and conduct'.[106] Perhaps the last of those causes is due for revision, in the light of an awareness that 'sexual literature' at any rate might sometimes have implications for equality.[107] If liberalism cares just as deeply about sexual equality as it cares about racial equality, it might be led to approve whatever measures are necessary to secure it.[108]

A second and alternative response is that what we have here is not an interesting conclusion about pornography and liberalism, but rather a conclusion about Dworkin. What I have shown is that a prohibitive policy is in harmony with *Dworkinian* liberal theory. Well, so much the worse for Dworkin. Since the conclusion about pornography is unacceptable (so this response runs), there must be something wrong with the Dworkinian premises. What has become evident here is not so much the compatibility of liberalism with restrictive policies on pornography as the weakness of Dworkin's own approach to civil liberties.

Those who are tempted to make this latter response might feel that their suspicions were confirmed if it appeared that these Dworkinian strategies could be used to undermine other liberties. Suppose we explore this possibility, confining ourselves for simplicity's sake to the right of free speech. Might these strategies be applicable to other forms of expression? Pornography is not, of course, the only form of expression that manifests a view about the worth of women; and one might ask whether the above strategies could be extended to other representations in the media that are not sexually explicit, but arguably manifest a certain view of women and promote that view. Would such speech be vulnerable in the ways I

---

[104] Dworkin, 'Liberalism', in *A Matter of Principle*, 181–204.   [105] Ibid., 187.   [106] Ibid.

[107] The 'content of political speech' might also have implications for equality; this is an issue I address briefly later in this essay, considering the example of incitement to racial hatred.

[108] Suppose, contrary to what I have said above, that some theoretical defense for the consumers of pornography can be found. A more modest variant of the above conclusion might still be plausible: namely, that the elimination of pornography is a liberal goal, to be pursued in whatever ways are legitimate, for example, through public education campaigns in the media.

have described? This is an interesting and important question, but rather than pursue it here, let me consider instead a rather different kind of speech, which is not sexually explicit, which is apparently constitutionally protected, and which does nonetheless seem to be vulnerable to the above strategies.

We are granting for the sake of the arguments in this article that Dworkin has *some* resources to defend a right to free speech. Such a defense might be a relatively simple matter where 'free speech' is spelled out as the 'freedom to speak unpopular or wicked thoughts'.[109] A restrictive policy based on an argument that 'most people want wicked thoughts not to be expressed' might well be a moralistic argument, based on external preferences, and therefore defeasible by a 'right to moral independence' of the kind derived in 'Do We Have a Right to Pornography?' Consider, however, the right that would be required to permit 'incitement to racial hatred', the example with which Dworkin began his discussion of pornography. Would Dworkin be able to defend a right of this kind? As a matter of fact, Dworkin takes incitement to racial hatred to be a special case of speaking 'unpopular or wicked thoughts',[110] speech which can easily be defended by Dworkinian strategies. But can a right to racist speech be so easily defended?

I suspect it cannot. I suspect moreover that an application of the principle of equal concern and respect will yield an 'illiberal' result about such speech. To see whether this is so, I invite the reader to consider the following imaginary story. The place is, once again, the University of Texas Law School; the story is set some time after Sweatt's successful suit; and the topic this time is not segregation but speech. The school has had a certain policy about the editorial content of student-run magazines and journals: it has given its students a completely free rein with regard to such content. We can suppose that the administrators have organized a referendum on the question, and have discovered that this is in fact what the majority of students prefer. The student population at this time consists of a small number of blacks, and a large number of whites, many of whom are racist and deeply resent the 'intrusion' of nonwhites into their traditional and elite school. The white editors of the student journals have been exploiting the permissive editorial policy to publish a constant (and popular) flow of hate literature, some of it crude, some of it subtle,

---

[109] Dworkin, 'Right to Pornography?', 335.   [110] Ibid.

but all of it directed against the black minority. The lives of the black students have been profoundly affected as a result. Can they mount an argument of principle against the school's permissive policy, and demand that it be changed? It all depends, of course, on the character of the preferences used by the policy: some student preferences for the policy may well be based on a distrust of any university interference; some may be based on a desire for a student voice that is independent of the administration in every way and at all costs; and some may be based on the knowledge that the policy would give a free rein to the racist editors, who would exploit the opportunity to attack, and perhaps in the long run drive away, students who were members of the despised minority. If racist preferences of the latter kind tipped the balance, then the answer is surely that the black students would indeed be able to mount an argument of principle against the permissive policy. This hypothetical example seems very similar in all the relevant details to the Sweatt case. What we have is a utilitarian policy, which disadvantages a certain group, and which relies on racist preferences—preferences that are, by the criteria described in the discussion of Sweatt, external preferences. This means that the black students would have rights against the policy.

The whites could claim no 'right to moral independence' in defense of their speech, since the restriction on their expression would be motivated by an argument of principle, not a moralistic majoritarian argument. The relevant fact about incitement to racial hatred is not that it is 'wicked' or 'unpopular' but that it embodies a view about the worth of people. This fact has implications for the question of whether those hurt by the speech have rights against it—rights, that is, of the kind Dworkinian theory identifies.[111]

The school could also offer an independent argument in support of a decision to restrict speech, modeled, as was the second of my arguments above, on the DeFunis case. Since the school (newly enlightened!) is interested in promoting the goal of equality on its campus, and has the not unreasonable empirical hypothesis that the old permissive policy

---

[111] I am not addressing here the question of whether a restrictive policy would be the best for all concerned in terms of other interests and goals; university administrators might decide that it would be better in the circumstances to invest resources in an alternative student magazine, in the hope that empowering the voice of the minority would enable speech to be answered with more speech. My point is simply that members of the minority would be *entitled* to bring an argument of principle in the way I have suggested.

was a barrier to the achievement of that goal; and since implementing a more restrictive policy would not obviously require violating any student's right to be treated as an equal, a more restrictive policy is permissible.

In order to bring out the analogy with the cases discussed in 'Reverse Discrimination', my imaginary story focused on a university situation. However, it is not implausible to think that governments might use similar arguments to support similar restrictions. Dworkin remarks in the opening paragraph of 'Do We Have a Right to Pornography?' that the United Kingdom Race Relations law 'makes it a crime to advocate racial prejudice'.[112] He appears to believe that in doing so, the law—which he says would be found unconstitutional in the United States—conflicts with a principle of equal concern and respect.[113] But the United Kingdom legislators might surely justify their policy by appeal to arguments of the very kind described above. To permit incitement to racial hatred would be to give weight to racist preferences of a kind that egalitarian governments have a duty to ignore, so such speech should not be permitted. Or: to prohibit such speech would be to make progress toward an important social goal, namely, equality, so such speech should be prohibited. If this were the case, then the United Kingdom policy would not conflict with a principle of equal concern and respect. It would, on the contrary, be in harmony with it.

What the Indianapolis ordinance and the United Kingdom Race Relations law appear to have in common is a concern for equality that runs very deep—so deep that the silencing of some speech is not regarded as too high a price to pay for it.[114] The Dworkinian commitment to equality appears to run equally deep. Recall that Dworkin said that there could be no real conflict between liberty and equality, since it is the right to equality that provides the wellspring for the rights to liberty. He also said that if we value liberty at all, then we have an interest in establishing a harmony between

---

[112] Dworkin, 'Right to Pornography?', 335.

[113] In 'Right to Pornography?', 335, Dworkin takes freedom to advocate racial prejudice as a case of freedom to speak 'unpopular or wicked thoughts', a liberty that he clearly supports (p. 352) and apparently thinks would be defended along lines similar to a defense of a right to pornography.

[114] As a matter of fact, members of the feminist antipornography movement in Britain have proposed (at the 1987 annual general meeting of the National Council of Civil Liberties) that 'the Race Relations Act 1976 be used as a model for legislating against pornography: making it unlawful to publish or distribute material likely to stir up sexual as well as racial hatred' (Itzin, 'Sex and Censorship', 46).

liberty and equality, since if there *were* any genuine conflict between the two, it would be a contest that liberty must lose.[115] It seems that Dworkin's prognosis about such a contest was correct. Where liberty and equality conflict in the ways I have described, it is indeed liberty that loses, assuming that one regards the conflict through the lens of Dworkinian liberal theory. That theory seems unable, in such circumstances, to supply a defense of free expression, even when that expression is of a kind to which the First Amendment extends its protection. Those of us who share the concern for equality expressed in the ordinance and the Race Relations law may welcome these results, happy to find in Dworkin an unexpected ally. Those of us who find the results unwelcome may conclude that Dworkin has not taken civil liberties seriously enough, and that rights to such liberties as free expression may need to be theoretically fundamental if they are to be successfully defended. Perhaps Dworkin has been hasty in dismissing as illusory all apparent conflict between liberty and equality. Perhaps, on the other hand, the apparent conflicts I have described are only that: apparent. I leave such questions to the reader's judgment.

[115] Dworkin, 'What Is Equality?', 9.

7

Equality and Moralism: Response to Ronald Dworkin

When traditional wars about pornography, waged between liberals and moralists, began to recede, Ronald Dworkin defended the on-going relevance of his classic defense of free speech as a significant weapon against a new and sinister feminist threat. His talk of 'old wars' and 'new armies' was surprisingly bellicose, given that the 'new armies' might easily have been on his own side, motivated as they were, and are, by principles of equality at the heart of his own philosophy. His optimism about the relevance of his earlier argument was ill-founded. It failed to justify the liberal, permissive conclusion he wanted, and helped to vindicate the feminist, restrictive conclusion he did not want, as I showed in 'Whose Right?'. More recently Dworkin has paid direct attention to feminist argument about pornography, in 'Liberty and Pornography' and 'Women and Pornography'. He considers, and rejects, two arguments developed by Catharine MacKinnon and others: the 'egalitarian' argument that pornography conflicts with a commitment to women's equality; and a 'silencing' argument, that pornography conflicts with a commitment to women's freedom of speech. (I address his response to the 'silencing' argument in 'Dangerous Confusion? Response to Dworkin'.) Here I shall look at his response to the argument about equality, and show how the feminist egalitarian argument can still succeed—by Dworkin's own lights.[1]

---

[1] This response to Ronald Dworkin is a revised extract from Langton, 'Pornography: A Liberal's Unfinished Business', *Canadian Journal of Law and Jurisprudence* 12 (1999), 109–33. Dworkin's remark is in *A Matter of Principle* (Cambridge, Mass.: Harvard University Press, 1977), 1. His classic defence is 'Do We Have a Right to Pornography?', *Oxford Journal of Legal Studies* 1 (1981), 177–212, reprinted in *A Matter of Principle*. But Dworkin's principles vindicate MacKinnon: see 'Whose Right?', this volume. His attention to feminist argument is in 'Liberty and Pornography', *The New York Review of Books*, 15 August 1991, 12–15 (page citations are to this version), published as 'Two Concepts of Liberty'

An argument that pornography threatens women's equality deserves careful attention from a philosopher who takes equality to be the starting point of liberal political philosophy, or so one might imagine. When MacKinnon said 'the law of equality and the law of freedom of speech are on a collision course in this country',[2] she found that some liberals agree with her: Bernard Williams, for example, said that this claim is no exaggeration.[3] How exactly is the feminist 'egalitarian' argument to be understood? In his broader philosophical work, Dworkin distinguishes two distinct roles that equality can play: equality can be invoked as a *right*; and it can be invoked as a *goal*. The feminist argument about equality could thus be construed in the two ways I have shown: first, as an argument of principle, claiming that pornography violates women's *right* to equality; second, as an argument of policy, claiming that pornography causally works to undermine women's equality, and that a government aiming to promote equality as a *goal* is justified in prohibiting pornography.

The stronger of these two argument forms would be the first, for Dworkin. If rights are trumps, the first gives women a trumping argument against pornography. If rights are trumps, the second argument, of policy, is potentially vulnerable to a trumping counter-argument of principle. Now Dworkin neither here, nor elsewhere, to my knowledge, considers a feminist *rights*-based argument against pornography, even when explicitly considering feminist 'egalitarian' argument. This is surprising, if only because the courts were obliged to consider precisely the question of whether pornography violates women's *right to equality* under the Fourteenth Amendment of the US Constitution. For a philosopher who sets such store by the right to equality, it seems a striking omission. If he has not considered a rights-based argument against pornography, he has not considered the feminist argument which, by his lights, should be the strongest. The feminist rights-based equality argument thus remains, for Dworkin, a major piece of unfinished business.

in *Isaiah Berlin: A Celebration*, eds., Edna and Avishai Margalit (Chicago: University of Chicago Press, 1991), 100–9. Dworkin's review of MacKinnon's *Only Words* appeared as 'Women and Pornography', in *The New York Review of Books*, 21 October 1993, 36, 37, 40–2.

    [2] Catharine MacKinnon, *Only Words* (Cambridge, Mass.: Harvard University Press, 1993), 71.

    [3] Bernard Williams, 'Drawing Lines' (review of MacKinnon's *Only Words*), *London Review of Books*, 16, no. 9, 12 May 1994, 9–10.

He interprets the equality argument in the weaker of the two ways just described. He construes the feminist egalitarian argument in general causal terms, and appears to accept its causal premise, at least for the sake of argument. The feminist egalitarian argument claims that 'pornography is in part responsible [for a] general and endemic subordination', and this is 'a matter of causal connection'.[4] Pornography works insidiously 'to damage the standing and power of women within the community', and

If pornography contributes to the general subordination of women....then eliminating pornography can...be defended as serving equality.[5]

He construes the feminist equality argument as a goal-based argument, based on an empirical hypothesis about what promotes equality.

Thus construed, it is the starting point of what could be a Dworkinian argument of policy of the kind I developed in 'Whose Right?': it is clearly analogous to the equality-promoting argument discussed and endorsed by Dworkin in 'Reverse Discrimination'.[6] A first step in considering it should therefore be to address the feminist 'egalitarian' argument as he addressed the reverse discrimination argument: ask whether the policy of prohibiting pornography, despite its apparent motivation in the goal of equality, may nonetheless violate some right to equality. Instead, there is a false start, and Dworkin initially does something remarkable. In both articles he says: if pornography does pose a conflict between liberty and equality, as feminists allege, then that is *a conflict that liberty must win*. If there were a conflict between liberty and equality, it could be 'resolved simply on the ground that liberty must be sovereign'.[7]

If we must make the choice between liberty and equality that MacKinnon envisages—if the two constitutional values really are on a collision course—we should have to choose liberty.[8]

---

[4] 'Liberty and Pornography', 14.   [5] 'Women and Pornography', 40.
[6] See Ronald Dworkin, 'Reverse Discrimination', in *Taking Rights Seriously* (Cambridge, Mass.: Harvard University Press, 1977), 223–39, for the distinction between rights-based and goal-based arguments of equality. Dworkin defends a goal-based strategy for justifying reverse discrimination policy. The general distinction between goal-based and rights-based arguments, and the relation of the latter to equality, is discussed in much of Dworkin's work, but see especially 'What Rights Do We Have?', in *Taking Rights Seriously*, 266–78.
[7] 'Liberty and Pornography', 14.   [8] 'Women and Pornography', 41.

This pronouncement would not be remarkable coming from the Court, which saw the issue in precisely those terms when it trumped women's equality by pornographers' liberty. It would not be remarkable coming from those liberals who take civil liberties such as free speech to be fundamental and absolute. But it *is* a remarkable pronouncement, coming from Dworkin: from a philosopher who has long taught that if there is ever a conflict between liberty and equality, that is a conflict which liberty must *lose*.[9] There is an inconsistency here, and 'Liberty and Pornography' leaves the reader with no better answer than this.

In 'Women and Pornography' Dworkin does go further, and considers the crucial question of whether the 'egalitarian' feminist policy might threaten someone else's right to equality. He concludes that there is no actual conflict between pornographers' liberty and women's equality: the right to pornography stems after all from the pornographers' right to equality.

First Amendment liberty is not equality's enemy, but the other side of equality's coin.[10]

Pornographers have an equal right to participate in forming the moral environment: no one may be prevented from influencing the shared moral environment on the grounds that his tastes and opinions disgust others. This is the 'right to moral independence' described by Dworkin in his earlier defence of the right to pornography, and, like all rights, it is derived from the right to equality. So it is censorship, after all, not pornography, which conflicts with equality.

Leaving aside the new question of why this does not simply pose a conflict between women's equality and pornographer's equality, it should be clear that Dworkin has failed to confront the feminist argument he is considering. Suppose we grant that there is an equality-based right to moral independence of the kind Dworkin describes, and suppose that everyone, including pornographers, has such a right. This right has no purchase on the feminist goal-based equality argument against pornography. Recall that we have here no absolute right to free speech: the right here is a right not to be prevented from influencing the moral environment, 'on the grounds

---

[9] Dworkin, 'What is Equality? Part 3: The Place of Liberty', *Iowa Law Review* 73 (1987), 9.
[10] 'Women and Pornography', 42.

that one's tastes and opinions disgust others'. And although Dworkin famously claims to be taking rights seriously, the rights he identifies are sensitive to context and background conditions, and hence vulnerable. Any rights claims must be identified against the backdrop of the countervailing argument that threatens them. One never has a right *simpliciter*, but always a right with respect to a particular kind of political argument. In arguing for the pornographer's 'right to moral independence', Dworkin imagined a background utilitarian argument for censorship, based on moralistic preferences of people who have contempt for pornographers and their way of life. Such preferences are external, so pornographers have rights against a utilitarian policy of censorship. This sensitivity of rights to context is what makes it so important for Dworkin to be precise about what the feminist argument is.

As described, it is an argument of policy whose goal is social equality: pornography contributes to a climate of inequality, so prohibiting pornography will probably help to make society more equal. Crucially, this argument does not say pornography should be prohibited *because it disgusts people*. Instead it is based on a causal empirical hypothesis: an admittedly fallible hypothesis about what is likely to happen if pornography is prohibited. On that hypothesis, society will become more equal if pornography is prohibited. The argument is not based on a claim that pornography disgusts and offends. Facts about current attitudes or preferences of people are not part of its justifying reason. One might object to this equality argument by saying that the empirical hypothesis is implausible. One might object by saying that a government should not be in the business of actively pursuing ideals like that of social equality. But one cannot object as Dworkin objects. One cannot object by saying there is a right which protects a group from moralistic preferences. Dworkin's 'right to moral independence' is, despite its generic-sounding label, a specialist tool, a weapon which can be used only against a moralistic threat. It is irrelevant to the goal-based feminist equality argument, and therefore gives us no reason to reject it. And since the feminist goal-based equality argument is structurally identical to the argument for reverse discrimination which Dworkin himself endorses, I conclude that Dworkin has every reason to positively endorse it.[11] If he

---

[11] In 'Reverse Discrimination'. Dworkin has not, to my knowledge, changed his mind about the conclusion of that paper.

thinks otherwise, he needs to say why. The feminist goal-based equality argument thus remains for him as more unfinished business.

There is a possible diagnosis for the trouble here. Dworkin may think the 'right to moral independence' is relevant after all to feminist argument, because he just assimilates the feminist argument with the old moralistic argument about offense and disgust. This assimilation appears in 'Women and Pornography', where an argument about equality simply *slides* into an argument about disgust and offense. Watch.

(a) *Equality:* Dworkin states the feminist goal-based 'egalitarian' argument clearly to begin with. He says, recall, that according to feminist egalitarian argument, pornography works insidiously 'to *damage the standing and power* of women within the community', and that

If pornography contributes to the general *subordination* of women . . . then eliminating pornography can . . . be defended as serving *equality*.[12]

As the italicized words show, this is unambiguously an argument about equality.

(b) *The Slide:* He says that if the feminist 'egalitarian' argument were taken seriously,

government could . . . forbid the graphic or *visceral* or *emotionally charged* expression of any opinion or conviction that might *reasonably offend* a *disadvantaged* group . . . Courts would have to balance the value of such expression . . . against the damage it might cause to the *standing or sensibilities* of its targets.[13]

Here the italicized words show an uneasy mixture: there is talk of equality in the suggestions that women are 'disadvantaged', and that their 'standing' may be damaged by pornography; but the new talk of emotion and offense and sensibilities gives hint of what is to come.

(c) *Disgust and Offense:* He says that the feminist egalitarian argument violates the principle that

no-one may be prevented from influencing the shared moral environment, through his own private choices, tastes, opinions and example, just because these tastes or opinions *disgust* . . . [The argument] allows a majority to define some people as *too corrupt or offensive* . . . to join in the informal moral life of the nation.[14]

---

[12] 'Women and Pornography', 40 (emphasis added).   [13] Ibid.
[14] Ibid., 41 (emphasis added).

The italicized words show the final metamorphosis. Dworkin's interpretation of the feminist equality argument is this, in short. Feminists say pornography subordinates women; that is, it damages the standing and power of women; that is, it damages the standing and sensibilities of women; that is, it disgusts and offends women.

Such equivocation, in the work of a leading liberal philosopher, is bewildering; and it disguises two things. It disguises Dworkin's continued failure to confront the feminist arguments of equality. With the disguise gone, we see that Dworkin is not, after all, a foe to feminists, but potentially a friend. His principle of equality does not undermine MacKinnon's conclusion, but can vindicate it, as I have shown. Second, the equivocation disguises the weakness, for more traditional liberals, of Dworkin's defense of free speech: if liberals want resources to combat the perceived perils of 'political correctness', they will not find them here. For all he has shown, the right to free speech works only when confronted with moralism, and offers no reply to restrictions on speech motivated by equality, even by equality as a goal. With the disguise gone, we see that Dworkin is not, after all, a friend to those liberals, but a foe.

In sum, then, Dworkin considers a feminist argument about equality and pornography, construes it in the weaker of two possible ways (weaker by his own lights, that is); and, through a mix of equivocation and bad philosophical management, has failed to answer even this. The goal-based equality argument against pornography stands unrefuted—though not for want of trying. And the rights-based equality argument against pornography stands unrefuted—for want of trying.

8

Scorekeeping in a Pornographic Language Game

(CO-AUTHORED WITH CAROLINE WEST)

1. Introduction

If, as many suppose, pornography changes people, a question arises as
to how.[1] One answer to this question offers a grand and noble vision.
Inspired by the idea that pornography is speech, and inspired by a certain
liberal ideal about the point of speech in political life, some theorists
say that pornography contributes to that liberal ideal: pornography, even
at its most violent and misogynistic, and even at its most harmful, is
political speech that aims to express certain views about the good life,
aims to persuade its consumers of a certain political point of view—and to
some extent succeeds in persuading them. Ronald Dworkin suggests that
the pornographer contributes to the 'moral environment, by expressing
his political or social convictions or tastes or prejudices informally', that
pornography 'seeks to deliver' a 'message', that it reflects the 'opinion' that
'women are submissive, or enjoy being dominated, or should be treated as
if they did', that it is comparable to speech 'advocating that women occupy
inferior roles'.[2] Pornography on this view is political speech that aims to

---

[1] This essay first appeared in the *Australasian Journal of Philosophy* 77 (1999), 303–19. Catharine
MacKinnon defines pornography as 'the graphic sexually explicit subordination of women in pictures
or words that also includes women dehumanized as sexual objects, things or commodities.' For full
definition see 'Francis Biddle's Sister', 176, in MacKinnon, *Feminism Unmodified* (Cambridge, Mass.:
Harvard University Press, 1987), cf. *Only Words* (Cambridge, Mass.: Harvard University Press, 1993),
121, n. 32. This definition is controversial, but for convenience we follow it here, ignoring for present
purposes the problems (political or philosophical) it may pose.

[2] Ronald Dworkin, 'A New Map of Censorship', *Index on Censorship* 1/2 (1994), 13, and 'Two
Concepts of Liberty', in *Isaiah Berlin: A Celebration*, eds., Edna and Avishai Margalit (London: Hogarth
Press, 1991), 104, 105. The mismatch between rhetoric and reality in Dworkin's analysis of pornography

persuade its listeners of the truth of certain ideas about women, and of course 'the government must leave to the people the evaluation of ideas'.[3]

Another answer offers a vision that is not grand and noble, but thoroughly reductive. Pornography is not politically persuasive speech, but speech that works by a process of psychological conditioning. This view seems common enough in the social science literature. Consider, for example, this description of an early experiment, from a time that pre-dates contemporary political debate.

Example (1).   An experimenter

...created a mild boot fetish in heterosexual male students by pairing slides of sexually provocative women with a picture of a pair of black knee-length women's boots. Not only did the boots become somewhat sexually arousing, but there was a slight tendency for this conditioned response to generalize to other footwear as well. The author concluded that there is little question that sexual responsiveness can be conditioned to external stimuli that initially fail to elicit any sexual arousal.[4]

Catharine MacKinnon, at least in some moods, offers this kind of answer. Pornography, she says, 'works as primitive conditioning, with pictures and words as sexual stimuli'.[5] More recently Danny Scoccia has agreed, saying that violent pornography produces misogynistic beliefs and violent desires by a process of conditioning. He also agrees, at least in part, with MacKinnon's political conclusion: since liberal principle 'does not protect speech insofar as it non-rationally affects its hearers' mental states', liberals can support a ban on violent pornography.[6] On this view, pornography

---

has been commented on by Jennifer Hornsby, 'Speech Acts and Pornography', *Women's Philosophy Review,* November 1993, 38–45, reprinted with a postscript in Susan Dwyer, ed., *The Problem of Pornography* (Belmont, Ca.: Wadsworth, 1995), 220–32.

[3] Dworkin, 'Two Concepts', 106, quoting with approval the words of Judge Frank Easterbrook, American Booksellers Assn., Inc. v. Hudnut 771 F.2d 323 (1985).

[4] Edward C. Nelson, 'Pornography and Sexual Aggression', in Maurice Yaffé and Edward Nelson, eds., *The Influence of Pornography on Behaviour* (London: Academic Press, 1982), 185, citing a 1966 study by S. Rachman, 'Sexual Fetishism: An Experimental Analogue', *Psychological Record* 16 (1966), 293–6.

[5] MacKinnon, *Only Words,* 16.

[6] Danny Scoccia, 'Can Liberals Support a Ban on Violent Pornography?', *Ethics* 106 (1996), 776–99. The quotation is from p. 777. Scoccia's focus, unlike MacKinnon's, is on violent desires produced by violent pornography, rather than on 'bigotry' produced by violent *and other* pornography. He provides an excellent discussion of the liberal 'persuasion principle', and how its application to pornography is undermined by the conditioning hypothesis. Other reductive accounts include Frederick Schauer's view that pornography is not really speech at all, but a kind of sex aid; and Cass Sunstein's view that since

is not political speech that aims to persuade its hearers of the truth of certain ideas. Instead, pornography is a stimulus that produces a response in subjects who seem to have more in common with the salivating dogs of Pavlovian fame than with the political agents of liberal utopia.

These two visions place pornography at opposite ends of a spectrum nicely described by Scoccia, at whose less rational end we might find spoken speech whose pitch and modulation 'excites the aggression centers in the brains of its listeners, causing in them strong urges to act violently even if they do not understand what is being spoken'; and at whose more rational end we might find 'most articles written by academics and published in scholarly journals'.[7] Whether or not one agrees with Scoccia's optimism about what lies at the rational end of the speech spectrum, his idea is a useful one. The grand and noble vision of pornography—the vision of Ronald Dworkin, in some moods—places pornography towards the end occupied by rational argument. The reductive vision—the vision of MacKinnon, in some moods—places pornography towards the irrational end. Neither of the two visions appears wholly plausible. Pornographers are not in the business of presenting arguments to persuade consumers that women are thus and so. Dworkin's rhetoric in particular seems ludicrous. Pornography is designed to generate, not conclusions, but orgasms. However, it seems hasty to rush to the other extreme, and equate pornography and its consumers with the bells and dogs of Pavlovian notoriety. If pornography is speech, then we can expect it to be at least partly continuous with other forms of human communication, and to produce its effects on beliefs, desires, and behaviour in a manner that is not utterly different from other speech.

In what follows we take up this moderate thought, and we use it to explore two well known feminist claims, that pornography *subordinates* and *silences* women.[8] In the course of our exploration, we hope to trace a

pornography aims at arousal and affects propositional attitudes by a process akin to subliminal suggestion, it is non-cognitive speech. See Schauer, 'Speech and "Speech"—Obscenity and "Obscenity": An Exercise in the Interpretation of Constitutional Language', *Georgetown Law Journal* 67 (1979), 899–933; Sunstein, 'Pornography and the First Amendment', *Duke Law Journal* (September 1986), 589–627. These views are discussed and rejected by Scoccia.

[7] Scoccia, 'Can Liberals Support a Ban?', 785.

[8] For some philosophical discussions other than those of MacKinnon, see e.g. Melinda Vadas, 'A First Look at the Feminist/Civil Rights Ordinance: Could Pornography be the Subordination of Women?', *Journal of Philosophy* 84 (1987), 487–511. Langton's 'Speech Acts and Unspeakable Acts',

middle path between the two extremes described. We do not so much argue for this path as pursue it, and any argument rests with the success, or otherwise, of its pursuit. We proceed on the assumption that pornography is speech—an assumption taken by the courts, and adopted here at least for the sake of argument. The assumption may be wrong. Perhaps pornography cannot be thought of as if it were continuous with other mundane human communications. Perhaps pornography does not work as speech after all. Notice that if this is so, then feminist arguments against pornography ought to have an easier time of it than they do, since it cannot be a right to free *speech* that protects pornography, if anything does. Alternatively, pornography may be speech, roughly continuous with other speech, but speech better understood in terms of an interpretative framework other than the one we choose here. We believe, however, that the approach we sketch here is a fruitful one, whose implications go beyond the debate about pornography which is our present focus.

In arguing that pornography can be speech that acts—speech that subordinates and silences—MacKinnon says this:

Together with all its material supports, authoritatively *saying* someone is inferior is largely how structures of status and differential treatment are demarcated and actualized. Words and images are how people are placed in hierarchies, how social stratification is made to seem inevitable and right, how feelings of inferiority and superiority are engendered, and how indifference to violence against those on the bottom is rationalized and normalized.[9]

Here we find MacKinnon in a different mood. She does not describe pornography as 'primitive conditioning'. She does not describe pornography as if it were a mere stimulus, like the ringing of a bell. She describes it as speech that has a certain content, and acts in a certain way. She describes it as if it were continuous with other sorts of 'words and images' that make certain attitudes become—or *seem* to become—rational and normal. Her idea

---

this volume offers a speech act analysis of the claims that pornography subordinates and silences women, and argues that free speech includes illocution. Jennifer Hornsby argues likewise with respect to the silencing claim, in 'Speech Acts and Pornography', 'Illocution and its Significance', in *Foundations of Speech Act Theory*, ed., S. L. Tsohatzidis (London: Routledge, 1994), 'Disempowered Speech', in *Philosophical Topics* 23 (1995) 127–47. See also Hornsby and Langton, 'Free Speech and Illocution', *Legal Theory* 4 (1998), 21–37, shortened version included as 'Freedom of Illocution: Reply to Daniel Jacobson', this volume.

[9] *Only Words*, 31.

seems to be in partial agreement with Ronald Dworkin's idea that pornography conveys a 'message' about women, but with one crucial difference. According to MacKinnon, when the 'message' is said by an authoritative speaker (together with certain 'material supports'), the saying can be a particular sort of doing, a particular sort of *illocutionary* doing—a legitimation of attitudes and behaviour, a subordination of women. On this view, pornography authoritatively says certain things: says that women are inferior, says that sexual violence is normal and legitimate. Given the authority of the saying, pornography has an illocutionary force which in some sense makes women socially inferior, and makes sexual violence normal and legitimate.

According to MacKinnon—in this mood—pornography says certain things, and says them with authority. Her claim thus raises a question about what pornography says, and a question about whether it speaks with authority. Our chief concern in what follows will be with the first question, the question of what pornography says. The second question is important too: MacKinnon's implication is that if pornography were not authoritative, it would still say these things—but without subordinating women. The saying would no longer be a doing, or rather, it would no longer be that sort of doing. So the conclusion about pornography's power to subordinate and silence women requires the premise about pornography's authority.[10] The first question, though, is really prior to the second. Before we consider whether pornography says something with authority we should consider whether it says it at all. Authoritative or not, does pornography even *say* the things that it is claimed by MacKinnon to say? Does it say that women are inferior, or that sexual violence is normal and legitimate?

There are two reasons for doubting that pornography says these things, and we aim to address both in what follows. One reason for doubt is that pornography does not seem to say such things *explicitly*. Little, if any, pornography will explicitly assert the propositions 'Women are inferior'

---

[10] Is pornography authoritative in the way MacKinnon claims? That question, which is partly empirical, is addressed by Langton, who argues in 'Speech Acts and Unspeakable Acts' that it is plausible to suppose pornography has the authority that is a condition of illocutions that subordinate and silence, and that it is therefore plausible to suppose MacKinnon is right in claiming that pornography subordinates and silences. The argument is challenged by Leslie Green in 'Pornographizing, Subordinating, Silencing', in *Censorship and Silencing: Practices of Cultural Regulation*, ed., Robert Post (New York: Getty Research Institute and Oxford University Press, 1998), 285–311, and Langton replies in 'Subordination, Silence and Pornography's Authority', in *Censorship and Silencing*, 261–83, a shortened version included as 'Pornography's Authority: Reply to Leslie Green', this volume.

or 'Sexual violence is normal' or 'Sexual violence is legitimate'. Much pornography will be in the form of pictures, not propositions. And while pornography that is words rather than pictures will have an explicit sexual content, it is doubtful that the 'message' identified by MacKinnon and Dworkin will ever be explicit. That is one reason for thinking pornography does not quite say these things.

Another independent reason for doubt is that much pornography purports to be fantasy or *fiction*: so even if it were to contain explicit propositions of the kind described, such propositions would not be assertions at all, but a kind of fictional story telling. That is a further reason for thinking pornography does not quite say these things.

We hope to offer an answer to the question of what pornography says, and to put to rest the two doubts provoked by it. We aim to gain a clearer understanding of how pornography might really say certain things which, at first sight, it may appear not to say: and hence that it might do certain things which, at first sight, it may appear not to do. We take this to be one necessary part of the task of showing that pornography is speech that subordinates and silences women. We aim to show that this important part of MacKinnon's case can be established. And if, in addition, MacKinnon is right to claim that pornography says these things *authoritatively*—the claim we do not address in detail here—then pornography may well be speech that subordinates and silences. Our conclusion thus locates pornography somewhere between the two extremes described above: neither at the reductive end of the speech spectrum, since pornography can be understood as at least partly continuous with other speech; nor at the grand and noble end of the speech spectrum, since pornography works in ways that are different to the ways of political argument, and it subordinates and silences women. An important question is raised by this location of pornography: whether speech that is located at this point on the spectrum, and that also subordinates and silences, ought be prohibited.[11] But this too is a question we must leave aside here, though we believe our conclusion offers broad support to that of MacKinnon.

In Section 2 we address the first doubt that pornography says the sorts of things it is claimed to say—the thought that since pornography does not

---

[11] This question is addressed by West in 'The Free Speech Argument Against Pornography', *Canadian Journal of Philosophy* 33 (2003), 391–422; and by Langton, in 'Pornography: A Liberal's Unfinished Business', *Canadian Journal of Law and Jurisprudence* 12 (1999), 109–33.

say them explicitly, it does not say them at all. We argue that this doubt is misguided, and we draw attention to the ways that things which are not explicitly said can nevertheless be said. In Section 3 we consider the implications of our suggestion for the claims that pornography subordinates and silences women. Section 4 takes up the second doubt—the thought that since pornography only says them fictionally, it does not really say them at all. We argue that this doubt too is misguided, and we draw attention to the ways in which things which are said as fiction can at the same time be said as purported fact. Our conclusion is that pornography may well say what MacKinnon claims it says, even if it does not say them explicitly, and even if it is fiction.

2. Saying, and What Pornography Says

Many philosophers have wanted to draw our attention to a distinction between what is explicitly said, on the one hand, and what is presupposed, or implied, or suggested, on the other. To give a familiar example, if I say 'The present King of France is bald', what I explicitly say is that 'The present King of France is bald'. But when I say 'The present king of France is bald', I presuppose, or imply, or suggest, that that there is a present King of France, even though I do not explicitly say so.[12] And if I am sincere, I will say such a thing only if I believe there is a present King of France. If I say 'Even Jane could pass', what I presuppose, or imply, or suggest is that Jane is comparatively incompetent; and I will sincerely say so only if I believe she is incompetent. If I say, 'That joke's as bad as Harry's', I presuppose, or imply, or suggest that Harry's jokes are bad, though I never explicitly say so; and I will sincerely say what I say only if I think that Harry's jokes are bad. These implications or presuppositions—Jane is incompetent, there is a present King of France, Harry's jokes are bad—are required in order to make sense, or to make best sense, of what I explicitly say. There would be something wrong with saying 'The present King of

---

[12] We are concerned here with presupposition at an informal level. Some say that the proposition 'the present King of France is bald' entails the proposition 'there is a present King of France', others say that the proposition 'the present King of France is bald' requires the truth of the proposition 'there is a present King of France' if it is to have a truth value. We do not wish, here, to take a particular stand on the logic of presupposition.

France is bald, and there is no present King of France'; or 'That joke's as bad as Harry's, and Harry's jokes are pretty good'. There might be different ways of making sense of what is explicitly said, but some ways will be more natural or obvious than others.

David Lewis, following Robert Stalnaker, has described the introduction of presupposition into conversation as a kind of move in a rule-governed language game. His analysis, in 'Scorekeeping in a Language Game,'[13] aims to show a common pattern exhibited not only by presupposition introduction, but by a variety of linguistic interactions, ranging from the moves made in informal conversations to the highly conventional illocutionary acts of the kind considered by J. L. Austin.[14] To say something in a speech-situation is more than to utter a string of words with a sense and reference; it is to make a certain move in a language game. What Lewis calls the 'score' of the language game adjusts itself in response to the moves speakers make, and the later moves that a speaker can make are in turn dependent upon the prior score of the game. Presuppositions figure as a prominent component of score.

Lewis compares a conversational language game with a baseball game. Both are rule-governed, and in both cases we can speak of the score of the game at any given time. The score of the game at any given time is given by the components of the score of the game at that time. In the case of baseball, the components of the score are numbers: the numbers of runs by the visiting team, runs by the home team, the half, the inning, the strikes, the balls, and the outs. In the case of conversational score, the components are similarly abstract entities—not numbers, but other set-theoretic constructs, such as sets of presuppositions.

Whether in a baseball game or a language game, Lewis thinks, score is determined in a more or less rule-governed fashion, and there are constitutive rules determining the kinematics of score, and determining correct play. The rules of the kinematics of score in baseball say how the score evolves over time: the score at one time is determined in a certain way by the score at an earlier time, and the behaviour of players in the intervening period. Likewise, the rules of the kinematics of score in language games say how the score evolves over time: the score at

---

[13] David Lewis, 'Scorekeeping in a Language Game', in *Philosophical Papers*, vol. i (Oxford: Oxford University Press, 1983), 233–49, first appearing in the *Journal of Philosophical Logic* 8 (1979), 339–59.
[14] J. L. Austin, *How to Do Things with Words* (Oxford: Oxford University Press, 1962).

one time is determined in a certain way by the score at an earlier time, and the behaviour of the players—the course of the conversation—in the intervening period. The rules determining correct play specify what counts as correct play, where correctness depends in part on the score at a particular time. In baseball, correct play after two strikes is not the same as correct play after three. Likewise, in a language game the truth value (or other acceptability value) of a sentence depends in part on the score at a particular time: correct play after a marriage proposal is typically not the same as correct play after a comment on the weather.[15]

However, there is one great difference between a language game and a baseball game, says Lewis. A game of baseball does not tend to evolve in whatever way is required to make the play that occurs count as correct. If a player walks to first base after three balls rather than four, his behavior does not make it the case that there *are* four balls and his behaviour *is* correct. Baseball is not governed by what Lewis calls a *rule of accommodation*. 'Baseball has no rule of accommodation to the effect that if a fourth ball is required to make correct the play that occurs, then that very fact suffices to change the score so that straightway there are four balls.'[16] Conversational score, however, *is* governed by a rule of accommodation. Conversational score, unlike baseball score, does tend to evolve in whatever way is required to make the play that occurs count as correct play. Such rules have the following general form. If at a given time something is said that requires a component of conversational score to be a certain way, in order for what is said to be true, or otherwise acceptable; and if that component is not that way beforehand (and if certain further conditions hold); then at that time, that score component changes in the required way, to make what is said true, or otherwise acceptable.

Presupposition provides a clear illustration. If I say 'even Jane could pass', and no one challenges ('Whadda ya mean, "*even* Jane"?'), the conversational score is immediately adjusted to include the new presupposition that Jane is incompetent. If someone says something which requires a missing presupposition, that presupposition is immediately established as part of the score, making the move count as correct play. In the case of presupposition,

[15] Lewis, 'Scorekeeping', 236. In addition to these constitutive rules, Lewis describes regulative rules directing the players to play correctly, and directing them to aim to make the score evolve in certain ways. (Team members should try to maximize the number of runs of their own team, and so forth.)
[16] Ibid., 240.

the correctness is not *truth*—my move does not on its own *make it true* that Jane is incompetent—but is some other sort of acceptability. The conversation will proceed with that presupposition in place—providing, of course, the move is unchallenged.

We can note at this point that when something is introduced as a pre-supposition it may be harder to challenge than something which is asserted outright. A speaker who introduces a proposition as a presupposition thereby suggests that it can be taken for granted: that it is widely known, a matter of shared belief among the participants in the conversation, which does not need to be asserted outright. Someone who says 'Even Jane could pass' conveys not simply the message that Jane is incompetent, but that everyone knows that Jane is incompetent. A challenger faces the cost of contradicting not simply the speaker, but the general opinion. That is surely part of the reason for presuppositions being more difficult to challenge than assertions.[17]

The phenomenon of accommodation is widespread, as Lewis observes: 'once we have this scheme in mind . . . we will find many instances of it'.[18] And he goes on to show that other linguistic interactions follow similar rules, ranging from the classic Austinian illocutions of marrying, christening, permitting, prohibiting, to the informal hatching of plans. When a speaker says, in felicitous circumstances, 'with this ring I thee wed', there is a rule of accommodation which makes it *correct* (in this case *true*) that the speaker weds. When a master says to a slave, 'you are not now permitted beyond the white line', there is a rule of accommodation which immediately adjusts the boundary of the permissible and impermissible to make it *correct* (in this case *true*) that the slave is not now permitted beyond the white line.

It is worth adding that once this phenomenon is noticed, one sees the possibility of moves which do more than one thing: the possibility of mixed cases. The master could make the move of prohibiting by using the performative tag 'I hereby prohibit . . . ', or he could make the same move more subtly. If he were all of a sudden to say something which merely *presupposed* that the slave was not allowed to cross the white line, that too could be a move of prohibiting the slave from crossing the white line. Likewise for permitting. 'Even Jane could pass' introduces the presupposition of Jane's incompetence, but it may also do other

---

[17] Thanks to Philip Pettit for emphasizing this point to us.   [18] Lewis, 'Scorekeeping', 240.

things—permit jokes at Jane's expense, legitimate further slurs on Jane's talents, and so on. The point is that such illocutionary moves as permissions and prohibitions may be explicit, or implicit: they may be introduced explicitly, or they may be introduced implicitly as presuppositions of what is said explicitly.

We agree with Lewis about the ubiquity of accommodation, and we wish to suggest that similar rules of accommodation might operate in the context of pornography—odd though it may sound to think of pornography in conversational terms. We suggest that Lewis's analysis can shed light on the question of what pornography says.

Recall the sorry tale of the slides and the footwear, in *Example (1)*. Even this most reductive story is open to a less Pavlovian, more conversational interpretation. Compare that study with some of the conversational situations described earlier. What I say about Jane ('Even Jane could pass') makes best sense on the assumption that she is an unpromising candidate. The presence of a bland pair of boots in an otherwise sexually exciting series of pictures makes best sense on the assumption that the boots are supposed to be exciting too. The conversation about Jane accommodates the new presupposition of her incompetence, making correct or acceptable that presupposition, and those taking part go on with the new score in place. In the 'conversation' about the footwear—a monologue rather than a dialogue—it seems likely that the same applies. The one-sided conversation with the slides accommodates the novel presumption about boots, and in doing so makes correct or acceptable the idea that boots are sexy. Perhaps some viewers challenge the move. ('Whadda ya mean, *boots?*') Perhaps many do not, and go on with that new score in place, responding appropriately. The sexiness of the boots is, so to speak, *presupposed* by the one sided 'conversation' with the slides. One can see even in this apparently most Pavlovian of interactions a pattern, which is at least partly continuous with other conversational situations.

More relevant to our present task are the rules of accommodation at play in the kind of pornography which concerns MacKinnon. It may be that we now have the resources to gain a better understanding of how pornography may say and do the things it may not, at first sight, appear to say and do.

While it may not explicitly be said in pornography that women are inferior, or that sexual violence is normal or legitimate, it may be that propositions like these are presupposed by what pornography explicitly says, because they are required for the hearer to make best sense of what is said. The explicit content of pornography may be one thing: may be sexually graphic depictions of women (whether in words or pictures) that include one or more of the details mentioned in the feminist definition (depictions of women 'cut-up, bruised, mutilated, penetrated by foreign objects, animals, reduced to body parts...').[19] But pornography may say more than it says explicitly, if we count what is implied or presupposed among the things that are said.

We illustrate with an example, not particularly extreme, but typical, perhaps, of the kind of pornography MacKinnon has in mind. The story, from *Hustler*, is called 'Dirty Pool'.

Example (2).   A waitress is pinched by a male pool player, while his companions look on with approval. The captions to the series of sexually graphic pictures read:

Though she pretends to ignore them, these men know when they see an easy lay. She is thrown on the felt table, and one manly hand after another probes her private areas. Completely vulnerable, she feels one after another enter her fiercely. As the three violators explode in a shower of climaxes, she comes to a shuddering orgasm.[20]

The story is an example of what is sometimes described in the social science literature as a 'favourable' rape depiction.[21] It is not explicitly said in the story that the female waitress says 'no' when she really means 'yes'; that, despite her protestations to the contrary, she wanted to be raped and dominated all along; that she was there as an object for the men's sexual gratification; that raping a woman is sexy and erotic for man and woman alike. Nevertheless the conversation—if we can call it that—follows certain patterns of accommodation which render acceptable

---

[19]   See definition in footnote 1.

[20]   The story is described by Catherine Itzin, drawing on work done by Jeanne Barkey and J. Koplin. See Itzin, ed., *Pornography: Women, Violence, and Civil Liberties* (Oxford: Oxford University Press, 1992). The story appeared in *Hustler*, January 1983 issue, about two months before the New Bedford pool hall rape took place (later dramatized in the film *The Accused*, starring Jodie Foster). Itzin's work also offers detailed descriptions of the kinds of pornography widely available in the United States and the United Kingdom, of which this story is in many ways typical; see especially 27–53.

[21]   Sometimes also described as a 'positive' depiction, see e.g. Edward Donnerstein, Daniel Linz, and Steven Penrod, *The Question of Pornography: Research Findings and Policy Implications* (New York, N.Y.: Free Press, 1987), especially chs. 5 and 6. An 'unfavourable' or 'negative' depiction would be one in which the woman's later enjoyment was absent.

these things that are not explicitly said. These presuppositions are required in order to make sense of what is explicitly said and illustrated—or at any rate they are required for one way, perhaps the most natural and obvious way, of making sense of it. One needs presuppositions like these to make sense of the way in which the initially reluctant young waitress gives in to immediate ecstasy upon being gang-raped. Poor sense could be made of the story if one were to add to it the negations of these presuppositions: if one were to add to the final sentence the conjunct 'and when she said no, she meant no; she never harboured a secret desire to be raped; when she ignored the men, she meant it; she did not want to have sex with them; she was physically hurt, terrorized, and psychologically traumatized as a consequence of what her violators did to her.'

In short, the story presupposes certain rape myths, just as surely as the comment about Jane presupposes her relative incompetence.[22] Although the story does not explicitly assert the propositions 'Gang rape is enjoyable for men', or 'Gang rape is enjoyable for women' or 'Sexual violence is legitimate', such messages are arguably presupposed by it. Our first conclusion, then, is that pornography can say such things, even if it does not explicitly say them.

3. Saying, Subordinating, and Silencing

What, if any, are the implications here for understanding the claims that pornography subordinates and silences women? Although the components of conversational score very often obey rules of accommodation, this is, as Lewis notes, only a tendency. And while Lewis's chief interest is in the *success* of accommodation, the occasional *failure* of accommodation is an equally interesting and relevant subject. Lewis is alert to the way rules of accommodation are sensitive to properties of the speakers, including such properties as relative power and authority. To take up one of his examples, the boundaries of the permissible and the impermissible instantly vary, not with what the slave says, but with what the master says. The authority of the speaker makes a great difference to the way in which this rule of

---

[22] In many pornographic conversations, such presuppositions will presumably be reinforced rather than introduced for the first time, but for purposes of simplicity we ignore this distinction.

accommodation operates. This bears on the two issues of subordination and of silence.

First, some implications for the question of subordination. The master's ability to subordinate the slave, using words, depends on his authority. What he says with his words is a certain kind of doing, only given his authority. If the arrangement changes, and the master loses his authority, the boundary of what is permissible and impermissible will *not* shift to match what he says. The same applies to pornography. Whether pornography introduces presuppositions that are also, for example, permissions, depends on its authority. To say 'Sexual violence is legitimate' (whether implicitly or explicitly) is not *on its own* to be an illocutionary move of permitting or legitimating sexual violence, and thus of subordinating women. For the saying to be that kind of doing takes authority. Recall MacKinnon's remarks: it is the *authoritative* saying that is the doing. Her argument rests on the premise that pornographic speech does have the authority to do this.[23]

Next, some implications for the question of silence. The slave's inability to make certain moves in the language game can be viewed as a kind of silence: his powerlessness is partly constituted by his inability to make certain moves. There are many moves that the master can make which the slave cannot. The master can say to the slave 'Cook dinner' or 'Your curfew is 6 p.m.' and these utterances count as acceptable moves—moves of ordering and permitting—in the game. The score of the master–slave language game moves to accommodate the master's utterances to make them count as correct. The slave, on the other hand, cannot say to the master 'Cook dinner' or 'Your curfew is 6 p.m.'. Of course, the slave can say these words, but his utterance will fail to count as an acceptable move in the master–slave language game. The rules of accommodation will not operate to adjust the score to make these utterances count as correct play, as

---

[23] Authority comes in different kinds and degrees, so that pornography may be authoritative in some contexts and not others. And acquiring the relevant authority for moves of permitting may sometimes be a relatively easy matter: we suggested earlier that 'Even Jane could pass' both presupposes her relative incompetence, and renders more *permissible* further slurs against Jane, without supposing that the speaker had quite the kind of authority the master has over the slave. See Mary Kate McGowan for subtle application of Lewis-style pragmatics to the question of permissibility facts and pornography, in ways that don't require strong Austinian assumptions about authority: 'Conversational Exercitives and the Force of Pornography', *Philosophy and Public Affairs* 31 (2003), 155–89; 'Conversational Exercitives: Something Else We Do With Our Words', *Linguistics and Philosophy* 27 (2004), 93–111.

moves of ordering and permitting. We have here one way of understanding what it is to be silenced—not to be prevented from uttering words (the slave could do that), but to be prevented from making certain intended moves in a language game.

Something similar applies to pornography, and in particular to the claim that pornography silences women. We have suggested that pornography introduces certain presuppositions about women, that these presuppositions figure as a component of score in language games, and obey rules of accommodation. And we have seen that in general the moves one can make in a language game can depend upon one's position of relative power in that language game. Suppose that women are often comparatively powerless in sexual language games, and pornographers and men are often comparatively powerful. Suppose that men and women are participants in language games in which moves are highly sensitive to the relative power and authority of speakers. Our suggestion is that, just as the master's speech affects the score of the game in the master-slave language game, so pornography affects the score of the sexual language game—a score which women cannot or do not adequately challenge. Perhaps the failure to challenge is due (in part) to the absence of women as speakers from the initial pornographic conversations—for although women appear in pornography, their speech is entirely scripted. Perhaps it is due (in part) to the comparative powerlessless of women, which undermines their attempts to alter the conversational score. Perhaps it is due (in part) to the nature of presupposition itself, which—as we remarked earlier—is inherently more difficult to challenge than outright assertion. Whatever the reason, pornography affects the presuppositional score of the sexual language game. The men who take part in pornographic conversations then take part in ordinary conversations with real women. Our suggestion is that the presuppositions introduced by the pornographic conversations persist in the conversations with real women. The result is that just as there are some illocutionary moves in the master-slave language game that the slave cannot make, so there are some illocutionary moves that a woman—in some contexts—cannot make. Certainly, like the slave, she can in one sense speak. She can utter or pen a string of words. She may, for example, say 'no' in a sexual context, and her intended move of refusal may fail to count as correct play. She may utter words when testifying in court about a rape, and her intended move of describing a rape may fail to count as correct play. She may utter words of protest, but her intended move may fail to count as correct play.

An example of the latter is provided by the case of Linda Marchiano (Lovelace), who wrote a book, *Ordeal*, intended as an indictment of the pornography industry. In it she tells the story of how she was abducted, beaten, tortured, and hypnotized in order to perform her starring role in the successful pornographic film *Deep Throat*. Now although *Ordeal* was meant to be a protest against the pornography industry, it has in fact been marketed *as pornography*.[24] This case appears to be one example in a familiar pattern to be found in the language games of many, including the sex offenders who twist women's words—who 'always reinterpret the behaviour of their victims [and] will say the victim encouraged them, or seduced them, or asked for it, or wanted it, or enjoyed it'.[25]

Women often find themselves unable to alter the score of language games in the ways that they intend—and find themselves altering the score in ways they did not intend—in both public and private sexual conversations, conversations whose score includes the presupposition, introduced and reinforced by pornography, that a woman's no often means yes. A woman's testimony in court about sexual violence and sexual harassment often goes awry. Judges and juries sometimes acquit men of sexually-related charges on the grounds that the victim was wearing a short skirt and so 'asking for it', or—in cases where the alleged offence was photographed or filmed—that she looked like she was enjoying it, or that, despite her words, she couldn't really have been refusing.[26] In the private contexts of date rape, a woman's 'no' sometimes fails to count as correct play—fails to count as the refusal it was intended to be. We have, it seems, a straightforward way to understand MacKinnon's idea that women are silenced by pornography.

---

[24] Linda Lovelace, with Mike McGrady, *Ordeal* (Secaucus, N.J.: Citadel Press, 1980). One of the authors received in her junk mail a catalogue of pornographic material in which *Ordeal* was marketed as pornography. This example, and those of testimony and sexual refusal, are discussed in Langton's 'Speech Acts and Unspeakable Acts' as examples of illocutionary disablement.

[25] Ray Wyre, 'Pornography and Sexual Violence: Working with Sex Offenders', in *Pornography: Women, Violence and Civil Liberties*, 236. See also Edna F. Einsiedel, 'Social and Behavioural Science Research Analysis', *Report of the Attorney General's Commission on Pornography*, vol. i (Washington, D.C.: United States Government Printing Office, 1986), 901–1033.

[26] MacKinnon describes many such examples throughout *Feminism Unmodified* and *Only Words*, particularly in 'Francis Biddle's Sister: Pornography, Civil Rights and Speech', in *Feminism Unmodified*, 163–97.

4. Fictional Saying

We concluded that pornography may well say what it does not explicitly say: that the 'messages' identified by Catharine MacKinnon and Ronald Dworkin may well be present as presuppositions of pornographic conversations between author and reader, introduced in roughly the rule-governed way that presuppositions are introduced in other conversational situations. The fact that pornography does not explicitly say these things is not a good reason for doubting that it says them. We also suggested that given a certain degree of authority, such presuppositions could indeed have the illocutionary dimension MacKinnon attributes to them: that they could be acts of permission, legitimation, subordination, and silencing.

However, we have so far entirely ignored the second, and independent, reason for doubting that pornography says the things MacKinnon claims that it says. It is time to remedy that. Pornography usually purports to be fantasy, or *fiction*. This fact does not undermine the preceding discussion, but it does introduce different grounds for skepticism. It does not undermine the preceding discussion, since rules of accommodation apply just as much to the speech acts of story-telling as they do to everyday conversations. Fiction too has its merely implicit content, introduced by the right sorts of authorial moves in the story-telling language game. The distinction between implicit and explicit propositions introduced by such moves applies as much to fiction as it does to everyday conversations. (It is true in the Sherlock Holmes stories, but not explicitly said, that Holmes lives closer to Paddington Station than to Waterloo, does not have a third nostril, etc.)[27] But there are different grounds for skepticism: for to number the *implicit* sayings of pornography among the things that pornography says will do MacKinnon's case no good, if they are *implicit* and *merely fictional* sayings. Even supposing the presuppositions of pornography to include such propositions as 'Sexual violence is legitimate' or 'Women enjoy rape',

---

[27] These examples are from Lewis's discussion in 'Truth in Fiction', *Philosophical Papers*, vol. i, 261–80, first published in *American Philosophical Quarterly* 15 (1978), 37–46. Our mention of 'the right sorts of authorial moves' is more hand-waving than we would like, but this is a large and complex topic beyond the scope of our project here. Sometimes, for example, the 'right' move for introducing implicit content in a fiction will really be an *absence* of a relevant countervailing move: as when the implicit content of a fiction includes the presupposition that the laws of nature operating in the fictional world are the same as the laws operating in our own.

if they occur within the scope of a fiction operator, pornography—it seems—does not actually *say* such things.

People do alter their beliefs and values as a result of exposure to (fictional) pornography, and in particular are more likely to believe rape myths; that is an empirical assumption of our discussion, and (we believe) fairly well supported by what evidence there is.[28] What we are considering then is whether and how people come to believe such things because pornography *says* them.

The question we face here is part of the more general question of how it is that one can learn from fiction. Many discussions of this topic treat it as the question of how one can gain *knowledge*—factual or moral—from fiction. Here we are concerned with ignorance rather knowledge, but the same principles apply. If we can gain true beliefs from fiction, we can also gain false beliefs from fiction. The simplest case will be where the fiction purports to be fact: where *all* of its propositions, implicit and explicit, purport to be true, and are taken to be true, of the actual world.

The idea can be illustrated by the contrasting stories of Wells and Welles. Readers of H. G. Wells's *The War of the Worlds* were left in no doubt that they were encountering fiction, because Wells made the authorial moves appropriate to fiction—whatever they may be. Listeners to Orson Welles's infamous 'news broadcast' of *The War of the Worlds* on radio thought they were encountering fact, because Welles did not make—or did not *adequately* make—the moves appropriate to fiction, and mayhem ensued.[29] Listeners believed that our world, and not some merely fictional world, was at war with the Martians. The story by Wells purported to be fiction; the story by Welles purported to be fact—or that, at any rate, is one way of interpreting events. This sort of thing happens rarely with ordinary fiction, but perhaps it happens more frequently with pornography. Autobiographical letters to pornographic magazines and internet chat groups, describing the elaborate

---

[28] See for example Donnerstein, Linz and Penrod, eds., *The Question of Pornography: Research Findings and Policy Implications* (New York: Free Press; London: Collier Macmillan, 1987): viewers of pornography appear to become more likely to view women as inferior, more disposed to accept rape myths (including the idea that women enjoy rape), more likely to see rape victims as deserving of their treatment, and more likely to say that they themselves would rape if they could get away with it.

[29] 'The War of the Worlds', directed by Orson Welles, Mercury Theatre of the Air, broadcast on CBS, 30 October 1938, an adaptation of H. G. Wells' novel, *The War of the Worlds* (1898) (London; NY: Penguin, 2005); Howard Koch, *The Panic Broadcast: Portrait of an Event* (Boston, Mass.: Little, Brown and Co., 1970).

sexual fantasies of their authors, often purport *not to be fiction*. In such cases the authors are what we can call for short (and oversimplifying) *liars*. In such cases there is nothing very surprising about people acquiring beliefs about the real world from pornographic fiction—false beliefs, since the purported fact is merely fantasy. However, much pornography both is *and* purports to be fiction, and some explanation is needed as to how anyone could learn from it.

Greg Currie, drawing on work by Lewis, observes that

there is truth—literal truth—in fiction, since most fictional stories play out against a background of fact. We can learn from that background of fact, as the reader of Patrick O'Brien will learn a good deal about Nelson's navy, and the reader of Hilary Mantel's *A Place of Greater Safety* will learn about revolutionary France.[30]

It is helpful to have our attention drawn to this class of *background* propositions, propositions which (whether implicit or explicit) are true in the fiction, and true in the world as well. However, it would be more accurate to say that most fictional stories play out against a background, not of fact, but of *purported fact*. It would be more accurate to say of members of this background class of propositions that they *purport* to be true in the fiction, and true in the world as well.[31]

If the authors mentioned are ill-informed, indifferent, or outright deceivers—for short (and over-simplifying), if the authors are *background liars*—then some propositions belonging to the background class may well be false. The reader, picking up on authorial moves signifying background propositions, may then learn falsehoods about (for example) revolutionary France. This gives us one straightforward way of seeing how it is that one could acquire false beliefs from fiction. Where the background propositions in a fiction are partly false, a reader expecting authorial reliability on background propositions may acquire false beliefs. It may be that if

---

[30] Gregory Currie, 'The Moral Psychology of Fiction', *Australasian Journal of Philosophy* 73 (1995), 250–9. The quotation is on p. 250. Currie himself is less interested in this factual learning than the moral learning he goes on to argue for. Currie's analysis, with its focus on the roles of simulation and the imagination, may well be relevant in ways we do not discuss here to the question of how one could learn from pornography, and the same may be true of some ideas in Kendall Walton's *Mimesis as Make-Believe* (Cambridge, Mass.: Harvard University Press, 1990).

[31] Lewis himself, in describing these background propositions, moves from an analysis which says they are true in the actual world, to an analysis which says they are true in what he calls the *collective belief worlds* of their community of origin: 'The proper background . . . consists of the beliefs that generally prevailed in the community where the fiction originated'. See 'Truth in Fiction', 272–3.

pornography says (implicitly) that 'Women enjoy rape' or 'Sexual violence is legitimate', such propositions have a background status: that is to say, they purport to be true not only in the fiction, but in the world as well. They are to the pornographic fiction as propositions about revolutionary France are to Mantel's novel, purported facts in both cases, but in the case of pornography *merely* purported facts.

On this suggestion the authors of pornography are background liars: pornography presents the reader with a combination, purely fictional propositions (e.g. about a particular waitress), and background propositions (e.g. about what women enjoy) that purport to be true in the fiction *and* true in the world. The propositions which concern MacKinnon belong to the latter class, and the authors of pornography, in presenting readers with false background propositions, are ill-informed, deceptive, or indifferent to the accuracy of the background they present. We don't dismiss this possibility, especially in circumstances where interests of profit may conflict with interests of truth, sincerity, accuracy, and the like.

However, there is another possibility which views the authors of pornography more charitably, should one choose to do so. Rather than being background liars, the authors of pornography may be *background blurrers*. It may be that such propositions as 'Women enjoy rape' or 'Sexual violence is legitimate' are presented as having the status of mere fiction, not purported factual background—but that the authorial moves which enable readers to distinguish background from mere fiction are inadequate. Such blurring, which may or may not be intentional, will have to do with both author and reader. One can expect it to be more likely in circumstances where authors are indifferent to a clear boundary between fiction and background, and where readers are likewise indifferent. The authorial moves which distinguish background from pure fiction are a complex matter, but they rely in part on what readers already know or believe.

When the line between the background and the fictional is blurred, two different kinds of mistake are possible: a reader may mistake background for mere fiction, or mere fiction for background. In the former case a reader would fail to learn what could be learned; in the latter he would learn what should not be learned. A reader of Mantel's novel who is ignorant of the French Revolution—ignorant even of its historical existence—might mistake background for mere fiction, and fail to learn what could have been learned about the French Revolution. Conversely a reader who believes the novel is partly about the French Revolution, but who is unable to tell the background from the fictional propositions, may mistake fiction for background and learn things about the French Revolution which should not have been learned. The latter mistake may happen with pornography. A reader ignorant of women and their desires may be unable clearly to tell background from fictional propositions in pornography, and as a result mistake fiction for background, and learn what should not be learned. Background blurring provides an alternative mechanism for bringing it about that rape myths purporting to be mere fiction are taken to be true of the world as well.

We conclude that pornography may well say that 'Women enjoy rape' and that 'Sexual violence is legitimate', even if it does not explicitly say these things, *and* even if it purports to be fiction. The fictional character of pornography is not a good reason for doubting that pornography says these things.

5. Concluding Remarks

As we observed at the outset, this conclusion about what pornography says appears to be shared by parties on both sides of the pornography debate, both in Ronald Dworkin's concessions about the 'message' of pornography, and in Catharine MacKinnon's claims about what pornography says and does. Our concern here has been to gain a better understanding of how pornography might *say* such things. In exploring this question we have drawn upon the idea that if pornography is speech, it works in ways that have something in common with the ways speech works in other circumstances. But as we indicated at the outset, our exploration brings us closer to Catharine MacKinnon's conclusion about pornography than to that of Ronald Dworkin. If pornography does say these things—and if, in addition, it says them authoritatively—then the score of sexual language games may be changed in ways that make plausible MacKinnon's claims that pornography subordinates and silences women. This is not speech that 'seeks to deliver' a 'message' in the manner of political speech, as Dworkin suggested; it does not—or not merely—express the 'opinion' that 'women are submissive, or enjoy being dominated, or should be treated as if they did'; it is not comparable to speech 'advocating that women occupy inferior roles'. Pornography, on the present suggestion, works in surreptitious ways by altering presuppositions, not by offering explicit political argument. It is speech that says things and—given its authority—does things. Women's utterances are made to count as the kind of move that is consistent with presuppositions about women, presuppositions established by pornography as a component of an on-going conversational score. In sexual conversations pervaded by such presuppositions, pornography prevents women from making the moves they intend to make. Pornography makes moves which subordinate and silence women, moves which women, as subordinate and silent, cannot then adequately challenge.

Our suggestion as to how pornography can change conversational score in life, notwithstanding its often merely implicit content, and notwithstanding its status as fiction, might seem over-simple. Pornographers, we have suggested, are liars, or background liars, or background blurrers. Presuppositions are introduced by pornography, authors innocently or otherwise fail adequately to indicate the line between fiction and background, readers innocently or otherwise take fiction for background, and accordingly come to believe certain rape myths. Women, as participants in conversations where rape myths are presupposed as a component of conversational score, are silenced and subordinated. The process, thus described, makes pornography seem continuous enough with other speech. That was our aim: for we were exploring a middle ground between the rationalism of Ronald Dworkin, for whom pornography is political argument, and the reductivism of the social scientists, for whom pornography is little more than a Pavlovian bell.

However, some readers might find that our approach places pornography towards an excessively rationalistic end of Scoccia's speech spectrum. Some might think we have not done justice to the more deeply irrational ways in which pornography changes people. We have, after all, said nothing about the important question of whether and how pornography changes *desires*, whether it produces violent desires, and what the relation between desire-change and belief-change might be. This question about desires is one to which the reductivist account—the account suggested by Scoccia, and by MacKinnon in a different mood—gives a very direct answer. Pornography changes desires through a process of conditioning. The question is well worth pursuing, but let it suffice for now to say this. If pornography does belong to a more deeply irrational end of the speech spectrum—if something closer to the reductivist vision is true—then MacKinnon's conclusion will receive even more support than we have given it. If we are wrong, then far from being political argument, as Dworkin suggested, pornography can barely be understood in ways that view it as continuous with conversational language games. Perhaps pornography has more in common with the Pavlovian bells than we expected. Or perhaps pornography is not *even* speech, in which case it is hard to see how a principle of free speech should protect it—especially if, as we have suggested, it is the free speech of women which is at stake.

9

Duty and Desolation

This is an essay about two philosophers who wrote to each other. One is famous; the other is not. It is about two practical standpoints, the strategic and the human, and what the famous philosopher said of them. And it is about friendship and deception, duty and despair. That is enough by way of preamble.[1]

1. Strategy and Friendship

In 1791 Kant received a letter from an Austrian lady whom he had never met. She was Maria von Herbert, a keen and able student of Kant's philosophy, and sister to Baron Franz Paul von Herbert, another zealous Kantian disciple. The zeal of her brother the Baron was indeed so great that he had left his lead factory, and his wife, for two years in order to study Kant's philosophy in Weimar and Jena. Upon his return, the von Herbert household had become a centre, a kind of *salon*, where the critical philosophy was intensely debated, against the backdrop of vehement opposition to Kant in Austria as in many German states. The household was, in the words of a student of Fichte's, 'a new Athens', an oasis of Enlightenment spirit, devoted to preaching and propagating the Kantian gospel, reforming religion, and replacing dull unthinking piety with a morality based on reason.[2] Here is the letter:

---

[1] This essay was first published in *Philosophy* 67 (1992), 481–505.
[2] According to Arnulf Zweig in his introduction to *Kant: Philosophical Correspondence, 1759–99* (Chicago: University of Chicago Press, 1967), 24.

1. To Kant, From Maria von Herbert, August 1791

Great Kant,

As a believer calls to his God, I call to you for help, for comfort, or for counsel to prepare me for death. Your writings prove that there is a future life. But as for this life, I have found nothing, nothing at all that could replace the good I have lost, for I loved someone who, in my eyes, encompassed within himself all that is worthwhile, so that I lived only for him, everything else was in comparison just rubbish, cheap trinkets. Well, I have offended this person, because of a long drawn out lie, which I have now disclosed to him, though there was nothing unfavourable to my character in it, I had no vice in my life that needed hiding. The lie was enough though, and his love vanished. As an honourable man, he doesn't refuse me friendship. But that inner feeling that once, unbidden, led us to each other, is no more—oh my heart splinters into a thousand pieces! If I hadn't read so much of your work I would certainly have put an end to my life. But the conclusion I had to draw from your theory stops me—it is wrong for me to die because my life is tormented, instead I'm supposed to live because of my being. Now put yourself in my place, and either damn me or comfort me. I've read the metaphysic of morals, and the categorical imperative, and it doesn't help a bit. My reason abandons me just when I need it. Answer me, I implore you—or you won't be acting in accordance with your own imperative.

My address is Maria Herbert of Klagenfurt, Carinthia, care of the white lead factory, or perhaps you would rather send it via Reinhold because the mail is more reliable there.

Kant, much impressed by this letter, sought advice from a friend as to what he should do. The friend advised him strongly to reply, and to do his best to distract his correspondent from 'the object to which she [was] enfettered'.[3] We have the carefully prepared draft of Kant's response:

---

[3] Letter to Kant from Ludwig Ernst Borowski, probably August 1791. The correspondence between Kant and Maria von Herbert, and the related letters, are in Volume XI of the Prussian Academy of Sciences edition of Kant's works (Walter de Gruyter, 1922). The English translations given in this paper are closely based on those of Arnulf Zweig, partly revised in the light of the Academy edition, and very much abridged. See Arnulf Zweig, *Kant: Philosophical Correspondence, 1759–99*. Readers who would like to see fuller versions of the letters than those given here should consult the Academy edition, or the Zweig translations now revised and published in Zweig, trans. and ed., *Immanuel Kant: Correspondence* (Cambridge: Cambridge University Press, 1999).

2. To Maria von Herbert, Spring 1792 (Kant's rough draft)

Your deeply felt letter comes from a heart that must have been created for the sake of virtue and honesty, since it is so receptive to instruction in those qualities. I must do as you ask, namely, put myself in your place, and prescribe for you a pure moral sedative. I do not know whether your relationship is one of marriage or friendship, but it makes no significant difference. For love, be it for one's spouse or for a friend, presupposes the same mutual esteem for the other's character, without which it is no more than perishable, sensual delusion.

A love like that wants to communicate itself completely, and it expects of its respondent a similar sharing of heart, unweakened by distrustful reticence. That is what the ideal of friendship demands. But there is something in us which puts limits on such frankness, some obstacle to this mutual outpouring of the heart which makes one keep some part of one's thoughts locked within oneself, even when one is most intimate. The sages of old complained of this secret distrust—'My dear friends, there is no such thing as a friend!'

We can't expect frankness of people, since everyone fears that to reveal himself completely would be to make himself despised by others. But this lack of frankness, this reticence, is still very different from dishonesty. What the honest but reticent man says is true, but not the whole truth. What the dishonest man says is something he knows to be false. Such an assertion is called, in the theory of virtue, a *lie*. It may be harmless, but it is not on that account innocent. It is a serious violation of a duty to oneself; it subverts the dignity of humanity in our own person, and attacks the roots of our thinking. As you see, you have sought counsel from a physician who is no flatterer. I speak for your beloved and present him with arguments that justify his having wavered in his affection for you.

Ask yourself whether you reproach yourself for the imprudence of confessing, or for the immorality intrinsic to the lie. If the former, then you regret having done your duty. And why? Because it has resulted in the loss of your friend's confidence. This regret is not motivated by anything moral, since it is produced by an awareness not of the act itself, but of its consequences. But if your reproach is grounded in a moral judgment of your behaviour, it would be a poor moral physician who would advise you to cast it from your mind.

When your change in attitude has been revealed to your beloved, only time will be needed to quench, little by little, the traces of his justified indignation, and to transform his coldness into a more firmly grounded love. If this doesn't happen, then the earlier warmth of his affection was more physical than moral, and would have disappeared anyway—a misfortune which we often encounter in life, and when we do, must meet with composure. For the value of life, in so far as it consists of the enjoyment we get from people, is vastly overrated.

Here then, my dear friend, you find the customary divisions of a sermon: instruction, penalty and comfort. Devote yourself to the first two; when they have had their effect, comfort will be found by itself.

Kant's letter has an enormously interesting and sensitive discussion of friendship and secrecy, much of which turns up word for word in *The Doctrine of Virtue*, published some six years later.[4] But what Kant's letter fails to say is as at least as interesting as what it says. Herbert writes that she has lost her love, that her heart is shattered, that there is nothing left to make life worth living, and that Kant's moral philosophy hasn't helped a bit. Kant's reply is to suggest that the love is deservedly lost, that misery is an appropriate response to one's own moral failure, and that the really interesting moral question here is the one that hinges on a subtle but necessary scope distinction: the distinction between telling a lie and failing to tell the truth, between *saying 'not-p'*, and *not saying 'p'*. Conspicuously absent is an acknowledgement of Herbert's more than theoretical interest in the question: is suicide compatible with the moral law? And perhaps this is just as well from a practical point of view. The sooner she gives up those morbid thoughts the better; the less said on the morbid subject, the less likely the morbid thoughts will arise. Perhaps it is also just as well, for Kant, from a theoretical point of view. Kant's conviction that suicide is incompatible with the moral law is not nearly as well founded as he liked to think; so here too, the less said, the better. What I want to talk about though is not the ineptitude[5] of an elderly bachelor in relieving a young woman's grief (for Kant is 67 by now, and Herbert 22), nor the ineptitude of an academic philosopher in addressing the realities of moral life. Instead, I want to follow Kant's lead for the moment, and think about friendship and deceit, in Kant's terms. What's good about friendship? And what's bad

---

[4] Immanuel Kant, *The Doctrine of Virtue*, Part II of *The Metaphysic of Morals*, trans. Mary Gregor (New York: Harper and Row, 1964). One wonders whether these parts of *The Doctrine of Virtue* may have been influenced by Kant's thoughts about Herbert's predicament. An alternative explanation might be that *The Doctrine of Virtue* and Kant's letter to Herbert are both drawing on Kant's lecture notes.

[5] Justin Oakley has commented on what he calls the 'moral ineptitude' of people who act from the motive of duty alone: an ineptitude that prevents them from achieving the very goal duty aims at, for example, that of comforting a friend. See 'A Critique of Kantian Arguments against Emotions as Moral Motives', *History of Philosophy Quarterly* 7 (1990), 441–59.

about deceit? The answers to these questions are connected. I'll begin with the latter.

Kant thinks it is always wrong to lie. Lying has a special place in his taxonomy of vices, meriting a special denunciation all of its own in an essay 'On a supposed right to tell lies from benevolent motives'.[6] When the murderer is at your door, and your friend hidden in your house, you must reply truthfully to the murderer: yes, my friend is here. The moral law commands categorically. The ifs and buts from anxious consequentialists—and anxious friends—must fall on deaf ears. Some have seen in this stringency a *reductio ad absurdum* of rationalist ethics, a blind and hideous attachment to principle that flies in the face of all moral decency. Others—notably Christine Korsgaard—have looked further and discovered, even in this apparently harsh aspect of the Kantian system, 'an attractive ideal of human relations',[7] an ideal that she finds to underpin Kant's views on both lies and friendship.[8] Now I must say from the outset that the Kant she finds is a warm and kind Kant, a Kant who thinks well of spontaneous natural sentiments, and thinks we should cultivate them, a Kant who shares much common ground with Aristotle. I will call him the *sane* Kant (for I need a technical term). Notoriously, there is another Kant to be found who thinks just the opposite, whom I shall call the *severe*, and we shall be encountering him too. My own opinion is that the sane Kant is partly a reconstruction, but a reconstruction well worth performing.

The 'attractive ideal of human relations' comes along with a more general picture of the world and the place of human beings in it, a picture that is as familiar as it is problematic. I shall not be addressing its problems. As human beings we find ourselves in a natural world that consists, first, of things, rocks and reindeer, corn and cotton, moulds and mistletoe. And we try as best we can to understand just how the world ticks; why corn grows when watered and not otherwise; why a rhinoceros is never born from a reindeer; why the big planetary rocks attract each other with a force that obeys an

---

[6] First published in 1797; an English translation is included as an addendum to L. W. Beck's translation of *The Critique of Practical Reason* (Chicago: University of Chicago Press, 1949).

[7] As she says on page 327 of 'The Right to Lie: Kant on Dealing with Evil', *Philosophy and Public Affairs* 15 (1986), 325–49.

[8] Korsgaard's views on Kant and lying are developed in 'The Right to Lie'. Her views on Kant and friendship are developed in 'Creating the Kingdom of Ends: Responsibility and Reciprocity in Personal Relations', in *Philosophical Perspectives 6: Ethics*, James Tomberlin, ed. (Atascadero, Calif.: The Ridgeview Publishing Company, 1992), 305–32. As will become evident, I owe a very great debt to Korsgaard's approach in both papers.

inverse square law. Science is good at finding out about things, and it goes about it by discovering more and more causal patterns in nature. Given the drought, given the dependence of living tissues on water, the corn had to wither. Given the facts about gene and species, the reindeer can only give birth to a reindeer. But we do more than try to understand how things tick. We use them. We do things with them. We build houses out of some of the smaller rocks. We smelt other rocks, to make hammers and needles. We eat the seeds of the corn plants. We make medicine out of some of the moulds, and inject it into our bodies to make us healthy. Things in the world are, on this picture, a resource, to be used as means for human ends. And this only works because we understand, at least partly, the causal laws in which the things feature. Broadly speaking, science makes technology possible. We predict that the corn will yield seeds for us to eat, if we give it water. We predict that our house will keep us safe, because we know how rocks behave. Furthermore, things we use have a certain worth that is captured in their price. Some rocks are better than others at serving human ends, and their price is higher. Industrial diamonds are priced higher than gravel. When something has a price, it can be exchanged for something else having the same price. When something is a tool, it can be exchanged for something else that will do the job just as well. Things, says Kant, are essentially replaceable.[9] Whether Kant's is the right stance to take towards the natural world—the world of things—is a question I'll leave aside.

Besides things, there are people. And in our dealings with people, we have a different way of going on, though it is hard to capture just what that is. I doubt that I could do better than Strawson, in *Freedom and Resentment*.[10] Strawson points out that in our dealings with people, we attribute responsibility to others in a way that manifests itself in a range of attitudes. We feel resentful when somebody hurts us on purpose. We do not (usually) feel resentful towards the rock that stubs our toe. We feel grateful when somebody helps us on purpose, out of good will, not as an accidental spin-off of something else he wanted to do. We do not (usually) feel grateful towards the sunshine that lifts our grey moods. We expect resentment for the hurt we cause, and try to excuse ourselves when we do not think we are responsible for the hurt. We don't simply observe people

[9] Kant is wrong about this. We often value particular items in such a way that they *aren't* replaceable by a duplicate: it is this very teacup that I value, this very house, this very painting.

[10] 'Freedom and Resentment', in *Freedom and Resentment* (London: Methuen, 1974), 1–25.

as we might observe planets, we don't simply treat them as things to be sought out when they can be of use to us, and avoided when they are a nuisance. We are, as Strawson says, involved.[11]

This standpoint is manifested in more than our attitudes, as Korsgaard is keen to point out.[12] It shows up in the way we act when we communicate and co-operate with others. When you hold someone responsible, you are prepared to work with them, view them as someone who has goals of their own that you might come to share, or as someone who might come to share your goals. You are prepared to *do something with them,* in a sense very different from the sense in which you might do something with a tool. When my friend and I make a cake, I'm *doing something with* my friend, and I'm *doing something with* flour, chocolate, cherries, brandy—but there is a difference. My friend, but not the flour, is doing something with me. My friend, and not the flour, is doing what I am doing, sharing the activity. As a human being, she can choose ends of her own, and can choose to make them coincide with mine. The standpoint we take towards human beings is interactive, and it is different from the standpoint we take with things. Kant thinks this is because human beings have an intrinsic worth that has its basis in our capacity for rational choice. Human beings are ends in themselves, who have a dignity, and not a price.[13] The moral law is the requirement to recognize and respect this dignity, and to act in a way consistent with it.

Of course, we don't adopt the moral standpoint—the interactive standpoint—towards everybody, all of the time. Suppose my neighbour forms a habit of vandalizing my car when it is parked outside his house. He emerges stealthily, at dead of night, and gently twists the wipers into intricate and elegant knots. The next day I stride to his door and knock, brimming with indignation, planning to ask him to be reasonable, hoping to reach mutual understanding. But if he responds with bulging eyes and a torrent of incoherent invective, and I see that he is a badly shell shocked war veteran, indignation instantly vanishes, to be replaced by pure alarm. I stop thinking of him as an agent, whose reasons, mysterious as they might be, I can in principle come to understand. My neighbour becomes a problem to be managed, an obstacle to be avoided, not a person to be argued with.

---

[11] Ibid., 9.   [12] op. cit., note 8.

[13] *Groundwork of the Metaphysics of Morals*, Paton (trans.) (New York: Harper and Row, 1964), 435.

He becomes just one more of the hazards of Elwood, along with the threat of the flooding canal. I have switched from the participant standpoint to what Strawson calls the *objective*. This is the attitude we have to things, items in the natural order, whose behaviour is explicable under causal laws, and manipulated if you know enough about them. To adopt it is to see a person as, perhaps, 'an object of social policy; as a subject for what, in a wide range of sense, might be called treatment; [someone] to be managed or handled or cured or trained.'[14]

Nor do we confine the objective attitude to these special cases where it seems to be forced upon us, where the person in question seems to be deranged or compulsive. The attitude is there for everyday use, if we want it. And typically we will often move from the objective to the interactive and back. Strawson says that although the two attitudes are deeply opposed to each other, they don't exclude each other. We *can* step back, and observe people as we observe the planets. We can observe a friend's rising anger as if it were the rising of the canal waters—something to be feared and avoided, not to be understood and respected. We can cast an objective eye on our students, our friends, our lovers, and no doubt we often do, when the interactive stance proves too exhausting. Kant would say that when we do this, we fail to treat people as human, as agents in the kingdom of ends, as ends in themselves.

Kant seems to think that this coincides with treating people as a *means to one's own ends*. But these don't, I think, have to coincide. My failure to treat my mad neighbour as an end—as a human being with reasons of his own to be respected—does not have to coincide with my using him as a means to further any goals of my own, partly because I do not at present see what he could be useful for. (False. What a useful philosophical example he's just proved to be.) But perhaps they often do coincide. When we look with the objective eye, and view people in the same way that we view natural phenomena, as items whose behavior is the subject for explanation and prediction, perhaps it does become easier to think of them as things in other respects: items that are there to be used. We can do things with people in just the same sense that we do things with flour and chocolate, when making a cake; or do things with rocks, when building a house. We can think of people as human resources. We can regard people and

---

[14] Strawson, op. cit., 9, note 10.

treat people as tools, things that are there to be used, things that do not control themselves, things whose 'nature is to be directed by something else'.[15] We can have a kind of human technology, otherwise known as management skills. To treat a person *merely* as a means would be to violate the categorical imperative, as captured in the formula of humanity: 'Act so that you treat humanity, whether in your own person or in that of another, always as an end, and never as a means only'.[16] Treating a person as an end, as a being who can form her own ends and act on them, does not entirely rule out treating her as a means. It does not rule out the possibility of human technology. The important thing is not to treat a person *merely* as a means. I treat a person merely as a means when I act towards her in a way that blocks her ability to form her own ends and act on them. I do this when I make it impossible for her to assent to my action towards her, impossible for her to share the goal I have in acting. I treat her as a means when I act in a way that prevents her from choosing whether to contribute to the realization of my end. This is a violation of duty, in Kant's terms.

One way that this can happen is through deception. Kant says in the *Groundwork* that the man who makes a lying promise to repay money he has no intention of repaying is making use of another 'merely as a means to an end he does not share. For the man whom I seek to use for my own purposes by such a promise cannot possibly share the end of the action'. The lender consents to the transaction under the description: 'giving the man temporary use of my money'. The action is in fact: 'giving the man permanent use of my money'. But the borrower's deceit has made it impossible for the lender to choose whether to consent to *that* action.[17] To deceive is thus to make a person thing-like: something that cannot choose what it does. We begin to have an inkling as to how Kant's apparently harsh pronouncements about lying might stem from an 'attractive ideal of human relations': the ideal of treating persons as persons, the ideal of maintaining, as far as possible, the interactive stance. What is distinctive about human beings is that we are authors of our actions, that we can form

---

[15] The phrase is Korsgaard's, op. cit., 335, note 7.

[16] op. cit., 429, note 13. Kant has many formulations of the categorical imperative. I restrict myself in this essay to the formula of humanity, partly because it best captures the 'attractive ideal' Korsgaard and I are hoping to find.

[17] Ibid., 430. This characterization draws heavily on Korsgaard.

ends and share them. What is bad about deception is that it blocks human agency, and in so doing, reduces persons to things.[18]

Think back to my cake-making endeavours. There is a sense in which I might indeed be using my friend as a means: she is an excellent cook, and without her my cake would be a dismal flop. But if she knows I want to exploit her culinary abilities, thinks baking is fun and still wants to do it with me, she shares my end; she is not *merely* a means. But now suppose my secret plan is to use the delectable cake as the *pièce de résistance* of this evening's romantic candle-lit dinner for two—a dinner to which her equally delectable and notoriously sweet toothed boyfriend is to be invited and, with luck, seduced. Now my friend is *merely* a means, merely a cog in the machine of my evil designs, just as surely as are the cherries and chocolate. Now I am *doing something with* my friend in the very same sense that I am *doing something with* cherries and chocolate, flour, and brandy. My deceit makes it impossible for my friend to assent to the action, to share my goal, to share that activity. Consent, outright enthusiasm, is there for our joint action under the description: 'making a delicious cake'; but not, sadly, under the description: 'helping Rae to seduce Otto'. My deceit makes it impossible for her to choose that end as her end.

Notice that I need not lie to my friend in order to deceive her. A dose of reticence will do the trick. Indeed, a dose of reticence will work far better for this plot than any lie. What would the lie be? I nonchalantly remark to my friend as we are busily sieving the cocoa, measuring out the brandy: 'Oh, and by the way Dora, let me assure you that the seduction of Otto is the last thing on my mind.' Hm. The lady doth protest too much, methinks. Far safer to keep quiet. This suggests that Kant's careful distinction between lying and reticence is not something that springs from his fundamental principles. The important question, as far as the formula of humanity is concerned, is whether you manage to deceive.

---

[18] To say this is not yet to address Kant's own characterization of what's wrong with lying in his letter, namely that it is a failure of duty to the self. That is because I think that what he says here is less plausible. He says, in *The Doctrine of Virtue*, that to lie is to violate humanity in one's own person. It is to use one's natural being, one's power of speaking, as a means to an end that is nothing to do with 'the intrinsic end' of speech, which is the communication of thought. In this respect, lying is an unnatural use of one's natural self, like masturbation (op. cit., note 4, 93, 94). Herbert's view, that honesty is something one owes to a friend, owes to others, has far more going for it, and finds independent support in Kant.

The important issue, to put it in terms borrowed from Habermas, is whether your speech acts are *communicative* or *strategic*. What matters is not whether your locutions have the right truth values: what matters is what your speech act is doing with people. Kant notes in *The Doctrine of Virtue*, in a characteristic outburst against lying, that the Bible calls the Devil the author of all evil, and the father of all lies.[19] Kant is right. But if you know your Bible, you know that what the Devil is *really* good at is not lies, but *strategic truth telling*. The Devil tries to achieve his nefarious ends by borrowing God's words. He challenges Jesus, during the Temptation, to cast himself down from the pinnacle of the temple: 'For it is written' he says, 'He shall give his angels charge concerning thee: and in their hands they shall bear thee up, lest at any time thou dash thy foot against a stone' (Matthew 4:6). It is indeed so written (Psalm 91: 11, 12), and if what is written is true, the Devil speaks the truth.

Kant's principles support not a rejection of lying *per se*, but a rejection of strategic speech in general, speech which treats people as things, not persons. This perspective finds added support in Kant's discussion of another vice, again in *The Doctrine of Virtue*. There we find that it can be a duty *not to speak the truth*. Kant is not so famous for this duty. But as we have just seen, to speak truly can be to speak strategically, and Kant says that it can be a duty to remain silent, rather than to tell the truth in a way that undermines the respect due to persons. The truth-telling vice we have a duty to avoid is that of calumny. 'By calumny I mean merely the inclination to bring into the open something prejudicial to respect for others. This is contrary to the respect due to humanity as such. The wilful spreading of something that detracts from another person's honour— ... even if what is said is true—diminishes respect for humanity as such'. We have a duty to 'throw the veil of benevolence over [people's] faults, not merely by softening our judgements but also by keeping these judgements to ourselves.'[20]

Contrary to Kant's letter, there is no principled distinction to be drawn between lies and reticence. The question—in this context—is whether actions were strategic, and whether deception occurred. Whether Herbert said 'not-p' or whether she failed to say 'p' is irrelevant in the face of the categorical imperative, construed in this way. The question is what she got her friend to believe. If he was deceived, and it seems he was, then she

---

[19] Ibid., 430. Kant is alluding to John 8:44.   [20] Ibid., 466.

forced him to perform actions he had no chance to choose. To that extent, she made him thing-like. She prevented him from being the initiator of his own action, and what is distinctive of things as opposed to people is that they do not choose what they do. Herbert failed to treat him as an end, in the Kantian sense: as a being who must be able 'to share the end of the action'.[21]

What actions did the friend choose to perform? Well, we can only speculate here, but let's suppose he chose to perform this action: 'courting a beautiful, intelligent young woman'. And this one: 'courting a beautiful intelligent young virgin'. It seems that that is what he thought he was doing. (The curious may skip to letter 4 for an explanation.)[22] But the action he performed was not the action he chose, if he chose the latter. The courtship he freely engaged in was not what he thought. Deceived, he was prevented from fully being the author of his actions. And that is just what is bad about deception, on the Kantian view.

I have been talking about how Kant would answer the question 'What's so bad about deception?' and about how his answer draws on a picture of human relations that is in many ways attractive. What of friendship? His answer here draws on just the same picture. Friendship (for the sane Kant of *The Doctrine of Virtue*) is a good thing because it is, as Korsgaard says, the moral relation 'in a perfected form'.[23] It is, in Strawson's terms, involvement at its best. We can take the objective standpoint occasionally towards friends, but the friendship will disappear if we take that attitude all the time, or even a significant part of the time. Kant thinks we have have a duty of friendship.[24] Friendship is not 'a union aimed at mutual advantage' but an 'intimate union of love and respect'.[25] Friends want to share their activities, and this means that friends choose their ends in such a way that the other can choose those ends too. Friends need to view themselves and the other as responsible if they are to share activities at all, and especially if they share activities that are on-going. Friends do not just predict that they will be together, do things together. They plan to be together, do things together. As well as sharing their activities, friends want to share their thoughts. Ordinarily, Kant says—both in the letter to Herbert, and in *The Doctrine of Virtue*—we have to 'lock up' our thoughts. The man

---

[21] op. cit., 429, note 13.   [22] See also Zweig, op. cit., 24, note 2.
[23] op. cit., 4, note 8.   [24] op. cit., 469, note 4.   [25] Ibid., 468, 469.

who is without a friend is the man who 'must shut himself up in himself', who must remain 'completely alone with his thoughts, *as in a prison*'.[26] But to a friend, one can—ideally—reveal oneself without anxiety or fear of betrayal. Friendship liberates, provides release from the prison of the self, enlarges the scope of the arena of virtue. When one is with a friend one is no longer 'completely alone with one's thoughts, as in a prison, but enjoys a *freedom* [otherwise] denied.'[27] The sphere of friendship is the sphere where one ideally has no temptation to lie, to remain reticent, to act strategically, but speaks one's mind: 'moral friendship is the complete confidence of two persons in revealing their secret thoughts and feelings to each other'.[28] In short, as Korsgaard puts it: 'to become friends is to create a neighbourhood where the Kingdom of Ends is real'.[29]

2. Duty and Desolation

Having posted his moral sedative off to Austria, and received no reply from the patient in more than a year, Kant enquired of a mutual friend who often saw her about the effect his letter had had. Herbert then wrote back, with apologies for her delay. This is her second letter:

3. To Kant, from Maria von Herbert, January 1793

Dear and revered sir,
Your kindness, and your exact understanding of the human heart, encourage me to describe to you, unshrinkingly, the further progress of my soul. The lie was no cloaking of a vice, but a sin of keeping something back out of consideration for the friendship (still veiled by love) that existed then. There was a struggle, I was aware of the honesty friendship demands, and at the same time I could foresee the terribly wounding consequences. Finally I had the strength and revealed the truth to my friend, but so late—and when I told him, the stone in my heart was gone, but his love was torn away in exchange. My friend hardened in his coldness, just as you said in your letter. But then afterwards he changed towards me, and offered me again the most intimate friendship. I'm glad enough about it, for his sake—but I'm not really content, because it's just amusement, it doesn't have any point.

[26] Ibid., 471, my italics. This is a remarkable metaphor for a philosopher who finds in the autonomous human self, and its self-legislating activity, the only source of intrinsic value.
[27] Ibid., 471.   [28] Ibid., 471.   [29] op. cit., 8, note 8.

My vision is clear now. I feel that a vast emptiness extends inside me, and all around me—so that I almost find myself to be superfluous, unnecessary. Nothing attracts me. I'm tormented by a boredom that makes life intolerable. Don't think me arrogant for saying this, but the demands of morality are too easy for me. I would eagerly do twice as much as they command. They only get their prestige from the attractiveness of sin, and it costs me almost no effort to resist that.

I comfort myself with the thought that, since the practice of morality is so bound up with sensuality, it can only count for this world. I can hope that the afterlife won't be yet another life ruled by these few, easy demands of morality, another empty and vegetating life. Experience wants to take me to task for this bad temper I have against life by showing me that nearly everyone finds his life ending much too soon, everyone is so glad to be alive. So as not to be a queer exception to the rule, I shall tell you of a remote cause of my deviation, namely my chronic poor health, which dates from the time I first wrote to you. I don't study the natural sciences or the arts any more, since I don't feel that I'm genius enough to extend them; and for myself, there's no need to know them. I'm indifferent to everything that doesn't bear on the categorical imperative, and my transcendental consciousness—although I'm all done with those thoughts too.

You can see, perhaps, why I only want one thing, namely to shorten this pointless life, a life which I am convinced will get neither better nor worse. If you consider that I am still young and that each day interests me only to the extent that it brings me closer to death, you can judge what a great benefactor you would be if you were to examine this question closely. I ask you, because my conception of morality is silent here, whereas it speaks decisively on all other matters. And if you cannot give me the answer I seek, I beg you to give me something that will get this intolerable emptiness out of my soul. Then I might become a useful part of nature, and, if my health permits, would make a trip to Königsberg in a few years. I want to ask permission, in advance, to visit you. You must tell me your story then, because I would like to know what kind of life your philosophy has led you to—whether it never seemed to you to be worth the bother to marry, or to give your whole heart to anyone, or to reproduce your likeness. I have an engraved portrait of you by Bause, from Leipzig. I see a profound calm there, and moral depth—but not the astuteness of which the *Critique of Pure Reason* is proof. And I'm dissatisfied not to be able to look you right in the face.

Please fulfil my wish, if it's not too inconvenient. And I need to remind you: if you do me this great favour and take the trouble to answer, please focus on specific details, not on the general points, which I understand, and already understood back when I happily studied your works at the side of my friend. You would like him, I'm sure. He is honest, goodhearted, and intelligent—and besides that, fortunate enough to fit this world.

I am, with deepest respect and truth, Maria Herbert.

Herbert's letter speaks for itself. The passion, the turbulence, has vanished. Desolation has taken its place, a 'vast emptiness', a vision of the world and the self that is chilling in its clarity, chilling in its nihilism. Apathy reigns. Desire is dead. Nothing attracts. Bereft of inclination, the self is 'superfluous', as Herbert so starkly puts it. Nothing has any point—except of course the categorical imperative. But morality itself has become a torment, not because it is too difficult, but because it is too easy. Without the counterweight of opposing inclination, what course could there be but to obey? The moral life is the empty, vegetating life, where one sees at a glance what the moral law requires and simply does it, unhampered by the competing attractions of sin. Herbert concludes that morality must be bound up with sensuality, that moral credit depends on the battle of the will with the sensual passions, a battle which, when there are no passions, is won merely, and tediously, by default—and where can be the credit in that? The imperative requires us never to treat persons merely as means to one's own ends. But if one has no ends, if one is simply empty, what could be easier than to obey? Herbert draws hope from her conclusion: if morality is bound to sensuality, with luck the next life will not be thus accursed.

This sounds like heresy. Is it? If so, Kant is blind to it. But perhaps it is not heresy at all. What Kant fails to see—what Herbert herself fails to see—is that her life constitutes a profound challenge to his philosophy, at least construed one way. Consider Kant's views on duty and inclination.

An action has moral worth when it is done for the sake of duty; it is not sufficient that the action conforms with duty.[30] Now, inclinations are often sufficient to make us perform actions that conform with our duty. To preserve one's life is a duty; and most of us have strong inclinations to preserve our lives. To help others where one can is a duty; and most of us are sympathetic enough and amiable enough to be inclined to help others,

---

[30] op. cit., 397, note 13.

at least some of the time. But—if we take Kant at his word here—actions thus motivated have no moral worth. The action of moral worth is that of 'the wretched man . . . [for whom] disappointments and hopeless misery have quite taken away the taste for life, who longs for death' but who, notwithstanding, preserves his life. The action that has moral worth is that of the misanthropist, 'the man cold in temperament and indifferent to the sufferings of others' who none the less helps others 'not from inclination but from duty'.[31]

This looks as though moral credit depends on both the absence of coinciding inclinations, such as sympathy; and the presence of opposing inclinations, like misanthropy. If so, Herbert is right: morality depends on there being inclinations to defeat. She has anticipated Schiller's complaint against Kant. An alternative reading, though, might be that the issue is epistemological: the presence of opposing inclinations helps us to *know* that we are acting for duty's sake.[32]

These views on the sympathetic inclinations take us far away from the 'attractive ideal of human relations' that Korsgaard hoped to find. The severe Kant is very far from the sane. It is important to see though that even here, what Kant says is not motivated by a kind of blind rule worship, but by a sense of the gulf between the two standpoints from which we must view ourselves. We are at once cogs in the grand machine of nature, and free agents in the Kingdom of Ends. We are persons, members of an intelligible world, authors of our actions; and at the same time animals, puppets of our genes and hormones, buffeted about by our lusts and loathings. Inclinations are *passions* in the sense that they *just happen* to us. And in so far as we let our actions be driven by them we allow ourselves to be puppets, not persons. We allow ourselves, to use Kant's own metaphors, to become marionettes or automata, which may appear to be initiators of action, but whose freedom is illusory, 'no better than the freedom of a turnspit, which, when once wound up also carries out its motions by itself'.[33] The inclinations are effects on us, they are *pathē*, and for that reason pathological. If we let them be causes of our behaviour, we abandon our personhood.

---

[31] op. cit., 397, note 398.

[32] For a defence of the latter reading, see Barbara Herman, 'On the Value of Acting from the Motive of Duty', *Philosophical Review* 90 (1981), 359–82.

[33] Immanuel Kant, *Critique of Practical Reason*, trans. L. W. Beck (New York: Macmillan, 1956), 97, 101.

Whether they lead us towards the action of duty or away from it, inclinations are among virtue's chief obstacles. When inclination opposes duty, it is an obstacle to duty's performance. When inclination coincides with duty, it is an obstacle at least to knowledge of the action's worth. 'Inclination, be it good-natured or otherwise, is blind and slavish... The feeling of sympathy and warmhearted fellow-feeling... is burdensome even to right-thinking persons, confusing their considered maxims and creating the wish to be free from them and subject only to law-giving reason.'[34] In the battle against the inclinations we can enlist the aid of that strange thing, respect, or reverence for the moral law. Reverence for the law serves to 'weaken the hindering influence of the inclinations'.[35] Reverence is a kind of feeling, but it is not something we 'passively feel', something inflicted upon us from outside. It is the sensible correlate of our own moral activity, the 'consciousness of the direct constraint of the will through law'.[36] Its function is not to motivate our moral actions, for that would still be motivation by feeling. Rather, its function is to remove the obstacles, to silence inclinations, something we should all look forward to. For inclinations are 'so far from having an absolute value... that it must... be the universal wish of every rational being to be wholly free from them'.[37]

Kant goes so far as to say we have a *duty of apathy*, yet another duty he is less than famous for. 'Virtue necessarily presupposes apathy', he says in *The Doctrine of Virtue*. 'The word "apathy" has fallen into disrepute', he continues, 'as if it meant lack of feeling and so subjective indifference regarding objects of choice: it has been taken for weakness. We can prevent this misunderstanding by giving the name *"moral apathy"* to that freedom from agitation which is to be distinguished from indifference, for in it the feelings arising from sensuous impressions lose their influence on moral feeling only because reverence for the law prevails over all such feelings'.[38] Something rather similar to apathy is described in the *Critique of Practical Reason*, but this time it is called not apathy, but 'bliss' (*Seligkeit*). Bliss is the state of 'complete independence from inclinations and desires'.[39] While it must be the universal wish of every rational being to achieve bliss, can we in fact achieve it? Apparently not, or not here. Bliss is 'the

---

[34] Ibid., 119.   [35] Ibid., 80.   [36] Ibid., 117.
[37] op. cit., 428, note 13.   [38] op. cit., 407, note 4.   [39] op. cit., 118, note 33.

self-sufficiency which can be ascribed only to the Supreme Being'.[40] The Supreme Being has no passions and inclinations. His intuition is intellectual, and not sensible. He can be affected by nothing, not even our prayers. He can have no *pathē*. God is the being more apathetic than which none can be conceived.

What of Kant's moral patient? She is well beyond the virtue of apathy that goes with mastery of the inclinations. She has no inclinations left to master. She respects the moral law, and obeys it. But she need not battle her passions to do so. She has no passions. She is empty—but for the clear vision of the moral law and unshrinking obedience to it. She is well on the way to bliss, lucky woman, and, if Kant is right about bliss, well on the way to Godhead. No wonder she feels that she—unlike her unnamed friend—does not quite 'fit the world'. She obeys the moral law in her day to day dealings with people from the motive of duty alone. She has no other motives. She is no heretic. She is a Kantian saint. Oh brave new world, that has such moral saints in it.[41]

What should Kant have said about inclinations? I have no clear view about this, but some brief remarks may be in order. A saner view is arguably to be found in Kant's own writings, a view that has been defended by Korsgaard and Herman. In *The Doctrine of Virtue*[42] Kant apparently advocates the cultivation of natural sentiment to back up the motive of duty. It is hard, though, to reconcile this with his other teachings, which tell us that inclinations, all inclinations, are to be abjured, as 'blind and slavish', in the graphic phrase from the *Critique of Practical Reason*. 'Blind' is an evocative word in the Kantian context, associated as it is with the blind workings of nature, with the sensual as opposed to the intellectual. It calls to mind the famous slogan of the first *Critique*: thoughts without content are empty, intuitions without concepts are blind. That slogan famously captures the synthesis of rationalism and empiricism Kant thought necessary for knowledge. It acknowledges the twin aspects of human creatures, as Kant sees us: we have a *sensible* intuition, a *passive* intuition,

---

[40]   op. cit., 118, note 33.

[41]   See Susan Wolf, 'Moral Saints', *The Journal of Philosophy* 79 (1982), 419–39, on the perils of sainthood.

[42]   See for example op. cit., 456, note 4.

through which we are affected by the world; and an active intellect. *We need both.* If only Kant had effected a similar synthesis in the moral sphere: for if it is true, as he says, that inclinations without reasons are blind, it seems equally true that reasons without inclinations are empty. The moral life without inclinations is a life of 'intolerable emptiness', as Herbert found. We need both.

I said that Herbert has no inclinations: but there are two exceptions. She wants to die. And she wants to visit Kant. She is, it seems, like the would-be suicide Kant describes in *The Groundwork*: her persistence with life has moral worth, because it is so opposed to her inclinations. But is she really like him? Not quite. For she is not even sure that duty points to persistence with life. Notice the change here. In her first letter she believed that self-respect, respect for 'her own being' required her to persist with life. But as her 'being' has begun to contract, as the self has withered, sloughed off, become superfluous—as the emptiness has grown—so too has her doubt. Now her conception of morality is 'silent' on the question of suicide. She wants to die. She has almost no opposing inclinations. And morality is silent. It takes no expert to wonder if she is in danger.

Why does she want to visit Kant? She says (letter 3) 'I would like to know what kind of life your philosophy has led you to'. In the *Critique of Practical Reason* Kant cites approvingly what he took to be the practice of the ancients: no one was justified in calling himself a philosopher—a lover of wisdom—'unless he could show [philosophy's] infallible effect on his own person as an example'.[43] Kant thinks we are justified in inquiring after the effect of philosophy on the philosopher, daunting as the prospect seems today. But what does Herbert have in mind? She wonders, perhaps, whether Kant's life is as empty as her own, and for the same reason. She discovered that love is 'pointless' when inclinations have withered, when you have no passions of your own and therefore no passions to share. And she wonders whether Kant's life reflects this discovery. She wonders whether Kant's philosophy has led him to think that it was simply 'not worth the bother' to marry, or to 'give his whole heart' to anyone. Perhaps she is right to wonder.

---

[43] op. cit., 109, note 33.

3. Shipwreck

In reply to an enquiry, Kant received this explanatory letter from a mutual friend, Erhard:

4. To Kant, from J. B. Erhard, January 17, 1793

I can say little of Miss Herbert. She has capsized on the reef of romantic love. In order to realize an idealistic love, she gave herself to a man who misused her trust. And then, trying to achieve such love with another, she told her new lover about the previous one. That is the key to her letter. If my friend Herbert had more delicacy, I think she could still be saved.

> Yours, Erhard.

Kant writes again, not to Herbert, but to someone about whom we know little:

5. From Kant, to Elisabeth Motherby, February 11, 1793

I have numbered the letters[44] which I have the honour of passing on to you, my dear mademoiselle, according to the dates I received them. The ecstatical little lady didn't think to date them. The third letter, from another source, provides an explanation of the lady's curious mental derangement. A number of expressions refer to writings of mine that she read, and are difficult to understand without an interpreter.

You have been so fortunate in your upbringing that I do not need to commend these letters to you as an example of warning, to guard you against the wanderings of a sublimated fantasy. But they may serve nonetheless to make your perception of that good fortune all the more lively.

I am, with the greatest respect, my honoured lady's most obedient servant,

> I. Kant.

Kant is unaware that he has received a letter from a Kantian saint. Indeed, it is hard to believe that he has read her second letter. He relies on the opinion of his friend, whose diagnosis of the patient resorts to that traditional and convenient malady of feminine hysteria. Herbert 'has capsized on the reef of romantic love'. The diagnosis is exactly wrong. Herbert has no passions. Her vision is clear. Her life is empty. But it is easier not to take this in,

---

[44] Letters 1, 3, and 4 above. Elisabeth Motherby was the daughter of Kant's friend Robert Motherby, an English merchant in Königsberg.

easier to suppose a simpler illness. She is at the mercy (aren't all women?) of irrational passions. She is evidently beyond the reach of instruction, beyond the reach of his moral sedatives; so Kant abandons her. It is hard to imagine a more dramatic shift from the interactive stance to the objective. In Kant's first letter, Herbert is 'my dear friend', she is the subject for moral instruction, and reprimand. She is responsible for some immoral actions, but she has a 'heart created for the sake of virtue', capable of seeing the good and doing it. Kant is doing his best to communicate, instruct and console. He is not very good at it, hardly surprising if he believes—as I think he does—that he should master rather than cultivate his moral sentiments. But there is little doubt that the good will is there. He treats her as a human being, as an end, as a person. This is the standpoint of interaction.

But now? Herbert is *die kleine Schwärmerin*, the little dreamer, the ecstatical girl, suffering a 'curious mental derangement', lost in the wanderings of a sublimated fantasy', who doesn't think, especially about important things like dating letters. Kant is here forgetting an important aspect of the duty of respect, which requires something like a Davidsonian principle of charity. We have 'a duty of respect for man even in the logical use of his reason: a duty not to censure his error by calling it absurdity . . . but rather to suppose that his error must yet contain some truth and to seek this out.'[45] Herbert, now deranged, is no longer guilty. She is merely unfortunate. She is not responsible for what she does. She is the pitiful product of a poor upbringing. She is an item in the natural order, a ship wrecked on a reef. She is a thing.

And, true to Kant's picture, it now becomes appropriate to use her as a means to his own ends. He bundles up her letters, private communications from a 'dear friend', letters that express thoughts, philosophical and personal, some of them profound. He bundles them up and sends them to an acquaintance under the title, 'Example of Warning'. The end is obscure and contradictory: it seems it is to warn somebody who, on Kant's own view, needs no warning. Is it gossip? Ingratiation? But the striking thing is that the letters are no longer seen as human communications. Far from it: Kant's presumption is that they *will not be understood* by their new recipient. For the letters 'refer to writings of mine that she read, that are difficult to

---

[45] op. cit., note 462, 4., my italics.

understand without an interpreter'. This is not the speech of persons, to be understood and debated; this is derangement, to be feared and avoided. These are not thoughts, but symptoms. Kant is doing something with her as one does something with a tool: Herbert cannot share the end of his action. She cannot be co-author. Kant's deceiving of her—neatly achieved by reticence—has made sure of that. Her action of pleading for help, asking advice, arguing philosophy, her action of writing to a well-loved philosopher and then to a friend—these have become the action of warning of the perils of romantic love. She did not choose to do *that*. Well may Kant have warned, 'My dear friends, there is no such thing as a friend'.

4. Strategy For the Kingdom's Sake

Enough. This is not a cautionary tale of the inability of philosophers to live by their philosophy. What interests me is what interested Kant at the outset: friendship and deception. What interests me is the very first problem: the 'long drawn out lie, disclosed'. Was it wrong for Herbert to deceive? Was it wrong for her to act strategically? Is it always wrong to deceive? Apparently, yes, from the Kantian perspective. In deceiving we treat our hearers as less than human. We act from the objective standpoint. We force others to perform actions they do not choose to perform. We make them things. If I reply to the the murderer, 'No, my friend is not here', I deceive a human being, use his reasoning ability as a tool, do something that has a goal (saving my friend) that I make impossible for him to share, make him do something (abandon his prey) that he did not choose to do. I have made him, in this respect, a thing.

But let's think about this some more. We want to say—though Kant did not want to say—that I *ought* to lie to the murderer. Christine Korsgaard proposes a way in which we can have what we want, and remain faithful to the Kantian spirit. She raises some important questions about the role of the idea of the Kingdom of Ends, a Kingdom of persons who always treat people with the dignity that is their due, a Kingdom where the performance of duty does not backfire. According to Kant, we must act as if we are already inhabitants of the Kingdom. We must obey the categorical imperative regardless of the consequences, regardless of the realities of life in this world, a world that is far from the Kingdom, a world that, as

Korsgaard says, is often evil. In such a world, acting in accordance with the moral law can lead to bad consequences, not simply in the prudential sense that Kant so despises, but in the sense of actively promoting evil. If I tell the truth to the murderer, I become an *instrument of evil*, as useful to his ends as the brandished axe. Kant thinks the evil that results is no responsibility of yours. But that is an impossible view. It is a terrible mistake for moral theory to blinker itself to the presence of evil, says Korsgaard, and she calls for revision—but a revision that makes sense in Kantian terms.

Much moral and political philosophy concerns itself with the construction of an ideal: we ask what a perfectly just, or a perfectly moral, society would look like. There are many answers. Kant's answer is the Kingdom of Ends. We then observe that the world we live in is very far from this ideal. And the question arises: what should we do? Should we live by our ideal now? Or should we do all that is in our power to make our ideal a reality? The questions are not the same: in an evil world, acting in accordance with the ideal may backfire, and make the achievement of the ideal more, and not less, remote. Acting justly in every circumstance may lead to more, not less, injustice. Telling the truth to the murderer will lead to more evil, not less. Kant thinks we must ignore this fact: the ideal of the Kingdom is an ideal to be lived by, not a goal to be sought after.

Korsgaard disagrees, and her proposed revision is this: when circumstances are far from the ideal, the ideal becomes a goal, something to strive towards, not something to live up to.[46] The Kantian ideal is one that should indeed guide us in daily life. But since we live in a world that is far from the Kingdom, we will sometimes encounter evil circumstances, and when we do, we must think of the Kingdom as an ideal to be worked towards, not lived by.[47]

---

[46] In the non-ideal case, she says, one's actions may be guided by a more instrumental style of reasoning than in ideal theory. But Korsgaard also wants to say that non-ideal theory is not a form of consequentialism. The goal set by the ideal is not one of good consequences, but of a just state of affairs (op. cit., 343, note 7.). I am unhappy with this defence: her view does apparently endorse a kind of consequentialism. It permits actions that are likely to have a certain good consequence, namely a just state of affairs. (Of course this is not consequentialism of a utilitarian variety.)

[47] Ibid. There are constraints on what we are permitted to do for the sake of this end. Briefly: on Korsgaard's view, the formula of universal law provides constraints on what we are permitted to do in our attempts to make the Kingdom a reality, when faced with evil. In the case of lying to the murderer, she believes that the formula of universal law, correctly applied, will yield a permissive conclusion. Korsgaard's reconstruction is subtle and complex, drawing on a Rawlsian distinction between ideal and

And the murderer? We are, first, allowed to lie. Lying is, ordinarily, impermissible. But in these evil circumstances it is permissible. Then other duties come in to play that make it not simply permissible, but required: duties of mutual aid, duties of self respect. To lie would be to be to allow yourself to be made an instrument for evil. 'You owe it to humanity in your own person', says Korsgaard, 'not to allow your honesty to be used as a resource of evil'. You will come closer to achieving the Kingdom of Ends if you lie, in this case, than if you do not. So that is what you should do. What we have here is something like: strategy for the Kingdom's sake.

I shall not comment on Korsgaard's proposal. But I suggest that it may have implications here. Herbert puts her dilemma like this: 'I was aware of *the honesty friendship demands* and at the same time I could see the terribly wounding consequences...The lie...was a...keeping something back *out of consideration for the friendship*.'[48] She is torn. Friendship demands honesty; and friendship demands dishonesty. Is she confused? Is she in contradiction? Not at all. It is the same old dilemma: having an ideal you want to live by, and an ideal you want to seek and preserve. You owe honesty to your friend; but the friendship will vanish if you are honest. Friendship is a very great good: it is, on the sane Kantian view we have been looking at, the Kingdom of Ends made real and local. One of the goods of friendship is that it makes possible the kind of relationship where one can unlock the prison of the self, reveal oneself to the compassionate and understanding eye of the other. But Kant sees true friendship to be a very rare thing, rare, he says as a black swan.[49] And what threatens friendship most is asymmetry, inequality with regard to love or respect, which can result in the partial breakdown of the interactive stance. This asymmetry can be brought about by the very act of self-revelation: if one person 'reveals his failings while the other person concealed his own, he would lose something of the other's respect by presenting himself so candidly'.[50] What Kant is pointing to is the very problem encountered, far more

---

non-ideal theory. I have not done Korsgaard justice here, and readers are referred to her article for the fuller picture. I should also say that my final conclusion, namely that in this case Herbert may have had a duty to lie, is not endorsed by Korsgaard herself.

[48] Letter 3, my italics.
[49] op. cit., 471, note 4. Kant's ignorance of Antipodean bird life is (just) forgivable.
[50] Ibid., 471.

acutely, by Herbert: in being a friend, in acting in the way that friendship demands, one can sometimes threaten friendship. To act as a member of the Kingdom can make the Kingdom more, and not less, remote. It resembles, in this respect, the problem of the murderer at the door. If Korsgaard is right, then it is sometimes permissible and even required to act strategically for the Kingdom's sake. Does that apply here?

Korsgaard says that we take this route when we are faced with evil. But she doesn't say what evil is. For Kant, what could evil be but this: the reduction of persons to things? Now consider Herbert's position. There is something we have been leaving out. Herbert is a *woman* in a society in which women start out on an unequal footing and then live out their lives that way, where women—especially women—must perpetually walk a tightrope between being treated as things and treated as persons. She must make her choices against a backdrop of social institutions and habits that strip her of the dignity due to persons, where what she does and what she says will always be interpreted in the light of that backdrop, so that even if she says 'my vision is clear', and speaks in a manner consistent with that claim, her speech will be read as the speech of the deranged, a mere plaything of the passions. Central among the institutions she must encounter in her life is that of the sexual marketplace, where human beings are viewed as having a *price*, and not a dignity, and where the price of women is fixed in a particular way. Women, as things, as items in the sexual marketplace, have a market value that depends in part on whether they have been used. Virgins fetch a higher price than second-hand goods. Such are the background circumstances in which Herbert finds herself. They are, I suggest, evil circumstances, evil by Kantian lights (though Kant himself never saw it).

Despite these handicaps, Herbert has achieved a great thing: she has achieved something like a friendship of mutual love and respect, found someone with whom she can share her activities and goals, become a partner in a relationship where ends are chosen in such a way that the ends of both agents coincide (prominent among which was, it seems, the happy study of Kant's works!). She has achieved a relationship where frankness and honesty prevail—with one exception. Her lie is the lie of 'keeping something back for the sake of the friendship'. If she tells the truth, evil circumstance will see to it that her action will not be taken as the honest self-revelation of a person, but the revelation of her thing-hood, her hitherto unrecognized status as used merchandize, as an item with a price that is lower than the usual. If she tells the truth, she becomes a thing, and the friendship—that small neighborhood of the Kingdom—will vanish. Should she lie? Perhaps. If her circumstances are evil, she is permitted to have friendship as her goal, to be sought and preserved, rather than a law to be lived by. So she is permitted to lie. Then other considerations come in. She has a duty to 'humanity in her own person', of which Kant says: 'By virtue of this worth we are not for sale at any price; we possess an inalienable dignity which instils in us reverence for ourselves'. She has a duty of self esteem: she must respect her own person and demand such respect of others, adjuring the vice of servility.[51] I think she may have a duty to lie.[52]

This is strategy, for the Kingdom's sake. Kant would not allow it. He thinks we should act as if the Kingdom of Ends is with us now. He thinks we should rely on God to make it all right in the end. But God will not make it all right in the end. And the Kingdom of Ends is not with us now. Perhaps we should do what we can to bring it about.

5. Coda

Kant never replied, and his correspondent, as far as I know, did not leave Austria.[53] In 1803 Maria von Herbert killed herself, having worked out at last an answer to that persistent and troubling question—the question to which Kant, and her own moral sense, had responded with silence. Was that a vicious thing to do? Not entirely. As Kant himself concedes, 'Self-murder requires courage, and in this attitude there is always room for reverence for humanity in one's own person.'[54]

---

[51] op. cit., 434, 435.

[52] For an argument challenging this conclusion, and my earlier claims about lies and reticence, see James Mahon, 'Kant and Maria von Herbert: Reticence vs. Deception', *Philosophy* 81 (2006), 417–44.

[53] There is one final letter from her on the record, dated early 1794, in which she expresses again a wish to visit Kant, and reflects upon her own desire for death.

[54] Ibid., 424.

10

Autonomy–Denial in Objectification

The idea of objectification has existed in philosophy for quite a while, and long before feminism got hold of it. It gains one of its first expressions in Aristotle's matter-of-fact remark that a slave is 'a living tool'. The thought that, Aristotle's complacency notwithstanding, there might actually be something *wrong* with treating a human being as a living tool is one that gains eloquent expression later, in the work of Immanuel Kant. For Kant, moral wrong-doing consists in a failure to treat humanity 'always as an end and never as a means only'—a failure to respect that humanity 'by virtue of [which] we are not for sale at any price'. This historically Kantian idea has gained new impetus in recent applications by feminist thinkers, who have observed its relevance to oppression, and to the varied ways that women might have been treated as a means only, and sometimes put up for sale. For feminists, unlike for Kant, there is a focus on treatment encountered by women, and a claim that women's oppression partly consists in women's being treated 'as objects'. Catharine MacKinnon says,

To be sexually objectified means having a social meaning imposed on your being that defines you as to be sexually used . . . and then using you that way.

That notion of sexual 'use' echoes the Kantian stricture against treating a person as a mere means or instrument; and Kant himself thought that sexual relationships presented special dangers about the 'use' of the other person.[1]

---

[1] A shortened version of this paper appeared as Part 3 of 'Feminism in Philosophy', *The Oxford Handbook of Contemporary Philosophy*, eds. Frank Jackson and Michael Smith (Oxford: Oxford University Press 2005), 231–57. Aristotle, *Nichomachean Ethics,* trans. David Ross (New York: Oxford University Press, 1998) 1161b; Immanuel Kant, *Groundwork of the Metaphysic of Morals* (1785), trans. H. J. Paton

In an enlightening essay, Martha Nussbaum draws together the Kantian and feminist ideas about what it might be to treat someone as an object.[2] Objectification is a cluster concept, on her way of thinking, in which the ideas of autonomy-denial and instrumentality are at the core; but the cluster also includes related notions of inertness, fungibility, violability, ownership, and denial of subjectivity. Nussbaum's proposal deserves careful attention, as an outstanding example of the kind of enquiry that is seamlessly feminist and philosophical. I shall be wanting to ask whether her proposal does justice to the Kantian and feminist heritage she claims for it, and if not, how it might best be augmented.[3] I shall be drawing special attention to the idea of 'treating' in that notion of 'treating someone as an object'. And while Nussbaum places the *denial* of autonomy at centre stage, I shall also investigate a possibility that smacks of paradox: whether one might treat someone as an object through *affirming* their autonomy.

This latter question is of philosophical interest, and of practical interest as well. One feminist application of the idea of objectification has been to pornography, which has been thought to deny women's autonomy, in its depiction of women 'as objects, things, or commodities'.[4] However, other pornography has been thought to affirm women's autonomy, representing women as not in the least object-like or subordinate, but as active sexual agents; and the suggestion has been that this, surely, is politically innocent. Joel Feinberg describes with nostalgia some 'comic strip pamphlets' of the 1930s and 1940s, which

portrayed... a kind of joyous feast of erotica in which the blessedly unrepressed cartoon figures shared with perfect equality. Rather than being humiliated or dominated, the women characters equalled the men in their sheer earthy gusto.[5]

(New York: Harper and Row, 1964), 428–9; *Doctrine of Virtue* (1797), trans. Mary Gregor (New York: Harper and Row, 1964), 101; Catharine MacKinnon, *Feminist Theory of the State* (Cambridge, Mass.: Harvard University Press, 1989), 122.

[2] Martha Nussbaum, 'Objectification', *Philosophy and Public Affairs* 24 (1995), 249–91.

[3] A further aspect of the feminist idea of objectification is epistemological. This is absent in Nussbaum, and in my opinion needs including; I do not address it in this essay, but it is the chief topic of 'Projection and Objectification', this volume.

[4] From the definition drafted by MacKinnon and Andrea Dworkin, see MacKinnon, *Feminism Unmodified* (Cambridge Mass.: Harvard University Press, 1987), p. 176. Note that if pornography is defined as subordination, the possibility of non-subordinating pornography is ruled out as a matter of terminology. I use a more vernacular sense of the term here.

[5] Joel Feinberg, *Offense to Others* (New York and Oxford: Oxford University Press, 1985), 144. He adds, 'the episodes had no butt at all except prudes and hypocrites. Most of us consumers managed to survive with our moral characters intact'.

The pornographic film *Deep Throat* was hailed for representing women as sexually autonomous, its heroine described as 'Liberated Woman in her most extreme form—taking life and sex on her own terms'.[6] Such descriptions aim to be vindications, aim to distinguish a liberating from a subordinating pornography. Indeed feminist antipornography legislation allows for just such a distinction, labelling non-subordinating pornography as 'erotica'. So in thinking about whether pornography might objectify women, it is tempting to think that the question must be about pornography that *denies* women autonomy—and not, surely, about pornography that *affirms* autonomy.

Well, the answer, as we shall see, is not so simple. Perhaps there really could be a liberating, autonomy-affirming pornography; certainly there are feminists who think the solution is not less pornography, but more—more pornography created by women, for women. Perhaps the 1930s and 1940s comic strips really were liberating; for present purposes we might as well accept Feinberg's rosy evaluation. But while allowing this, one can also allow that it is not the whole story. The description of *Deep Throat* as representing 'Liberated Woman in her most extreme form' must in the end be resisted, not because its affirmation of autonomy is a sham, but because, as I shall argue, objectification sometimes *depends* on affirmation of autonomy. This may sound strange at first, but it turns out to be a natural enough consequence of the plurality of ways in which someone can be treated as object.

1. Treating as an 'Object'

Nussbaum herself begins with a plurality, naming seven features that form a cluster concept of objectification—seven ways to treat something, or someone, as a thing:

1. *Instrumentality*: one treats it as a tool of one's own purposes.
2. *Denial of autonomy*: one treats it as lacking in autonomy and self-determination.
3. *Inertness*: one treats it as lacking in agency and activity.

---

[6] The words of a commentator quoted in a documentary made by Mark Kermode and Russell Levin, 'The Real Linda Lovelace', first broadcast on Channel 4 in the UK, 26 September 2002.

4. *Fungibility*: one treats it as interchangeable (a) with other things of the same type, and/or (b) with things of other types.
5. *Violability*: one treats it as lacking in boundary-integrity, as something that it is permissible to break up, smash, break into.
6. *Ownership*: one treats it as something that is owned by another, can be bought or sold, etc.
7. *Denial of subjectivity*: one treats it as something whose experience and feelings (if any) need not be taken into account.[7]

I take this to be a particularly helpful proposal about what 'object' amounts to, in the notion of 'treating as an object', and this is, in my view, at least half the story. The other half, as we shall see, rests not on what an 'object' *is*, but on what 'treating *as*' amounts to. Nussbaum's proposal gives content to the idea of objectification by teasing out a number of features associated with objecthood: an object lacks autonomy, lacks subjectivity, is inert, an appropriate candidate (sometimes) for using as a tool, exchange, destruction, possession.

Nussbaum observes, interestingly, that objects themselves are not always candidates for 'objectifying' treatment. A painting is not treated as violable, or fungible, nor is its value merely instrumental, though it may be treated as an object in the other ways. Certain parts of the natural world are not merely instruments, not fungible, nor violable, nor ownable. Not all objects are to be 'treated as objects'; it depends on the nature of the object and the context.

However it is in the application to persons that the idea of objectification gets its chief point. And in the case of persons, she thinks treatment relating to autonomy is central in a distinctive way, partly because of its implications for other modes of object-making. When you treat a person as autonomous, you are treating them as someone capable of choice: and that seems to imply not treating them merely as instrument. It seems to imply treating them as not simply inert, not owned, not something whose feelings need not be taken into account. To put her suggestion another way, the ideas of instrumentality, inertness, ownership, and denial of subjectivity each imply

---

[7] Nussbaum, 'Objectification', 257. I have slightly adapted Nussbaum's own formulation. My neutral pronoun 'one', in subject position, replaces her term 'objectifier', which is more appropriate given that (on Nussbaum's own account) someone engaging in such treatment needn't be an objectifier, if e.g. the treatment is directed towards an object rather than a person, or if insufficiently many features of the 'cluster' are in play.

the denial of autonomy. So that is one reason for putting autonomy-denial at the core of objectification.

Instrumentality seems central too, she thinks, and in a different distinctive way. On the face of it, the other modes of object-making do not immediately imply instrumentality. Many things are treated as lacking in autonomy which nonetheless ought not to be treated as mere means to one's ends. For example, children are treated as lacking in autonomy, but it would be wrong to treat them instrumentally. The same perhaps applies to pets, and to certain objects such as paintings. These examples suggest that while instrumentality implies autonomy-denial, the converse does not in general hold. That said, however, when it comes to the treatment of adult human beings, the connections between instrumentality and autonomy-denial are very much closer. She goes so far as to suggest that, when we restrict ourselves to the domain of adult human beings, there is an implicit biconditional connecting these two modes of object-making. She suggests that autonomy-denial and instrumentality are mutually entailing: one treats an adult human being as mere means if and only if one denies their autonomy.

Nussbaum does not explicitly say quite this, but it seems to be implied by what she does say. One half of the biconditional is implied by her view that 'treating an item as autonomous seems to entail treating it as non-instrumental', i.e. (by contraposition) *instrumentality entails autonomy-denial*. The other half of the biconditional is implied by her view that 'treating as autonomous [may] be a necessary feature of the non-instrumental use of adult human beings': non-instrumentality entails treating as autonomous, or (by contraposition) *autonomy-denial entails instrumentality*, for adult human beings.[8] Now, if Nussbaum is indeed claiming that instrumentality and autonomy-denial are mutually entailing, in the domain of treatment of adult persons, that claim is much too strong, as we shall be in a position to see in Section 2.

Having spelled out this 'cluster concept', Nussbaum applies it illuminatingly to sexual objectification, attending to a variety of texts, from the relatively highbrow (D. H. Lawrence, James Joyce, Henry James) to the low (*Playboy*, and a sadistic sample from the work of one 'Laurence St. Clair'). She uses it to defend many aspects of the feminist understanding of

<hr>

[8] Nussbaum, 'Objectification', 260–1.

women's subordination developed by Catharine MacKinnon and Andrea Dworkin, together with their associated critique of pornography. While for Kant, all wrong-doing is, in a sense, objectification, Nussbaum narrows her focus to the special kind of wrong-doing that most of us, somewhat informed by feminist thinking, would describe as objectification. So not all wrong-doing is objectification. Not all objectification is wrong-doing either: for Nussbaum also argues that some sorts of objectification, including some sorts of denial of autonomy, may be 'a wonderful part of sexual life'—a surprising result, if our initial thought was that objectification is a distinctive moral failure. She argues that, in a manner sensitive to context, in background conditions of equality, a mutual 'denial of autonomy' may be valuable, and she offers as an example a kind of sexual self-surrender, described by D. H. Lawrence.

If we are interested in whether Nussbaum's proposal does justice to the feminist philosophical understanding of 'treating someone as an object', it is worth asking whether there are aspects of the idea of an 'object' that are relevant to feminist thinking, but absent from Nussbaum's proposal. There is a methodological point to this: for when dealing with a cluster concept, something counts as coming under the concept in case it satisfies a vague 'sufficiently many' of the listed features. This means there can be reason to add features especially associated with objectification, even if (in some cases) they imply or are implied by existing members of the cluster. In the remainder of this section, I'll propose and defend three additions.

One absence from Nussbaum's list, notwithstanding its prominence in her illustrative examples, is the idea of reducing someone to their body. So let us put this down this as an eighth feature.

8. *Reduction to body*: one treats it as identified with its body, or body parts.

This idea appears as a clause of the famous feminist anti-pornography ordinance from which she takes inspiration, according to which (some) pornography treats women 'dehumanized as sexual objects, things, or commodities...reduced to body parts'. The idea is also important to Kant's own concern about sexual objectification. As Barbara Herman has commented, Kant finds moral difficulty in the fact (as he sees it) that sexual interest in another is not interest in the other as a person, but as a body.[9]

Here is one more idea:

9. *Reduction to appearance*: one treats it primarily in terms of how it looks, or how it appears to the senses.

This is worth including for its importance, in different ways, to both Kantian and feminist thinking. It appears in Nussbaum's illustrative examples too, whether in the objectifying character of soft core pornography, or in the relationship of a couple described by Henry James, who value each other in a purely aesthetic way, appropriate for fine paintings and antiques.

And here is another idea:

10. *Silencing*: one treats it as silent, lacking the capacity to speak.

Speech is a distinctive capacity of persons, just as distinctive perhaps as autonomy and subjectivity. Admittedly, this was not a particularly important idea for Kant, but it has been important to feminists, who hold that women's subordination is partly constituted by the fact that women have been silenced, for example, by pornography.

Pornography makes [women's] speech impossible, and where possible, worthless. Pornography makes women into objects. Objects do not speak. When they do, they are by then regarded as objects, not as humans.[10]

Leaving aside the question of what exactly this silencing amounts to, the idea of silence has been central to feminist thinking about women's situation, and it is worth adding independently to Nussbaum's list.

Including these features has some advantages. Not only do they pick up on some ideas that have been important in feminist thinking; they also provide us with resources to address some possible counter-examples to Nussbaum's initial proposal. Of course since Nussbaum offering a 'cluster concept' rather than a definition of objectification, it is not open to counter-example in the usual way. Nevertheless, we would expect that if a way

---

[9] Barbara Herman, 'Could it be Worth Thinking about Kant on Sex and Marriage', in *A Mind of One's Own*, eds., Louise Antony and Charlotte Witt (Boulder, Co.: Westview Press, 1993), 55.

[10] MacKinnon, *Feminism Unmodified*, 182.

of treating someone happens to possess the core features of objectification, plus a decent number of the others, it ought to count as an objectifying way of treating someone. These expectations are sometimes frustrated.

Example 1: Burglar

If someone burgles my house, he does something that arguably denies my autonomy, and violates my choice. He treats me as a mere tool for his purposes. He disregards my experiences and feelings, thereby denying subjectivity. Fungibility is in play, since as far as he is concerned, any house sufficiently well-equipped and ill-secured will do. Perhaps violability is in play, in his invasion of a personal space. One would expect something satisfying so many features of the cluster to deserve the concept. But in this case, I think it does not: we would not normally think of burglary as objectification.

Example 2: Management

A university bureaucrat introduces new and absurdly time-wasting policies, arrogantly steam-rolling them through without consulting his colleagues. His policies are rather pointless, but he wants to leave his mark. He denies the autonomy of his colleagues, in forcing them to go his way. He is not interested in what they think or want, and ignores their subjectivity. He perhaps uses them as the tools of his petty ambition. Many of the features of Nussbaum's cluster are in play; yet we would not think of this as objectification.

How to respond to these examples? One could ask whether there already are resources to address them in Nussbaum's initial proposal. A feature on Nussbaum's list absent in both of these examples is that of *possession*. Suppose we include that feature—suppose, for example, in a different employment situation, the employees are sports stars who are in effect bought and sold. Might that be objectification? Perhaps. If so, perhaps the feature of possession could be given greater weight. But one can also ask whether it helps to have the additions I just proposed. Suppose we adjust the example further still, so that, for example, employees are treated merely as *bodies*. Some feminists will perhaps think of prostitution as illustrating such a case, and of being more obviously objectifying. But the idea has wider application. Readers of Charles Dickens' *Hard Times* may recall the exploitative Mr. Gradgrind, and his habit of regarding his factory workers as 'the Hands'.[11] He, unlike the bureaucrat, really does objectify his employees. My suggestion is not, of course, that any of my proposed additions are necessary for objectification; but that the presence of these features raises the likelihood that the behaviour will count as objectification, on a par with such features as possession and fungibility.

With these inclusions, the relevant idea of an 'object' turns out to be of something lacking in subjectivity and autonomy, something inert, something that is an appropriate candidate for using as a tool, exchange, destruction, possession, all as Nussbaum suggested; and in addition it is something that is *silent*, something that is just an *appearance*, just a *body*.

Teasing out a plurality of features associated with objecthood is, I suggest, only half the task. In this idea of 'treating someone as an object', we need to look not only at the notion of an object, but also at the notion of *treatment*. Here too we confront a plurality, albeit a different one. 'Treat' is a wide-ranging verb that has so far been functioning as a dummy, standing in for a host of different attitudes and actions. 'Treating' may be a matter of attitude or act: it may be a matter of how one depicts or represents someone, or a matter of what one more actively does to someone.

2. 'Treating' as an Object

Suppose we restrict our attention to treatment relating to autonomy. This is partly for reasons of simplicity, and partly because of its core status in the concept of objectification. Suppose we agree with Nussbaum that lack of autonomy is a salient feature of objects, and that 'denying autonomy' is therefore an important aspect of 'treating as an object'. Suppose too that we can postpone contested questions about what autonomy might actually be. Let us think about what the 'treating' part of that idea involves: what exactly does *denying* autonomy amount to?[12]

---

[11] Charles Dickens, *Hard Times* (1854) (Oxford: Oxford University Press, 1989).

[12] There is a vast literature on autonomy, to which I am not doing justice here, but for some significant feminist contributions, see e.g. Catriona Mackenzie and Natalie Stoljar, eds., *Relational Autonomy: Feminist Perspectives on Autonomy, Agency and the Social Self* (Oxford: Oxford University Press, 2000); Alison Assiter, 'Autonomy and Pornography', in *Feminist Perspectives in Philosophy*, eds., Morwenna Griffiths and Margaret Whitford (London: Macmillan, 1988); Marilyn Friedman, *Autonomy, Gender, Politics* (Oxford: Oxford University Press, 2003).

On Nussbaum's description, denial of autonomy takes place when one treats something 'as lacking in autonomy and self-determination'.[13] Here are some examples she uses to illustrate autonomy-denial. One (permissibly) denies autonomy when one treats a pen, a painting, one's pets, or one's small children, as non-autonomous. Ownership is by definition incompatible with autonomy, so slaves are denied autonomy: and 'once one treats as a tool and denies autonomy, it is difficult to say why rape or battery would be wrong, except in the sense of rendering the tool a less efficient tool of one's purposes'. Aspects of slavery anticipate, as she rightly says, the MacKinnon–Dworkin understanding of sexual objectification. Slavery

shows us how a certain sort of instrumental use of persons, negating the autonomy that is proper to them as persons, also leaves the human being so denuded of humanity, in the eyes of the objectifier, that he or she seems ripe for other abuses as well—for the refusal of imagination involved in the denial of subjectivity, for the denial of individuality involved in fungibility, and even for bodily and spiritual violation and abuse, if that should appear to be what best suits the will and purposes of the objectifier.

The relationship between the Brangwens, described by D. H. Lawrence, also involves 'a mutual denial of autonomy', 'a kind of yielding abnegation of self-containment and self-sufficiency'. An example of hard-core sadistic pornography 'represents women as creatures whose autonomy and subjectivity don't matter at all', the woman's 'inertness, her lack of autonomy, her violability' is eroticized.[14]

Is autonomy-denial a matter of attitude, or act, or both? Nussbaum's examples exploit a number of different ways of treating. An agent presumably *believes* the pen, the painting, the small child, are lacking in autonomy—that is why they then *act as if* they are lacking in autonomy—and act rather differently, depending on whether it is the child or the pen whose autonomy is 'denied'. In buying the slave, an agent thereby 'denies' autonomy: but in what sense? The act may presuppose an attitude, of failing to *regard* the slave as autonomous. The act of buying may be an act of autonomy-denial that *violates* the slave's autonomy, preventing him from having any choice in the matter. Or perhaps slavery does something even worse to the slave's autonomy—*stifles* it, or *destroys* it.

---

[13] Nussbaum, 'Objectification', 257.   [14] Ibid., 261, 264, 265, 273, 280.

To make a start, in considering autonomy-denial, *non-attribution of autonomy* needs to be distinguished from *violation of autonomy*. I take it that non-attribution is primarily a matter of attitude, while autonomy-violation is something more—a more active doing, perhaps one that prevents someone from doing what they choose. The distinction between non-attribution and violation is somewhat obscured by allowing 'autonomy-denial' to label both. The two are quite independent: there can be autonomy-denial *qua* non-attribution, without autonomy-denial *qua* autonomy-violation—and vice versa.[15]

To illustrate the first possibility, there can be non-attribution of autonomy without violation of autonomy, in the 'objective' attitude described so well by P. F. Strawson, the attitude of the doctor or social scientist:

To adopt the objective attitude to another human being is to see him, perhaps, as an object of social policy; as a subject for what, in a wide range of sense, might be called treatment; as something . . . to be managed or handled or cured or trained.[16]

Someone denying autonomy in this attitudinal way need not deny autonomy in other ways. A doctor viewing his patient from what Strawson calls the 'objective' stance *may* act in ways that override his patient's choices, but he may well not: perhaps institutional procedures of securing informed consent will prevent autonomy-violation, notwithstanding the shortfall in the doctor's attribution of autonomy. When doctors attributed hysteria to women, they were attributing something that was, in part, supposed to be an affliction of autonomy; but they were not *ipso facto* violating women's autonomy.[17] And consider the failure to attribute autonomy to beings that actually lack autonomy (the pens, paintings, and small

---

[15] For a related discussion of the relationship between using someone and failing to treat them as a person, see Onora O'Neill: 'Making another into a tool or instrument in my project is one way of failing to treat that other as a person; but only one way', 'Between Consenting Adults', in *Constructions of Reason* (Cambridge: Cambridge University Press, 1990), 105.

[16] P. F. Strawson, 'Freedom and Resentment,' in *Freedom and Resentment and Other Essays* (London: Methuen, 1974), 9. Strawson would not wish to reduce such attitudes to e.g. metaphysical beliefs about whether the person is free or autonomous.

[17] For a surprising discussion of how women occasionally exploited diagnoses of hysteria to find a limited outlet for their own sexual expression, see work by Jennifer Saul, 'On Treating Things as People: Pornography, Objectification, and the History of the Vibrator', *Hypatia* 21 (2006), 45–61; drawing on Rachel Maines, *The Technology of Orgasm: 'Hysteria,' the Vibrator, and Women's Sexual Satisfaction* (Baltimore, Md and London: Johns Hopkins University Press, 1999). Saul's work includes criticism of the argument in 'Sexual Solipsism', this volume.

children of Nussbaum's examples): such failure is not just compatible with non-violation of autonomy; it is presumably incompatible with violation of autonomy, there being no autonomy there to violate. These examples illustrate in different ways how there can be failure to attribute autonomy without violation of autonomy.

To illustrate the second possibility, there can be autonomy-violation without failure to attribute autonomy, as in the classic examples from Kant's *Groundwork*, where autonomy is attributed, *and* violated. Someone who makes a lying promise to repay his friend's money does not suppose his friend lacking in autonomy, but does violate his friend's autonomy, on the Kantian view.

Another kind of example relevant to feminist work might be sadistic rape, by which I mean rape where non-consent is actively sought, rather than disregarded or ignored. In this sort of case, it's not that he doesn't *listen* to her saying 'no'—he *wants* her to say 'no'. Here there is violation of a woman's autonomy committed by someone who affirms her autonomy, attributes to her a capacity for choice, and desires precisely to overcome that choice, make her do what she chooses not to do. In sadistic rape, someone is 'treated as an object' in part by attributing autonomy to them in one way—so that autonomy can be denied a different way. A certain kind of autonomy-affirmation is thus a necessary feature of this way of treating as an object. Notice an important difference between this sexual example and those typically described by Kant. For Kant, autonomy-violation is in the service of some other purpose (for example, gaining money) achievable innocently by other means. Sadistic rape violates autonomy, not in the service of some other purpose (for example, achieving sexual pleasure), but partly for its own sake. So we might even be motivated to draw a further contrast, *within* the category of violation of autonomy, distinguishing whether it is done as a means or as an end.[18]

Reflection suggests that *deliberately* violating someone's autonomy (whether as a means or as end) is not just compatible with not affirming their autonomy, but requires it. Deliberate violation of someone's choice presupposes attribution of a capacity for choice. This underlines even more

---

[18] For discussion of a related contrast in the social psychology literature, see Roy Baumeister, *Evil: Inside Human Violence and Cruelty* (New York: W.H. Freeman, 1997), chs. 4 ('Greed, Lust, Ambition: Evil as a Means to an End') and 7 ('Can Evil be Fun? The Joy of Hurting'), a psychological study of, roughly, a contrast between evil as means (ch. 4) and as end (ch. 7).

clearly the distinctness of the two 'autonomy-denials' of non-attribution, and violation.

Some of the examples illustrating the distinctness of these 'autonomy-denials' also serve to illustrate the distinctness of autonomy-denial and *instrumentality*. Recall that Nussbaum suggested a mutual entailment between autonomy-denial and instrumentality, when it comes to the treatment of adult human beings: that whenever one denies a person's autonomy, one treats them as an instrument; and whenever one treats them as an instrument, one denies their autonomy. We can see now why this suggestion is too strong.

Does instrumentality entail autonomy-denial? I think it may well entail autonomy-denial construed as autonomy-violation; but it does not entail autonomy-denial construed as non-attribution of autonomy. A liar or rapist may treat someone as a mere means, while attributing autonomy to them.

Does autonomy-denial entail instrumentality? Clearly not; there can be autonomy-denial of either kind without instrumentality. There can be non-attribution of autonomy without instrumentality. A kindly, paternalistic doctor who takes an 'objective' attitude to his patient denies autonomy via non-attribution, but he does not use the patient as a mere tool, or a means to his ends. There can be violation of autonomy without instrumentality. Suppose the kindly, paternalistic doctor goes too far, and has the patient admitted to hospital against his will: the patient's autonomy is violated 'for his own good', but this is not rightly described as a *use* of the person. From Nussbaum's examples it is clear that she wishes 'autonomy-denial' to cover non-attribution and violation of autonomy, but neither of these have quite the intimate conceptual link with instrumentality she suggests.

Our main business here has been to show that non-attribution of autonomy, and autonomy-violation, are two importantly different ways of denying autonomy. However, still further modes of treatment are implicit in Nussbaum's discussion: for example, *self-surrender* of autonomy, and relatedly a *demand* for another's self-surrender of autonomy. These are features of Tom Brangwen's sexual experience, as described in *The Rainbow*, 'a kind of yielding abnegation of self-containment and self-sufficiency' offered by himself, and hoped for from his partner. This self-surrender, and the demand for it, are not failures to attribute autonomy, nor violations of autonomy. These are characterized by Nussbaum as potentially 'wonderful' parts of sexual life, in conditions of mutuality and equality; but an asymmetric version of the demand for surrender is perhaps less wonderful, being a feature of a different sadism, which seeks surrender of autonomy, the 'abjuration' described unforgettably by Sartre:

The spectacle which is offered to the sadist is that of a freedom which struggles against the expanding of the flesh, and which freely chooses to be submerged in the flesh. At the moment of abjuration . . . a freedom chooses to be wholly identified with this body; this distorted and heaving body is the very image of a broken and enslaved freedom.[19]

The result sought by the sadist is that the other abjure herself, abjure her autonomy, freely choose to become thing-like. I think it misses something to place this demand for surrender under the generic label of 'autonomy-denial', as if it were a version of what is going on when someone 'denies' autonomy to small children and inanimate objects.

Still further possibilities include the *destruction* or *stifling* of autonomy, perhaps implicit in the sexual slavery of *The Story of O*, described by Andrea Dworkin, and discussed by Nussbaum.

O is totally possessed. That means that she is an object, with no control over her own mobility, capable of no assertion of personality, her body is a body, in the same way that a pencil is a pencil, a bucket is a bucket.[20]

This presents a deeper damage to autonomy, a snuffing out of the capacity for choice; or a stifling of that capacity, if it is prevented from growing in the first place.

We have been observing how varied are the modes of 'treating', even when the aspect of 'object-hood', namely absence of autonomy, is held constant. This variation allows for the possibility of treatment that denies autonomy in one way, while affirming it in another. It probably allows for variation in moral significance: thinking of someone as lacking in autonomy is occasionally appropriate, and always less invasive than violating or destroying someone's autonomy. Such variations are due not just to the context-sensitivity which Nussbaum rightly emphasizes, but to differences in what the agent is doing to autonomy itself: failing to

---

[19] Jean-Paul Sartre, *Being and Nothingness* (1943), trans. Hazel Barnes (London: Methuen, 1966), 404. I discuss this passage in 'Sexual Solipsism', this volume.

[20] Nussbaum, 'Objectification', 269, quoting Andrea Dworkin, *Woman Hating* (New York: E.P. Dutton, 1974), 58.

attribute it, violating it, surrendering it, demanding that another surrender it, destroying it, stifling it.[21]

We can note that this plurality of modes of treatment probably extends to other listed features of objecthood. Subjectivity-denial, for instance, may be failure to attribute subjective mental states; sytematically attributing the wrong subjective mental states; manipulating someone's subjective mental states; even perhaps invading, destroying, or stifling their subjectivity. Silencing may be failure to attribute a capacity to speak, preventing someone from speaking, destroying or stifling someone's capacity to speak. The diverse ways of *treating as* an object link up with the diverse aspects of *being* an object, creating combinatorial possibilities whose surface we have barely begun to scratch.

3. Autonomy-denial in Pornography

In applying this to the question of pornography, we can begin with Nussbaum's comment on a violent sexual tale in the work of 'Laurence St. Clair', material which in her view would fall clearly in the scope of MacKinnon's definition. Nussbaum agrees with MacKinnon that such material is objectifying, notwithstanding an 'assuaging fiction' that this violating treatment 'is what she has asked for'—i.e. notwithstanding an 'assuaging fiction' that violation is *the woman's choice*. Nussbaum dismisses the affirmation of autonomy as, in this case, an 'assuaging fiction', but her remark brings us to the issue of pornography that 'affirms autonomy'.

Recall that *Deep Throat* was hailed as presenting 'Liberated Woman in her most extreme form, taking life and sex on her own terms'. Should that description likewise be dismissed, as a mere 'assuaging fiction'? It is tempting to say yes, that the autonomy-attribution is a sham: Linda Lovelace is hardly affirming her autonomy when she embarks on a life driven by nothing more than an insatiable desire for throat sex. That is a possible option, but it is not the only one. For there is a clear sense in which it is not completely a sham: *Deep Throat* attributes genuine choices

---

[21] It would be worth thinking about how these interact, the relevance of repetition and pervasiveness, and institutional support; whether repeated and widespread autonomy-violations may, for example, destroy autonomy; how a one-off autonomy-violation (e.g. being lied to once) is vastly different to a systematic pattern that requires institutional support (e.g. slavery).

to its fictional heroine. There is also the real Linda to consider: and here too, the film may have attributed real choices, affirming the autonomy of the *real* Linda. It claimed to be 'introducing Linda Lovelace as herself' (so the billing went), and in so doing, it portrayed not only the fictional but the real Linda as acting autonomously. Extending further afield, there are women more generally to consider: and here again, if Linda is an iconic 'Liberated Woman', standing for all women, the film in a certain sense affirms the autonomy of women in the wider world.

Do these affirmations of autonomy (of the fictional Linda, the real Linda, or other women) settle the question of whether the film affirms autonomy, *tout court*? No. There is scope for treatment that at once denies and affirms autonomy, as we have just seen. A paternalistic attitude may deny autonomy through non-attribution, without denying autonomy through violation. Certain sorts of rape may seek to override refusal, and seek to violate an autonomy whose existence they at the same time affirm. Certain kinds of sadism may seek the willing self-subjugation of an autonomy that abjures itself. Various kinds of autonomy-affirmation are compatible with various kinds of autonomy-denial, once the plurality of possible modes of treatment are recognized. Even if *Deep Throat* were to affirm women's autonomy in all the above ways, that would not settle whether it affirms autonomy *tout court*.

The film does not affirm autonomy, *tout court*. First, the claim that the film affirmed the real Linda's autonomy, even if true, requires instant qualification: for the film also denied her autonomy, as documented in her own testimony, *Ordeal*, and as more or less admitted by her one time husband and pimp, Charles Traynor. Autonomy was attributed to her in the film, but denied her in life. In a remarkable set of televised interviews, Traynor admitted the autonomy-denial:

She was pretty dumb. So everything she did, she had to be told how to do it, when to do it, and why she was doing it, and how to dress, and it just kinda rolled along like that, y'know . . . it was always a matter of telling her what to do.[22]

What she was told to do was (among other things) to *deny* that she was being told what to do. The message was, 'look as though it's your choice—or

---

[22] This and the later quotations from Traynor and Marchiano are from interviews in the documentary made by Kermode and Levin, 'The Real Linda Lovelace'.

else.' Autonomy sells. Linda couldn't choose, but was more saleable if she looked like she could. She was a useful object, more useful if it looked like a subject. There is an odd sense in which her autonomy was *itself* commodified, thwarted in life but exaggerated, in fiction, for its cash value.

The film's autonomy-attribution served autonomy violation. According to Linda's testimony in *Ordeal*, it took violence, rape, and death threats to make her play her role. Traynor admitted the violent relationship:

> I was the dominant figure, she was a submissive figure, so if it reached the point where dominance had to take over, then dominance took over. ... If you argue to a point and somebody keeps pushing you, you know, fists are bound to fly. I don't mind somebody putting in their two cents worth, but I don't want them to argue with me to the point where I get upset or violently upset, and ... yeah, that happened, on occasion. [...] I think she didn't enjoy us getting in arguments with each other, but they say if you don't want me to get into an argument, don't argue with me.

Her interviews with the press, scripted by Traynor, convey not just violation of autonomy, but other kinds of autonomy denial, perhaps destruction or stifling of autonomy. Linda later said of those interviews:

> I was just like a robot, I was told what to say and I said it, because if I didn't I was beaten, brutally.

Traynor admitted the scripting:

> I schooled her on what to say. Always sound sexy. Always look cute. Wink at the camera. Wink at the interviewer ... Always be titillating. You'd rather be having sex than doing anything. Y'know, it was just schooling, teaching her what to say, how to say it, and when to say it.

This is autonomy-denial, and it is silencing too. What she was told to say was (among other things) to deny that she was being told what to say. Linda's own voice is silenced, in the scripted interviews, and silenced in a different way later on when her own testimony about abuse, in *Ordeal*, was sold as pornography.[23]

Finally, there is the autonomy of other women to think about. Linda is not just *a* woman, but *woman*, 'Liberated Woman in her most extreme

---

[23] *Ordeal* was sold as pornography: this example of illocutionary disablement is discussed in 'Speech Acts and Unspeakable Acts', this volume, where a distinction is made between locutionary silencing due to threats (e.g. the scripted interviews), and illocutionary silencing (e.g. of *Ordeal*).

form, taking life and sex on her own terms': there is autonomy attribution here, a vision of what autonomy is, not just for Linda, but for women in the wider world. But it can be argued that this autonomy-affirmation serves autonomy-denial, a false vision of autonomy being, after all, among the most potent enemies of autonomy. According to MacKinnon, and to testimony at the Minneapolis Hearings, the film legitimated a series of real-life autonomy-violations, provoking an increase in throat rape (with associated suffocation), and an increase in unwanted and sometimes coercive attempts at throat sex.[24] In affirming women's autonomy one way, and identifying that autonomy with sexual freedom, *Deep Throat* style, it legitimated autonomy-denial a different way, when the pornographer's image of women's choices was used to thwart real women's choices.

Some pornography, I conclude, might objectify even as it affirms autonomy: indeed, it might objectify through its autonomy-affirmation, the way it objectifies depending on the distinctive way it affirms autonomy. The autonomy-affirmation in *Deep Throat* (of a fictional Linda, a real Linda, or real women elsewhere) is one that serves autonomy-denial (of a real Linda, and real women elsewhere). These denials of autonomy—the violations, silencings or stiflings of autonomy—depend, substantially, on the affirmation of autonomy. That attribution of sexual autonomy to Linda was a structural feature of her oppressive circumstances, making abuse easier, hiding it, and hindering escape. That attribution of sexual autonomy to an iconic Liberated Woman, and thereby to other women, likewise facilitated violation of at least some other women's autonomy. Now whether *Deep Throat* is a typical or significant sample of autonomy-affirming pornography is a question I shall not, here, take time to address. But it is enough to suggest, I think, that pornography's way of affirming women's autonomy could, at least sometimes, be a way of denying women's autonomy; and there would be no paradox, at all, about that.

---

[24] See Minneapolis City Council, *Pornography and Sexual Violence: Evidence of the Links* (London: Everywoman, 1988), transcript of *Public Hearings on Ordinances to Add Pornography as Discrimination Against Women*, Committee on Government Operations (Dec. 12–13, 1983).

11

Projection and Objectification

1. Autonomy and Projection in Feminist Philosophy

It is hard to say anything uncontroversial about present feminist work in philosophy, let alone about prospects for the future. All the same, I shall begin by picking up two ideas, and saying something about why they have mattered, and will continue to matter. They are the ideas of *autonomy*, and of *projection*. These two have mattered to different camps within feminist philosophy, camps that have sometimes disagreed in ways that roughly, though not exactly, mirror an older division between analytic and continental philosophers. I shall be wanting to see how the two ideas unite in a phenomenon of wider interest: that of sexual objectification.[1]

Pioneer feminists viewed women's oppression in terms of women's autonomy and its thwarting, and this concern has remained central to the work of many liberal feminists, and those working in analytic philosophy. On this view, the basic problem has been that women have been cast in the role of human tools, as Aristotle described slaves: women have been treated as beings whose nature is to be directed by another, and whose purpose is instrumental; women have been treated as lacking in autonomy, and have had their autonomy systematically violated or stifled. This links the idea of oppression with that of objectification: when women are treated as tools, they are treated as things, items lacking in agency. Feminists tend in general to have few warm words for Kant, but these might find it in their hearts to concede he was on the right track when he said that 'autonomy is . . . the ground of the dignity of human nature, and of every rational nature'; and that we should therefore 'always treat humanity,

---

[1] This essay originally appeared in *The Future for Philosophy*, ed., Brian Leiter (Oxford: Oxford University Press, 2004), 285–303.

whether in our own person or in the person of any other, never simply as a means, but always at the same time as an end'.[2] They may disagree about what, exactly, autonomy is, and how, exactly, it matters; but they agree that it matters. Martha Nussbaum, to take a recent example, offers an illuminating study of objectification that places autonomy-denial at centre-stage. Connected with autonomy-denial, through a variety of different entailments, are a cluster of other features: instrumentality; ownership or possession; fungibility, or replaceability; subjectivity-denial; violability; and denial of agency. I shall be drawing on her study in what follows.[3]

The second idea I want to pick up is the idea of projection implicit in certain feminist accounts of social construction. Women's oppression stems from the operation of large-scale psychological or linguistic forces, shaped by unconscious and irrational desires, or shaped by the structure of language itself, a 'language of the fathers'. While feminists in this camp are if anything less likely to find warm words for Kant, and would view with suspicion his pronouncements on autonomy and the dignity of human nature, they might find it in their hearts to concede he was on the right track when he said, on a different topic, that 'the order and regularity in the appearances, which we entitle nature, we ourselves introduce'—and when he showed an interest, not in how our cognitions conform to objects, but in how objects conform to our cognitions.[4] Taking this thought to the social world, they might ask how women conform to the cognitions or representations men have of them. They might add that Kant was mistaken in taking projective construction to be a product of reason, rather than irrational desire, mistaken in supposing it yields necessary constraints, and mistaken above all in his blindness to its political significance.

Those who draw on certain theories of language might speak in terms of the constructive power of certain concepts, or the projection of certain

[2] Immanuel Kant, *Groundwork of the Metaphysics of Morals*, trans. H. J. Paton, in *The Moral Law* (New York: Harper and Row, 1964), 436, 429.

[3] Martha Nussbaum, 'Objectification', *Philosophy and Public Affairs* 24 (1995), 249–91. See also Barbara Herman, 'Could It Be Worth Thinking about Kant on Sex and Marriage?' in *A Mind Of One's Own: Feminist Essays on Reason and Objectivity,* eds., Louise M. Antony and Charlotte Witt (Boulder, Co.: Westview Press, 1993). For some alternative interpretations of autonomy, see e.g. *Relational Autonomy: Feminist Perspectives on Autonomy, Agency and the Social Self,* eds., Catriona Mackenzie and Natalie Stoljar (Oxford: Oxford University Press, 2000).

[4] Immanuel Kant, *Critique of Pure Reason*, trans. Norman Kemp Smith (London and Basingstoke: Macmillan, 1980), A126 and Bxvi.

grammatical categories; in an extreme example, Luce Irigaray tries to convey the oppressive potency of grammar by proposing that 'I love *to* you' is an improvement on 'I love you', the latter after all making a direct 'object' of the loved one. Those who draw upon psychoanalysis (sometimes the same theorists) might speak in terms of the projection of unconscious desires.[5] Descartes' dualistic metaphysics, with its denigration of matter, gets interpreted as the projection of unconscious desires to reject one's mother, and insist on separation. Philosophy itself is put on the couch, interpreted as desire-driven belief which unconsciously expresses and perpetuates hostility to women, shaping thought about the world in general and women in particular. (Needless to say, a liberal focus on autonomy receives a similar projective and debunking explanation.) Distinctive features of this approach include the assumptions that belief is driven by desire; that desire-driven belief shapes and constructs the social world; and that the process is largely invisible to the participants. In this camp too one finds a link with a notion of objectification, understood rather differently, drawing on grammatical notions of an object, or conceptual associations of women with matter.

Feminist thinkers in one camp sometimes get impatient with feminist thinkers in the other. One side finds the other's preoccupation with autonomy naive, a relic of oppressive, dualistic ways of thinking; finds naive her apparent focus on individual action, and local manifestation of prejudice; and finds naive her apparent neglect of the invisible forces of desire and language. The other in turn finds naive her sister's exaggeration of the power of desire and language; finds frustrating the poetic style which seeks an alternative to the language of the fathers, an authentic woman's voice which in practice thwarts communication; and finds naive her apparent neglect of norms, whether of reason or morality, by which a case for feminism can be argued. Moreover the background assumptions of psychoanalytic feminism can look philosophically suspicious. The claim

---

[5] Luce Irigaray proposes implausibly dramatic theses about linguistic and psychoanalytic projection in e.g. *I love to you* (London: Routledge, 1995); and *Speculum of the Other Woman* trans. Gillian Gill (Ithaca: Cornell University Press, 1985), which puts Descartes and other philosophers on the couch. It is impossible to refer adequately to the vast literature here, but for another salient example see Jane Flax, 'Political Philosophy and the Patriarchal Unconscious', eds., Sandra Harding and Merrill Hintikka, *Discovering Reality* (Dordrecht: Reidel, 1983). Genevieve Lloyd's *The Man of Reason* (London: Methuen, 1984) is a classic study of the conceptual (though not particularly psychoanalytic) associations between women and matter in philosophy's history.

that belief is driven by desire, and that belief shapes and constructs the world—these appear to violate rules of direction of fit. Belief aims to fit the world; desire aims for the world to fit it. But the psychoanalytic story violates these rules: instead of belief coming to fit the world, belief comes to fit desire, and the world, somehow, comes to fit the belief.

It is not my aim to referee these disagreements here. Instead I want to look at the twin themes of autonomy and projection, each emphasized by one camp, neglected by another. I shall say something brief about their on-going importance, and consider, in conciliatory spirit, how they unite in an adequate understanding of sexual objectification. I shall be assuming, but not arguing, that each camp is at least partly right. Yes, autonomy does indeed matter. And yes, belief can indeed come to fit desire; the world can indeed come to fit belief; the process can indeed go on in ways invisible to the participants. I shall be interested in the implications of this projective process for autonomy, in sexual objectification.

Section 2 considers how projection might *help* sexual objectification through its generation of certain desire-driven beliefs. I distinguish a number of projective mechanisms, and explore how these projective mechanisms might assist in the treating of women as things.[6] Section 3 considers how projection might *hide* sexual objectification. I focus here on the epistemology of objectification, and how projection might help to mask itself, and the objectification it assists.

Unwise though it is to speculate, it seems unlikely that the importance of autonomy and projection will go away. One needs no crystal ball to guess that the forces of global capitalism will be around for a while, and with them a tendency to treat people not only as consumers but as commodities, items for use and consumption, and that this is likely to have a continuing effect on women's lives, as the ever-burgeoning sex industry illustrates. One can anticipate on-going scope for a feminist version of the Kantian idea that there is a dignity in human nature having its ground in autonomy,

---

[6] The distinctions and arguments of Section 2 build on work in 'Humean Projection in Sexual Objectification' (forthcoming), which looks in more detail at Hume. It was presented as my inaugural lecture as Professor of Moral Philosophy (Edinburgh, January 2002), a position for which Hume himself was, in 1755, turned down—salutary reminder of another prejudice. Other feminist work draws on Hume, see e.g. Annette Baier, 'Hume: The Reflective Women's Epistemologist?', in *A Mind of One's Own: Feminist Essays on Reason and Objectivity*, eds., Louise M. Antony and Charlotte Witt (Boulder, Co.: Westview Press, 1993), but I am not aware of material that draws on his views of projection.

and that by virtue of this worth 'we are not for sale at any price'.[7] And one needs no crystal ball to guess that the substitution of the virtual for the real will become an increasing fact of life; and that projection will be a topic of increasing importance, as people increasingly substitute virtual action for action, virtual experience for experience, and virtual human relationships for human relationships.

The pornography industry again provides an illustration. But whether projection should matter here is perhaps less obvious. For even if pornography use does involve projection, and even if pornography also objectifies women in ways that deny autonomy, that would not show that the projective aspect of pornography matters. Projection could be a merely incidental feature of pornography, of as little moral interest as other accidental facts about pornography—as, for example, the uninteresting fact that its images supervene on dots of ink, or pixels on a screen.

To see how the ideas of autonomy and projection might connect, I turn now to an account of sexual objectification offered by Catharine MacKinnon which draws explicitly upon both ideas, and in so doing, unites elements from each of the camps I have described.[8] The hope is that this will enable us to see how projection might help, and hide, sexual objectification.

2. How Projection Helps Sexual Objectification

MacKinnon describes sexual objectification as 'the primary process of the subjection of women', and says:

To be sexually objectified means having a social meaning imposed on your being that defines you as to be sexually used. . . and then using you that way.[9]

This notion of sexual objectification draws in recognizable ways on the first of the two ideas, conveying a Kantian heritage in that notion of

[7] Kant, *Doctrine of Virtue*, trans. Mary Gregor (New York: Harper and Row, 1964), 435.

[8] Notwithstanding the fact that MacKinnon's proposals have been viewed skeptically by members of each camp. See e.g. Nussbaum, 'Objectification', whose skepticism is directed not so much against the analysis but the legal proposal; Judith Butler, *Excitable Speech: A Politics of the Performative* (New York and London: Routledge, 1997), ch. 2.

[9] MacKinnon, *Toward a Feminist Theory of the State* (Cambridge, Mass.: Harvard University Press, 1989), 122, 140.

'use', which picks up on idea autonomy–denial and instrumentality. Sexual objectification emerges as the idea (drawing here on Nussbaum's elucidation) that certain sexual ways of treating someone may be ways of denying their autonomy, ignoring their subjective inner life, treating them as readily replaceable, treating them as the kinds of things that can be bought and sold, treating them as something merely to be used, something that is a mere tool.

MacKinnon also describes sexual objectification in terms that draw on the second idea: sexual objectification is, she says, 'an elaborate projective system'.[10] She is interested in how objectification 'unites act with word, construction with expression, perception with enforcement, myth with reality'.[11] She is interested in how different modes of treatment 'unite': for example when speech 'unites' with act, and when thought 'unites' with coercion. She is also interested in how desire 'unites' with belief and perception: those who exert power over women see the world as a certain way because they '*want* to see' the world that way; they believe the world is a certain way because they '*want* to believe' it is that way. What she describes, I suggest, is a kind of *desire-driven* projection.[12]

This theme of projection, desire-driven or otherwise, tends to be absent in the accounts of objectification offered by analytic or liberal feminists; it seems, for example, to be missing in Nussbaum's otherwise admirably comprehensive study.[13] It receives plenty of attention elsewhere in analytic philosophy however, for example in analyses of the epistemology of colour, and of value. Indeed the projective process is given the very label 'objectification' by J. L. Mackie, when he complains of our tendency 'to objectify values', complains of the propensity of the mind to project itself—to 'spread itself on external objects', as Hume put it.[14] Mackie and

---

[10] MacKinnon, *Feminist Theory*, 140–1.

[11] MacKinnon, *Feminist Theory*, 122.

[12] MacKinnon, *Feminist Theory*, 122, 140; *Feminism Unmodified: Discourses on Life and Law* (Cambridge, Mass.: Harvard University Press, 1987), 164, emphasis added.

[13] An important exception is Sally Haslanger, whose work on this topic has substantially inspired and influenced me; see Haslanger, 'On Being Objective and Being Objectified', in *A Mind of One's Own*, eds., Louise Antony and Charlotte Witt (Boulder, Co.: Westview Press, 1993). I draw on this in 'Beyond A Pragmatic Critique of Reason', *Australasian Journal of Philosophy* 71 (1993), 364–84; and 'Feminism in Epistemology: Exclusion and Objectification', *The Cambridge Companion to Feminism in Philosophy*, eds., Jennifer Hornsby and Miranda Fricker (Cambridge: Cambridge University Press, 2000) 127–45, the latter reprinted here.

[14] J. L. Mackie, *Ethics: Inventing Right and Wrong* (Harmondsworth: Penguin, 1990), ch. 1; David Hume, *A Treatise of Human Nature*, ed., L. A. Selby-Bigge, rev. P. H. Nidditch (Oxford: Clarendon Press, 1978), 167.

MacKinnon share an interest in the way desire and belief may unite to create something both wish to call 'objectification', notwithstanding their different concerns; and they share an interest, too, in desire-driven projection. According to Mackie, in objectifying value, we ascribe 'a fictitious external authority' to features that are nothing more than projections of our 'wants' and 'demands', our 'appetites' and 'desires'.[15]

How are we to understand the idea of a desire-driven projection, as it bears on sexual objectification? In what follows I shall describe and distinguish three varieties of desire-driven projection, none of which should seem too unfamiliar. They all have in common a capacity to generate a belief, given a desire. And they all have in common a potential involvement in sexual objectification, or so I shall suggest, drawing on MacKinnon in each case to illustrate their possible workings. My purpose is analytical and exploratory, rather than polemical. I shall assume, without defending, the adequacy of some projective explanatory hypotheses MacKinnon proposes, though I am aware that more defence is needed.

The first mechanism I shall call the *phenomenological gilding* of desired objects, recalling Hume's description of our activity of 'gilding or staining all natural objects with the colours, borrowed from internal sentiment'.[16] This mechanism is distinctive in generating beliefs about *value* in particular. The second is the familiar mechanism of *wishful thinking*, which can generate a belief that something is so, given a desire that it be so. Its scope goes beyond beliefs about value to beliefs about almost anything. The third mechanism I shall call *pseudo-empathy*, which is an over-hasty disposition to attribute features of one's own mind to other people, animals, or even inanimate objects (I don't address the question of when exactly such a leap counts as 'over-hasty'). Pseudo-empathy can generate a belief, given a desire, when it leaps from one's own desire that something be so to a belief that someone else desires that it be so. While these mechanisms can all generate belief, given desire, they vary in the sorts of belief they can in principle generate, given a desire—phenomenological gilding generating beliefs about value, wishful thinking generating beliefs about almost anything, and pseudo-empathy generating beliefs about the desires of others. To the extent that these mechanisms generate belief, given desire, they violate the

---

[15] Mackie, *Ethics*, 34, 42, 43, 45.

[16] David Hume, *Enquiries Concerning Human Understanding and Concerning the Principles of Morals*, ed., L. A. Selby-Bigge, rev. P. H. Nidditch, 3rd edn (Oxford: Clarendon Press, 1975), 294.

aforementioned rule about direction of fit: belief aims to fit the world, not to fit desire. But these beliefs fit desire.[17]

There is a question about what sorts of desires will be relevant to a projective belief implicated in sexual objectification; and I shall be considering broadly sexual desires. More sinister desires might be equally relevant, or more relevant: for example, explicit desires to maintain or exercise power, to dominate or humiliate, to cause pain; but I shall not be attending much to these. This is a very substantial omission, since such desires may well have an important role to play in sexual objectification, given that some of them presumably *aim* to objectify someone, reduce someone to a thing. I am hoping the omission can be viewed as a dialectical strength: presumably if sexual objectification can be generated by more ordinary sexual desires, without help of sinister desires to exert power or humiliate, it could all the more readily be generated with their help.

2.1. *Phenomenological gilding*

Sometimes projective belief may have its source in a distinctive phenomenology of experience. Our beliefs about color, for example, are thought by some philosophers to be mere projections based on the phenomenological character of our color experience. Our beliefs about color do not, of course, have their source in desire, so this example is different to the projective beliefs we shall be considering. But I want to ask whether there might be something about the phenomenology of desire—by analogy with the phenomenology of color—which could yield certain beliefs. If there were, this would be a desire-driven mechanism quite different to the familiar mechanism of wishful thinking: my wishful belief in the immortality of the soul does not arise from any phenomenological feature of my desire to avoid death: my life does not *look* to be immortal, in the way that objects *look* to be colored. If the phenomenology of desire has the capacity to generate beliefs, possible candidates for such beliefs are beliefs about value.

Hume applied his metaphor of 'gilding and staining' to color and value alike, and may partly have had this phenomenological parallel in mind when he pursued his extended analogy between them. Describing 'the impulse to desire', he said

---

[17] See 'Exclusion and Objectification', this volume, for further discussion.

it has a productive faculty, and gilding and staining all natural objects with the colours, borrowed from internal sentiment, raises in a manner, a new creation.[18]

Mackie, following Hume, regards the desire-generated projection of belief about value as partly phenomenological. He also quotes Hobbes—'whatsoever is the object of any man's Appetite or Desire, that is it, which he for his part calleth Good'—and comments on how (in his view) we reverse the direction of dependence, regarding the desire as depending on the goodness, rather than the goodness on the desire. In parallel manner, but for aversion rather than desire, Mackie says we attribute independent disvalue, a foulness, to the fungus that fills us with disgust.[19] To the extent this occurs, Mackie's account of the projection of value (whose skeptical implications don't concern us here) can be seen as describing a projective response to phenomenological features of desire. The thing desired can appear phenomenologically as having independent qualities that justify, demand, or legitimate the desire, making it almost literally *appear* to have independent value, just as a strawberry appears to be independently red. When you desire something, you can project its desirability, aware less of your attitude than of an apparent feature of the object of your attitude. The phenomenology is quasi-perceptual. (To the eye of a hungry Goldilocks, the porridge literally *looks* delicious.) Belief about value may sometimes be belief that is responsive to this distinctive phenomenology of desire. This phenomenological gilding presents us with one sort of desire-generated belief: belief about the value of what is desired.

Let us think about the possible role of phenomenological gilding in sexual objectification. MacKinnon says,

Like the value of a commodity, women's sexual desirability is fetishized: it is made to appear a quality of the object itself, spontaneous and inherent, independent of the social relation that creates it, uncontrolled by the force that requires it.[20]

MacKinnon is here attempting to describe a certain phenomenology of desire, of men's sexual desire, in an oppressive political context. A woman's 'value', a woman's 'desirability' is 'made to appear a quality of the object, spontaneous and inherent'. The sexual value of a woman appears,

---

[18] Hume, *Enquiry*, 294. He is here describing taste as the first impulse to desire.
[19] Mackie, *Ethics*, 42, 43.   [20] MacKinnon, *Feminist Theory*, 123.

phenomenologically, as an 'inherent', independent feature, independent of the desire and independent of relevant social forces, seeming authoritative, seeming to justify the belief in the value, and seeming to justify the sexual desire it provokes. This is what I have described as phenomenological gilding. And so far, so innocuous: there is nothing yet to indicate sexual objectification, nothing yet to indicate how this valuing might be involved in treating a woman as a thing. But now: a woman's value, a woman's desirability, is somehow 'like the value of a *commodity*'. What does she mean? Perhaps this. A massive commercial industry, namely the pornography industry, makes certain objects of sexual desire into commodities, items for commercial buying and selling, a sexual tool for easy satisfaction of appetite, for ownership; and it shapes men's desires too so that they become attracted to these sexual commodities. When this occurs, men's sexual desires can themselves become, so speak, commodifying desires: the phenomenology of men's sexual desire comes to be, in certain aspects, a desire for this kind of commodity, to the extent that their sexual desires for real women can come to resemble, in certain aspects, their desires for the pornographic commodities.[21]

What then would be the implications for belief about a woman's value? If phenomenological gilding is possible, desire can be a source of projective evaluative belief. So a commodifying desire could be a source of a commodifying evaluative belief. The result would be that the value women are seen as having, and believed to have, will be the sort of value that commodities, especially pornographic commodities, are seen as having, and believed to have.

This in turn would have implications for questions about whether and how phenomenological gilding is implicated in sexual objectification. In many contexts, phenomenological gilding is innocent in moral terms (whether or not dubious epistemologically); indeed it may be better than innocent. Nussbaum wanted to allow that the objectification she describes could, in certain contexts, be a 'wonderful' part of sexual life,

---

[21] In Pamela Paul's interviews with pornography consumers, it is clear that consumers of pornography can have their desires shaped by pornography, to the extent that their sexual enjoyment with real women can come to depend on treating women as pornography: whether by running pornography in their imaginations while treating their partners as a prop; or demanding that their partners act like the women in pornography; or some combination of both. Pamela Paul, *Pornified: How Pornography is Transforming Our Lives, Our Relationships, Our Families* (New York: Henry Holt, 2005), throughout, but see especially e.g. ch. 3.

as, for example, when lovers (as described by D. H. Lawrence at any rate) might seek a mutual abandonment of autonomy.[22] The same applies here: when one thinks of the power of sexual love to transfigure perception of the loved one, so that through its eyes every bodily feature appears as precious, every gesture illumined—this 'gilding' of the loved one through desire likewise appears as a potentially 'wonderful' part of sexual life.

But with commodified desire, things will be altogether more bleak. Phenomenological gilding allows a transition from desire to belief about value, via the phenomenology of desire; and MacKinnon's thought seems to be that, to the sexually objectifying eye of the pornography consumer, women appear, phenomenologically, a certain way—they, so to speak, 'look' the way pornography looks, not (or not just) because pornography tries to resemble women (which would make the idea trivial), but because pornography's commodified view of women gets transferred, through the eye of the consumer, to women themselves. That is perhaps why MacKinnon says elsewhere that pornography shapes a 'gaze that constructs women as objects for male pleasure . . . that eroticizes the despised, the demeaned, the accessible, the there-to-be-used, the servile'.[23] If phenomenology of desire can prompt belief about value, and commodifying sexual desires lead to women being seen and valued in the way that commodities—especially pornographic commodities—are seen and valued, this would result in women being treated as things, along many of the dimensions Nussbaum identifies. Women would be valued as instruments for the easy satisfaction of desire, as ownable, readily exchangeable; and those who value women as sexual commodities would be more likely to treat them that way in their behaviour. One could expect these attitudes to result in autonomy-denying action, as women's autonomy is inadequately attributed, and violated, through harassment and rape.

2.2. *Wishful thinking*

Wishful thinking is a phenomenon so familiar it needs little in the way of introduction, and while it poses many difficult philosophical questions, they will not be our topic here. It presents a different aspect of Hume's idea of the mind 'spreading itself' on the world. Hume himself thought many

---

[22] Nussbaum, 'Objectification'.   [23] MacKinnon, *Feminism Unmodified*, 53–4.

of our beliefs have such wishful origins, including, for example, belief in the immortality of the soul:

All doctrines are to be suspected which are favoured by our passions; and the hopes and fears which gave rise to this doctrine are very obvious.[24]

Our question is whether wishful thinking might have a role to play in sexual objectification. What salient beliefs might be wishfully prompted by sexual desire? Candidates might be beliefs that help the desire to persist, that seem to fulfil the desire, or that make the desire seem more likely to be fulfilled. A belief in a *matching desire* seems a likely candidate: the belief of the form 'she desires to do what I desire to do' will legitimate the initial desire and make its satisfaction seem more likely. Moreover, it has plausibly been suggested (by Thomas Nagel) that a constitutive component of an ordinary sexual desire is the aim for a matching desire in the other person.[25] (There will be other, more pathological, cases where the desire of the other person is irrelevant, or relevant negatively, as for a sadist who might desire an *absence* of matching desire.) Belief in matching desire would then convey the belief that this component is already satisfied, as well as conveying hope of the desire's complete fulfillment. So we might antecedently expect wishful incentives for belief in matching desire, and in a source that is far from sinister, namely the very desire for mutuality which is so central to sexual life, but that can go awry, if it helps generate merely wishful belief.

We turn now to some candidate examples, most of which are drawn from MacKinnon, though the first is not. They are examples which also make 'wishful thinking' appear a sadly inadequate label (which is perhaps why MacKinnon does not use it).

Example 1: Attribution of matching desire, in a scene from *The Innocent*, by Ian McEwan . . . Leonard, a young and 'kindly' Englishman, and Maria,

---

[24] David Hume, 'On the Immortality of the Soul', from *Essays Moral and Political* (1741–2), reprinted in *David Hume: Selected Essays*, eds., Stephen Copley and Andrew Edgar (Oxford: Oxford University Press, 1998), 331.

[25] Thomas Nagel, 'Sexual Perversion', in *Mortal Questions* (Cambridge: Cambridge University Press, 1991)—describing not merely a matching desire, but a matching desire which has a complex and iterative Gricean structure.

who is German, meet and fall in love in post-war Berlin. Later on Leonard begins to have a fantasy:

It began . . . with a simple perception. He looked down at Maria, whose eyes were closed, and remembered she was a German . . . Enemy. . . . Defeated enemy. This last brought with it a shocking thrill. He diverted himself momentarily. . . . Then: she was the defeated, she was his by right, by conquest, by right of unimaginable violence and heroism and sacrifice. . . . He was powerful and magnificent. . . . He was victorious and good and strong and free. In recollection these formulations embarrassed him. But next time round the thoughts returned. They were irresistibly exciting . . . she was his by right of conquest and then, *there was nothing she could do about it.* She did not want to be making love to him, but she had no choice.

Still later, he begins to imagine himself a soldier forcing himself on a defeated German enemy; and then he found himself

tempted to communicate these imaginings to her . . . He could not believe she would not be aroused by it. . . . His private theatre had become insufficient. . . . He wanted his power recognized and Maria to suffer from it, just a bit, in the most pleasurable way. . . . Then he was ashamed. What was this power he wanted recognized? It was no more than a disgusting story in his head. Then, later, he wondered whether she might not be excited by it too. There was, of course, nothing to discuss . . . He had to surprise her, show her, let pleasure overcome her rational objections . . . [26]

Leonard uses Maria's body as, so to speak, a screen, his 'private theatre', on which to project the fantasy of Maria (or: anonymous German enemy) as victim of his rape. The process, as it develops, involves wishful thinking: first in the desire-driven attitude which falls short of belief (he does not believe she is a victim of rape, it is merely 'as if'); then in the desire-driven genuine belief that she will find the fantasy exciting too.

The example brings out an important ambiguity in the notion of a 'matching' desire, which is roughly the contrast between 'same desire' and 'complementary desire'. Depending on how it is described, the projected 'matching' desire may look like the same desire as the man's, or it may

---

[26] Ian McEwan, *The Innocent* (London: Picador, 1990), taken from 83–5. This scene is also discussed in 'Humean Projection' (where the examples from MacKinnon are also discussed); and in 'Sexual Solipsism', this volume.

look like a desire that complements his. The desire that Leonard attributes to Maria is under one description the same as his: 'a desire to entertain this rape fantasy'. When thought of in these terms, it looks like a hoped-for mutuality. But the desire he attributes is, under another, more careful, description, very different from his. Leonard's is a desire to *imagine raping*; the one he projects on to Maria is a desire to *imagine being raped*. 'He could not believe that she would not be aroused by it'; but the 'it' for her is hardly the same as the 'it' for him.

Does this example involve sexual objectification? Surely yes. There is instrumentality and autonomy-denial merely in this use of Maria as a projective screen, especially given the fantasy's hidden content. And when Leonard still later succumbs to the temptation to share his solipsistic theatre and 'show' her his imaginings, what ensues is something both parties view, or come to view, as attempted rape. This brings us to the more general issue provided by the next example.

Example 2: Attribution of matching desire, in certain kinds of rape. MacKinnon says, of the 'system' that is sexual objectification,

In this system...women men want, want men....Raped women are seen as asking for it: if a man wanted her, she must have wanted him.[27]

In a case where a woman is genuinely believed to have 'wanted him', either at the time, or later on in *post hoc* rationalization, the rapist desires to have sex with the woman, and projects a matching desire, perhaps wishfully generated.[28] (I shall not speculate about how common such cases of genuine belief are.) Wishful belief that 'she wanted it' may also be projected by other people, including, perhaps, jury members and other ordinary women, prompted in the latter case by a rather different sort of desire—a desire, perhaps, that the world should be a safe one. To the extent that wishful thinking is responsible for the attribution of matching desire in such contexts, it would be implicated in sexual objectification, in particular the profound autonomy-denial and violation which is rape.

---

[27] MacKinnon, *Feminist Theory*, 140–1.

[28] Such cases may be more common in date rape, and raise issues that parallel the Morgan case in British law (where Morgan's friends claimed genuine belief that his wife consented to sex with them), discussed briefly in Langton, 'Pornography: A Liberal's Unfinished Business', *Canadian Journal of Law and Jurisprudence* 12 (1999), 109–133; part reprinted as 'Equality and Moralism: Reply to Dworkin', this volume.

Example 3:   Attribution of matching desire, in the pornographic film *Deep Throat.*

This elaborate projective system of demand characteristics—taken to pinnacles like fantasizing a clitoris in a woman's throat so that men can enjoy forced fellatio in real life, assured that women do too—is surely a delusional structure deserving of serious psychological study.[29]

This is a peculiar case, in which something like wishful thinking may well be implicated, first in the desire-driven generation of an attitude that falls short of belief, the entertainment of the fiction that Linda Lovelace madly desires throat sex, due to a quirk of anatomy. Genuine beliefs are also generated, according to MacKinnon (who cites evidence about subsequent behaviour), among them a belief that the star, Linda Marchiano, enjoyed what she was doing; and that women, more generally, are likely to enjoy throat sex.[30] Wishful thinking provides a possible explanation (plus the fact that desire is assisted by genuine belief that pornography 'actors' enjoy what they do). Sexual objectification is described here as 'an elaborate projective system', where 'demand characteristics' are projected first on to a fictional protagonist, the projected desire sustaining and legitimating the viewer's own arousal. The wishful shaping of belief is mediated by the shaping of desire: MacKinnon suggests that pornographic fantasy conditions and alters sexual desire; a consumer may subsequently find desirable the prospect of throat sex, which desire in turn provides incentives for attributing matching desire to Marchiano herself, and to other women—notwithstanding the real world absence of science-fiction anatomy. A projective pattern like this is, MacKinnon remarks, a 'delusional structure deserving of serious psychological study'.

How would this projective pattern be implicated in sexual objectification? A small part of the question is whether the envisaged desire attribution objectifies the merely fictional Linda, and here one might be

---

[29] MacKinnon, *Feminist Theory*, 140–1.

[30] Cf. MacKinnon on the 'realism' of *Deep Throat*: '[B]efore "Linda Lovelace" was seen performing deep throat, no one had ever seen it being done that way, largely because it cannot be done without hypnosis to repress the natural gag response. *Yet it was believed.* Men proceeded to demand it of women, causing the distress of many and the death of some. Yet when Linda Marchiano now tells that it took kidnapping and death threats and hypnosis to put her there, that is found *difficult to believe*'; (see *Feminism Unmodified*, 181, and associated references to relevant empirical data).

tempted to think it does not: there is (in Nussbaum's terms) no denial of subjectivity or autonomy, but an affirmation, an attribution to the fictional character of an avid and independent desire for throat sex. The process may still be objectifying, though, in its instrumental view of a woman desperate to make herself sexually available to anyone who wants her. A more important part of the question is whether the desire-attribution to the real Linda objectifies her, and here the answer is surely affirmative: her testimony in *Ordeal* tells how she suffered threats to her life, sexual torture, and rape, in the film's making, and that it took that plus hypnosis (to reduce the gag response) to make her do it. The attribution of matching desire to the real Linda obscures all this, and is thus a denial of subjectivity which assists the deep instrumentality and autonomy-denial involved in her abuse, and silences her later testimony.[31] Thirdly, there is the question of whether desire-attribution to other real women by consumers later on objectifies those women.[32] Here again the answer again may be affirmative, if one accepts testimony that some consumers later attributed, or tried to attribute, matching desires for throat sex to their partners (resulting sometimes in 'deep throat' assault): such attitudes and consequent behaviour are likely to instantiate particularly serious versions of (in Nussbaum's terms) subjectivity-denial, instrumentality and autonomy-denial.[33]

Example 4: Attribution of matching desire, through women's supposed capacity for vaginal orgasm—a science fiction about women that was long accepted as orthodox science. MacKinnon's explanation is that because 'men demand that women enjoy vaginal penetration', they acquire the belief, dressed up as science, that 'vaginal orgasms' are the only 'mature' sexuality; and accordingly the belief that women desire penetrative sex

---

[31] In 'Autonomy-Denial in Objectification' (this volume) I add the notion of silencing to Nussbaum's 'cluster concept' of objectification. Cf. 'Objects do not speak. When they do, they are by then regarded as objects, not as humans, which is what it means to have no credibility,' MacKinnon, *Feminism Unmodified*, 182. For an understanding of what the silencing amounts to, and how Marchiano is silenced, see 'Speech Acts and Unspeakable Acts', this volume.

[32] There is also the question of the attribution of desire to women more generally by the film itself: despite being fiction, it may attribute to real women the sorts of desires the fictional Linda is represented as having, in which case the attitude to women in general is at the least an instrumental one. See 'Scorekeeping in a Pornographic Language Game' (co-authored with Caroline West) and 'Autonomy Denial in Objectification', both in this volume.

[33] Such testimony was given at the Minneapolis Hearings (I *Hearings* 60), cited by MacKinnon in *Feminism Unmodified*, 286 n. 65.

because this is their natural route to orgasm.[34] Wishful thinking projects an imagined biological basis for a conveniently matching desire on the part of the woman, and adds whatever legitimation is granted by a scientific establishment—an eery pseudo-science parallel to the science-fiction biology of *Deep Throat*. Does such attribution of matching desire objectify women? One might suppose again that the attitude itself is not objectifying, that on the contrary it attributes an active independent desire to women, a distinct source of pleasure unique to women, that however erroneous, it is at least subjectivity-affirming and autonomy-affirming. This would be too hasty, given that the attitude denies that women have the sexual experiences they have, and asserts they have sexual experiences they lack—something that may count as subjectivity-denial, rather than affirmation.[35] There may also be instrumental thinking involved; how much more useful if the shape of women's sexual desire were the perfect match to that of men! The theorizing in turn perhaps helped to legitimate instrumental sexual use of women by other parties, by silencing, as 'immature' those women whose desires were apparently less convenient.

Example 5:   Attribution of matching desire in Freud's 'seduction theory'. The Freudian interpretation of women's testimony about abuse as children bears comparison, according to MacKinnon, with the projective 'system' in pornography use:

Both the psychoanalytic and the pornographic 'fantasy' worlds are what men imagine women imagine and desire because they are what men, raised on pornography, imagine and desire about women. . . . Perhaps the Freudian process of theory-building occurred like this: men heard accounts of child abuse, felt aroused by the account, and attributed their arousal to the child who is now a woman. . . . Classical psychoanalysis attributes the connection between the experience of abuse (hers) and the experience of arousal (his) to the fantasy of the girl

---

[34] MacKinnon, *Feminist Theory*, 123, 140–1. Elisabeth Lloyd cites blindness to 'orgasm-intercourse discrepancy' for women as an example of bias in evolutionary explanations of women's sexuality, 'Pre-Theoretical Assumptions in Evolutionary Explanations of Female Sexuality', *Philosophical Studies* 69 (1993), 139–53: 'Not to have orgasm from [unassisted] intercourse is the experience of the majority of women the majority of the time' (p. 144), citing studies according to which 30% never have orgasm from unassisted intercourse, 20–35% always or almost always do. For discussion of Lloyd, see Langton, 'Feminism in Philosophy', *The Oxford Handbook of Contemporary Philosophy*, eds., Frank Jackson and Michael Smith (Oxford: Oxford University Press, 2005), 231–57.

[35] See 'Autonomy-Denial in Objectification', this volume.

child. When he does it, he likes it, so when she did it, she must have liked it. Thus it cannot be abusive to her. Because he wants to do it, she must want it done.[36]

The psychoanalyst hears a sexual narrative which he experiences as arousing; since sexual desire aims for a matching desire, he desires the woman likewise to experience the narrative as arousing and accordingly to desire to entertain it. Such desire, on the part of the woman, would sustain and legitimate his own desire. Through a process of wishful thinking, there is a transition to belief: he believes the woman herself experiences the telling of the narrative as arousing, and desires to entertain it; and he believes that as a child, she had that sort of experience and that desire. This belief offering in turn a sufficient explanation for the narrative's existence, the narrative is interpreted as desired fantasy, rather than testimony of child abuse. MacKinnon suggests that a similar projective pattern can destroy testimony of rape in the courts today; and that fear of it contributes to the known reluctance of rape victims to testify—the fear that in effect, their testimony becomes pornography.

How would this desire-attribution be sexually objectifying? Despite the fact that it attributes an active independent desire, the attribution nonetheless exemplifies sexual objectification: the attitude is (in Nussbaum's terms) subjectivity-denying in its blindness to the experience of women who had suffered sexual abuse as children. It is also, perhaps, instrumental, in treating the women and their actions—speech acts of testimony about sexual abuse—as if they were themselves pornographic artifacts, as if they were items whose function is to stimulate arousal. As an action of discounting a woman's testimony, the theorizing that followed was a speech act that denied their subjectivity and autonomy, and silenced them. The implications go beyond the particular woman to women more generally: seduction theory perhaps legitimates other sexual abuse and violence by undermining women's credibility, conveying the thought that women's testimony is probably a lie, that women find the thought of abuse arousing, but are too repressed to say so. The most salient initial feature here seems to be that of subjectivity-denial, leading then to significant instrumentality and autonomy-denial, to the extent that it also makes sexual violence more likely, and redress against it more difficult.

---

[36] MacKinnon, *Feminist Theory*, 152.

2.3. Pseudo-empathy

In arguing for the projective origins of many of our beliefs, Hume cites yet another disposition; he complains of the

universal tendency among mankind to conceive all beings like themselves, and to transfer to every object those qualities, with which they are familiarly acquainted, and of which they are intimately conscious.[37]

Such pseudo-empathic tendencies provide an anthropomorphic explanation for belief in primitive deities; and also for over-hasty belief about the mental states of other people—though how precisely it is to be distinguished from sympathy is a question I shall here leave aside.

Where wishful thinking makes a transition from 'I desire that she desires to do this', to the belief, 'She desires to do this', pseudo-empathy makes a transition from 'I desire to do this' to the belief 'She desires to do this', the agent's own desire directly prompting belief in a matching desire. While pseudo-empathy can be desire-generated, it need not be: any datum about oneself, whether a desire, a belief, an emotion, or a pain, could prompt pseudo-empathic attribution to another of a similar desire, or belief, or emotion, or pain. We are confining our attention to what these projective mechanisms can generate, given a desire.

Observe again the potential ambiguity in the idea of a 'matching desire': pseudo-empathy may project the *same* desire, in an apparent hope of mutuality; or it may project a *complementary* desire, not the same thing at all.

Most of the examples just considered under the heading of wishful thinking are as open to a pseudo-empathic as to a wishful interpretation, given that what is attributed in each case is a matching desire, a desire that appears to mirror the desire of the person attributing it. Leonard's belief about what Maria desires could be wishful; and it could as easily be the result of an over-hasty leap from his own experience. 'He could not believe she would not be aroused by it. . . . He had to surprise her, show her, let pleasure overcome her rational objections'. Is it a wishful move from 'I desire her to desire it; so I believe she desires it'; or a pseudo-empathic move from 'I desire it; so I believe she desires it'? Quite possibly both, working

[37] David Hume, *The Natural History of Religion* (1757), ed., H. E. Root (London: Adam and Charles Black, 1956), 141.

in tandem. The projective belief might be prompted by pseudo-empathy, and sustained by wishful thinking; in both cases blind to the fact that the 'it' he imagines for himself is not the 'it' he imagines for her.

Likewise for the examples from MacKinnon. 'Raped women are seen as asking for it: if a man wanted her, she must have wanted him.' Is this the wishful 'I want her to want it; so I believe she wants it'; or the pseudo-empathic, 'I want it, so I believe she wants it'? Again, quite possibly both, working together. The projection of matching desire to the real Linda Marchiano could be a pseudo-empathic leap from what the viewer finds desirable, to belief about what she finds desirable. Pseudo-empathy could similarly be part of the explanation for projection of matching desire in scientific theorizing about vaginal orgasm; and it could be part of the explanation for the projection of matching desire in MacKinnon's hypothesis about the origins of the seduction theory.

How is pseudo-empathy implicated in sexual objectification? This question exactly parallels the question just considered, of whether wishful thinking might be so implicated; and the answer stands or falls with the answer given for wishful thinking. If it seemed plausible that these are indeed examples of sexual objectification, when construed as wishful projection, because of their subjectivity denial, instrumentality, and autonomy-denial; then it should seem equally plausible that they are examples of sexual objectification, when construed as pseudo-empathic projection. So I shall not rehearse the examples case by case, but shall simply assume that the argument about wishful thinking can be extended to pseudo-empathy.

I said I would be sharing some assumptions of psychoanalytic feminists (though leaving aside their substantive proposals): they are right to emphasize the significance of projective desire-driven belief; right also think that such belief can shape the world; and right to suppose that these processes can be substantially invisible to the participants. In this section I have looked at the first of these, distinguishing three ways in which desire might projectively generate belief, and showing how each can, in certain circumstances, be implicated in sexual objectification. How widespread or systematic their significance might be, how far their importance extends beyond these particular examples, are questions I don't address, but I suspect

MacKinnon is right to give projection a central place in the notion of sexual objectification.

There remain the questions of how such projection may help shape the world, and in ways that are in part invisible: and this bears on the issue of how projection may not only help sexual objectification, but also hide it.

3. How Projection Hides Sexual Objectification

Suppose an Evil Genius were to invent a social system that benefits one group of people at the price of subordinating or objectifying another; suppose he were to realize that the system could be helped along by means of a complex pattern of desire-driven projective beliefs on the part of those people; and suppose he were to want the system to evade notice. He ponders, and, after taking advice from the Devil, dreams up a nearly perfect Plan from Hell. It goes like this.

Step 1: Genesis. Make genesis of the projective belief invisible. Nobody will notice where the belief came from, nobody will wonder about its possibly dubious origins.

Step 2: Subjective appearance. Let the mind create a subjective appearance of confirming evidence for the projective belief. Make it look as though there is confirming evidence for the projective belief to the eye of the observer, by helping the observer see the world a certain way. And make counter-evidence subjectively hard to see, so that evidence proving the belief wrong will not be noticed.

Step 3: Objective appearance. Let the world create an objective appearance of confirming evidence for the projective belief. Make the world change, so that it produces evidence that really is genuine evidence for the belief, notwithstanding the belief's falsity.[38]

---

[38] Assuming here one can have evidence for something that is false; for an alternative view about evidence, according to which one cannot, see Timothy Williamson, *Knowledge and its Limits* (Oxford: Oxford University Press, 2000).

Step 4: Reality.   Let the world make the projective belief true. Make the world change, so that it fulfills the projective belief; in which case it will keep supplying all the evidence one could ever want.

The beauty of this Plan from Hell is that it will work whether or not it is planned (indeed better the less it is planned), and will work just as well in the absence of Evil Genius and his devilish advisor; so one need be no conspiracy theorist to see how effective it might be. Let us take a look at how projection might help to implement it.

Step 1: Genesis.   Make genesis of the projective belief invisible. This trick is achieved by the very nature of projective belief. A distinctive feature of projective belief is that it does not convey to the believer its own best explanation.[39] Such beliefs have their origin in non-epistemic features of the believer's psychology, they are not epistemically receptive—but to the believer, they will seem as good as any other belief. This is partly because of belief's direction of fit. Belief, even projective belief, aims to fit the world; and although projective belief fits desire, rather than fitting the world, it must seem to the believer to be aiming to fit the world, or it would not be belief. Desire-driven projection must make its origins invisible if it is to be belief at all: one cannot (usually) be a merely wishful thinker and believe one is a merely wishful thinker. Of course, that does not make wishful thinking, and the like, immune to discovery. But, with some special exceptions, the moment it is detected, it disappears. Its existence depends on its invisibility, to the believer.

This invisibility is not enough to protect a belief in the face of compelling evidence to the contrary. Even a wishful belief *aims* to fit the world, and enough evidence that the world is not as wished will make the belief go away. So the next step, indeed all the next steps, involve doing something about the evidence.

Step 2: Subjective appearance.   Let the mind create a subjective appearance of confirming evidence for the projective belief, which seems also to make

---

[39] For futher discussion, see e.g. Peter Kail, 'Projection and Necessity in Hume', *European Journal of Philosophy* 9 (2001), 24–54; and *Projection and Realism in Hume's Philosophy* (New York: Oxford University Press, 2007); to both of which I am indebted.

counter-evidence disappear. The projective attribution of matching desire, in rape, meets counter-evidence in a woman's refusal, a woman's 'no'. She does not want it, and says so. This counter-evidence will seem to disappear, if from the subjective viewpoint it may not sound as though she is refusing—if, for example, her refusal has been disabled by pornography's lie that women who say no mean yes. Her 'no' will not look like counter-evidence, and may even look like confirming evidence. The projective attribution of matching desire to the real Linda Marchiano meets counter-evidence in her testimony about abuse, in *Ordeal*. This counter-evidence will seem to disappear, when it looks as though she is not describing abuse, but producing more pornography (*Ordeal* was sold as pornography).[40] The projective attribution of matching desire, based on women's supposed capacity for vaginal orgasm, meets counter-evidence in many women's descriptions of their actual sexual experience. This counter-evidence will disappear, if those descriptions sound instead like descriptions of repression, frigidity, or immaturity. The projective attribution of desire to women who narrated to Freud how they were abused as children meets counter-evidence in that very narration. The women were abused, and said so. This counter-evidence too will disappear the minute the projective belief is adopted, and it will appear to be transmuted into confirming evidence; the narrative sounds like an arousing fantasy that anyone would enjoy making up. Belief is supposed to fit the world: but here the world—at least the world *as subjective appearance*—has come to fit projective belief.

Step 3: Objective appearance.   Let the world itself change, so that it creates an *objective* appearance of confirming evidence for the projective belief, evidence that goes beyond how things happen to look to the theory-laden eye of a projection-influenced observer; genuine evidence for the belief, even if the belief is false. Pornography will be helpful in supplying it, and so too, sadly, will women themselves.

If one is looking for evidence about what sex is like, pornography may seem to be as authoritative a source as any. True, it is often fiction: but it also makes claims about what real women desire. Pornography's fictional narratives are made against a backdrop of claimed truths about the world, just as a novelist's fictional narrative about Sherlock Holmes

---

[40] It was marketed that way in junk mail I once received: see 'Speech Acts and Unspeakable Acts'.

are made against a backdrop of claimed truths about London. Pornography will be a source of independent testimony that women's desires are the desires they are projected to be. Coercion and other incentives in the background can help, as when Marchiano and other women are forced or simply paid to be false witnesses about what gives women pleasure. On this way of thinking, pornography has at least two distinct roles to play in projective objectification, in shaping desire (as discussed in Section 2) and in confirming belief. Yes, says pornography, women *do* have the desires you desire, therefore believe, women to have.

Women too will be helpful in supplying the objective appearance of confirming evidence, and what better authoritative source for evidence about women's sexuality than women? Here the projective beliefs will themselves assist the process, in a context of oppression. Women will sometimes be aware of those projective expectations, and—depending on their circumstances—will sometimes respond in a confirming way. In conditions of relative vulnerability and powerlessness, and with penalties for non-cooperation, some women will act in ways that confirm the belief. Had Maria been less assertive, more dependent and vulnerable, she might have had incentives to behave in ways that confirmed Leonard's expectations, notwithstanding their falsity. Women of whom vaginal orgasms are expected, and who are penalized as repressed or immature without them, will, as MacKinnon says, have incentives to fake them.[41] Belief is supposed to fit the world, but here again the world—at least the world *as objective appearance*—has come to fit the belief.

Step 4: Reality. Let the world make the projective belief true. If the world changes, so that it fulfills the projective belief, it will keep on supplying all the evidence needed. MacKinnon says,

[The] beliefs of the powerful become [proven], in part because the world actually arranges itself to affirm what the powerful want to see. If you perceive this as a process, you might call it force, or at least pressure or socialization or what money can buy. If it is imperceptible as a process, you may consider it voluntary or consensual or free will or human nature, or just the way things are. Beneath this, though, the world is not entirely the way the powerful say it is or want to believe it is.[42]

---

[41] MacKinnon, *Feminist Theory*, 123, 140–1.   [42] MacKinnon, *Feminism Unmodified*, 164.

We are considering here the thought that the world *as reality* might come to fit the projective objectifying belief: not simply the world as subjective appearance, or the world as objective appearance. This is what MacKinnon has in mind when speaking of how the world 'arranges itself to affirm' the projective belief. MacKinnon describes this as a sort of projective seeing, and a sort of projective belief, that has a self-fulfilling aspect. This fits in with a broader view about how gender works.

If a woman is defined hierarchically so that the male idea of a woman defines womanhood, and if men have power, this idea becomes reality. It is therefore real. It is not just an illusion or a fantasy or a mistake. It becomes embodied because it is enforced.[43]

The idea that the world 'actually arranges itself to affirm what the powerful want to see' is not the transcendental idealism Kant was proposing in saying that objects must conform to our cognitions: the projective attitudes we are considering become true, partly because of the responsiveness of human beings to the attitudes themselves, and to the modes of treating those attitudes generate. The seeing, and the belief, are themselves part of the constraint, given the woman's awareness of them, and given background conditions of oppression. Marilyn Frye makes a similar point:

The arrogant perceiver . . . coerces the objects of his perception into satisfying the conditions his perception imposes . . . He manipulates the environment, perception and judgment of her whom he perceives, so that her recognized options are limited, and the course she chooses will be such as coheres with his purposes. . . . How one sees another and how one expects the other to behave are in tight interdependence, and how one expects the other to behave is a large factor in determining how the other does behave.[44]

For example, a wishful attribution to a woman of submissive desire may be self-fulfilling: the woman in question may not merely fake such desire, but actually acquire it. MacKinnon says, 'Subjection itself, with self-determination ecstatically relinquished, is the content of women's sexual desire and desirability,'[45]—and she means that this is the content

---

[43] MacKinnon, *Feminism Unmodified*, 119.

[44] Marilyn Frye, *The Politics of Reality* (Trumansburg, NY: The Crossing Press, 1983), 67. I am leaving aside other important ways of understanding construction which draw on language, e.g. speech act theory, or the semantics of natural kind terms.

[45] MacKinnon, *Feminism Unmodified*, 148. The projective attribution of submissiveness is a central theme of Haslanger's discussion, see 'On Being Objective'.

of women's desire, as projected by men, and also as really instantiated by some women. Desire is constrained by what is perceived to be possible; if it seems that any other than submissive desires are futile, desire may conform to this restricted world, and lower its sights. This, by the way, seems like yet another violation of rules about direction of fit: desire is supposed to aim for the world to fit it: desire is not supposed to aim to fit the world. But as the Stoics showed long ago, it can be a wise course to fit one's desires to the world, at least to some degree. The projective expectation of submissive desire can help create submissive desire; and if the desire is really there, of course it will supply evidence that it is there. Belief is supposed to fit the world, but here again the world—this time the world *as reality*—has come to fit the belief.

By way of a less gloomy conclusion, we can note that there will be limits on the extent to which the world can come to fit projective beliefs, limits on the extent to which the world will make those beliefs true. As MacKinnon puts it, 'the world is not entirely the way the powerful say it is or want to believe it is.' For example (and here I draw on Sally Haslanger) projective beliefs that women are *naturally* or *essentially* submissive will be false: there are likely to be mistakes in the modal content of the beliefs in question.[46] Moreover, there are likely to be mistakes in meta-beliefs about projective beliefs. The 'arrogant perceiver' believes the reason his belief is true is that it has come to fit the world; really it is true because the world has come to fit the belief.

If projective beliefs are bound to be at least partly mistaken, that makes sexual objectification epistemologically vulnerable. Its masking can be discovered. The Plan from Hell is, thankfully, not perfect. But, vulnerable or not, the projective system does make sexual objectification harder to notice—and noticing it is surely a first, and necessary, step to doing something about it.

[46] Haslanger, 'On Being Objective'.

12

Feminism in Epistemology: Exclusion and Objectification

1. Introduction

Philosophy leaves everything as it is, or so it has been said.[1] Feminists do not leave everything as it is. We are always interfering, always fighting for something, always wanting things to be otherwise and better—even in philosophy itself. But if philosophy leaves everything as it is, shouldn't feminists leave philosophy as it is? If philosophy leaves everything as it is, then it cannot hurt women, and it cannot help women. To be sure, if philosophy leaves everything as it is, it leaves oppression as it is, but one should no more hope otherwise than one should hope for the stones to cry out for justice. Shouldn't feminists let philosophy be? Well, not everyone agrees with the one who said philosophy leaves everything as it is. Someone else began his meditations thus:

Some years ago I was struck by the large number of falsehoods that I had accepted as true in my childhood, and by the highly doubtful nature of the whole edifice that I had subsequently based on them. I realized it was necessary, once in the course of my life, to demolish everything completely and start again . . .

He thought that philosophy can shore up prejudice—but can also uproot it, 'demolish everything completely', destroy 'the habit of holding on to old opinions'.[2] Descartes has been a villain of the story for many feminists, but on this question at least—on the question of philosophy's passivity or power—we are perhaps on the same side.

[1] This essay first appeared in the *Cambridge Companion to Feminism in Philosophy*, eds., Jennifer Hornsby and Miranda Fricker (Cambridge: Cambridge University Press, 2000), 127–45. 'Philosophy leaves everything as it is', see Ludwig Wittgenstein, *Philosophical Investigations*, trans. G. E. M. Anscombe (Oxford: Blackwell, 1958), §124.

[2] René Descartes, *Meditations on First Philosophy*, 12, 34, trans. John Cottingham (Cambridge: Cambridge University Press, 1986).

Many a woman has experienced vividly at first hand that demolition, that shaking of established belief, which Descartes thought necessary for the acquisition of knowledge—and it has happened not because she is a philosopher, retreating to a room of her own, but because she is a woman in the wide world. At some, usually early, point in her life, the news of women's oppression arrives as a shock, a sudden discovery that things are not as they had seemed to be. The discovery can be an exhilarating one for someone to whom the world had seemed gloomy. Life had seemed to offer little opportunity and adventure, no future fate but keeping house and raising babies, and then all of a sudden something—a friendship made, a scholarship won, a mountain scaled—reveals the perception of fate to be an artefact of oppression. Things are much better than they had seemed to be. The same discovery can also be a depressing one for someone to whom the world had seemed rosy. Life had seemed to offer a level playing field, full of opportunity and adventure, and then all of a sudden something—exclusion from the team, rape, unexpected pregnancy—reveals that the cards are stacked. Things are much worse than they had seemed to be. Foundations in either case are shaken, not by reflections on demons and sensory delusion, but by a life under inequality or oppression—a life which suddenly reveals for what they are those many falsehoods one had accepted as true. If doxastic shock is supposed to have the therapeutic effect Descartes ascribed to it, one might expect women to have an antecedent advantage as knowers. Perhaps oppression is a help to knowledge.[3]

The questioning of prejudice, and the philosophical method itself, have seemed to some feminists to go hand in hand. Mary Astell, writing in 1700, confronted the 'error' underpinning women's oppression, the '*Natural Inferiority* of our Sex, which our Masters lay down as . . . Self-Evident and Fundamental', and presented with typical eloquence the philosophical remedy for it.

Error, be it as antient as it may, [cannot] ever plead Prescription against Truth. And since the only way to remove all Doubts, to answer all Objections, and to

---

[3] This thought motivates feminist standpoint epistemology. See e.g. Nancy Hartsock, 'The Feminist Standpoint Theory: Developing the Ground for a Specifically Feminist Historical Materialism', in Sandra Harding and Meryl Hintikka, eds., *Discovering Reality* (Dordrecht: Reidel, 1983); Sandra Harding, 'Rethinking Standpoint Epistemology: What is "Strong Objectivity"?', in L. Alcoff and E. Potter, eds., *Feminist Epistemologies* (London: Routledge, 1993); Alison Jaggar, *Feminist Politics and Human Nature* (Totowa, N.J.: Rowman and Allanheld, 1983).

give the Mind entire Satisfaction, is not by *Affirming*, but by *Proving*, so that every one may see with their own Eyes, and Judge according to the best of their own Understandings, [the author] hopes it is no presumption to insist on this Natural Right of Judging for her self... Allow us then as many Glasses as you please to help our Sight, and as many good Arguments as you can afford to Convince our Understandings: but don't exact of us we beseech you, to affirm that we see such things as are only the Discovery of Men who have quicker Senses; or that we understand and Know what we have by Hear-say only; for to be so excessively Complaisant is neither to see nor to understand.[4]

More recently Michele le Doeuff has said that ' "thinking philosophically" and "being a feminist" appear as one and the same attitude: a desire to judge by and for oneself.'[5] These are feminists who see that an insistence on judging for oneself can be a powerful tool against prejudice, whether of the sort challenged by foundational philosophy or the sort challenged by feminism.[6] Viewed this way, epistemology is a friend to feminism, in its ability to uproot 'the habit of holding on to old opinions', and to reveal women as rational knowers. The discovery of one's ability to judge for oneself—and the subsequent discovery that one is a thinking thing—can be at the same time a discovery that women are not made for servitude. Astell drew a feminist moral from her own Cartesian reflections, and drew it with her usual irreverence:

[A] Rational Mind is too noble a Being to be Made for the Sake and Service of any Creature. The Service [a woman] at any time becomes oblig'd to pay to a Man, is only a Business by the Bye. Just as it may be any Man's Business and Duty to keep Hogs...[7]

---

[4] Mary Astell, *Reflections Upon Marriage* (London: John Nutt, 1700), reprinted in *Astell's Political Writings*, ed., Patricia Springborg (Cambridge: Cambridge University Press, 1996), 9, 10. See also Ruth Perry's classic account of Astell, *The Celebrated Mary Astell: An Early English Feminist* (Chicago: University of Chicago Press, 1986); and Jacqueline Broad, *Women Philosophers of the Seventeenth Century* (Cambridge: Cambridge University Press, 2003).

[5] Michele le Doeuff, *Hipparchia's Choice*, trans. Trista Selous (Oxford: Blackwell, 1990), 9, also discussed by Linda Martin Alcoff, in 'Is the Feminist Critique of Reason Rational?', *Philosophical Topics* 23 (1995).

[6] See also Louise Antony, 'Sisters, Please, I'd Rather Do it Myself: A Defense of Individualism in Feminist Epistemology', in *Philosophical Topics* 23 (1995), 59–94.

[7] Astell, *Reflections*, 11. The passage continues: 'he was not Made for this, but if he hires himself out to such an Employment, he ought conscientiously to perform it'. Astell took the Cartesian meditations to reveal women as essentially thinking things—and hence as beings entitled to an education. On feminism and Cartesian rationalism see Margaret Atherton, 'Cartesian Reason and Gendered Reason', in

The duties a woman might owe to a man are like the duties of a swineherd to his charges, a 'Business by the Bye', and not what she is made for. Astell is not simply a feminist who happens to be a philosopher, or a philosopher who happens to be a feminist: her feminism and her philosophy are allies. When what stands between oppression and liberty is 'the habit of holding on to old opinions', especially when the opinion that women are incapable of rational thought is an old one, rationalist methodology can be revolutionary. Given the non-accidental connection between her epistemology and her feminism, it would be churlish to deny that Astell is doing one sort of feminist epistemology.

If relations between feminism and epistemology were entirely friendly, then feminism's contribution to the subject would be to point this out, as Astell did. 'Feminist epistemology' would be epistemology aware of its own feminist implications. But there is more to the story than this, and there are many ways in which relations have not been entirely friendly. One central strand of the feminist contribution to epistemology has been to show how, when it comes to knowledge, women get left out. Another has been to show how, when it comes to knowledge, women get hurt. These partly overlap, since women may be hurt by being left out, but may be hurt in other ways too. To say that women get left out when it comes to knowledge is to say something vague, to say something that does duty for many things—which suggests already that we have here not so much a strand, but a rope, whose strands tend in the same direction; or not a rope, but a web, whose strands tend in different directions. Likewise for the second claim: to say that when it comes to knowledge women get hurt is to say something vague, something that does duty for many things. In what follows, these two claims—that women get left out, and that women get hurt—form the topics of Sections 2 and 3 respectively.

2. Knowledge and How Women Might Be Left Out

The concern that women have been left out, when it comes to knowledge, might be a concern about women as objects of knowledge—are women

A Mind of One's Own: Feminist Essays on Reason and Objectivity, eds., Louise Antony and Charlotte Witt (Boulder, Co.: Westview Press, 1993), 19–34.

known? It might be a concern about women as subjects of knowledge—are women knowers? Or more subtly—do women count as knowers? Let us look at these in turn.

2.1. Are women known?

A first way in which women might be left out is that women might fail to be known. Women might get left out, as objects of knowledge, in its various institutionalized branches. Women's lives may be rendered invisible by particular bodies of knowledge, such as history, economics, medicine, and philosophy itself.[8] When historians chronicle only kings and dates and battles, women are left out. When economists analyze the relations between capital and labor, ignoring unpaid labor in the home, women are left out. When scientists study heart disease using male-only samples, women are left out. When philosophers define human beings as rational animals, assuming all the while that women are not rational, women are left out. To the extent that these things happen, women remain a kind of *terra incognita*.

This status of *terra incognita* has sometimes been viewed as distinctive of, even essential to, one's being as a woman. On this way of thinking it will appear no accident that women are unknown, for women appear as unknowable. Simone de Beauvoir wrote that of all myths about women,

none is more firmly anchored in masculine hearts than that of the feminine 'mystery'. It has numerous advantages. And first of all it permits an easy explanation of all that appears inexplicable; the man who 'does not understand' a woman is happy to substitute an objective resistance for a subjective deficiency of mind; instead of admitting his ignorance, he perceives the presence of a 'mystery' outside himself: an alibi, indeed, that flatters laziness and vanity at once... [I]n the company of a living enigma man remains alone... [This] is for many a more attractive experience than an authentic relationship with a human being.[9]

When women are not known, there is ignorance on the part of men—'a subjective deficiency of mind', as de Beauvoir puts it. The lazy way out is to say that the ignorance is not the fault of the ignorant subject, but of the

---

[8] See for example Dale Spender's *Women of Ideas and What Men Have Done to Them* (London: Routledge and Kegan Paul, 1982).

[9] Simone de Beauvoir, *The Second Sex* (1949) (London: Pan, 1988), 285–6. See also Michèle le Doeuff, *Hipparchia's Choice*, 52, 102; Langton, 'Love and Solipsism', this volume; and 'Sexual Solipsism', this volume.

unknown object: woman is a living enigma. If women are *terra incognita*, that is not the fault of ignorant men, but of unknowable women. An objective resistance is substituted for a subjective deficiency, and women's absence from the objects of knowledge appears to be an inevitability. De Beauvoir describes this as a kind of solipsism. The bridge to other minds—the bridge to women's minds—remains unbuilt. Solipsism is not simply a problem in epistemology, but a political problem: in the company of a living enigma, man remains alone.

2.2. Are women knowers?

A second way that women might get left out is by failing to be knowers: women might get left out as subjects of knowledge, rather than as objects of it. Here are some ways this might happen.

Women might fail to be knowers because they are deprived of the knowledge men have. From the earliest days of feminism it has been eloquently argued that women's subordination is constituted in part by barriers to the knowledge to which men have access. Here is Astell once again:

Boys have much Time and Pains, Care and Cost bestow'd on their Education, Girls have little or none. The former are early initiated in the Sciences, are made acquainted with Antient and Modern Discoveries, they Study Books and Men, have all imaginable encouragement.... The latter are restrain'd, frown'd upon, and beat, not for but from the Muses; Laughter and Ridicule that never-failing Scare-Crow is set up to drive them from the Tree of Knowledge. But if in spite of all Difficulties Nature prevails, and they can't be kept so ignorant as their Masters wou'd have them, they are star'd upon as Monsters...[10]

If some of us are more fortunate today, the complaint will remain that many women still lack knowledge: that women are deprived of the epistemological resources of the written word through lack of the requisite language, literacy, time, power, or economic resources; or that women are excluded, overtly or covertly, from particular fields of knowledge such as medicine or physics; or (more subtly) that a woman's under-confidence—her lack of what we might call subjective authority—means that even when she apparently knows, she does not know she knows,

---

[10] Astell, *Reflections,* 28.

and therefore (given a certain principle about knowledge) does not really know.[11] The remedy for the complaint that women lack knowledge would be to remove the barriers to knowledge, whatever they may be. It would mean working for women's literacy and education, and removing the overt and covert discrimination which excludes women from particular fields of knowledge. It would mean creating the conditions that allow women to gain confidence, to gain the subjective authority required for knowledge, so that they can indeed 'see with their own Eyes, and Judge according to the best of their own Understandings', as Astell put it. A special role has been ascribed by some feminists to this claiming of subjective authority, with Marilyn Frye going so far as to call it 'the first and most fundamental act of our own emancipation.'[12]

Women may be left out both as subjects and as objects of knowledge if they are deprived of knowledge of themselves. One important strand in feminist thinking has been an argument that women lack knowledge of their own lives and experiences as women—precisely the knowledge one might antecedently expect to be the most accessible. Here the deprivation is not a lack of what men already have, for men lack it too. It is a lack of what women should be the first to have. Thus Betty Friedan wrote of an amorphous and gnawing 'problem that has no name'. She wrote of the desperation of women who felt the problem obscurely, though lacked the conceptual resources to bring it to full awareness—until, that is, they learned to communicate with one another and learned to name the hitherto nameless.[13]

Opinions about the appropriate remedy to this problem differ; opinions differ as to how one can come to name the hitherto nameless. Part of the solution will be the achievement of the confidence and authority just alluded to. But to the extent that there are conceptual constraints on what women can know, more will be needed. Some feminists suppose that women's ignorance of their own lives and experiences can be remedied by the ordinary talk that takes place among women at a grass-roots level, the sort that sometimes goes by the name of 'consciousness raising'. Others

[11] According to the so-called 'KK Principle' you know something only if you know that you know it. I don't do justice to this thought here.

[12] 'For feminist thinkers of the present era the first and most fundamental act of our own emancipation was granting ourselves authority as perceivers', Marilyn Frye, 'The Possibility of Feminist Theory', reprinted in *Women, Knowledge and Reality*, eds., Ann Garry and Marilyn Pearsall (London and New York: Routledge, 1996), 34–47 (quotation from p. 35).

[13] Betty Friedan, *The Feminine Mystique* (New York: Dell, 1964).

think that the conceptual resources for such knowledge will only become available with radical reforms of language, or with radical reforms of the symbolic order of the imagination. They say that if the words we use, or the symbols with which we think, come from a 'man-made' language, or a 'language of the fathers', then that will be a bar to women's knowledge of themselves as women. At this point feminist questions in epistemology will overlap with their cousins in philosophy of language and psychoanalysis.

These are ways in which women get left out as subjects of knowledge because they really fail to be knowers.

2.3. Are women counted as knowers?

Women may be left out as subjects of knowledge, not by failing to be knowers, but by failing to be counted as knowers, even when they do know. Here are some of the ways in which this might happen.

Women may fail to be counted as knowers because of a lack of credibility—a lack of what we might call intersubjective authority. Because of this lack, even when women are knowers, they are not known by others to be knowers. Some philosophers say that credibility is of more than incidental interest to an account of knowledge as such. Miranda Fricker argues that the notion of credibility is crucial to the concept of a knower, properly understood.[14] Once one acknowledges that where there are unequal distributions of social power, the distribution of credibility is likely to be distorted, one sees that an understanding of social power is crucial to a proper understanding of the concept of a knower. This in turn enables one to identify a phenomenon of epistemic injustice, which can arise from an unjust distribution of credibility, and which could serve to exclude women from the class of those who fully function as knowers.[15] The remedy for this problem is not to remove barriers to women's knowledge (women already have that, more or less), but to remove the barriers to credibility.[16]

---

[14] Miranda Fricker, 'Rational Authority and Social Power: Towards a Truly Social Epistemology', *Proceedings of the Aristotelian Society* (1998), 159–77.

[15] Fricker draws on Edward Craig's work in arguing that being a participant in the spread of knowledge is central to our conception of knowledge, and uses this framework to develop her notion of epistemic injustice. See also Fricker, *Epistemic Injustice: Power and the Ethics of Knowing* (New York: Oxford University Press, 2007); Marilyn Frye, *The Politics of Reality: Essays in Feminist Theory* (Freedom, CA: The Crossing Press, 1983), especially, 'In and Out of Harm's Way: Arrogance and Love'.

[16] Louise Antony suggests a kind of epistemic affirmative action as a remedy, 'Sisters, Please, I'd Rather Do It Myself', 89.

Women may fail to be counted as knowers in a different way—because of a spurious universality ascribed to a merely partial story of the world as told by men, which means that even when women know, they are not known by men to know. Women are left out, because women's perspectives on the world are left out. Marilyn Frye says,

Imagine that a single individual had written up an exhaustive description of a sedated elephant as observed from one spot for one hour and then, with delighted self-satisfaction, had heralded that achievement as a complete, accurate and profound account of The Elephant.

That story of the elephant is, she says, like the traditional story of the world.

The androcentrism of the accumulated philosophy and science of the 'western' world is like that. A few, a few men, have with a like satisfaction told the story of the world and human experience—have created what pretends to be progressively a more and more complete, accurate and profound account of what they call 'Man and his World'.[17]

What women know about the world fails to enter this official story about life, the universe, and everything, and the incompleteness and partiality of the story goes unnoticed. So even when women do achieve knowledge—do break free from the various material and conceptual constraints on knowledge described above—their knowledge may fail to look like knowledge to men, so that women, again, fail to be counted as knowers. Seen this way, one goal of feminism is to correct the partiality of existing knowledge:

The project of feminist theory is to write a new Encyclopaedia. Its title: The World, According to Women.[18]

There is yet a different way in which women may fail to be counted as knowers, which has not so much to do with women, or with the incompleteness of knowledge, but with a conception of knowledge itself. Women may fail to be counted as knowers because there is something wrong with traditional conceptions, or traditional ideals, of knowledge. Something about knowledge, as it is traditionally understood, is mistaken, and it is this mistake—not women's ignorance, or women's lack of credibility, or the omission of women's perspectives on the world—which prevents women

---

[17] Frye, 'Politics of Reality', 34.   [18] Ibid., 35.

from being counted as the knowers they really are.[19] Just what the mistake is will depend on what the traditional conception is interpreted to be, and the remedy likewise. It is at this point that feminist critique of reason becomes more radical, and—sometimes questioning the uncritical use of notions of truth, knowledge, and reason, with which early feminists like Astell argued for liberation—advocates reform, supplementation, or outright rejection of the epistemological status quo.

To take one example, made famous by Carol Gilligan, it may be that moral knowledge is defined by some theorists in such a way that women and girls are made to seem ignorant or immature, and the remedy might not be to change women, but to change the conception of knowledge. Once it is recognized that women have a 'different voice' when it comes to moral knowledge, which speaks in an idiom of care rather than justice, and that this voice is as good if not better than its male counterpart, then women and girls will be recognized for the moral knowers they are.[20] Or, to take an example discussed by Vrinda Dalmeyer and Linda Alcoff, it may be that assumptions about the propositional character of knowledge have served to discredit the knowledge of illiterate midwives whose knowledge is more a matter of knowing how than knowing that.[21]

What have these claims to do with the idea that when it comes to knowledge, women get hurt? To the extent that women are left out in any of the ways just described, women are also hurt. If women are left out as objects of knowledge, whether in the history books or in medical research, that is one of the ways in which women are hurt; and if women are viewed as essentially mysterious and unknowable, then that too is a

---

[19] Lorraine Code has done a great deal to expose biases in traditional epistemology; see e.g. *What Can She Know? Feminist Theory and the Construction of Knowledge* (Ithaca, New York: Cornell University Press, 1991). For an important recent contribution see Michèle le Doeuff, *What Can She Know?* trans. Kathryn Hamer and Lorraine Code (New York: Routledge, 2003). Genevieve Lloyd traces the historical association of maleness with rationality in her classic *The Man of Reason: 'Male' and 'Female' in Western Philosophy* (London: Methuen, 1984). Karen Green identifies some women through history who rebelled in *The Woman of Reason: Feminism, Humanism and Political Thought* (Cambridge: Polity Press, 1995).

[20] Carol Gilligan, 'In a Different Voice: Women's Conceptions of Self and of Morality', in *The Future of Difference,* eds., Hester Eisenstein and Alice Jardine (Boston, Mass.: G. K. Hall and Co., 1980), 247–317.

[21] Vrinda Dalmeyer and Linda Alcoff, 'Are "Old Wives' Tales" Justified?', in *Feminist Epistemologies,* eds., Linda Alcoff and Elizabeth Potter (London and New York: Routledge, 1993), 217–44; the authors draw on work by Lorraine Code, e.g. in 'Taking Subjectivity into Account', in *Feminist Epistemologies,* 15–48.

way in which women get hurt. In addition there will be the hurts arising from these, when ignorance of women is acted upon. If women get left out as subjects of knowledge—whether because they lack the knowledge men have, or because they lack knowledge of themselves as women, or because they lack credibility, or because their perspectives on the world are omitted, or because they are excluded by a mistaken traditional conception of knowledge—these are all ways in which women get hurt. In addition there will be the hurts arising from these, when women's exclusion as subjects of knowledge has consequences for their wider social lives—for example when lack of knowledge, or of credibility, undermines their status and their job prospects. In so far as the problem is one of women being left out (and of the consequences of being left out) the sin looks to be a sin of omission, whose remedy is simple: let women in. Let women into the stories of those who are known—let women into the history books, and the rest. Let women in to the treasures of knowledge, let women in to the club of the credible, let women's knowledge count as the knowledge it is.

However, there might be hurts that accrue to someone which go beyond the hurt of being left out, and its consequences. Perhaps there could be something about knowledge—as traditionally pursued, under patriarchal conditions—that does not merely leave women out, but hurts women in a more active way. Some feminist writers have claimed that some traditional norms of knowledge objectify women. If this is so, we have here not a sin of omission, but a sin of commission which cannot be remedied simply by letting women in.

3. Knowledge and How Women Might Be Hurt

The thought that some traditional ideals of knowledge objectify women finds one expression in the work of Catharine MacKinnon.

The stance of the 'knower'...is...the neutral posture, which I will be calling objectivity—that is, the nonsituated distanced standpoint...[This] is the male standpoint socially...[The] relationship between objectivity as the stance from which the world is known and the world that is apprehended in this way is the relationship of objectification. Objectivity is the epistemological stance of which objectification is the social process, of which male dominance is the politics, the acted out social practice. That is, to look at the world objectively is to objectify it.[22]

MacKinnon says there is something wrong with knowledge as it is traditionally pursued or understood, and to that extent her complaint belongs with those just discussed. But there is more, for her complaint is also that women are actively hurt. Objectivity, she says, is the stance of the traditional male knower; and objectivity objectifies. Now MacKinnon's point is overstated, but there may be something right about it, and it is worth thinking about how an assumption of objectivity might help to objectify women.[23] To do this we would need a clearer sense of what might be meant by objectivity, and what might be meant by objectification. Sally Haslanger has suggested an interpretation of MacKinnon which offers a more detailed grasp of each of these, which she puts to use in defending MacKinnon's claim.[24]

3.1. Objectivity

Objectivity—that 'non-situated distanced standpoint'—can be thought of as an epistemological norm that has its place in a familiar picture of the world, says Haslanger. Things in the world are independent of us, and their behavior is constrained and determined by their natures. We can best discover those natures by looking for the regularities that reveal them in normal circumstances. In abnormal circumstances things may be distorted, and the regularities we see may not reveal their natures. But the usual circumstances are the normal circumstances, so we should infer the natures of things from how things usually are. When it comes to practical matters, our actions will of course need to accommodate the natures of things, if we are to achieve our practical goals.

Thus understood, objectivity seems to be an innocuous enough collection of epistemic and practical norms governing one's reasoning about the world and how to get about in it. In so far as it has any distinctive feature, it is the default assumption that one's epistemic circumstances are normal—which

---

[22] Catharine MacKinnon, *Feminism Unmodified* (Cambridge, Mass.: Harvard University Press, 1987), 50.

[23] The argument of this section draws on Langton, 'Beyond a Pragmatic Critique of Reason', *Australasian Journal of Philosophy* 71 (1993), 364–84.

[24] Sally Haslanger, 'On Being Objective and Being Objectified', in *A Mind of One's Own*, 85–125.

is why Haslanger dubs it 'Assumed Objectivity'. The collection of norms, she says, consists of these:

1. Epistemic neutrality: take a genuine regularity in the behavior of something to be a consequence of its nature;
2. Practical neutrality: constrain your decision-making and action to accommodate things' natures;
3. Absolute aperspectivity: count observed regularities as genuine regularities just in case the observations occur under normal circumstances;
4. Assumed aperspectivity: if a regularity is observed, assume that circumstances are normal.[25]

Attending to the notion of 'normal circumstances' that appears in conditions 3 and 4, we can note that there are many ways in which observational circumstances could fail to be normal, an important one among them being that the regularities observed fail to be independent of the observer—that they are an artefact, created by, or conditioned by, the observer or the process of observation. The observer may render the circumstances abnormal in a variety of different ways: the properties of the observed items may be altered by the observer's sheer physical presence; by his social features, for example his power or rank; by his propositional attitudes, his beliefs and desires. So when the norm directs one to assume, among other things, the observer-independence of what is observed, it directs one to assume that the observer is not rendering the circumstances abnormal in any of these ways.

The norm of Assumed Objectivity directs an observer to assume that circumstances are normal. But if an observer's *beliefs* can render observational circumstances abnormal by helping to alter the properties of the observed, then implicit in the norm is an assumption about *direction of fit*: that one's belief about perceived regularities conforms to the world.

3.2. Belief, desire, and direction of fit

By saying that the norm assumes that one's belief conforms to the world, I do not mean simply that the belief corresponds to how the world is—for

---

[25] Haslanger, 'On Being Objective', 107. I have abbreviated and slightly paraphrased the conditions. Haslanger adds to the notion of normal circumstances what I take to be included in that notion, namely that the observations are not conditioned by the observer's social position, and that the observer has not influenced the behavior of the items under observation.

short, that it is true. For there are two ways in which a belief could correspond to how the world is: the belief might conform to the world; or the world might conform to the belief. A believer might believe that p because p is the case—her belief thus conforming to the world; or p might be the case because the believer believes it—the world thus conforming to her belief. In the latter situation there would be something self-fulfilling about the belief: there would be a belief whose direction of fit was the reverse of the normal case, 'normal' in a sense to be considered in a moment.

Elizabeth Anscombe used a nice example to explain the notion of what has come to be called direction of fit. Imagine a shopper, filling his trolley with the things on his shopping list, and a detective following him, writing a list of the things in the trolley. The shopper's list and the detective's list both match the things exactly, but there is a difference in direction of fit.[26] If the things in the trolley fail to correspond to the shopper's list, the mistake is in his performance: he ought to make the world fit his list. If the things in the trolley fail to correspond to the detective's list, the mistake is in the list: he ought to make his list fit the world. Assuming there are no mistakes, the things in the trolley conform to the shopper's list; and the detective's list conforms to the things in the trolley. Another difference: the shopper's list is a list of the things he *wants* to be there; the detective's list is a list of the things he *believes* are there. These latter differences are no accident: a difference in direction of fit is widely thought to be constitutive of the difference between belief and desire. Belief aims to fit the world; desire aims for the world to fit it. There is an assumption in epistemology generally—and in the norm of Assumed Objectivity in particular—that the knowing subject is like the detective, molding his list to the way the world is, and not like the shopper, molding the world to the way his list is. And that makes sense, because the subject matter of epistemology is not desire, but belief, and whether or not belief is true and justified. The norm of Assumed Objectivity directs one to assume, among other things, that one's observations about the world have the normal direction of fit—which is to say, the direction of fit that beliefs aim to have.

---

[26] Elizabeth Anscombe, *Intention* (Oxford: Blackwell, 1957), 56. See also Lloyd Humberstone, 'Direction of Fit', *Mind* 101 (1992), 59–83.

But even if beliefs do aim to fit the world, beliefs sometimes fail to fit the world, sometimes for the ordinary reason that they are false, as when the detective makes a mistake; and sometimes for the more complicated reason that they have an anomalous direction of fit—perhaps the belief has come to fit something other than the world, or perhaps the world has come to fit the belief, or perhaps both. Here are the sorts of anomalies I have in mind.

Sometimes beliefs arrange themselves to fit desires. I want to believe I can jump across a crevasse, and gritting my teeth, come to believe it.[27] Pascal wants to believe there is a God, goes to church, and ends up believing it. I want to believe that every day, in every way, I am getting better and better, and—with the help of some New Age motivational tapes—talk myself into believing it. There is something odd about these examples, because of belief's 'normal' direction of fit: if belief aims to fit the world, how can it be produced by desire rather than by perception of the world? Such cases tend to be relegated to the margins of epistemology, where they are discussed, if at all, under the heading of wishful thinking and self-deception.

Sometimes the world arranges itself to fit beliefs. I believe I can jump across the river, and, freshly emboldened, do indeed jump across the river. I believe that every day, in every way, I am getting better and better, and—with luck, and with the help again of my New Age motivational tapes—do indeed get better and better. There is something odd about these examples too, again because of belief's 'normal' direction of fit: if belief aims to fit the world, how can there be a belief whose direction of fit has the pattern distinctive of desire—how can there be a belief which alters the world, so as to make the world fit the belief? Such cases again tend to be relegated to the margins of epistemology, and discussed, if at all, under the heading of the psychology of self-fulfilling belief.

The ordinary reason for failure of fit in a belief—namely outright falsehood—receives plenty of attention in epistemology; these more complicated anomalies receive less. But it is these which will be of special interest to anyone who wants to think about how an assumption of objectivity may help to objectify women.

---

[27] The example is from William James, *The Will to Believe and Other Essays in Popular Philosophy* (London: Longman's and Green, 1891).

3.3. Objectification

If objectivity is about how mind conforms to world, objectification is about the opposite: objectification is, roughly, about some of the ways in which world conforms to mind. Objectification is a process in which the social world comes to be shaped by perception, desire, and belief: a process in which women, for example, are made objects because of men's perceptions and desires and beliefs. To say that women are made objects is to speak in metaphors, albeit familiar ones; but, to make a start, it has something to do with how some men see women. MacKinnon says,

> Men treat women as who they see women as being... Men's power over women means that the way men see women defines who women can be.[28]

Marilyn Frye describes something similar, and calls it 'The Arrogant Eye'.

> The arrogant perceiver... coerces the objects of his perception into satisfying the conditions his perception imposes... He manipulates the environment, perception and judgment of her whom he perceives, so that her recognized options are limited, and the course she chooses will be such as coheres with his purposes. The seer is himself an element of her environment. The structures of his perception are as solid a fact in her situation as are the structures of a chair which seats her too low or of gestures which threaten. How one sees another and how one expects the other to behave are in tight interdependence, and how one expects the other to behave is a large factor in determining how the other does behave.[29]

MacKinnon and Frye describe a sort of perception that works to objectify women, where seeing women as subordinate helps to make women subordinate: a kind of self-fulfilling perception, where seeing it as so makes it so, when it is backed up by power. The perception does not work in isolation from other things. It is there because of what men believe, and in that sense it is a theory-laden perception. And to the extent that the perception is self-fulfilling, the underlying belief is too. MacKinnon says,

> [The] beliefs of the powerful become [proven], in part because the world actually arranges itself to affirm what the powerful want to see. If you perceive this as a process, you might call it force, or at least pressure or socialization or what money can buy. If it is imperceptible as a process, you may consider it voluntary or consensual or free will or human nature, or just the way things are. Beneath this,

---

[28] MacKinnon, *Feminism Unmodified*, 122.   [29] Frye, 'In and Out of Harm's Way', 67.

though, the world is not entirely the way the powerful say it is or want to believe it is.[30]

The world 'arranges itself'—at least in part—to fit what the powerful believe. Believing women to be subordinate can make women subordinate: thinking so can make it so, when it is backed up by power.

Such beliefs have an anomalous direction of fit, anomalous in both of the ways considered earlier. Instead of belief arranging itself to fit the world, it arranges itself to fit desire. On MacKinnon's description, when the powerful desire that p, they come to believe that p—in the manner of the wishful thinker. And instead of belief arranging itself to fit the world, the world arranges itself to fit belief. When the powerful believe that p, things alter to make it the case that p. Unlike most examples of wishful thinking, the result here is not mere projection accompanied by self deception, for there is a sense in which the wishfully thought beliefs become *true*. The powerful are described as doing what the unusually fortunate wishful thinker does: for example, the crevasse-leaper of William James's example, who desires that p, consequently believes that p, consequently makes it the case that p.

How does the world 'arrange itself' to conform to what is seen or believed? Men *treat* women as who they see women as being, says MacKinnon. How men treat women is affected by men's perceptions, desires, and beliefs about women. Part of the treatment will just be a matter of making known one's beliefs—making known one's expectations. Those expectations can exert the sort of pressure that Frye described so vividly in the passage quoted above, so that how women are will come to fit what is believed about women—what is expected of women. Part of the treatment will be a matter of what men *say* to women and about women. This brings us to questions about language, thus to questions beyond our present project, but a brief glance in their direction suggests that here again one would discover the same anomalous direction of fit: that saying so can, in conditions of oppression, make it so.[31]

[30] MacKinnon, *Feminism Unmodified*, 164. I follow Haslanger in substituting 'proven' for 'proof', 'On Being Objective', 103.

[31] Cf. Frye, 'The voice of the men's world story is the voice of the speaker who does not have to fit his words to the truth, because the truth will fit his words,' 'Politics of Reality', 44; MacKinnon, *Feminism Unmodified*, 131. See Langton, 'Speech Acts and Unspeakable Acts'; 'Pornography's Authority: Reply to Leslie Green'; 'Pornography's Divine Command: Reply to Judith Butler', this volume.

Described this way, objectification is a process of projection supplemented by force, whose result is that women are made subordinate. The projection involves desire, belief, and perception all working together: men desire certain qualities in women, believe women have them, see women as having them. But this projection, says MacKinnon, 'is not just an illusion or a fantasy or a mistake. It becomes embodied because it is enforced'.[32] Women really come to have at least some of the qualities that are projected onto them. Haslanger draws on these ideas in MacKinnon's work to reach a general view of what it is to objectify someone or something. One objectifies a thing or person when one satisfies these conditions:

1. One views it and treats it as an object for the satisfaction of one's desire;
2. Where one desires it to have some property, one forces it to have that property;
3. One believes that it has that property;
4. One believes that it has that property by nature.[33]

For example, men objectify women if they view and treat them as objects of male sexual desire; they desire them to be submissive, and force them to submit; they believe that women are in fact submissive; and they believe that they are submissive by nature.

The belief of the final condition—namely the belief that women are submissive by nature—is quite illusory. But there is something interesting about the belief of the third condition. On my reading of MacKinnon and Haslanger, that belief is wishful, having its source in desire (mentioned in the second condition). Under conditions of oppression, that belief—say, the belief that women are submissive—will be a true belief, an accurate descriptive belief. That belief is, as MacKinnon says, 'not just an illusion or a fantasy or a mistake': It is a belief that corresponds to the world. It is not, though, a belief that conforms to the world: it is a belief to which the world has conformed. The belief of the third condition is part of the force (mentioned in the second condition). Wishfully thinking that women are so has—suitably supplemented by power—made women so.

---

[32] MacKinnon, *Feminism Unmodified*, 119.
[33] Haslanger, 'On Being Objective', 100–4, 109. Again, I have paraphrased her analysis.

3.4. Explaining objectifying belief

On this proposal, the process of objectification has something in common with the process of wishful thinking. Ordinarily, of course, wishfully thinking so doesn't make it so. But sometimes it can make it so, when the thinking is, say, the faith described by William James—or the objectification described by MacKinnon.

The fact that the relevant belief becomes true may help to explain a puzzle about how it can even be believed. In general, wanting something to be true, or wanting to believe something is true, isn't enough to get you to believe it. In this way belief and action are different. If I offer to pay you twenty dollars to *act* like Elvis, you might do it. If I offer to pay you twenty dollars to *believe* you are Elvis, you won't do it, because you can't—not even if I put up my offer to a hundred. You can decide to act, but you can't as simply decide to believe, as many philosophers have pointed out. Bernard Williams says:

> it is not a contingent fact that I cannot bring it about, just like that, that I believe something... Why is this? One reason is connected with the characteristic of beliefs that they aim at truth. If I could acquire a belief at will, I could acquire it whether it was true or not; moreover, I would know that I could acquire it whether it was true or not. If in full consciousness I could will to acquire a 'belief' irrespective of its truth, it is unclear that before the event I could seriously think of it as a belief, i.e. as something purporting to represent reality.[34]

Since belief aims at truth, aims to fit the world, you can't just believe something because you want to, for reasons 'irrespective of its truth'. Wishful thinking does happen—but it happens when there is less than 'full consciousness'. If self-deception allows you to turn a blind eye to counter-evidence, that will help you maintain the wishful belief. Better would be if there were no counter-evidence. Better still would be if there were confirming evidence. But confirming evidence is exactly what you do get, if the belief becomes true.

In short, a self-fulfilling aspect to the belief makes an important epistemological difference. The wishful thinker whose belief is outright false—the wishful thinker whose belief is *mere* projection—must keep turning a blind

---

[34] Bernard Williams, 'Deciding to Believe', *Problems of the Self* (Cambridge: Cambridge University Press, 1973), 148.

eye to the evidence, which is what makes it difficult to see how it can even *aim* to fit the world, and hence how it can even be a belief at all. But suppose an objectifier's belief that a woman has some property helps to make her acquire it: he expects her to be submissive, say, and she is. To the extent that the belief is self-fulfillingly true, he need turn no blind eye: to the extent that the evidence confirms the belief, the belief can aim to fit the world. There is little need for self-deception. The objectifier's self-fulfilling belief will be rational—or at any rate, more rational than the beliefs of the ordinary wishful thinker.[35]

3.5. Objectivity and objectification

MacKinnon says that to look at the world objectively is to objectify it. Haslanger argues that there is something right about this: to look at the world objectively can certainly *help* one to objectify it. For suppose a man were to look at the social world objectively: that is, suppose he were to follow the norm of Assumed Objectivity in his dealings with the social world. Suppose it is a world in which gender hierarchy exists. Such a man will observe that women appear, in general, to be sexually submissive. Following the norm of assumed aperspectivity, he assumes that circumstances are normal. Following the norm of absolute aperspectivity, he concludes that this is a genuine regularity. Following the norm of epistemic neutrality, he attributes the regularity to the workings of the nature of women. Following the norm of practical neutrality, he structures social arrangements to accommodate those natures, and, for example, dominates women in sexual encounters. Will this help him objectify women? Yes—to a degree. If he is an objectifier, following the norm of Assumed Objectivity will help to make him a more successful one. His interpretations of the regularities he encounters will lead him to the sorts of beliefs possessed by the objectifier: he will satisfy the third and fourth conditions that the objectifier satisfies, because he will believe that women are submissive, and believe that women are submissive by nature. Moreover, acting on those beliefs will help him satisfy the second condition: acting on the beliefs that

---

[35] Non-voluntarism about belief, with its implications for feminist critiques of reason, is a topic of Langton, 'Beyond a Pragmatic Critique of Reason', *Australasian Journal of Philosophy* 71 (1993), 364–84. I do have reservations, not expressed here, about the rationality of wishful self-fulfilling beliefs: see 'Intention as Faith', in *Agency and Action*, eds., John Hyman and Helen Steward (Cambridge: Cambridge University Press, 2004), 243–57.

women are submissive by nature, he will help make women submissive. In acting on the assumption that his mind conforms to an independent world, he will play his part in making that world conform to his mind—and to the minds of other objectifiers. Being objective helps to make him a more successful objectifier.[36]

When objectification is going on, in place of a world-sensitive observer there is an observer-sensitive world: a social world distorted by the physical, social, and mental properties of those who are doing the observing. When that social world is distorted by the beliefs of the observers to the extent that the world comes to fit the observers' beliefs, the knowing subject is less like the detective of Anscombe's example, molding his mind (his mental 'list') to the way the world is, and more like the shopper, molding the world to the way his mind is. And Assumed Objectivity masks all this: it allows the observer to rest secure in an assumption that his beliefs are a mirror, not a template.

The conclusion that objectivity can help the objectifier is more modest than MacKinnon's, as Haslanger points out: although being objective can help one be an objectifier, one can be objective without being an objectifier. Following the norm of Assumed Objectivity in other everyday activities—gardening, for instance—will have no untoward results.[37] But if being objective can even help one be an objectifier, surely that is bad enough. We have grounds, surely, for a political critique of a certain epistemological norm: when men follow it, women get hurt.

Understood this way, the feminist critique of a certain ideal of knowledge is based on the harm it does to women. We can add to this critique an epistemological one: the norm of Assumed Objectivity is not just bad for women, it is also bad by the lights of reason. Applied in conditions of gender hierarchy, although it leads some objectifiers to self-fulfillingly *true* beliefs, it also reliably leads them to *false* beliefs. As MacKinnon says, 'the world is not entirely the way the powerful say it is or want to believe it is'.

---

[36] This description leaves out the wishfulness of his objectifying belief. Perhaps Haslanger would not after all accept the above reading of her proposal, as involving wishful belief; perhaps for MacKinnon wishful belief should be thought of as one objectifying process, among others. I leave these issues unresolved.

[37] Haslanger also suggests that following the norm could help one be a collaborator, rather than an objectifier: for example, a woman following the norm would observe the same regularities about women, and interpret women's subordination as natural and inevitable, without herself desiring it or forcing it to be that way (109–10).

It is only in part that 'the world actually arranges itself to affirm what the powerful want to see'. Something about the world is different to what the powerful say and believe.

Some of their ordinary beliefs *about women* are false. Guided by Assumed Objectivity, objectifiers believe falsely that women possess by *nature* the properties they acquire through objectification.[38] For example, they believe falsely that women are submissive by nature. That is one way in which their beliefs fail to fit the world. Moreover, some of their more complex beliefs are false: some of their beliefs *about their beliefs* are false. Guided by Assumed Objectivity, objectifiers believe that their true beliefs have come to fit the world, when in fact it is the world that has come to fit their beliefs. For example, while they believe truly that women are submissive, their belief about that belief is false. They believe they believe it because women are submissive. Wrong: they do not believe it because women are submissive; women are submissive because they believe it. Believing so, with the aid of power and action, has made it so. That is another way in which their beliefs fail to fit the world. Assumed Objectivity has led them away from the truth—the truth about women, and the truth about their own beliefs.

Armed now with two critiques, a political and an epistemological, we can say that the epistemological norm of Assumed Objectivity is a bad one: it hurts women, and it gets in the way of *knowledge*.[39] To say that it is bad because it gets in the way of knowledge is to suppose knowledge to be a good thing—just as Mary Astell supposed when she argued so eloquently against the ancient error, and for the truth. Is this to fall prey once again to an uncritical allegiance to knowledge, of the sort that feminists are supposed to question? I hope not. Astell is right: what has hurt women is not knowledge but ignorance masked as knowledge. What has hurt women is not objectivity after all, but pretended objectivity. The hurt is in the complacent assumption, and not, surely, in the ambition.

---

[38] Haslanger identifies this as the major illusion generated by the norm (103–4).

[39] It does get in the way of some knowledge; but, as a source of true belief, it may be a source of other knowledge. I take up this concern in 'Speaker's Freedom and Maker's Knowledge', this volume.

13

Speaker's Freedom and Maker's Knowledge

1. Introduction

This is an essay about speaker's freedom, and maker's knowledge. By 'speaker's freedom' I have in mind the special freedom someone has to speak about something, in virtue of a right to free speech, as captured in the theories of political philosophers and philosophers of law. By 'maker's knowledge' I have in mind the special knowledge someone has of something, in virtue of making that thing, as captured in the theories of certain epistemologists and theologians. I shall be asking what, if anything, the ideas of speaker's freedom and maker's knowledge have to do with each other. You might think the answer is, nothing at all, and you may turn out to be right. After all, one idea comes from political philosophy, and a rather applied region of it at that; the other comes from arcane regions of theology and moral psychology. But I think they might well bear upon each other, especially if you suppose, as did John Stuart Mill, that *knowledge* may be among the theoretical justifications of free speech.[1]

My focus will be on the implications for pornography, the sort of material described by some feminists as 'the graphic, sexually explicit subordination of women in pictures and words'.[2] Now, we are familiar with the thought

---

[1] 'Speaker's Freedom and Maker's Knowledge' has not been previously published. J. S. Mill, *On Liberty* (1859) ch. 2, in *On Liberty and Other Writings*, ed., Stefan Collini (Cambridge: Cambridge University Press, 1989), 53–4.

[2] From a Minneapolis ordinance drafted by Catharine MacKinnon and Andrea Dworkin, see MacKinnon, *Feminism Unmodified* (Cambridge, Mass.: Harvard University Press, 1987), 176; also described by Judge Easterbrook, in Hudnut, 771 F.2d 329 (7th Cir. 1985), where the Minneapolis Ordinance was found unconstitutional. See also Andrea Dworkin, *Pornography: Men Possessing Women* (London: The Women's Press, 1981).

that some of Mill's ideas might apply to debate about pornography. We are familiar with the thought that his *harm principle* might be relevant. Mill famously argued that,

the only purpose for which power can be exercised over any member of a civilised community against his will, is to prevent harm to others.[3]

Feminist claims that pornography subordinates women are, of course, controversial, and need to be assessed in their own right. But if pornography subordinates women, then its consumption is not simply personal matter: it does, in Mill's terms, 'harm others'. Many liberals have doubted that the harm attributed to pornography is direct enough, or certain enough, to justify sanctions against it. But some have argued with care and eloquence that Mill's harm principle can in principle justify restrictions of just the kind that feminists have proposed. David Dyzenhaus, for example, brings together Mill's arguments in *On Liberty* with those of *The Subjection of Women*, and identifies on Mill's behalf 'a rich conception of harm, one which embraces harm to fundamental interests, such as the interest in an autonomous life under conditions of equality'. When the harm principle is understood in light of this substantive conception of harm, it turns out, so he argues, that 'there is little or no difference in principle between [Mill] and procensorship feminists'.[4]

I shall be taking up a less familiar thought, looking at how a Millian *knowledge*-based argument might bear on pornography. But we shall get around, in the end, to the question of how issues of knowledge connect up with issues of harm. Some caveats are in order here. I do not aim to defend the premises from which conclusions about knowledge and harm may follow, even though the premises are contested. Nor do I aim for a detailed defense of a principle of free speech, either as offered by the historical Mill, or as required by contemporary political theory. My project here is a philosophical one, and exploratory rather than polemical. I want to draw out some little-noted connections between pornography and knowledge, and some little-noted connections between knowledge and harm. And while my aims are modest, there will be some broad implications for free speech, given the two aforementioned Millian assumptions, on the one

---

[3] Mill, *On Liberty*, ch. 1, 13.

[4] David Dyzenhaus, 'John Stuart Mill and the Harm of Pornography', *Ethics* 102 (1992), 534–51, at 550. See also a response by Robert Skipper, 'Mill and Pornography', *Ethics* 103 (1993), 726–30.

hand, that the point of free speech is partly the generation of knowledge; and on the other hand, that significantly harmful speech should not be free.

How might a knowledge-based argument for free speech apply to pornography? Here is one way. Perhaps pornographic speech *destroys* knowledge, in which case there may be a *prima facie* knowledge argument against it. Here is another way. Perhaps pornographic speech *creates* knowledge, in which case there may be a *prima facie* argument in its favor.

The latter possibility would be surprising, given our starting definition of pornography as 'the graphic, sexually explicit subordination of women'; but it is a possibility that I am going to be taking seriously. It is not one that is likely to attract the attention of either party to the debate. Feminist critics have tended to regard pornography as the enemy of knowledge, saying that pornography tells lies about what women are like.[5] Pornography's defenders tend to defend it in quite other terms, saying not that pornography is truthful, but that it is mere fantasy. Since neither lies nor fantasy seem conducive to knowledge, there has been little reason for either party to think about a knowledge argument in pornography's favor.

However there does indeed appear to be a knowledge argument in favor of pornography, as we'll see in due course. I do not mean that pornography creates knowledge in the usual way, for example by having an educative role—although it is true that when children are asked why they watch pornography, their answer is 'to find out about sex'.[6] It might have such a role, but that is not my topic. Nor do I mean that it is political speech, offering a contribution to a truth-seeking debate about how to live the good life, though that has been suggested by at least one eminent liberal theorist.[7] I doubt it has such a role, but in any case that is not my

---

[5] This can ground a comparison with group libel, see Susan Brison, 'The Autonomy Defense of Free Speech', *Ethics* 108 (1998), 312–39, at 315.

[6] Jon Henley, 'Pornography Forms French Children's Views on Sex', *Guardian*, 25 May, 2002. This answer deserves more attention than I am going to give it.

[7] For example, Ronald Dworkin says pornography contributes to the 'moral environment, by expressing... political or social convictions or tastes or prejudices informally', that it 'seeks to deliver' a 'message', that it reflects the 'opinion' that 'women are submissive, or enjoy being dominated, or should be treated as if they did', that it is comparable to speech 'advocating that women occupy inferior roles'. See 'A New Map of Censorship', *Index on Censorship* 1/2 (1994), 13, and 'Two Concepts of Liberty', *Isaiah Berlin: A Celebration*, eds. Edna and Avishai Margalit (London: Hogarth Press, 1991), 104, 105.

topic either. The contribution to knowledge I have in mind is of a quite different kind.

And there is a twist of dialectical irony about it. The argument about knowledge that interests me here is one that should bother pornography's feminist critics, since it will turn out that the positive conclusion about knowledge arises from explicitly *feminist* premises: in particular, premises about the role of pornography in social construction. How could such an argument arise from feminist premises? We think knowledge is good. We think pornography is bad. How could our arguments demonstrating the badness of pornography turn pornography into a source of something good?

Whether the knowledge in question is indeed 'something good' remains to be seen. There is certainly something peculiar about it—something odd, and interesting, and perhaps sinister. What I shall argue is, briefly, this. The knowledge pornography creates has the distinctive features of what I am calling *maker's knowledge*. What is distinctive about maker's knowledge is that it not only aims at truth, but *makes* its truth. I shall try to show why this matters both philosophically and politically. And I shall try to show why, even if most knowledge is good, in this case the knowledge is bad, because the knowledge is itself, oddly enough, a kind of harm. This means that while there might well be a Millian knowledge argument in favour of pornography, it will in the end be constrained by a Millian argument about harm.

2. Speaker's Freedom

Many political philosophers have wanted to say that speech merits special protection, because of the contribution it makes to human interests and values. Sometimes a special justification for free speech is sought in the value of autonomy. Our opinions about how to lead our lives are somehow not our own, if there are constraints on speech. Our opinions are imbided blindly, unreflectively, if they are absorbed without due consideration of the alternatives that would be provided by the expressed opinions of others. Free speech is a condition of our being able to live our lives from the inside, autonomously. Sometimes a special justification for free speech is sought in the value of equality. A principle of equal concern and respect requires that speaker's voices are granted equal concern and respect, and it requires a right to moral independence that protects unpopular speech from the tyranny of majority opinion.[8]

Sometimes, however, a special justification for free speech is sought in the value of knowledge, and this is our present topic. Here, for example, is the celebrated four-fold argument from John Stuart Mill's *On Liberty*:

> We have now recognized the necessity to the mental well-being of mankind ... of freedom of opinion, and freedom of the expression of opinion, on four distinct grounds ...
>
> First, if any opinion is compelled to silence, that opinion may, for aught we can certainly know, be true. To deny this is to assume our own infallibility. Secondly, though the silenced opinion be an error, it may, and very commonly does, contain a portion of the truth; and since the general or prevailing opinion on any subject is rarely or never the whole truth, it is only by the collision of adverse opinions that the remainder of the truth has any chance of being supplied.
>
> Thirdly, even if the received opinion be not only true, but the whole truth; unless it is suffered to be, and actually is, vigorously and earnestly contested, it will, by most of those who receive it, be held in the manner of a prejudice, with little comprehension or feeling of its rational grounds. And not only this, but fourthly, the meaning of the doctrine itself will be in danger of being lost or enfeebled, and deprived of its vital effect on the character and conduct; the dogma becoming a mere formal profession, inefficacious for good, but cumbering the ground and preventing the growth of any real and heartfelt conviction from reason or personal experience.[9]

Mill's argument is better known as the 'Argument from Truth'—understandably enough, given the number of times the words 'true' or 'truth' appear in it. It is really, though, an argument from knowledge, notwithstanding the fact that the word 'knowledge' appears, in this passage, not at all; and if we agree that knowledge matters, then Mill's argument should matter.

[8] See e.g. Thomas Scanlon 'A Theory of Freedom of Expression', *Philosophy and Public Affairs* 1 (1972); Joshua Cohen, 'Freedom of Expression', *Philosophy and Public Affairs* 22 (1993); Susan Brison, 'The Autonomy Defense of Free Speech'; Ronald Dworkin, 'Do We Have a Right to Pornography?', in *A Matter of Principle* (Cambridge, Mass.: Harvard University Press, 1985), 335–72. Mill's justification of free speech also includes assumptions about the value of autonomy, see Dyzenhaus, 'John Stuart Mill'.

[9] J. S. Mill, *On Liberty* (1859), ch. 2, Paras. 41–3.

What is worth having, according to Mill, are not opinions that are merely *true*. If truth were all that mattered, a *true prejudice* would be good enough, and he says explicitly it is not. Even if received opinion is true, and even it is the whole truth, that is no good if the opinion is held merely 'in the manner of a prejudice, with little comprehension or feeling of its rational grounds'. A little later Mill condemns those

who think it enough if a person assents undoubtingly to what they think true, though he has no knowledge whatever of the grounds of the opinion, and could not make a tenable defence of it against the most superficial objections.

If the true opinion 'abides as a prejudice, a belief independent of, and proof against, argument', this is not something worth having, because this

is not the way in which truth ought to be held by a rational being. This is not knowing the truth. Truth, thus held, is but one superstition the more, accidentally clinging to the words which enunciate a truth.[10]

What is worth having is *knowledge*—opinion that has 'rational grounds', indeed rational grounds of which the believer has 'feeling' and 'comprehension'. Freedom of speech matters, according to Mill, because it provides the conditions for knowledge, conditions for the emergence of opinions that are true, and have rational grounds. Free speech allows the expression of unpopular opinions that help the cause of knowledge, either because they are themselves true, or partly true; or else because, though false, they provide the tests and challenges that transform true opinions into true and justified opinions. Free speech matters because free speech helps us get knowledge, and knowledge matters.

Why does knowledge matter? Well, knowledge is, as a general rule, a *useful* sort of commodity, and you might expect this be salient to someone of Mill's utilitarian persuasion. But the answer given by Mill is not that answer, at least here. Knowledge, he suggests, is not just useful, but constitutive of the 'mental well-being of mankind'. Given the kinds of creatures we are—creatures vulnerable to suffering, capable of happiness, but also 'rational beings', driven by a thirst to know—knowledge is part and parcel of well-being, for us.

[10] J. S. Mill, *On Liberty*, ch. 2.

3. A Knowledge Argument against Pornography?

Feminists (but not all or only feminists) have doubted whether the values which justify freedom of speech will justify freedom of pornographic speech.[11] Indeed, they suggest, the values that justify freedom of speech in general seem to justify *restriction* of pornographic speech. Perhaps there is an autonomy argument for freedom of speech: but there is an autonomy argument *against* pornography. If pornography is something that (in Judge Easterbrook's words) 'perpetuates subordination [and] leads to affront and lower pay at work, insult and injury at home, battery and rape on the streets', then pornography thwarts women's autonomy.[12] Perhaps there is an equality argument for freedom of speech: but there is an equality argument *against* pornography. If pornography is the 'graphic, sexually explicit subordination of women in pictures or words', which 'perpetuates subordination', then permitting pornography is incompatible with a commitment to equal concern and respect.[13]

Perhaps there is also a knowledge argument for freedom of speech, just as Mill declared. But it seems unlikely, antecedently, that there could be a knowledge argument in favor of pornography. On this feminists and liberals apparently agree. The concern from feminists has been, as already noted, that pornography tells dangerous *lies* about women—for example, 'rape myths' as the social scientists call them, descriptive lies about what women want and need, and normative lies about how women ought to be treated.[14] Pornography's defenders do not defend it in terms of its contribution to knowledge. In response to a feminist charge that pornography tells lies, the

---

[11] Many feminists oppose the MacKinnon/Dworkin strategy on pornography, see e.g. V. Burstyn, ed., *Women Against Censorship* (Vancouver: Douglas and MacIntyre, 1985); Judith Butler, *Excitable Speech: A Politics of the Performative* (New York and London: Routledge, 1997).

[12] The words of the MacKinnon/Dworkin ordinance; and of Judge Easterbrook, in Hudnut, 771 F.2d 329 (7th Cir. 1985). For some autonomy-related arguments, see Brison, 'The Autonomy Defense'.

[13] Equality has a special role for liberals such as Ronald Dworkin, who locates a right to freedom of speech in a right to moral independence, derived in turn from a right to equality, see 'Do We Have a Right to Pornography?' For a response, see Langton, 'Whose Right? Ronald Dworkin, Women, and Pornographers', this volume.

[14] For a review of the social science evidence, and concern about propagation of 'rape myths', see Edward Donnerstein et al., *The Question of Pornography: Research Findings and Policy Implications* (New York: Free Press, 1987); and for a survey of important and more recent meta-studies confirming the effects of pornography, Neil Malamuth et al., 'Pornography and Sexual Aggression: Are there Reliable Effects and Can we Understand Them?', *Annual Review of Sex Research* 11 (2000), 26–91.

defense is not that pornography tells truths, but that pornography doesn't tell anything. Pornography is fiction, pornography is fantasy. It doesn't aim to represent reality; it doesn't aim to be even a small step on the path to truth.

There are plenty of reasons for feminists to persist in casting pornography as an enemy of knowledge, even in the face of this response. First, pornography might well tell lies, even if it is fictional. Second, pornography might somehow subvert rational thought processes. And third, pornography might somehow undermine women's standing as knowers.

Looking at these briefly, one at a time: pornography may still tell lies, even if it is fictional. Works of fiction, after all, can make claims about reality, implicitly or explicitly. Stories in general are told against a claimed real-world backdrop: the fictional world is claimed to match the real world in, for example, its geography of London, or in its laws of nature, or in its social structure.[15] And that is how even fictional works can tell or presuppose untruths about the actual world, whether about London, or the laws of nature—or about the desires, behavior, and social status of women. So pornography, though fictional, might tell lies about real women; and if pornography is lies, perhaps there is a knowledge argument against it.

Put that way, the envisaged knowledge argument against pornography sounds over-hasty. Mill's knowledge argument does not, after all, require an opinion to be true for it to be free. On the contrary, the expression of even false opinions can serve truth, because it 'contests' the truth and encourages comprehension of its 'rational grounds', helping what would otherwise be mere prejudice acquire the status of knowledge. So it will not do simply to say: pornography is false, so the knowledge argument opposes it. Even if pornography were to tell hateful lies about women, perhaps its presence could make its hearers apprehend the truth all the more vividly.

But here the next point might come in. Pornography may be the enemy of knowledge not just because of its falsity, but because of its irrationality. Pornography does not work by offering reasons for false opinions: it works, perhaps, by a process of conditioning. Cass Sunstein argues that violent pornography works by 'subliminal suggestion'. Danny Scoccia points

---

[15] See David Lewis, 'Truth in Fiction', in his *Philosophical Papers* (Oxford: Oxford University Press, 1983) vol. i, 261–80; for application to pornography, see Langton and Caroline West, 'Scorekeeping in a Pornographic Language Game', this volume.

to evidence that violent pornography works by 'operant conditioning', altering desires and beliefs in ways that bypass the normal processes of reason. According to Scoccia, it should receive no First Amendment protection, because a free speech principle 'does not affect speech insofar as it non-rationally affects its hearer's mental states'.[16] MacKinnon says that pornography 'works as primitive conditioning, with pictures and words as sexual stimuli'.[17] The suggestion would be that pornography thwarts knowledge not only through its falsity, but through its interference in the very reasoning processes of its consumers. And if pornography interferes with reasoning, it can hardly be in the business of playing the helpful epistemological role that even false opinions are able to play, according to Mill.

A knowledge argument against pornography might be augmented, if one attends to the effects on knowledge more widely, and in particular the effects on the standing of *women* as knowers. On a certain social picture of knowledge, proposed for example by Edward Craig, what matters for knowledge is not just whether your beliefs are true, justified, and so on. In addition, social facts matter, including facts about whether you are counted as a credible witness. Miranda Fricker draws out some political implications of this idea. Suppose that someone, through no fault of her own, is accorded no credibility: then she has her very standing as a knower undermined, even if her own beliefs are true and justified. Such a person could suffer *epistemic injustice*, a phenomenon that Fricker identifies as an unjust distribution of credibility.[18] This idea, interesting in itself, has implications for our reflections about pornography. It opens up the possibility that not only pornography's consumers, but women themselves, may have their standing as knowers adversely affected. Pornography arguably undermines women's credibility, for example when it comes to testifying about sexual violence in court. Pornography make its viewers less likely to notice violence, less likely to take seriously the testimony of rape victims, and more disposed

---

[16] Cass Sunstein, 'Pornography and the First Amendment', *Duke Law Journal* (1986), 589–627; Danny Scoccia 'Can Liberals Support a Ban on Violent Pornography?', *Ethics* 106 (1996), 776–99, at 777.

[17] MacKinnon, *Only Words* (Cambridge, Mass.: Harvard University Press, 1993), 16.

[18] Miranda Fricker, *Epistemic Injustice* (Oxford: Oxford University Press, 2007) and 'Rational Authority and Social Power: Towards a Truly Social Epistemology', *Proceedings of the Aristotelian Society* (1998), 159–77; Edward Craig, *Knowledge and the State of Nature: An Essay in Conceptual Synthesis* (Oxford: Clarendon Press, 1990). The Craig/Fricker view of knowledge is attractive, but I am not sure that I endorse it; and of course would not attribute it to Mill.

to assign lower sentences to convicted rapists.[19] If pornography does these things, then it might well be an agent of 'epistemic injustice', in Fricker's terms, in which case there could be a different kind of knowledge argument against it. Pornography in that case would undermine knowledge not just because it is false, not just because it engenders irrationality, but because it undermines women's credibility; and on this social picture of knowledge, credibility matters to one's standing as a knower.

At first sight, then, it seems that a knowledge argument for freedom of speech is unlikely to generate a knowledge argument for freedom of pornographic speech; meanwhile, a knowledge argument *against* pornography looks rather promising.

4. A Knowledge Argument for Pornography?

There is something that we have been missing, however, a possibility missed both by the liberals for whom pornography is escapist fiction, and by the feminists for whom pornography is irrational lies. It is the possibility that pornography, even defined as 'the graphic sexually explicit subordination of women', helps create knowledge; and accordingly that there might be a Millian knowledge argument in its favor—indeed a Millian argument drawing on feminist anti-pornography premises.

We can make a start on this with Catharine MacKinnon's remarks on the epistemology of pornography.

[The] beliefs of the powerful become [proven], in part because the world actually arranges itself to affirm what the powerful want to see. If you perceive this as a process, you might call it force, or at least pressure or socialization or what money can buy. If it is imperceptible as a process, you may consider it voluntary or consensual or free will or human nature, or just the way things are. Beneath this, though, the world is not entirely the way the powerful say it is or want to believe it is.[20]

---

[19] See Donnerstein et al., *The Question of Pornography*.

[20] MacKinnon, *Feminism Unmodified*, 164. I follow Sally Haslanger in substituting 'proven' for 'proof', see 'On Being Objective and Being Objectified', in *A Mind Of One's Own: Feminist Essays on Reason and Objectivity* (Boulder, Co.: Westview Press, 1993), 103. Haslanger emphasizes the epistemological implications of MacKinnon's understanding of objectification, and this essay is partly inspired by her work. She anticipates some themes of the present essay, in a footnote speculating whether an objectifier is 'infallible' with respect to his beliefs about the objectified.

Again:

If a woman is defined hierarchically so that the male idea of a woman defines womanhood, and if men have power, this idea becomes reality. It is therefore real. It is not just an illusion or a fantasy or a mistake. It becomes embodied because it is enforced.[21]

On this way of thinking, pornography is 'not just an illusion or a fantasy or a mistake': pornography is not just a fiction, as some liberals want to say; not just libellous lies, not just irrational conditioning. MacKinnon is talking here about a process of social construction, a process in which the world of women conforms to the beliefs, perceptions, and speech of powerful men. This social construction has implications for knowledge.

On MacKinnon's way of thinking, pornography claims to be a mirror. Look, it says, *women are like this*. In reality, pornography acts as a blueprint. Look, it says, *let women be like this*. The difference between a mirror and a blueprint is a difference in direction of fit: a mirror conforms to fit the world; the world conforms to fit a blueprint. A blueprint can seem to be a mirror, because treating women as if they *are* 'like this' can be a way of making women seem to become 'like this', or indeed genuinely become 'like this'. In conditions of oppression, expectations of how a subordinate will behave can be self-verifying or self-fulfilling. Marilyn Frye comments on this phenomenon:

The arrogant perceiver...coerces the objects of his perception into satisfying the conditions his perception imposes.... He manipulates the environment, perception and judgment of her whom he perceives, so that her recognized options are limited, and the course she chooses will be such as coheres with his purposes.... How one sees another and how one expects the other to behave are in tight interdependence, and how one expects the other to behave is a large factor in determining how the other does behave.[22]

Combining these ideas from MacKinnon and Frye, the thought is that pornography shapes a kind of 'arrogant perception' of women, which in

---

[21] MacKinnon, *Feminism Unmodified*, 119.

[22] Marilyn Frye, *The Politics of Reality* (Freedom, Ca.: The Crossing Press, 1983), 67. See also Haslanger's work on social construction in e.g. 'Ontology and Social Construction', *Philosophical Topics* 23 (1995), 95–125; 'Feminism and Metaphysics: Negotiating the Natural', in *Cambridge Companion to Feminism in Philosophy*, eds., Miranda Fricker and Jennifer Hornsby (Cambridge: Cambridge University Press, 2000).

turn shapes women themselves, so that women conform to the identities pornography assigns them.

We might distinguish the idea that pornography is self-verifying from the idea that it is self-fulfilling. Let us say that if a belief is self-verifying, it provides evidence for itself (given a certain context). If it is self-fulfilling, it makes itself true (again, given a certain context).

Beliefs that are self-verifying may be false, but justified: the evidence may be misleading, but being evidence, it supports the belief, even if the belief is false. To take an example often cited by MacKinnon: belief in the so-called 'vaginal orgasm', long endorsed by Freud and orthodox sexologists, casts women's sexual desires as a convenient match to men's desires, satisfied, at least for the 'mature' woman, by penetrative sex alone. Such belief may be false, but self-verifying, in part because it is verified by the behavior of women themselves, who learn to fake the kinds of sexual pleasure expected of them, given the incentives for doing so.[23] More generally, being ranked or believed to be inferior can make someone act as if they are inferior, even when they are not. Beliefs that are merely self-verifying are not knowledge, but they are perhaps somewhere on the road to knowledge: they are, arguably, justified belief. This yields one way, an important way, in which the beliefs of the powerful are, in MacKinnon's words, 'not just an illusion or a fantasy or a mistake'.

Beliefs that are self-fulfilling go further along the road to knowledge, since they are true as well. A pornography-inspired belief that a woman will be sexually servile may be true because it becomes true, when a woman acts in ways that fulfill expectation. A pornography-inspired belief that young girls will welcome adult sexual advances may be true, because it becomes true, when a girl acts in ways that fulfill expectation. In oppressive conditions, some pornography-inspired beliefs may be self-fulfilling in the way that Frye describes, when someone with limited power and opportunities conforms to the expectations had of her. And again, more generally, being ranked or believed to be inferior can make someone not only act as if they are inferior, but actually become inferior—as illustrated in the Pygmalion studies on school children, where expectations of stupidity

---

[23] See e.g. MacKinnon, *Toward a Feminist Theory of the State* (Cambridge, Mass.: Harvard University Press, 1989), 123, 140–2.

helped to create stupidity.[24] In such cases, the relevant belief is true; once true, there is evidence that it is true; so it becomes justified as well. This yields a further way, a different way, in which the beliefs of the powerful are 'not just an illusion or a fantasy or a mistake'.

If we are supposing that pornography helps generate beliefs that are 'not just an illusion or a fantasy or a mistake', we are supposing that pornography is not just irrational lies. We are taking seriously the thought that pornography generates at least some justified beliefs, some true and justified beliefs, and, perhaps, some knowledge.

And now we face the uncomfortable prospect advertised at the outset: there appears to be a knowledge argument *for* pornography. Pornography helps bring it about that 'the beliefs of the powerful' become *knowledge*, given that, as MacKinnon puts it, 'the world actually arranges itself to affirm what the powerful want to see'.

5. Maker's Knowledge

A first question to consider is whether the prospect is one of knowledge after all. When you peer at your rear-view mirror, you have knowledge of the approaching car whose reflection you see. In this case the representation, the image in the mirror, has come to fit the world. Your belief is true, and justified. That is the pattern for ordinary knowledge, of which perceptual knowledge is a paradigm. When, at the General Motors boardroom, you draw the blueprint of next year's model, you perhaps have knowledge of next year's car. But in this case, the direction of fit runs the other way, for the world will come to fit the blueprint. Your belief is true, and justified. But *is* it knowledge?

I suspect untutored intuition suggests the answer 'yes'. This knowledge is *maker's* knowledge, the special knowledge you have of something in virtue of making it. When Mill thought of knowledge he naturally had in mind the other direction of fit: Mill thought of opinion as mirror, not as blueprint. The truth is out there, independent of our opinions, but free

---

[24] Robert Rosenthal and Lenore Jakobson, *Pygmalion in the Classroom* (New York: Holt, Rinehart and Winston, 1968).

speech is going to help our opinions become more accurate mirrors of reality. Opinion is in the business of conforming to truth. It doesn't cross Mill's mind that truth may be in the business, sometimes, of conforming to opinion. But opinions made true the blueprint way might be knowledge just the same.

Admittedly, philosophers often caution that knowledge needs something else besides truth and justification, though they cannot agree on what the something else might be. Examples from Bertrand Russell, Edmund Gettier, and their successors, have made it clear that *something* more is needed. When, at 11.00 o'clock, I look at the railway station clock to learn the time, and see the hands pointing to 11.00 o'clock, my belief that it is 11.00 o'clock is true and justified—but it is not knowledge, since (unbeknownst to me) the clock has stopped.[25] Philosophers have wanted to say that knowledge needs truth, justification, plus a 'something else' that they have tried to capture in the idea of *non-accidentality*, or the idea of a *reliable connection* between the belief and the belief's truth.

Note that these two extra conditions provide no bar to counting self-fulfilling beliefs as knowledge. Such conditions seem to be satisfied by the boardroom blueprint. It is no accident that next year's model conforms to the blueprint; the connections that ensure the conformity can be as reliable as one could wish. The conditions could likewise be satisfied by some of the beliefs engendered by pornography: when oppression is systematic enough, there is nothing accidental about a correlation between beliefs that women are servile, and women's servility; and the connection between beliefs and the truth of those beliefs can be as reliable as one could wish. What is anomalous, what does set this 'knowledge' apart from the usual variety, is the peculiar direction of fit.

Some philosophers have worried about the epistemological standing of beliefs that are true because the world 'arranges itself' to affirm them. Some have denied that a blue-print-like direction of fit is compatible with knowledge. Thus Lloyd Humberstone asks us to

consider the case of a subject, S, whose beliefs about the future are monitored by a supernatural being who, taking (for whatever reason) a special interest in

---

[25] Drawing on Russell's original example, in *Human Knowledge: Its Scope and Limits* (New York: Allen and Unwin, 1948), 170–1; this kind of example was taken up by Edmund Gettier, 'Is Knowledge Justified True Belief?', *Analysis* 23 (1963), 121–3.

minimizing falsity amongst S's beliefs, intervenes in the course of history so as to make these future-oriented beliefs of S true. Note that we do not suppose that S has the slightest inkling that this is going on. It does not seem correct to say that S, who believes, for example, that Islam will be the state religion of a United Europe by the year 2100, knows this to be the case, even though it is not at all accidental that S's belief here is true. The trouble is that the non-accidentality pertains to a matching of the world to S's mental state rather than in the converse direction.[26]

Here we have a philosopher's thought experiment, whose conclusion is that an opinion's being true, justified, and non-accidentally true, is not good enough for knowledge. In casting the net for that elusive 'something else' which knowledge requires, Humberstone's suggestion is that knowledge, to be knowledge, in fact needs a mirror-like direction of fit.

There is, however, an ancient and still thriving tradition which stands opposed to Humberstone's suggestion. God knows his creation because he makes it. God can have maker's knowledge of creation. We can have maker's knowledge of our own actions. Car designers can have maker's knowledge of next year's model. Maimonides described this distinctive knowledge in these terms:

There is a great difference between the knowledge which the producer of a thing possesses concerning it and the knowledge which other persons possess concerning the same thing. Suppose a thing is produced in accordance with the knowledge of the producer. The producer was then guided by his knowledge in the act of producing the thing. Other people, however, who examine this work and acquire a knowledge of the whole of it, depend for that knowledge on the work itself. For instance an artisan makes a box in which weights move with the running of water and thus indicate how many hours have passed. . . . His knowledge is not the result of observing the movements as they are actually going on; but on the contrary, the movements are produced in accordance with his knowledge.[27]

The producer of the water-clock has maker's knowledge of the water-clock, in the same way that God has knowledge of us. Anscombe draws upon the idea of maker's knowledge in describing the knowledge we have, as agents, of what we are doing.

[26] Lloyd Humberstone, 'Direction of Fit', *Mind* 101 (1992), 59–83, 62.
[27] Moses Maimonides, *The Guide for the Perplexed,* trans. M. Friedländer, Part III, ch. XXI (New York: Pardes Publishing House, 1946).

Imagine someone directing a project, like the erection of a building which he cannot see and does not get reports on, purely by giving orders.... His knowledge of what is done is practical knowledge. But what is this 'knowledge of what is done'? First and foremost, he can say what the house is like.[28]

The architect of the building has maker's knowledge, which enables him to know (sight unseen) just what the house is like. David Velleman places the idea of maker's knowledge at the heart of practical reason: the self-fulfilling nature of a belief about what we are going to do is what enables that belief both to aim at truth, and to count as knowledge.

[W]hen I make a choice, a question is resolved in the world by being resolved in my mind. That I am going to do something is made true by my representing it as true. So choice has the same direction of fit as belief but the same direction of guidance as desire: it is a case of practical cognition.[29]

William James is interested in a different kind of self-fulfilling belief about what one is going to do, which he describes as faith. A famous example: imagine a mountain climber, whose belief that he will successfully leap enables him to do so. A more salient example, if we are interested in self-fulfilling beliefs about what someone *else* will do:

How many women's hearts are vanquished by the mere sanguine insistence of some man that they must love him! he will not consent to the hypothesis that they cannot. The desire for a certain kind of truth here brings about that special truth's existence; and so it is in innumerable cases of other sorts.... There are then, cases where a fact cannot come at all unless a preliminary faith exists in its coming.[30]

Faith and intention are not the same, but with each there is a belief that is reliably and non-accidentally connected with its truth, because it makes itself true. And, like Velleman, James takes the self-fulfilling feature of

---

[28] Elizabeth Anscombe, *Intention* (1957); reprint (Cambridge, Mass.: Harvard University Press, 2000). Anscombe also remarks upon the dual direction of fit that speech acts and mental states may have: 'When a doctor says to a patient in the presence of a nurse "Nurse will take you to the operating theatre", this may function both as an expression of his intention ... and as an order, as well as being information to the patient', p. 3. As speech act, it is assertion and order; the corresponding mental state is at once a belief about what will happen, and an intention that it will.

[29] David Velleman, *The Possibility of Practical Reason* (Oxford: Clarendon Press, 2000), 25.

[30] James, 'The Will to Believe', in *The Will to Believe and Other Essays in Popular Philosophy* (Norwood, Mass.: Plimpton Press, 1896), 23–4.

such belief to earn it the title of knowledge.[31] So thinkers as different as Maimonides, Anscombe, James and Velleman, give us some reasons for thinking that having an anomalous direction of fit is no bar to knowledge.

Notice how there are close structural parallels between these descriptions of maker's knowledge and MacKinnon's account of sexual objectification. The beliefs of the powerful become proven, she says, because the world 'arranges itself' to affirm them, just as the building, in Anscombe's story, 'arranges itself' to affirm what the architect plans; and just as the world, in Humberstone's story, 'arranges itself' to affirm what S believes, thanks to the power and benevolence of his divine epistemological guardian. If a creative direction of fit is no bar to knowledge in general, it should be no bar to S's knowledge after all, contrary to Humberstone; and it should be no bar to pornography's knowledge either. If we accept that maker's knowledge is knowledge, we should accept that pornography may be a source of knowledge. It may be a source of self-fulfilling belief, that is non-accidentally and reliably self-fulfilling: belief, for example, about the sexual servility of women, or the sexual receptiveness of children. That is admittedly not the kind of knowledge Mill had in mind, when he spoke so glowingly about the search for the truth; but it is, perhaps, knowledge nonetheless.

So yes, it seems that we do face that uncomfortable conclusion. There is a knowledge argument *in favor* of pornography, generated by the very premises of feminists who oppose it. End of story? Not quite.

6. Maker's Knowledge and Harm

First, we have done nothing, so far, to adjudicate the balance of error and knowledge that pornography engenders. Pornography may help a man know a woman is sexually servile, because it may help to make that true, where it would not otherwise be true. Pornography may help a sexual abuser know that a young girl will welcome his advances, because it may help to make that true, where it would not otherwise be true. But what of

[31] James, 'The Will to Believe', 12. He thought that when we have faith, we know, but we do not know that we know. See Langton, 'Intention as Faith', in *Agency and Action*, eds., John Hyman and Helen Steward (Cambridge: Cambridge University Press, 2004), 243–57.

pornography's lies, for example the lie that women are *naturally* servile, or that a young girl will *naturally* welcome adult sexual advances?[32] It seems that knowledge argument in favor of pornography supplements, but does not outright contradict, the earlier knowledge argument against it. And we are now in a position to add a further error to those earlier noted, namely a false meta-belief about the direction of fit between knowledge and the world. The knower fails to notice that the world is coming to fit his beliefs: he falsely believes that his knowledge has a mirror-like direction of fit, that it reflects, in MacKinnon's words, 'just the way things are'. It would take considerably more thought to adjudicate this mix of error and knowledge, and reach a reasonable conclusion about whether, on balance, pornography is a greater enemy or friend to knowledge.

More importantly, though, there are values other than knowledge at stake, as we observed right at the outset. Freedom is never an absolute, for Mill, but always constrained by the harm principle. Power can be exercised over a member of a civilized community against his will, if his speech would otherwise cause harm to others. Among the freedoms constrained by the harm principle is that of freedom of expression, as shown, perhaps, in Mill's famous remarks about the opinions of the hater of corn-dealers:

Even opinions lose their immunity when the circumstances in which they are expressed are such as to constitute their expression a positive instigation to some mischievous act. An opinion that corn dealers are starvers of the poor ... ought to be unmolested when circulated through the press, but may incur just punishment when delivered ... to an excited mob assembled before the house of a corn dealer, or when handed about the same mob in the form of a placard.[33]

Harmful speech will incur just punishment, and the difference between that hateful opinion circulated through the press, and delivered to an excited mob, lies in the degree and the certainty of the ensuing harm.

We have already seen how some liberals think that Mill's harm principle justifies restrictions on pornographic speech. Our interest here is not, however, in how the harm principle might bear on pornography as

---

[32] See Haslanger, 'On Being Objective and Being Objectified', for some careful work distinguishing the truths from the falsities in objectifying belief, with a special focus on the falsity of the modal beliefs that women are *necessarily* or *naturally* thus-and-so. The falsities, and in general the power of objectification to thwart knowledge, are discussed in Langton, 'Feminism in Epistemology: Exclusion and Objectification', this volume.

[33] Mill, *On Liberty*, ch. 3, 56.

such, but how the harm principle might bear on this Millian knowledge argument. For there are different ways in which a harm principle might constrain a knowledge argument for freedom of speech. We can distinguish four.

First, it might be thought, simply, that the independent harm of a particular kind of speech simply outweighs the good of any knowledge it helps create. Second, it might be thought that the knowledge in question is instrumentally harmful. Wartime posters warned that 'Careless talk costs lives', because knowledge, in the wrong hands, can have bad consequences. Third, it might be thought that the knowledge in question is intrinsically harmful, because merely knowing certain things is bad. Consider, for example, a stalker's invasive knowledge of his target's personal life. Whether or not he acts on the knowledge, the mere fact that someone knows very private and personal facts can be a violation.

One can imagine these sorts of connections being potentially relevant to any judicious weighing up of knowledge and harm, by the lights of Mill's commitments. However, my interest is in yet a fourth relationship. Maker's knowledge, as manifested by pornography, presents us with a yet different connection between knowledge and harm—a more intimate, and more subtle, connection than any of the three just described.

It is tempting to put the point thus. Pornography's knowledge *is* harm, because the creation of knowledge, through pornography, and the objectification of women by pornography are two sides of the very same phenomenon. On MacKinnon's way of thinking, pornography is a certain kind of self-fulfilling projection. That is what makes it a source of knowledge, and that is what makes it a kind of objectification. Part of the harm is in the *shape* that is projected: the vision of what women are like—servile, inferior, less-than-human. And part of the harm is also in the *shaping*, the fact that the projection becomes, in contexts of oppression, a self-fulfilling one. In shaping women, pornography undermines a woman's autonomy, undermines the power a woman might otherwise have had to shape herself. On this way of thinking, it looks as thought there is a connection between the blueprint-like direction of fit, and the harm to women.

Should this make us wonder whether there is an association between harm and 'maker's knowledge' as such? At first sight, that seems implausible. Those who find nothing epistemologically amiss in maker's knowledge will surely find nothing morally amiss either. After all, the 'maker's knowledge' God has of his creations is supposed to be compatible with his supreme benevolence. The 'maker's knowledge' we each have of our own future actions is supposed to be a requirement of our own practical rationality, with no untoward implications for ethics. There seems to be nothing morally, or politically, amiss with maker's knowledge *as such*.

But wait! God-like knowledge of one's creations? Practical knowledge of one's own actions? If the pattern of pornography-inspired belief matches, in certain respects, the pattern of divine knowledge, or of practical knowledge, this should surely ring some alarm bells. Harm may lurk in the wings after all—harm, via damage to autonomy.

Here is the thought. For an agent to have maker's knowledge of his own actions suggests an agent who is maker of his own actions. But for an agent to have maker's knowledge of the actions of others suggests an agent who is somehow a maker of the actions of *others*. Is it just a coincidence that the way a pornographer knows what a woman will do sometimes matches, structurally, the way he knows what he will do himself? Perhaps not. Perhaps it is an epistemological reflection of the moral fact that she is somehow being made an extension of himself: that her autonomy has been excluded from the picture.

Where does this leave us if, with Mill, we care about knowledge and we care about harm? If knowledge is good, and harm bad, what do we do about a kind of knowledge that is also a kind of harm? I don't resolve this here, but a natural response to this question would be to take the harm principle seriously: if the maker's knowledge in pornography is harm, that fact should trump what value, if any, it might otherwise have as knowledge.

These connections between knowledge and harm are implicit in MacKinnon's analysis of objectification as social construction. The ideas about social construction are familiar, if controversial; the task here has been just to spell out their epistemological implications. For MacKinnon, there is a close relationship between the blue-print-like direction of fit, and the damage to women, both there in the idea of objectification. When she describes how the beliefs of the powerful become proven in part because 'the world actually arranges itself to affirm what the powerful want to see', what she describes is objectification. The harm of pornography lies in the way it objectifies women—the way it makes the world arrange itself to match the pornographic vision. That creates knowledge, *and* it creates harm. When objectification is going on, there is a pattern of self-fulfilling, projective attitudes, which project a certain shape on to women, and alter women to conform to that shape. When objectification is going on, it is no accident, after all, that the way a pornographer knows what a woman will do matches the way he knows what he will do himself. The harm and the knowledge are, in a sense, the very same thing.

14

Sexual Solipsism

1. Introduction

Solipsism finds its best known philosophical expression in the predicament of Descartes's meditator, which is where we are going to begin. But a variety of solipsisms are going to occupy us here—more local, and sexual, counterparts of the lonely meditator. We shall be thinking about escape from solipsism, and what Kant had to say about it (Section 2). We shall be taking a closer look at the solipsism that bothered Kant, which involves treating people as things, and which might be taken to include objective attitudes, objectifying attitudes, and sadism (Section 3). And finally, we shall look more closely at a claim that, in pornogaphy, two sexual solipsisms are united: things are treated as people, and people are treated as things (Section 4).[1]

1.1. Two solipsisms

Suppose I were the meditator, and the Cartesian nightmare were the truth. The beings beneath my window, in their hats and coats, would be mere machines. Would I treat them as mere machines? No. I would call to them, laugh with them, talk with them, just the same. I would treat these things as people. But my world would be, in one way, solipsistic. Suppose now the reverse. Suppose the Cartesian nightmare were false, but I believed it true. The beings beneath my window would be people, but I would treat them as machines. Solipsism would be false, but I would act as though

---

[1] This is a slightly revised version of 'Sexual Solipsism', *Philosophical Topics* 23 (1995), special issue 'Feminist Perspectives on Language, Knowledge and Reality', ed., Sally Haslanger, 181–219. It has a companion piece, 'Love and Solipsism', this volume. The solipsist's predicament is in René Descartes, *Meditations on First Philosophy* (1641), trans. John Cottingham (Cambridge: Cambridge University Press, 1986), e.g. at p. 32.

it were true. And my world would be, in a different way, solipsistic. If both worlds are solipsistic, then one aspect of solipsism concerns the world itself, and another concerns an attitude to the world. One aspect concerns the nature of the beings beneath the window: are they people? Another aspect concerns my attitude: do I treat them as people? If one is to avoid the solipsistic worlds, some of the beings with whom one interacts must *be* people (not things); and one must *treat* them as people (not as things).

1.2. Two local solipsisms

The two global solipsisms just described may have local counterparts. Someone may *treat some things as people*. Someone might treat a doll as if it is hungry. Someone might treat a river as if it is angry, and can be appeased with gifts. Someone might beg help from a statue. Someone might take an axe to a recalcitrant motor car (there, smash, that'll teach you, smash). Someone might treat a piece of paper as if it were a sexually desirable, and desiring, human being. It is a familiar, if mysterious, fact of human experience that we project human qualities onto the inanimate, whether in games, or fantasy, or outright mistake.

What can be said about this treating of things as people? When it involves outright mistake, it may perhaps be faulted on grounds of rationality; but if we owe moral duties only to people, not to things, then, at first sight, no case is obviously to be faulted on moral grounds. I cannot really hurt a thing that I treat as a human being, no matter how I treat it. I cannot help or harm a statue that I treat as a friend. I cannot help or harm the car upon which I vent my rage, though I may damage it. Perhaps that is why the elevation of things to persons attracts little philosophical attention, with some exceptions.[2] It is not obvious that this local solipsism is to be condemned in the way that its global counterpart deserves, and it may be that human life would be the poorer if no one ever treated some things as people. Besides, the treating of things as people is usually a rather piecemeal affair, involving the attribution (serious or otherwise) of only *some* human qualities. I might treat a statue as an especially kind and powerful friend, but am unlikely to wonder what it had for lunch. I might treat my car as an

---

[2] For one lively exception see Rosalind Hursthouse's discussion of some similar examples, in 'Arational Actions', *Journal of Philosophy* 88 No. 2, 1991, 57–68. She observes that there can be something touching and endearing about them.

appropriate target for reactive attitudes of blame and rage, but am unlikely to apologize to it later. I might treat things as people in some respects, and not in others. I shall speak of this treating of things as people, this animation of things, as a solipsism nonetheless. In the small world of my reactive relationship with a statue, or a car, there is only one real person. So I see this local solipsism as a microcosm of the first global solipsism I described: the solipsism of one who attributes (seriously or otherwise) human qualities to an inanimate thing.

There is a second local solipsism. Someone may *treat some people as things*. This reduction of people to things attracts attention from philosophers. They say it is wrong to treat a person as a thing, because such an attitude fails to treat the other person as an end in herself, or because it violates the autonomy of the other person, or because it objectifies the other person, or because it makes an Other of the other. They say that it fails to do justice, both morally and epistemically, to the humanity of the person who is treated as a thing. The treating of people as things is likewise a rather piecemeal affair, involving only *some* non-human qualities. I might treat people as things in some respects, and not in others. I shall speak of this treating of people as things, this objectifying of people, as a form of solipsism nonetheless. In the small world of an objectifying relationship, there is more than one real person: but it is, for one, as if he were the only person. So I see this local solipsism as a microcosm of the second global solipsism described above: the solipsism of one who ignores—and perhaps diminishes, or destroys—some human qualities of the person whom he treats as a thing.

Feminists too are concerned about a local solipsism. Many say that women, in particular, are treated as things, objectified, made Other. Mary Wollstonecraft wrote that the oppression of women produces creatures who are 'alluring objects' and 'slaves', and that relations between men and women can be solipsistic as a result. She wrote of 'the man who can be contented to live with a pretty, useful companion, without a mind', and said that 'in the society of his wife he is still alone'.[3] The theme is famously developed by Simone de Beauvoir, who says that oppression is the degradation of a free human being into an object.

---

[3] Mary Wollstonecraft, *A Vindication of the Rights of Woman* (1792), ed., M. B. Kramnick (Harmondsworth: Penguin, 1992), 191–2.

What peculiarly signalizes the situation of woman is that she—a free and autonomous being like all human creatures—nevertheless finds herself living in a world where men compel her to assume the status of the Other. They propose to stabilize her as an object...

In the company of a living enigma *man remains alone*. [This] is for many a more attractive experience than an authentic relationship with a human being.[4]

If a failure to recognize the humanity of others amounts to a solipsism, then one message of feminist writers is that solipsism is not a mere problem in epistemology, but a moral and political problem, and one we have yet to fully escape.

1.3. Two sexual solipsisms

Among these local versions of the global solipsisms with which I began are two that have a sexual aspect. In the first, someone treats a thing as a human being, in a context that is sexual; in the second, someone treats a human being as a thing, in a context that is sexual. Feminists have been concerned with both sexual solipsisms, and so has Kant.

First there is a solipsism of animating things. When someone treats a thing as a human being, in a sexual context, he does not believe outright it is a human being, but he may act as if it were. He may talk with it, he may praise it, or blame it; he may attribute to the thing beliefs about himself, and desires. He may direct a range of reactive attitudes towards it. And he has sex with it. The talk, praise, blame, belief/desire attribution, is in some sense make-believe. The sexual experience is not. Perhaps the thing is a piece of paper, a doll, or, more elaborately, the electronically created virtual being imagined in Jeanette Winterson's novel:

If you like, you may live in a computer-created world all day and all night. You will be able to try out a Virtual life with a Virtual lover. You can go into your Virtual house and do Virtual housework, add a baby or two, even find out if you'd rather be gay. Or single. Or straight. Why hesitate when you could simulate?

---

[4] The two quotations are from Simone de Beauvoir, *The Second Sex* (1949) trans. H. M. Parshley (London: Pan, 1988), 29, 286. More precisely, oppression is (as discussed below) the *inflicted* degradation of a free human being into an object. In interpreting de Beauvoir, Michèle le Doeuff discusses the existentialist notion of a 'de facto solipsism' which reduces people to their functions in relation to a subject, and she compares the conceptual status of woman to the status of a secondary quality. See *Hipparchia's Choice*, trans. Trista Selous (Oxford: Blackwell, 1990), 52, 102.

And sex? Certainly. Teledildonics is the word. You will be able to plug in your telepresence to the billion-bundle network of fibre optics criss-crossing the world and join your partner in Virtuality. Your real selves will be wearing body suits made up of thousands of tiny tactile detectors per square inch. Courtesy of the fibre optic network these will receive and transmit touch. The Virtual epidermis will be as sensitive as your own outer layer of skin.

For myself, unreconstructed as I am, I'd rather hold you in my arms . . . Luddite? No, I don't want to smash the machines but neither do I want the machines to smash me.[5]

Technology may be catching up with the thought experiments that philosophers, since Descartes, have half-seriously entertained—brains in vats, experience machines, the rest. And Winterson's description nicely captures the liberal dream. A thousand possible experiments in living, and cost free. The Cartesian nightmare becomes utopia. Why not plug in from the start? Why hesitate, when you could simulate?

In short, one sexual solipsism might involve the treating of things as if they are human, when pornography is used as a sexual partner. This idea is clearly present in certain feminist discussions, and in Kant's writing, though I postpone discussion of Kant's version until later. Catharine MacKinnon says that the use of pornography is 'sex between people and things, human beings and pieces of paper, real men and unreal women'.[6] Melinda Vadas defines pornography to be 'any object that has been manufactured to satisfy sexual desire through its sexual consumption or other sexual use as a woman' where 'as' means 'in the role, function, or capacity of' a woman.[7] She says that the use of pornography is the sexual consumption of a manufactured artifact, a thing, a piece of paper, that is treated as a human being, and in particular, as woman. There may well be something piecemeal about this treating of things as if they are human that is involved in pornography: there may be some reactive attitudes and not others, there may be a projection of some human qualities and not others, so that although this sexual solipsism may involve the treating of a thing as a woman, it falls short of treating a thing as a person. That, indeed, is a point that Vadas wants to emphasize, and we will return to it later.

[5] Jeanette Winterson, *Written on the Body* (London: Jonathan Cape, 1992), 97−8.

[6] Catharine MacKinnon, *Only Words* (Cambridge, Mass.: Harvard University Press, 1993), 109.

[7] Melinda Vadas, 'The Manufacture-for-use of Pornography and Women's Inequality,' *Journal of Political Philosophy* 13 (2005), 174−93 (published posthumously), 21−2.

To describe the feminist argument in this way is to risk missing the main point, which is not that pornography *animates things*, but that it *objectifies women*, not that pornography elevates things to human beings, but that it reduces human beings to things—in other words, that pornography instantiates the second sexual solipsism. Let us think briefly (for the moment) about what this latter solipsism might involve.

In addition to the solipsism of animating things, there is a solipsism of objectifying people, and this, like the first, can have a sexual aspect. Feminists see a sexual aspect to the treating of women as things, as the remarks from Wollstonecraft and de Beauvoir show. Women are treated as things, when they are treated as sex objects. What this amounts to is a matter of debate, but let us say provisionally that in sexual contexts, women are treated as things to the extent that women are treated as merely bodies, as merely sensory appearances, as not free, as items that can be possessed, as items whose value is merely instrumental.

Feminists say that women are often treated as things, in sexual contexts, and ought not to be: the claim has a descriptive and a normative role. Kant says that people are often treated as things, in sexual contexts, and ought not to be: the claim has a descriptive and normative role for him as well. In pessimistic moments Kant suggests that sexual desire carries, in itself, a tendency to this kind of solipsism. He says that when a human being becomes an object of someone's sexual desire, the 'person becomes a thing and can be treated and used as such'. He says, notoriously, that 'sexual love makes of the loved person an object of appetite; as soon as that appetite has been stilled, the person is cast aside as one casts away a lemon that has been sucked dry'.[8] The bleakness of Kant's descriptive claim echoes the bleakness of some feminist claims, as Barbara Herman has noted.[9]

It is in the context of a general view about objectification that the main feminist claims about pornography have their place. The claim is that pornography, in particular, makes women objects, helps to bring it about that women are treated as merely bodies, merely sensory appearances, not free, as items that can be possessed, as items whose value is merely instrumental.

---

[8] Immanuel Kant, *Lectures on Ethics* (1775–1780), trans. Louis Infield (London: Methuen, 1930), from notes made by Brauer, Kutzner, and Mrongovius, ed., Paul Menzer, 163.

[9] Barbara Herman, 'Could It Be Worth Thinking about Kant on Sex and Marriage?', in *A Mind Of One's Own: Feminist Essays on Reason and Objectivity,* eds., Louise M. Antony and Charlotte Witt (Boulder, Co.: Westview Press, 1993).

Now MacKinnon herself says that pornography instantiates both solipsisms, though not in quite those words. She says that in pornography
use, things are treated as women, and women are treated as things—in
pornography use, things are animated, *and* women are objectified. The use
of pornography involves 'sex between people and things, human beings and
pieces of paper, real men and unreal women';[10] and when sex is solipsistic
in one way, it becomes solipsistic in the other:

What was words and pictures becomes, through masturbation, sex itself. As the
industry expands, this becomes more and more the generic experience of sex. . . . In
other words, *as the human becomes thing* and the mutual becomes one-sided and
the given becomes stolen and sold, objectification comes to define femininity, and
one-sidedness comes to define mutuality, and force comes to define consent as
pictures and words become the forms of possession and use through which women
are actually possessed and used.[11]

When sex is something you do with a thing, 'the human becomes thing'.
Notice that this phrase is exactly ambiguous between the two sexual
solipsisms I have described. When MacKinnon says that 'the human
becomes thing', she means both (a) that a pornographic artifact is used in
place of a human sexual partner, and (b) that a human sexual partner is
used as if she were a pornographic artifact, a thing. It may be tempting to
think that there is a pun here, or an equivocation, or that MacKinnon has
somehow mistaken the one solipsism for the other. A better alternative is
that we have here a substantive claim: that there is a connection between
these two solipsisms; and that the solipsism of treating things as people,
in pornography, in some way leads to the solipsism of treating people as
things.

In these preliminary thoughts I have described two sexual solipsisms: one
of treating things as human beings, in sexual contexts; and one of treating
human beings as things, in sexual contexts. What is involved in each of
these? And might the two be connected, generally, or in pornography?
A wholly adequate response to these questions would analyze each of the
two solipsisms in detail, firmly distinguish their moral and epistemological
dimensions, make plain their implications for philosophy and feminism,
and discover whether and exactly how they are related. But my response,

---

[10] MacKinnon, *Only Words*, 109.   [11] Ibid., 25–6 (emphasis added).

in what follows, is more modest. I consider in Section 3 the solipsism of treating people as things, drawing on Kant and other writers, and I distinguish, in a far from exhaustive taxonomy, four kinds of object-making attitude: objective attitudes, objectifying attitudes, self-objectifying attitudes, and the attitudes of sadism. The discussion of that section is partly interpretive (in its exploration of Kant), partly analytical (in its distinctions between attitudes), and partly critical (in its attack on a recent account of sadism). As for the solipsism of treating things as people, I consider in Section 4 MacKinnon's suggestion that there is a connection between solipsism of the one kind and solipsism of the other, and that through pornography 'the human becomes thing' in more ways than one.

First, though, let us turn our thoughts to escape.

2. Escape From Solipsism

Descartes said that the path to solipsism, and hopefully beyond, required the temporary abandoning of practical life. The meditator should leave his normal activities, since the task before him 'does not involve action'.[12] He should leave, for the moment, his friends. Imagine how disquieting it would otherwise be for the friend. Imagine what it would be like to meet the solipsist. Imagine how it would feel to converse with someone, hitherto my friend, who seriously entertains the hypothesis that I, in my hat and coat, am a mere machine. Imagine how it would feel to converse with someone who seriously entertains the hypothesis that thoughts are being constantly inserted into his mind by a malevolent spirit—that the thoughts which I *myself* put in his mind (using a traditional technique known as 'speech') have their source in the actions of the same malevolent spirit. It would be disquieting, to say the least. Better leave behind ones friends, or one is unlikely to be left with many.

2.1. Kant on friendship and sexual love

If an effective remedy for (and proof against?) solipsism can be found, it is in practice, and one remedy is in friendship itself. Kant suggests that friendship provides escape from solipsism. He describes the man without a

---

[12] First Meditation, in Descartes, *Meditations*, 22.

friend as if he were the Cartesian meditator. The man without a friend is the man who is all alone, who 'must shut himself up in himself', who must remain 'completely alone with his thoughts as in a prison'.[13] Kant says that friendship provides 'release' from the 'prison' of the self, and that we have a duty 'not to isolate ourselves', but to seek release from the prison of self by seeking out friendship. Kant says, in short, that we have a moral duty to escape solipsism.

In friendship the reciprocity characteristic of moral relations in general is present in a distinctive way: friendship is 'the maximum reciprocity of love', an 'intimate union of love and respect', an ideal of 'emotional and practical concern' for another's welfare.[14] In her illuminating discussion of Kant's views on friendship, Christine Korsgaard notes the metaphors of self-surrender and retrieval in Kant's description of reciprocity.[15] Kant says, of an ideal friendship,

Suppose that I choose only friendship, and that I care only for my friend's happiness in the hope that he cares for mine. Our love is mutual; there is complete restoration. I, from generosity, look after his happiness and he similarly looks after mine; I do not throw away my happiness, but surrender it to his keeping, and he in turn surrenders his into my hands.[16]

The escape from the prison of the self is bought, in part, by a surrender of the self—a surrender that is no one-sided abdication, but a generous gift offered and reciprocated. The friendships of practical life do not achieve this ideal of reciprocity, but friendships aim for that ideal, in Kant's opinion, and can sometimes approach it.

Since friendship is an escape from solipsism, it has aspects that are both practical and epistemic. If I am to respect the beliefs and intentions of my friend, I must learn what those beliefs and intentions are. If I am to share his goals, I must learn what they are. If I am to bring him happiness, I must learn what his desires are. And if our love and respect is reciprocal, he must know the same about me. That is why Kant says that one needs epistemic

---

[13] Kant, *Doctrine of Virtue* (1797) trans. Mary Gregor (New York: Harper and Row, 1964), 144.

[14] Kant, *Lectures on Ethics*, 202.

[15] My understanding of Kant's views about friendship owes a great debt to Christine Korsgaard's work in 'Creating the Kingdom of Ends: Responsibility and Reciprocity in Personal Relations', *Philosophical Perspectives 6: Ethics* (1992), 305–32. She discusses the reciprocity common to friendship and sexual love, and some of Kant's suspicions about sexual desire. Herman too discusses Kant on the mutual self-surrender and retrieval of sexual reciprocity in 'Kant on Sex and Marriage'.

[16] Kant, *Lectures on Ethics*, 202–3.

virtues to pursue the moral life: one must exercise an 'active power' of sympathy, a practically oriented capacity that provides one with knowledge of the beliefs and desires and feelings of others as a means of 'participating actively' in their fate.[17] In friendship this capacity is especially necessary, since the duty of friendship is in part a duty to know and to make oneself known. The best kind of friendship involves 'the complete confidence of two persons in revealing their secret thoughts and feelings to each other'[18] Kant says that because of the basic human need to 'unburden our heart',

...each of us needs a friend, one in whom we can confide unreservedly, and to whom we can disclose completely all our dispositions and judgments, from whom we can and need hide nothing, to whom we can communicate our whole self.[19]

If friendship provides an escape from solipsism, and there can be sexual solipsisms, we can conclude that not all sexual relations are friendly—but we are left wondering about the relation between sex and friendship.

Kant, in optimistic mood, writes that friendship and sexual love can provide the same escape from solipsism, and that sexual love can be as potent as friendship in its capacity to unlock the 'prison' of the self.

Love, whether it is for a spouse or for a friend...wants to communicate itself completely, and it expects of its respondent a similar sharing of heart, unweakened by distrustful reticence.

Whether it is for a spouse, or for a friend, love presupposes the same mutual esteem for the other's character.[20]

This is from Kant's letter to Maria von Herbert, a young woman who believes she has been abandoned by someone, but whether friend or lover is unclear. 'It makes no difference' anyway, says Kant, since these relationships share the same moral core of communication, respect, and 'sharing of heart'.[21] In his *Lectures on Ethics*, Kant's description of the reciprocity of sexual love has the very same features as his description of friendship, as Christine Korsgaard points out—the same talk of surrender and retrieval. Of friendship, Kant writes that if I love my friend 'as I love myself', and he loves me 'as he loves himself', 'he restores to me that with

---

[17] Kant, *Doctrine of Virtue*, 126.   [18] Ibid., 471.   [19] Kant, *Lectures on Ethics*, 205–6.

[20] Kant's letter to Maria von Herbert of spring 1792. See *Kant: Philosophical Correspondence*, trans. Arnulf Zweig (Chicago: University of Chicago, 1967).

[21] The exchange of letters between Kant and Maria von Herbert is the topic of 'Duty and Desolation', this volume.

which I part and I come back to myself again'. Of sexual love, Kant writes 'if I yield myself completely to another and obtain the person of the other in return, I win myself back'.[22] If sexual love and friendship are similar, as Kant suggests, then a lover can be a

friend...in whom we can confide unreservedly, and to whom we can disclose completely all our dispositions and judgments, from whom we can and need hide nothing, to whom we can communicate our whole self.[23]

There is reason for thinking that Kant is an optimist, who believes that sexual love and friendship are alike in their power to provide an escape from solipsism, through mutual knowledge, affection, respect, and the trust which makes knowledge possible.

2.2. Interlude

The sense of discovery in love and friendship can be brought to life by novelists in ways that no philosopher can hope to do, and this section tells a story from *The Innocent*, by Ian McEwan.

She sat across from him and they warmed their hands round the big mugs. He knew from experience that unless he made a formidable effort, a pattern was waiting to impose itself: a polite enquiry would elicit a polite response and another question. Have you lived here long? Do you travel far to work?...Only silences would interrupt the relentless tread of question and answer. They would be calling to each other over immense distances, from adjacent mountain peaks...Rather than tolerate more silence, he settled after all for more small talk and began to ask, 'Have you lived here long?'

But all in a rush she spoke over him, saying, 'How do you look without your glasses? Show me please.' This last word she elongated beyond what any native speaker would have considered reasonable, unfurling a delicate papery thrill through Leonard's stomach. He snatched the glasses from his face and blinked at her. He could see quite well up to three feet, and her features had only partially dissolved. 'And so,' she said quietly. 'It is how I thought. Your eyes are beautiful and all the time they are hidden. Has no one told you how they are beautiful?'...

His voice sounded strangled in his ears. 'No, no one has said that'...

'Then I am the first to discover you?' There was humour, but no mockery, in her look. She interlocked her fingers with his.... Their hands fitted well, the grip was intricate, unbreakable, there were so many points of contact. In this poor

[22] Kant, *Lectures on Ethics*, 167, 202–3.   [23] Ibid., 205–6.

light, and without his glasses, he could not see which fingers were his own. Sitting in the darkening, chilly room in his raincoat, holding on to her hand, he felt he was throwing away his life. The abandonment was delicious. . . . Something was pouring out of him, through his palm and into hers, something was spreading back up his arm, across his chest, constricting his throat. His only thought was a repetition: So this is it, it's like this, so this is it . . .[24]

Leonard knows from experience how the encounter will proceed. They will be remote as adjacent mountain peaks, a vast space of awkward good manners and English reserve floating between them, despite his best hopes. He doesn't know at all, of course. He hadn't begun to factor into the equation what Maria herself might think, or want, or do.

He began to explain himself . . . 'Actually, I didn't know whether you'd want to see me, or if you'd even recognise me'.
   'Do you have another friend in Berlin?'
   'Oh no, nothing like that' . . .
   'And did you have any girlfriends in England?'
   'Not many, no.'
   'How many?'
   He hesitated before making a lunge at the truth. 'Well, actually, none.'
   'You've never had one?'
   'No.' Maria leaned forwards. 'You mean, you've never . . .'
   He could not bear to hear whatever term she was about to use. 'No, I never have.'
   She put her hand to her mouth to stifle a yelp of laughter. It was not so extraordinary a thing in nineteen fifty five for a man of Leonard's background and temperament to have had no sexual experience by the end of his twenty-fifth year. But it was a remarkable thing for a man to confess. He regretted it immediately. She had the laughter under control, but now she was blushing. It was the interlocking fingers that had made him think he could get away with speaking without pretence. In this bare little room with its pile of assorted shoes belonging to a woman who lived alone and did not fuss with milk jugs or doilies on tea trays, it should have been possible to deal in unadorned truths.

Maria's directness, her evident delight in him, her indifference to feminine niceties, her physical closeness, make him trust her. Leonard has a feeling

---

[24] Ian McEwan, *The Innocent* (London: Picador, 1990), 54–60.

of throwing away his life in a 'delicious abandonment', the surrender Kant described which is perhaps more typical of lovers than friends. He has the impulse of which Kant wrote, the desire love has to 'communicate itself completely', that 'expects of its respondent a similar sharing of heart, unweakened by distrustful reticence.' But the relations of lovers are at once more intimate and more convention-governed than the relations of friends. And it is not at all obvious that a lover can always be a 'friend . . . in whom we can confide unreservedly, and . . . from whom we can and need hide nothing', especially at first. Margaret Atwood once asked a group of men, what is it that you fear most from women? The reply was, we're afraid that they'll laugh at us.[25] There was no mockery at first, but Maria is surely laughing at him now.

The story continues:

. . . it should have been possible to deal in unadorned truths.

And in fact, it was. Maria's blushes were brought on by shame at the laughter she knew Leonard would misunderstand. For hers was the laughter of nervous relief. She had been suddenly absolved from the pressures and rituals of seduction. She would not have to adopt a conventional role and be judged in it, and she would not be measured against other women. Her fear of being physically abused had receded. She would not be obliged to do anything she did not want. She was free, they both were free, to invent their own terms. They could be partners in invention. And she really had discovered for herself this shy Englishman with the steady gaze and the long lashes, she had him first, she would have him all to herself. These thoughts she formulated later in solitude. At the time they erupted in the single hoot of relief and hilarity which she had suppressed to a yelp.

Leonard took a long pull of his tea, set down the mug and said 'Ah' in a hearty, unconvincing way. He put his glasses on and stood up.

Maria's laughter, if only he could read it, spells joyful relief: a relief at a release from convention, and something else—a relief that accompanies the vanishing of fear. The story about Margaret Atwood had another chapter. She asked the women, what is it that you most fear from men? The reply was, we're afraid that they'll kill us. Maria has known violent soldiers and

[25] This anecdote is told by Naomi Wolf, *The Beauty Myth* (London: Vintage 1991), 153, who gives no further citation. I report it as illustrative of contrasting concerns about danger and embarrassment. Note a relevant ambiguity in the question of what one 'fears most', between severity and probability of the thing feared.

an abusive husband, after which the innocence of Leonard is a treasure. But innocence is partly ignorance, and Leonard takes the laughter to be his worst fear fulfilled. Convinced of his 'humiliating tactical blunder', Leonard invents an excuse and turns to leave.

He was fumbling with the unfamiliar lock and Maria was right at his back. . . . The man scrabbling to leave by her front door was less like the men she had known and more like herself. She knew just how it felt. When you felt sorry for yourself, you wanted to make things worse . . . .

He opened the door at last and turned to say his goodbyes. Did he really believe that she was fooled by his politeness and the invented appointment, or that his desperation was invisible? He was telling her he was sorry he had to dash off, and expressing gratitude for the tea again, and offering his hand—a handshake!—when she reached up and lifted his glasses clear of his face and strode back into her sitting room with them . . . .

'Look here,' he said, and, letting the door close behind him, took one step then another into the apartment. And that was it, he was back in. He had wanted to stay, now he had to. 'I really do have to be going.' He stood in the centre of the tiny room, irresolute, still attempting to fake his hesitant English form of outrage.

She stood close so he could see her clearly. How wonderful it was, not to be frightened of a man. It gave her a chance to like him, to have desires which were not simply reactions to his. She took his hands in hers. 'But I haven't finished looking at your eyes.' Then, with the Berlin girl's forthrightness . . . she added, 'Du Dummer! Wenn es für dich das erste Mal ist, bin ich sehr glücklich. When this is your first time, then I am a very lucky girl.'

It was her 'this' which held Leonard. He was back with 'this'. What they were doing here was all part of 'this', his first time.

Leonard's revelation is not after all a tactical error. His innocence, his ignorance about tactics and conventions, his awkwardness—all are utterly endearing to Maria. Without the trammels of convention and fear, there is room for discovery. She can know how he feels, she knows herself how stubborn self-pity can be, that when you feel sorry for yourself, you want to make things worse. There is room for ordinary friendship: she has a chance to like him. There is room for desire: a chance for her to have desires which are not simply reactions to his. The two of them are free to be lovers who are partners in invention, which is what they indeed become.

3. The Solipsism of Treating People as Things

The optimism about friendship and sexual love occasionally to be found in some of Kant's writings must be placed against a pessimism which is his more common attitude.

3.1. Kant on sexual objectification

Kant more often writes as though sexual love does not provide an escape from solipsism at all. Sexual desire, he says in the passage partly quoted above,

> ... is *an appetite for another human being* .... Human love is good will, affection, promoting the happiness of others and finding joy in their happiness. But it is clear that when a person loves another purely from sexual desire, none of these factors enter into love. Far from there being any concern for the happiness of the loved one, the lover, in order to satisfy his desire, may even plunge the loved one into the depths of misery. Sexual love makes of the loved person an object of appetite; as soon as that appetite has been stilled, the person is cast aside as one casts away a lemon that has been sucked dry.[26]

Sexual love is not a species of 'human love' but is opposed to it: or so Kant seems to say here. Sexual love is not the cure for solipsism, but the disease. Sexual desire makes of the loved person an 'object of appetite'. What does he mean?

Clearly there is one, innocuous, sense in which sexual desire makes of the loved person 'an object'. Any intentional attitude directed towards a person makes of that person an 'object' of that attitude: an intentional object. A person can be an object of someone's thought, or love, or loathing, or respect, or desire. This sense of 'object' yields no grounds for moral alarm. On the contrary, we have duties to make persons into objects, in some of these ways. We have duties to make persons into objects of knowledge, and love, and respect. These ways of making persons into objects are implied by the duty we have to escape solipsism. So while it may well be that sexual desire makes a person into an object in this intentional sense, since the same can be said of the intentional attitudes of knowledge, and love, and

---

[26] Kant, *Lectures on Ethics*, 163.

respect, we have no explanation yet for Kant's moral dismay. Kant must mean something more by the claim that sexual love makes of a person 'an object of appetite', and two different suggestions have made, by Korsgaard, and by Herman.

According to Korsgaard, Kant believes that sexual desire takes as its intentional object not a mere body, but a person in his or her entirety. Kant says,

Amongst our inclinations there is one which is directed towards other human beings. They themselves, and not their work and services, are its objects of enjoyment. . . . There is an inclination which we may call an appetite for enjoying another human being. We refer to sexual impulse. Man can, of course, use another human being as an instrument for his service; he can use his hands, his feet, and even all his powers; he can use him for his own purposes with the other's consent. But there is no way in which a human being can be made an object of indulgence for another except through sexual impulse . . . it is an appetite for another human being.[27]

Kant says here that the sexual inclination is 'directed towards other human beings': that 'they themselves', and not their services, or their bodies, are its objects of enjoyment. Korsgaard says that what troubles Kant is the idea that sexual love demands that the beloved put not simply her body but her *entire self* at the lover's disposal. 'Viewed through the eyes of sexual desire another person is seen as something wantable, desirable, and therefore inevitably possessable. To yield to that desire, to the extent it is really that desire you yield to, is to allow yourself to be possessed'.

Herman suggests an alternative interpretation. She draws attention to the evident common ground between Kant and the feminist writers who say that sexual relations can make women into objects: that sexual relations can objectify women. On this interpretation, Kant thinks that there is something about sexual desire that can cast the desired person in the role of a thing, a mere body, something whose value is merely instrumental. Kant says,

Because sexuality is not an inclination which one human being has for another as such, but is an inclination for the sex of the other, it is a principle of the degradation of human nature . . . That [the woman] is a human being is of no

---

[27] Kant, *Lectures on Ethics*, 162–3.

concern to the man; only her sex is the object of his desires. Human nature is thus subordinated. Hence it comes that all men and women do their best to make not their human nature but their sex more alluring and direct their activities and lusts entirely towards sex. Human nature is thereby sacrificed to sex.[28]

Kant's claim that in sexual love a person is somehow made thing-like finds an echo in claims of MacKinnon and Andrea Dworkin, and Herman offers the reader some samples from the latter, for comparison:

It is especially in the acceptance of the object status that her humanity is hurt; it is a metaphysical acceptance of lower status in sex and in society; an implicit acceptance of less freedom, less privacy, less integrity . . . a political collaboration with his dominance . . . [In intercourse] he confirms for himself and for her what she is; that she is something, not someone; certainly not someone equal.[29]

Sexual desire makes a woman 'something, not someone'. On Herman's interpretation of Kant, sexual desire takes as its intentional object a body, rather than a person. It may view the body as an object of beauty, or it may view the body as an anonymous instrument, but in either case, it ignores the person who is partly constituted by her body.

On Herman's interpretation, sexual love can be reductive: it can make of the loved person an object by making her something, not someone. On Korsgaard's interpretation, sexual desire can be invasive: it can make of the loved person an object by viewing her as someone (not something), a person in her entirety (not merely a body)—but a person to be invaded and possessed.

Neither description is plausible, as a description of the essential and inevitable character of sexual relationships, even according to Kant: for Kant says that sexual love can be like friendship in its power to unlock the prison of the self, nourish the epistemic and moral virtues, provide escape from the hell of solipsism. However, both interpretations are evidently plausible as descriptions of different pathologies of sexual love. Perhaps sexual desire can indeed be invasive, in the way that Korsgaard describes. That possibility is addressed in this essay's companion piece.[30] Perhaps sexual desire can indeed be reductive, in the way that Herman describes. To consider this possibility is to consider in closer detail the

---

[28] Ibid., 163.

[29] Andrea Dworkin, *Intercourse* (New York: Free Press, 1987), 122–3, 140–1.

[30] Langton, 'Love and Solipsism'.

solipsism of treating people as things, the solipsism of making someone an object.

3.2. Making someone an 'object'

The notion of an object draws its weight from a particular picture of the world and the place of human beings in it, a picture which has been in the background of the discussion so far, and which, as I have painted it, is broadly Kantian. There is the world of natural phenomena—things bright and beautiful, creatures great and small, purple mountains, rivers running by, sunset, morning, bright sky. Things dance inexorably to a score laid down by the laws of nature. Their movements are explained and predicted by scientists and engineers, cooks and gardeners. Things appear to our senses, they dazzle and bewitch with color and noise and smell. Things provide us with tools. We take them, fix them up, make them more amenable to our purposes, and use them for whatever we want without so much as a by your leave. Things don't talk back, argue, communicate. Things may be noisy, but when it comes to speech, things are silent. Things are bought and sold in the marketplace. They have a price fixed by their usefulness to a buyer. When things are worn out, you throw them away. If you lose a thing, you can always replace it with another thing that will do the job just as well.

Despite the fact that people are to be counted amongst the creatures great and small, our attitude to people is not the same. And although people are undubitably part of the great dance whose score is laid down by laws of nature, people—somehow—get to make up their own steps. People are viewed as responsible for what they do. We feel resentful when they hurt us deliberately, grateful when they help us deliberately, and in general have a range of reactive attitudes that show that we are, as Strawson says, involved.[31] The movements of human beings are to be explained, not by a physicist, but by someone who understands the pattern of beliefs, desires, reasons, and decisions, that motivate the human beings. People talk back, argue, communicate. People appear to our senses, just as other sensory phenomena do, and a person can be more dazzling and bewitching than any rainbow. But there is always more to a person than meets the eye or

---

[31] P. F. Strawson, 'Freedom and Resentment', in *Freedom and Resentment* (London: Methuen, 1974), 1–25.

ear, there is an inner life, a garden enclosed, which may be very different to the appearance presented at the gate. With a person there is a potential gap between appearance and reality that makes room for shyness, reticence, hypocrisy, and deception, one reason why the problem of other minds is not simply the problem of the external world. A person who is an object of appearance for me is someone for whom I in turn am an object of appearance. And on the Kantian vision, what most sets human beings apart from the world of natural phenomena is their capacity for choice, a capacity which endows each person with 'an inalienable dignity', and prohibits the treating of persons as things.

To be an object, on this picture, is to be a natural phenomenon: something which is not free, something whose movements could be explained and predicted by science, something whose movements are not determined by reason and choice. It is to be something incapable of the activities of knowledge, communication, love, respect. It is to be something that is merely a sensory appearance, something whose qualities are exhausted by how it can look, feel, sound, and taste to a perceiver. It is to be merely a body, something solid and extended in space. It is to be a tool, something whose value is merely instrumental, something which is a potential possession. These different aspects of the notion of an object are related: it is no coincidence that the realm of determined things, the realm of sensory appearances, the realm of bodies, and the realm of potential tools and possessions are, for Kant at least, one and the same. But these are all conceptually, and modally, distinct. And since they are distinct, a person may be made an object in some of these ways, but not others. That is why the solipsism of treating people as things can be a piecemeal, partial affair.

3.3. 'Making' someone an object

What sense can be attached to the idea that someone whose humanity is inalienable can nonetheless be *made* an object in some or all of the above ways? This is a vast topic, but here I want to describe four overlapping ways of object-making.[32]

---

[32] See also Martha Nussbaum's excellent study, 'Objectification', *Philosophy and Public Affairs* 24 (1995), 249–91. The thoughts expressed in this section are further developed in Langton, 'Autonomy-denial in Objectification', this volume, the author having by then had the advantage of engaging with Nussbaum's proposal.

Objective attitudes   One might make someone an object, in one sense, when one takes an objective attitude towards her, in the manner that Strawson described in 'Freedom and Resentment'. This is to view someone as if she were a natural phenomenon in the first sense—lacking in responsibility, not (or not fully) free, autonomous, or responsible for what she does.

To adopt the objective attitude to another human being is to see him, perhaps, as an object of social policy; as a subject for what, in a wide range of sense, might be called treatment; as something . . . to be managed or handled or cured or trained.[33]

Strawson says that the objective stance can be contrasted with the stance of the engaged participant, and an important sign of the difference between them is the absence or presence of certain reactive attitudes. In general, the absence of such reactive attitudes as resentment indicates the presence of an objective attitude. One does not resent the (hurtful) behavior of a human being who is not held to be responsible.

It that always so? It is plausible enough for the cases Strawson considers: the benign social scientist, the teacher, the psychiatrist, who can afford the distance required by the objective attitude. But there are exceptions to Strawson's rule. Consider cases where one is in a relation of on-going dependence on, or vulnerability to, a person who is not responsible for the pain they cause, and is known not to be responsible. One views them as not responsible, and in that sense takes an objective attitude towards them: however, one may still feel resentment even though the hurtful actions are not viewed as the result of reasoned choice. One might resent a person who innocently, and deafeningly, snores. One might resent a cruel jailer, even if the cruelty were viewed as a result of Maoist indoctrination. One might resent an infant who guiltlessly, and inexplicably, screamed for months on end. The resentment here is not always dissipated by knowledge that the person is not responsible. Such knowledge can even, rightly or wrongly, exacerbate the resentment. Where the vulnerability is towards a loved person who was once responsible, but is no longer, resentment can come from a feeling that one has been robbed, a feeling that something precious has been torn away. What can provoke resentment is the very fact that the loved one *is no longer a participant*. One can feel not only grief but anger towards a loved person who has become senile, or insane, or

---

[33] Strawson, 'Freedom and Resentment', 9.

alcoholic. And the death of a loved person can provoke a potent mixture of grief and rage. How *dare* she die! How *dare* she leave me! Such resentment is a datum of human experience, and rational or not, it seems relevant to a Strawsonian task of a purely descriptive metaphysics.

To take an objective attitude towards someone is one way of treating a person as a thing: but the objective attitude described by Strawson is rather benevolent, notwithstanding its lack of respect. It is the attitude of the impartial social scientist, the kind teacher, the concerned psychiatrist. What has this attitude to do with the treating of women as things? Something, certainly. But it is unlikely that this is what Kant and feminist writers have in mind when they say that sexual desire can make a person an object. They do not mean that in sexual contexts one person looks upon another with an eye of benign and dispassionate concern, viewing the person as not responsible for their behavior and thus 'an object of social policy'. There is something else.

Objectifying attitudes   Someone might display, not the objective attitude which Strawson described, but what we can call an objectifying attitude. Someone might view a person as thing-like: view her not merely as lacking in responsibility, but view her as if there were nothing more to her than an appearance, nothing more to her than how she looks, and generally manifests herself to the senses. Someone might view a person as being nothing more than a body, nothing more than a conveniently packaged bundle of eyes, lips, face, breasts, buttocks, legs. Someone might view a person as if she were a mere tool, a mere instrument to serve his own purposes, or property that belonged to him. The benign social scientist imagined by Strawson would not view a person in these ways. But these latter ways come closer to the sexual solipsism described by Kant, MacKinnon, and Dworkin. An objectifying attitude may well have in common with the objective attitude a lack of respect, and a tendency to view a person as not fully responsible, but other aspects of the notion of an object may be in play: mere sensory appearance, mere body, possession, tool. One who takes an objective attitude sees a person in terms of certain well-meaning relational gerundives: he sees him as to be handled, to be managed, to be cured, to be trained. One who takes the objectifying attitude sees a person in terms of different relational gerundives: something to be looked at, to be pursued, to be consumed, to be used, to be possessed.

I remarked that, contrary to Strawson, it seems possible to resent someone while at the same time 'seeing' them as an object, in his sense, that is, as lacking in responsibility—resentment seems compatible with the objective attitude. It is worth noting that resentment seems compatible with an objectifying attitude as well. Someone who views women reductively, as brutish creatures whose purpose is the satisfaction of men's lusts, may also manifest resentment towards women. Misogyny may sometimes present just this combination. And perhaps the connection between the resentment and the objectifying attitude is not coincidental. Perhaps it is caused by a horror that one's desires put one in the power of such contemptible creatures.

There are objective and objectifying attitudes, but this emphasis on attitudes as ways of 'seeing' a person may suggest mere states of mind, not in themselves harmful to the person who is 'made an object' in these attitudinal ways. As Strawson says, though, it matters to us very much that we are viewed as people, and not as things. Strawson says that in much of our behavior, 'the benefit or injury resides mainly or entirely in the manifestation of attitude itself'.[34] If one is injured by being made the object of an objective attitude, one can also be injured by being made the object of an objectifying attitude, and a person is injured when she is viewed as if she were a thing—unfree, mere appearance, body, tool, or property. But there is more than 'seeing' involved.

Strawson somewhat blurs the distinctions between attitude, action, and effect in his use of the gerundives: one adopts the objective attitude when one 'sees' a person as 'an object of social policy...as something...to be managed or handled or cured or trained'. Is it a matter of seeing, or doing? Clearly, both. The person who sees someone as to-be-managed, to-be-cured, to-be-trained, will translate that attitude into action, and will (assuming power and resources) actually manage, cure, or train. He will act in a certain way. And he will achieve certain effects. The objectifying attitude likewise will involve both seeing and doing. MacKinnon says, 'Men treat women as who they see women as being'. Objectification is a stance, a way of looking at the world, and a social practice.[35] Someone

---

[34] Strawson, 'Freedom and Resentment', 5.

[35] *Feminism Unmodified* (Cambridge, Mass.: Harvard University Press, 1987), 50, 122. See Sally Haslanger, 'On Being Objective, and Being Objectified', in *A Mind Of One's Own: Feminist Essays on Reason and Objectivity,* eds., Louise M. Antony and Charlotte Witt (Boulder, Co.: Westview Press, 1993), 85–125.

who adopts an objectifying attitude may do things to the people he views as objects. He may turn people into objects, in so far as that is possible. If human beings have an 'inalienable' dignity, as Kant says, then there will be limits on how far this process can go: one cannot turn a human being into something that is entirely unfree, a mere tool, something that is exhausted by its sensory appearance, its body. But a person can be made less free, more tool-like, and a person's appearance and bodily qualities can be made to play a more exaggerated role in her own social identity.

When MacKinnon says that 'men treat women as who they see women as being', she means, in part, that men see women as beings whose purpose is the satisfaction of desire. Perhaps men see women as being submissive by nature; they want women to be that way; and they treat women accordingly. And in conditions of gender hierarchy, seeing can become doing. Men attribute certain qualities to women, see women a certain way, and that projection of qualities 'is not just an illusion or a fantasy or a mistake. It becomes embodied because it is enforced'.[36]

Sally Haslanger has drawn upon this theme in MacKinnon to offer one conception of what it is to objectify someone. To objectify someone is to take a (practical) attitude that has four dimensions: it is to view and treat someone as an (intentional) object for the satisfaction of one's desire; to force her to have a property that one desires her to have; to believe that she has that property; and to believe that she has that property by nature.[37] It is worth noting that of these four conditions, the first, second and fourth would each independently appear among the objectifying attitudes described by Kant. To view someone as an object for the satisfaction of *desire* is to treat her as a thing: 'as soon as a person becomes an object of appetite for another, all motives of moral relationship cease to function, because as an object of appetite for another, a person becomes a thing'.[38] To *force* someone to have some property is to violate her autonomy, and in that sense to treat her as a thing. To believe that someone has some property *by nature* is to view her as determined, lacking in responsibility, part of the natural order, and this too would be to treat her as a thing. On Haslanger's conception

[36] MacKinnon, *Feminism Unmodified,* 119.
[37] Haslanger, 'On Being Objective and Being Objectified'. Her proposal is discussed in Langton, 'Feminism in Epistemology: Exclusion and Objectification', this volume; and 'Beyond a Pragmatic Critique of Reason', *Australasian Journal of Philosophy* 71 (1993), 364–84.
[38] Kant, *Lectures on Ethics,* 163.

of objectification, the objectifying attitude requires the satisfying of all four conditions. On this conception, men objectify women if, for example, they view and treat women as objects of sexual desire, desire them to be submissive, force them to submit, believe that women are in fact submissive, and believe that they are submissive by nature. The 'seeing' involved is partly accurate, and partly inaccurate. The attribution of qualities is 'not just an illusion or a fantasy or a mistake', as MacKinnon says: women do indeed have the qualities in question, because they are forced to have them. There is an accurate descriptive belief, combined with an illusory projective belief. The illusion is to think women have the enforced qualities by nature.

Haslanger's analysis offers us one way to understand Kant's moral dismay about the character of (some) sexual desire. It may be that sexual desire can sometimes 'make a person an object' by instantiating the four-fold attitudes of objectification: viewing a woman as an object of sexual desire, desiring her to be submissive, believing that she is submissive, and believing that she is submissive by nature. This would be to make the desired person into a mere instrument to serve one's own purposes, a mere means to satisfy one's own pleasure, something less free, and more like a thing, whose behavior is dictated by the will of another.

Self-objectification   It is possible for someone to make *herself* an object, and this is a central theme of de Beauvoir's analysis of the subjection of women, and of many who speak of women's complicity in oppression. Perhaps someone could make herself an object in any of the ways that we have described. Perhaps someone could take an objective attitude to herself by viewing herself as unfree, as having no choice. Perhaps someone could take, not only the objective, but the objectifying attitude towards herself: view herself as being nothing more than how she appears to someone else, nothing more than her body, nothing more than a thing whose (relevant) properties are bodily and sensory, shape, weight, textures, and looks.[39] She may view herself as determined, as having the qualities she has by nature. She may take herself to have value only in so far as she can be used, or possessed, by someone else. She may view herself as a being whose purpose is to satisfy the desire of another. The self-objectifying attitude will be a

---

[39] The tyranny of the 'beauty myth' on women's attitudes to themselves has been described by many, including Naomi Wolf, *The Beauty Myth*.

matter of both seeing, and doing. Someone who has it may actually turn herself into an object—so far as that is possible. She may bring it about that she is in fact less free, more tool-like, more thing-like. She may become passive, she may become submissive, she may become a slave.

To view oneself in these ways is to be in bad faith, according to existentialists, and they say that it presents a constant temptation to us all. Each of us would like 'to forgo liberty and become a thing'.[40] We would each prefer the role of the automaton, in the hat and coat, to the role of the free and conscious agent, the Cartesian ego, the meditator doing battle with his goliath. When Herman says that Kant and feminist writers share a common ground, she has partly this self-objectification in mind. Andrea Dworkin says that a woman's humanity is hurt by her own 'acceptance of the object status'. She says that sexual desire is implicated in a woman's making an object *of herself*. Kant is likewise concerned about what a person does to himself or herself: he is concerned that 'men and women do their best to make not their human nature but their sex more alluring,' and that 'human nature is thereby sacrificed to sex'. Kant wastes no sympathy on the person who objectifies himself or herself. 'One who makes himself a worm', he says, 'cannot complain if others step on him'. Such a person violates a self-regarding duty, the duty of self-esteem, and is guilty of servility. Such a person fails to show respect for the humanity in one's own person, by virtue of which 'we are not for sale at any price, and possess an inalienable dignity'.[41] Kant's words about servility are harsh, but they find a later echo in the fine line de Beauvoir attempts to draw between bad faith and oppression: the downfall to thing-hood 'represents a moral fault if the subject consents to it; if it is inflicted . . . it spells frustration and oppression'.[42]

It is oppression 'if it is inflicted'. One way to do something is to make someone else do it. One way to hurt someone is to get someone else to hurt them. One way to hurt someone is to get them to hurt themselves. (The death of Socrates was an execution and a suicide.) One way to make someone an object is to make her make herself an object. This misuse of a person would go beyond the usual vices, in Kantian terms. When you lie to someone, you fail to respect their humanity, and you prevent them from being the authors of their actions. When you steal from someone,

---

[40] De Beauvoir, *The Second Sex*, 21.   [41] Kant, *Lectures on Ethics*, 163; *Doctrine of Virtue* 101, 103.
[42] De Beauvoir, *The Second Sex*, 29.

the same is true. However, while the liar and the thief do treat a person as a mere instrument, they do not desire the person in question to identify *herself* as a mere instrument. They do not desire the person to throw off her personhood with abject abandonment. But perhaps that is what sexual desire can sometimes demand. When Andrea Dworkin says that a woman's humanity is hurt by her own 'acceptance of the object status', she takes this acceptance to be demanded by a man's desire. Dworkin (famously) sees this as a feature of 'normal' sexual intercourse, but what seems clear is that sexual desire in its sadistic guise at any rate can have the character she describes.

Sadistic attitudes   I take my description of sadistic sexual desire from the work of a well-known contemporary analytic philosopher (let him be temporarily nameless) who attempts in a lengthy book to analyze the complex terrain of sexual desire. Sadistic desire, he says, is a desire to 'vanquish the other in his body, to force him to abjure himself for his body's sake'; it aims 'to show the ease with which another's perspective can be invaded and enslaved by pain, to humiliate the other by compelling the self to identify with what is not-self', to 'go under' in the stream of bodily suffering. It aims, through the infliction of pain, 'to overcome the other in the act of physical contact'. The author approvingly quotes Sartre as an accurate reporter on the attitude of the sadist.

The spectacle which is offered to the sadist is that of a freedom which struggles against the expanding of the flesh, and which freely chooses to be submerged in the flesh. At the moment of abjuration, the result sought is attained: the body is wholly flesh, panting and obscene; it holds the position which the torturers have given to it, not that which it would have assumed by itself; the cords which bind it hold it as an inert thing, and thereby it has ceased to be the object which moves spontaneously. In the abjuration a freedom chooses to be wholly identified with this body; this distorted and heaving body is the very image of a broken and enslaved freedom.[43]

In Sartre's description, the 'result sought' by sadistic desire is that the person will turn herself into a thing, 'abjure' herself, become 'wholly identified' with a 'broken and enslaved freedom'. Sadistic desire aims that the desired person should make herself as thing-like as it is possible for a person to be. Sartre's 'incomparable description' in fact applies to the attitudes of

[43] Jean-Paul Sartre, *Being and Nothingness* (1943); trans. Hazel Barnes (London: Methuen, 1966), 404.

torturer and sadist alike, according to our author. The torturer and the sadist both aim to be seen by their victims in a dominating light, both aim to inflict pain. But what distinguishes the two is that the sexual sadist (unlike the mere torturer) has in addition a desire for the victim to have a certain desire: he 'wants the other [person] to want the pain inflicted, and to be aroused by it'. He wants the other person to desire the pain and domination, and to be aroused by it. He wants the other to want to submit, he wants the other to want to abjure herself. The attitude has some aspects of solipsism, and not others. In so far as it is a desire for the other person to be identified as a thing, it is solipsistic. In so far as it is a desire for the other person to have a certain desire, it demands that the other should retain some human qualities. But the desired desire is a desire to be a thing, a desire to become the 'very image of a broken and enslaved freedom'. The sadist is a solipsist who wants the other to *want* to be a machine. He is a solipsist who demands that the other choose to be a mere machine, that she choose to become a thing that cannot choose. The project, as Sartre says, is doomed. If she wants and chooses anything, she is no machine.

One hopes that the words used by our author—vanquish, force, abjure, invade, enslave, humiliate, suffer, overcome—describe some rare variety of violent rape, punishable by law. But no: the author distinguishes this 'normal' attitude from a 'perverted' sadism which cares nothing about the desires of its victim, but seeks rather to 'abolish the personal object of desire . . . and replace him with a compliant dummy'. The 'ideas of dominance and submission' manifested in the 'normal' sadism 'form a fundamental part of the *ordinary understanding* of the sexual performance'. Sadism is, he says, a 'normal' variant of this 'ordinary understanding' of sexual performance. It is part of a 'common human condition'.

The author tries to offer a gender-neutral story about the phenomenon of 'normal' sadism, and presents a man, Count Sacher Masoch, as chief among masochists. But it is hard to credit this attempt at neutrality, given the kind of sexual encounter that the author offers as a paradigm. He takes seriously the hypothesis that sadism 'lies in the very structure of the sexual urge'. Whose 'sexual urge'? He cites expert social science testimony according to which

the paradigm example is the practice of 'marriage by capture'—in which a woman is pursued by her suitors and forced to yield by the strongest . . . The girl . . . submits only to that force which she also desires. The aggression of the male, and the submission of the female, here combine to fulfil an archetype of sexual encounter.

The games of an aristocrat, and the forcible rape of a woman, are presented by the author as expressions of the same unitary sexual phenomenon. In both, a desire to dominate, and be dominated, are desires that lie 'in the very structure of the sexual urge'. The paradigm case he offers shows how this is to be understood. It is the submission of the female to force that is supposed to provide the 'archetype' of sexual encounter.

These descriptions of the 'ordinary understanding of the sexual perform-ance' and its 'normal' variant might have been lifted from the works of MacKinnon and Dworkin. The author seems to share their bleak view about the paradigm sexual encounter: that the sexual desire of a man is a desire to dominate another person, a desire to overcome her, a desire to make her abjure her personhood; that it is, for women, a desire to submit to force. Indeed, the view of this author is bleaker than that feminist view, since he appears to see the 'ideas' of dominance and submission not as a contingent product of oppressive but changeable social relations, but as arising from the very structure of sexual desire.

The philosopher is Roger Scruton.[44] It is interesting to learn of such unanimity between radical feminists and a conservative philosopher. It is true that assertions of common ground between some feminists and conservatives are not unusual: there are critics who complain of an allied opposition to pornography, for example. But this particular unanimity seems new. Here there is an agreement, not about the 'immorality' of pornography, but about the *normality of domination*. MacKinnon, and Dworkin, and Scruton, agree that domination is 'normal', that it is the dynamic which underlies ordinary sexual relations. If this opinion were right, then Kant would be right to be concerned about the morality of sexual desire. Kant would be right if he thought that 'normal' sexual desire aims to reduce people to things.

The appearance of unanimity is interesting, and perhaps gratifying for any seeker of consensus—until, of course, one realises that 'normal' is here being used by Scruton not in its descriptive but its *normative* sense. Scruton

---

[44] Roger Scruton, *Sexual Desire: A Philosophical Investigation* (London: Weidenfeld and Nicolson, 1986; reprint, London: Phoenix, 1994), earlier quotation at p. 173. He describes on p. 302 the perverted variety of sadism, which seeks only a 'compliant dummy'.

says that the ideas of dominance and submission so fundamental to our ordinary understanding of sexuality are '*moral* ideas'. He says that sadistic desires 'can easily be accounted for, in terms of the conscious structure of desire, as an *interpersonal emotion*', and that they aim at 'an *intelligible moral relation*'.[45] The 'marriage by capture', and the games of the count, instantiate 'an intelligible moral relation between effective equals'.[46] The contrast drawn between 'normal' sadism, and the 'perverted' variety which seeks a 'compliant dummy', is not a contrast between the common and the exotic, but a contrast between the morally appropriate, and the morally inappropriate. Well, well. The most facile ascent from fact to value is the ascent from the normal to the normatively appropriate, and Scruton would hardly be the first to infer the rightness of an activity from its ordinariness. However, our author is usually rather more fussy about this kind of normative ascent, and his standards for sexual 'normality' are hardly generous. A homosexual, a masturbator, a woman who (heaven forbid) touches her clitoris while having sex with her partner—none of these people are, in his view, 'normal'—their ordinariness notwithstanding. They, unlike the sadist, are *perverts*, and their actions are cowardly and obscene.[47]

Scruton is right to describe the emotion of the sadist as a kind of interpersonal relation: if a woman were a mere puppet, or doll, or dummy to start with, there would be nothing to 'vanquish'. If by describing a relation as 'moral' he were to mean that it falls within the scope of morality, then it is a 'moral relation'—as indeed are all relations of objectification. That would hardly be grounds to approve them. The sadism Scruton describes begins with an acknowledgement of the humanity of the desired person. Sartre's sadist acknowledges the desired other as a person with a unique inner life, a 'freedom', a being that 'chooses', and 'moves spontaneously'. The desired person is not regarded as unfree or thing-like to begin with, as with other forms of reductive objectification, or sadism of the 'perverted' variety. The person is regarded as free and to-be-*willingly*-enslaved. The desire distinctive of normal sadism, the desire

---

[45] Scruton, *Sexual Desire*, 173–9, italics added. The book as a whole has more to offer than my own discussion may suggest: it is sometimes interesting, illuminating, acutely perceptive—and sometimes bewildering, ignorant, one-sided, depressing.

[46] Ibid., 298.

[47] Ibid., 305, 317. All three activities are, he says, obscene; the homosexual and the solitary masturbator are cowardly as well.

that one's partner should want the pain and domination, and be aroused by it—this desire, according to Scruton, transforms the action entirely, and raises it to new moral heights. This production of a 'broken and enslaved freedom' is not obscene. This new dimension elevates the action from mere torture to a morally intelligible interpersonal relation which is 'an affirmation of mutual respect'.[48] The action of the sadist thereby becomes a mere 'extended version of the lovebite'.[49] The solipsist who wants the other to *want* to be a machine is a superior sort of fellow, on a moral plane far above the solipsist who views the other as a machine from the start.

Scruton adds that the strategy adopted by the sadist is a reasonable solution to a serious practical problem that can plague sexual relations: namely, the problem of embarrassment. The infliction of pain enables a person to do what he 'would otherwise be too embarrassed to do: to overcome the other in the act of physical contact'.[50] Embarrassment. One person plans to 'overcome' another in an 'act of physical contact'—and the problem is embarrassment. One person contemplates turning another into something bound, tortured, distorted, inert, heaving, broken, enslaved—and the problem is embarrassment. Here we have the Atwood story all over again: 'we're afraid that they'll laugh at us'. That was Leonard's response to Maria, in McEwan's story. It is also a response of liberals to pornography. The real victim of pornography law, according to Ronald Dworkin, is the 'shy pornographer'. Poor chap, will he, or will he not, be permitted a brown paper bag for his magazine?[51] The real, and serious, problem about pornography is embarrassment, and Scruton shows the same touching sympathy for the 'normal' sadist. What a helpful advice column a philosopher could run here. Imagine.

'Dear sir, I am attracted to someone. So I really would like to overcome her in the act of physical contact. But I find the prospect embarrassing. What can I do? Signed, Embarrassed.' 'Dear Embarrassed: Yes, I understand your problem perfectly. Here's what to do. Make her suffer. Bind her with

---

[48] Scruton, *Sexual Desire*, 302.   [49] Ibid., 177.

[50] Ibid., 177. Scruton is purporting to speak here of the couple, not only the sadistic partner, but his reference to the goal of 'overcoming the other' shows that it is the sadistic partner he mainly has in mind.

[51] See Ronald Dworkin, in 'Do We Have a Right to Pornography?', in *A Matter of Principle* (Cambridge, Mass.: Harvard University Press, 1985), 335–72. His article and (briefly) the problem of embarrassment, are discussed in my 'Whose Right? Ronald Dworkin, Women, and Pornographers', this volume.

cords, make her into a distorted and heaving body, make her wholly flesh, panting and obscene, the very image of a broken and enslaved freedom. And make her want it. You'll find that will relieve your embarrassment, and put a stop to unseemly mirth. With best wishes, from your friendly Agony Uncle.'

Appearances notwithstanding, Scruton is an earthling like the rest of us. That means he comes from a small planet in which sexual violence against women is rife, where many marriages are violent, many women have their first sexual experiences under conditions of force, many women are raped. He comes from a planet where the 'moral ideas' of dominance and submission are popular, even fashionable, where many adolescents apparently believe it acceptable for a man to rape a woman if he is sexually aroused by her, and where many young men find faces of women displaying distress and pain to be more sexually attractive than faces showing pleasure.[52] Why not, if pain and domination are thought to be what a woman wants, and human sexual relations find their paradigm in a ritual where a woman 'submits...to that force which she also desires'? Recall that the story about Margaret Atwood had another chapter. She asked the women: What is it that you most fear from men? The reply was, 'we're afraid that they'll kill us'. Why not, if in the 'archetype of sexual encounter' a woman is 'pursued' by a gang, captured, and 'forced to yield' to 'the strongest'—forced to yield to 'the aggression of the male'? Social scientists and pornographers, psychiatrists and judges, have often preached the gospel that men dominate and women not only submit, but like it that way. It was only a matter of time, perhaps, before a philosopher should join their illustrious ranks.

---

[52] The following figures are cited by Naomi Wolf, in *The Beauty Myth,* 159–60, 166. A 1980 study of marriages in the US suggested that there had been assault in twenty eight per cent of those surveyed; other US studies suggest violence in twenty one per cent of relationships, ninety five per cent of it directed towards women; Diana Russell, *Rape in Marriage* (Bloomington: Indiana University Press, 1982). In a Toronto survey one in four girls in their final year of high school reported having been sexually forced; Jane Caputi, *The Age of Sex Crime* (London: The Women's Press, 1987), 119. One in four women students at Auburn University reported having been date raped, with similar figures for other US universities; Robin Warshaw, *I Never Called it Rape* (New York: Harper and Rowe, 1988), 13–14. More than half of adolescent boys in a UCLA study think it okay to force sex on woman if he is sexually aroused by her, e.g. if 'she gets him sexually excited', according to Goodchild et al., cited in Warshaw, 120. A proportion of male college students perceived faces expressing distress to be more attractive than faces showing happiness, Wolf (p. 166) and Warshaw (p. 197) giving the proportion as thirty per cent (a relativized figure), but better read as twelve per cent (see footnote 40, 'Speech Acts and Unspeakable Acts', this volume).

I said that feminist writers Andrea Dworkin and Catharine MacKinnon seem to share Scruton's opinion that there is something 'normal' about the dynamic of dominance and submission. Kant may share this opinion too, and it may be what he means when he says that sexual desire makes of a person an object: he may mean that it aims to reduce a person to a thing, because it aims to dominate. There are crucial differences. Kant and the feminist writers appear to share the descriptive part of Scruton's story, but they reject the normative part. Unlike Scruton, they both acknowledge the moral bleakness of this story, and refuse to accept it as inevitable. For Scruton the story is not bleak, but fine and morally intelligible; it is not avoidable, but 'lies in the very structure of the sexual urge'. This deterministic fantasy belongs on the dust heap with the mouldering fantasies of original sin, which Kant would have detested with equal vehemence. Despite Kant's occasional pessimism, human beings have, he thinks, a 'splendid disposition for good',[53] and it would be an inhuman pessimism that failed to agree. As for the normative part of Scruton's verdict, enough is enough. Domination may be 'normal' in one sense. To say it is therefore 'normal' in the other would be to make a more than philosophical mistake.

3.4. Interlude, again

One might wonder what, if anything, these abstract descriptions of object-making have to do with the sexual love which Kant regards as an escape from solipsism. One might wonder what they have to do with the ordinary lovers described so well by McEwan. Perhaps it is a foolish philosopher who would rush in where even novelists might fear to tread.

As a matter of fact McEwan paints sexual solipsism as eloquently as he paints its escape.[54] There is a new development in the relationship between Leonard and Maria.

It began . . . with a simple perception. He looked down at Maria, whose eyes were closed, and remembered she was a German. The word had not been entirely prised loose of its associations after all . . . German. Enemy. Mortal enemy. Defeated enemy. This last brought with it a shocking thrill. He diverted himself momentarily . . . . Then: she was the defeated, she was his by right, by conquest, by right of unimaginable violence and heroism and sacrifice . . . . He was powerful and magnificent . . . . He was victorious and good and strong and free. In recollection

---

[53] Kant, *Doctrine of Virtue*, 107.   [54] Ian McEwan, *The Innocent*, 83–5.

these formulations embarrassed him. . . . They were alien to his obliging and kindly nature, they offended his sense of what was reasonable. One only had to look at her to know there was nothing defeated about Maria. She had been liberated by the invasion of Europe, not crushed . . .

But next time round the thoughts returned. They were irresistibly exciting . . . she was his by right of conquest and then, there was nothing she could do about it. She did not want to be making love to him, but she had no choice. . . . She was struggling to escape. She was thrashing beneath him, he thought he heard her call out 'No!' She was shaking her head from side to side, she had her eyes closed against the inescapable reality . . . she was his, there was nothing she could do, she would never get away. And that was it, that was the end for him, he was gone, finished . . .

Over the following days, his embarrassment faded. He accepted the obvious truth that what happened in his head could not be sensed by Maria, even though she was only inches away. These thoughts were his alone, nothing to do with her at all.

Eventually, a more dramatic fantasy took shape. It recapitulated all the previous elements. Yes, she was defeated, conquered, his by right, could not escape, and now, he was a soldier, weary, battle-marked and bloody, but heroically rather than disablingly so. He had taken this women and was forcing her. Half terrified, half in awe, she dared not disobey.

Leonard has a kindly nature. He knows there is nothing defeated about Maria. Nevertheless he finds that a certain cluster of thoughts makes him feel good and powerful and strong and free: the thought that she is his by right; the thought that she is a defeated enemy; the thought that she is half terrified; the thought that she is obeying him from fear and awe; the thought that she wants to get away and cannot; the thought he is raping her. This cluster of thoughts could have been plagiarized from Scruton's description of the archetypical conquest, and Leonard finds it irresistably exciting.

There is something intensely solipsistic about this sexual encounter. But what? The events take place in a private theatre, the theatre of Leonard's mind: they happen 'in his head', 'his alone, nothing to do with her at all'. What makes them possible is 'the obvious truth', the Cartesian truth, that other minds are less accessible than one's own. Leonard is like the man Kant describes, who 'must shut himself up in himself', who must remain 'completely alone with his thoughts as in a prison'.[55] The two might as

---

[55] Kant, *Doctrine of Virtue*, 144.

well be 'on adjacent mountain peaks', as they were before they came to know each other. But it is not quite true that the events have 'nothing to do with her': the 'she' of his fantasy is, in some sense, Maria herself. Her own actual actions, her movements, her speech, are all interpreted (in make-believe) as the actions, movements, speech, of a woman being raped. If the Cartesian meditator were to encounter a friend among the automata in their hats and coats, he would hear friendly words as the words of a demon. Leonard hears loving words as the words of a woman in pain and terror. And not just any woman, but Maria herself (or Maria in so far as she is female and German—not perhaps the same at all). Is Leonard treating her as thing? It is at least *as if* he is treating her as a thing: the thoughts that are irresistably exciting are thoughts in which she features as something that is conquered, possessed, owned by right, captured against her will, violated against her will, in short (to borrow a phrase) 'the very image of a broken and enslaved freedom'. And there is surely more than 'as if': Maria is indeed being treated as a thing. Her body is being treated as a kind of tool, or instrument; so too are her actions. That is shown not just in the absence of her consent to their joint activity (under the description 'pretending that Leonard is raping Maria') but in the deliberate deception. Sex has ceased to be something he is *doing with her*, in the sense that one does something with another human being, shares an activity. It has become something he is *doing with her*, in the sense that one does something with a thing, uses an instrument. The scene has a more than epistemological claustrophobia: it is a solipsism of treating a person as a thing.

Treated as what kind of thing? As a canvas on which to project a particular fantasy, an object that has the convenient advantage of possessing in fact some of the qualities in fantasy: warm, female, human, German, etc. Perhaps there is something reminiscent here of the solipsism involved in pornography: perhaps Leonard is treating Maria as he would treat a pornographic artifact, the locus of a projective fantasy. MacKinnon's words about pornography seem uncannily apt here: 'the human becomes thing, and the mutual becomes one-sided and the given becomes stolen'.

If Leonard is treating Maria as he would treat a pornographic artifact, then there is a sense in which the two sexual solipsisms have met. In treating her as an instrument, in treating her as if she were an artifact, he treats her as a thing. And in treating that thing as a human being who is in terror, says 'no', submits, he animates that thing again, attributes to it human qualities absent in the original. Flattened to an instrument, Maria is then reanimated with a different human life, one in which she is then again, and in a different way, reduced to a thing. She is treated as a thing (a mere canvas) that is treated as a human being (a German enemy) that is treated as a thing (through rape). He really does treat her as if she were an instrument, a canvas. The rest is a kind of make-believe: but, as with pornography, the sexual experience that depends on the make-believe is real.

One could say, in Leonard's defense, that what Maria doesn't know can't hurt her. But that is a barren thought. One can be harmed by an objectifying attitude, whether one is aware of it or not. One could say, in Leonard's defense, that this is really a matter of seeing rather than doing: an attitude rather than an action. That seems dubious. Leonard is using Maria as a screen for his private theatre. And Leonard is in the end not satisfied with his private theatre.

He found himself tempted to communicate these imaginings to her . . . he wanted her to acknowledge what was on his mind, however stupid it really was. He could not believe she would not be aroused by it. . . . His private theatre had become insufficient. . . . Telling her somehow was the next inevitable thing. . . . He wanted his power recognized and Maria to suffer from it, just a bit, in the most pleasurable way. . . . Then he was ashamed. What was this power he wanted recognized? It was no more than a disgusting story in his head. Then, later, he wondered whether she might not be excited by it too. There was, of course, nothing to discuss. There was nothing he was able, or dared, to put into words. He could hardly be asking her permission.

What does Leonard want? Notice that what he wants is precisely what the 'normal' sadist wants: he wants Maria to recognize his power, suffer from it, and be excited by it. The presence of this desire is precisely what elevates sadistic desire to a reciprocal moral relation, according to Scruton. Leonard is becoming the 'normal' sadist, who desires that the other identify herself as a thing, desires that she should find that identification arousing. If Scruton were right, readers should all at this point heave a sigh of relief. At last we have an aim for reciprocity, at last we have an intelligible moral relation, at last Leonard's ideas have become *moral* ideas. But readers do not heave a sigh of relief. We wait with dread for the (inevitable?) disaster that ensues when Leonard—already blurring fact and fiction in his demand that his actual power be recognized, and that Maria actually suffer—tries to communicate his imaginings through actions, rather than words. Can readers hope for a happier ending? Well . . . yes, and no. But that is another story.

4. Two Sexual Solipsisms, and Their Possible Connection

MacKinnon describes a sexual solipsism when she says that the use of pornography amounts to 'sex between people and things, human beings and pieces of paper'. She not only describes this solipsism, but condemns it. Sex 'between people and things' will not exist 'in a society in which equality is a fact, not merely a word'.[56] Vadas likewise does not merely describe this solipsism, but condemns it. She argues that the pornography which she defines as something 'that has been manufactured to satisfy sexual desire though its sexual consumption . . . as a woman' is the very same as the pornography MacKinnon defines in her ordinance: namely, 'the graphic, sexually explicit subordination of women in pictures or words'. What is used as a woman, she says, also subordinates women. There is a connection between the two solipsisms in pornography.

Kant discusses a solipsism similar to the pornographic in his remarks about solitary sexual experience. Sexual desire can occur, he says, when a person 'is aroused to it, not by its real object, but by his imagination of this object, and so in a way contrary to the purpose of the desire, since he himself creates its object'.[57] And Kant does not merely describe this solipsism, he condemns it. He says that imaginary objects are treated as people, sexually, and ought not to be. He says that such behavior is 'unnatural', and worse. Are Kant and MacKinnon discussing the same phenomenon? Not quite. The fantasy MacKinnon describes is anchored to a particular thing: the object of the fantasizer's attention is an existing thing, a pornographic artifact, and he (perhaps) makes believe that *it* is a woman. He (perhaps) pretends of something that exists, that it is other than it is: which is to say that the fantasy is existentially conservative (like the make-believe of mud-pies).[58] The fantasy Kant describes is not anchored to

---

[56] MacKinnon, *Only Words*, 109. [57] Kant, *Doctrine of Virtue*, 88.
[58] These labels are from Gareth Evans, *The Varieties of Reference,* ed., J. McDowell (Oxford: Clarendon Press, 1982), 358. The make-believe game of mud-pies and of shadow-boxing are his illustrations of fantasies that are (respectively) existentially conservative and creative.

a particular thing: the object of the fantasizer's attention is not an existing thing, but a merely intentional object. He pretends that there is something which there isn't: which is to say that the fantasy is existentially creative (like the make-believe of shadow-boxing). There is little doubt, however, that Kant would have agreed with some of MacKinnon's conclusions about the use of pornographic sexual partners. Pornography is not the 'real object' of sexual desire, in Kant's sense, and the use of pornography would presumably be equally 'unnatural' in his opinion. However, Kant's hostility to this sexual solipsism seems unjustified, by his own lights, as he seems uneasily to acknowledge.[59] And Kant does not condemn this solipsism by saying it coincides with the other. He does not go on to say that treating imaginary objects as people is a way of treating other people as objects. The claim that there is a *connection* between the two sexual solipsisms is unique, as far as I know, to feminist discussion of pornography.

Feminist condemnation of pornography depends on the claim that through the use of pornography, women are treated as things. That is what distinguishes the feminist approach to pornography from the moralistic hostility displayed by Kant towards solitary sexual activity. There are different arguments for the feminist claim that through pornography, women are treated as things. Perhaps pornography makes women objects in virtue of its power as a kind of speech act, a kind of authoritative hate speech that ranks women as sub-human, legitimates violence against women, deprives women of powers and rights. Perhaps it makes women thing-like by silencing women, depriving women of the power to perform the speech acts we want to perform, including crucial speech acts of sexual refusal, and protest. Perhaps it makes women more thing-like by producing changes in the beliefs and desires and behaviour of those who consume it, with results of the kind acknowledged by Easterbrook, who rejected feminist anti-pornography legislation while affirming its premises. He said that depictions of subordination 'tend to perpetuate subordination. The subordinate status of women in turn leads to affront and lower pay at work, insult and injury at home, battery and

---

[59] Kant says 'it is not so easy to produce the rational proof that the unnatural . . . use of one's sexual power is a violation of duty to oneself'. He then goes on to assert that such a use is incompatible with respect for humanity in one's own person, *Doctrine of Virtue*, 88. So he does say that it involves treating *oneself* as a thing.

rape on the streets', all of which proved the power of pornography as speech.[60]

These ways of understanding the idea that pornography objectifies women do not obviously depend on thinking that in pornography things are treated as women. If what is crucial to feminist argument is only the claim that pornography objectifies, or subordinates, women, what are we to say of the *two* sexual solipsisms in pornography? Is it a mere coincidence that pornography instantiates them both? According to MacKinnon, it is no coincidence that pornography instantiates both. She says that in pornography 'the human becomes thing', meaning both that a pornographic artifact is used in place of a human sexual partner, and that a human sexual partner is used as if she were a pornographic artifact, a thing—and I said that this is not an equivocation, but a substantive thesis. When sex is something you do with a thing, she says, it becomes something you do with a thing, even when you do it with a person. When you treat things as human beings, you end up treating human beings as things. The solipsism of animating things *leads to* the solipsism of objectifying people. But why should pornography, as defined by Vadas, be pornography, as defined by MacKinnon: what reason is there for thinking that what is sexually consumed 'as a woman' also subordinates women? *Is* there a connection between the two solipsisms in pornography?

One possible answer is negative. There is no connection of any kind between the two claims: contrary to MacKinnon, it is after all a mere coincidence that pornography happens to instantiate them both. Other possible answers are affirmative, and various, but I will divide them into two broad types.

---

[60] See American Booksellers, Inc. v. Hudnut, 771 F2d 329 (7th Cir. 1985). For discussion of pornography's effects, see Edward Donnerstein, Daniel Linz, and Steven Penrod, *The Question of Pornography: Research Findings and Policy Implications* (New York: Free Press; London: Collier Macmillan, 1987); for a discussion of causation in this context, Frederick Schauer, 'Causation Theory and the Causes of Sexual Violence', *American Bar Foundation Research Journal* 4 1987, 737–70. For sample feminist argument see Catharine MacKinnon, *Feminism Unmodified*, and *Only Words*; Andrea Dworkin, *Pornography: Men Possessing Women* (London: The Women's Press, 1981); Melinda Vadas, 'A First Look at the Pornography Civil Rights Ordinance: Could Pornography Be the Subordination of Women?', *Journal of Philosophy* (1987), 487–511; Langton, 'Speech Acts and Unspeakable Acts', this volume; Jennifer Hornsby, 'Speech Acts and Pornography', *Women's Philosophy Review* 10 1993, 38–45, reprinted in *The Problem of Pornography*, ed., Sue Dwyer (Belmont, CA: Wadsworth, 1995).

4.1. There is a causal connection

As a matter of human psychology, when men sexually use objects, pornographic artifacts, as women, they tend to use real women as objects. Because of this causal fact, pornography that is used *as a* woman also *subordinates* women: pornography as defined by Vadas is pornography as defined by MacKinnon. One weaker variant of this causal claim might be restricted to a subset of the pornography defined by Vadas. As a matter of human psychology, when men sexually use objects as women, and those objects are pornographic artifacts *whose content is violent or misogynistic,* then they will tend to use real women as objects. Other variants may give stronger or weaker interpretations to the talk of a *tendency*: perhaps the causal connection is a matter of psychological law; perhaps it is a matter of mere raising of probabilities. What all of these have in common is that the sense in which one solipsism 'leads to' the other is a *causal* sense.

4.2. There is a constitutive connection

When pornographic artifacts are treated as women, *ipso facto* women are treated as objects. Because of this constitutive fact, pornography that is used *as a* woman also *subordinates* women: pornography as defined by Vadas is pornography as defined by MacKinnon. Although the two solipsisms look different, the one implies the other. One weaker variant of this constitutive claim might be restricted to a subset of the pornography defined by Vadas. When objects are used as women, and those objects are pornographic artifacts *whose content is violent or misogynistic,* then *ipso facto* women are treated as objects. Another weaker variant of the constitutive claim might be restricted not only to a subset of the pornography defined by Vadas, but also to certain background conditions. When objects are used as women, and those objects are pornographic artifacts whose content is violent or misogynistic, and whose status as speech is *authoritative*, then *ipso facto* women are treated as objects. What all of these have in common is that the sense in which one solipsism 'leads to' the other is a *constitutive* sense.

Let me consider first the constitutive variants of the claim that in pornography 'the human becomes thing' in two ways. I have some sympathy for a constitutive version of the claim that one solipsism 'leads to' the other, that what is used as a woman also subordinates women. If an argument I develop elsewhere is correct, then pornography may be an illocutionary act of subordination: in certain conditions pornography (of a certain kind) constitutes an act of subordination—in conditions, for example, when its speakers have authority.[61] This amounts to the weakest of the constitutive claims described above. On this view, there is a connection between the two solipsisms: when objects are treated as women, women are indeed treated as objects, since pornography ranks women as inferior, legitimates discriminatory behaviour and violence, deprives women of powers and rights. On this view, one solipsism 'leads to' the other only in certain conditions: if pornography were to lack authority, for example, then pornography would not subordinate.

A stronger constitutive variant is that one solipsism *ipso facto* leads to the other: that the treating of pornographic objects as women is, in and of itself, the treating of women as objects, whether or not the content of the pornography is violent or misogynistic, whether or not the pornographic speech is authoritative. If this claim could be defended, then pornography would threaten women's equality not in virtue of its content ('depictions of subordination', etc.), nor in virtue of its force as authoritative hate speech, but in virtue of its basic and essential role as an inanimate sexual partner.

This strong constitutive interpretation of the claim would contradict the views of conservatives, liberals, and also many feminists. It would contradict the views of pro-pornography feminists who say that an egalitarian pornography might liberate women. It would contradict the views of feminists opposed to pornography who think there may be conditions in which objects sexually used as women would not subordinate women. It would (apparently) contradict the opinion of MacKinnon herself, in so far as a distinction between pornography and erotica was allowed in the ordinance she drafted—where erotica was defined to be sexually explicit material that does not subordinate women. (If the use of erotica were to involve sex 'between people and things', then on MacKinnon's premise that the one solipsism implies the other, there could be no erotica that does not subordinate, hence there could be no erotica.) On all these views, there could be graphic, sexually explicit pictures and words, designed for sexual consumption, that are liberating for women, or at any rate neutral.

[61] See 'Speech Acts and Unspeakable Acts', this volume.

If pornography's power to subordinate depends in part on its content, then material with a different, egalitarian, content would not subordinate. Or if pornography's power to subordinate depends on its authority, then in the absence of that authority pornography would not subordinate. If the strong constitutive claim could be defended, then that would be interesting both philosophically and dialectically. It is uncontroversial that pornography is used as a sexual partner; it is controversial that pornography subordinates women. If the former can be shown to imply the latter, then there would be a path from the uncontroversial to the controversial.

4.3. Vadas on a constitutive connection

The strong constitutive claim has been vigorously defended by Melinda Vadas, and although no brief summary can do her argument justice, what follows may convey something of her strategy. The definition with which she begins is by now familiar: pornography is 'any object that has been manufactured to satisfy sexual desire through its sexual consumption or other sexual use as a woman.'[62] The definition makes it clear that pornography is an inanimate, non-sentient artefact, that is sexually used in the role, function, or capacity of a human being. The definition has advantages of neutrality and realism. It is fairly neutral, since it does not stack the deck in favor of a particular feminist conclusion. It is realistic, since it focuses on the (often ignored) purpose and function of pornography. Vadas wants to say that pornography, on this definition, is the same as pornography on MacKinnon's definition: that what is used as a woman subordinates women. She considers a question left open by her definition, about whether pornography is representational (and hence speech). One way, the usual way, for us to distinguish between things that are representational and things that are not is by considering their uses in human life:

What is typically used or usable as a gun is a gun and not a representation of a gun. ... A gun, by definition, is able to fire projectiles of some sort, typically lethal, while a representation of a gun can, as such, fire nothing.[63]

---

[62] Melinda Vadas, 'The Manufacture-for-use of Pornography'. Jennifer Saul interprets and criticizes Vadas, and offers an alternative account of the connection in 'On Treating Things as People: Objectification, Pornography, and the History of the Vibrator', *Hypatia* 21 (2006), 45–61. Saul agrees that any case of 'personification' of pornography will be a case of 'objectification' of women—but she argues that this is because the former *presupposes* the latter, so will only occur if consumers are already objectifiers.

[63] Vadas, 'The Manufacture-for-use of Pornography', 185.

There can be ambiguous cases. There can be an object that is a gun *and* a representation of a gun. A toy gun may be able to fire projectiles, and might also be used to represent a real gun in a court re-enactment. Whether the toy gun is a representation or not depends on its use, in a particular context. In general, 'an object's use dictates whether it is an *a* or a representation of an *a*'. Imagine a thing that can be used in the way that a gun is used, but made from materials typically used to *represent* guns: imagine a gun made of paper. If it can be used as a gun, it is a gun.

Apply these principles now to the question about pornography. If something is used as a female sex object, then even if made of paper it *is* a female sex object, and not a mere depiction of one.

> Within its context of sexual consumption, the pornography used *as* a woman *is* a woman, and not a representation of one.[64]

Vadas draws two conclusions, both controversial, and it is the second which concerns us here. She says that pornography is not speech; and she says that pornographic objects are in the same ontological class as flesh and blood women. When pornography is manufactured for use, she says, a new category of reality is created and populated: the category of individuals who are both women and non-persons. It then becomes true that *women are not necessarily persons*. In this way the treating of things as human beings has implications for the status of real human beings. The harm to flesh-and-blood women is that they are now members of a class of beings that are not necessarily persons. And this has implications, she says, for the way that flesh-and-blood women are treated in sexual contexts:

> Since, where pornography is manufactured-for-use, men's sexual relations with women are conceptually unrelated to their female partner's personhood, it follows that men's sexual relations with women will, under these conditions, be conceptually unrelated to any and all person-related characteristics or abilities their female partners might have . . . Now consent, everyone would agree, is a person-related ability. . . . it follows that under these conditions women's consent is conceptually outside the practice of the sexual.[65]

The real harm done to flesh and blood women is that we are placed in the same ontological category as pornographic objects; that person-related properties are not essential to women; and that person-related actions

---

[64] Vadas, 'The Manufacture-for-use of Pornography', 186.   [65] Ibid., 190.

such as consent are therefore conceptually irrelevant to sex with women. If I understand Vadas correctly, her conclusion is that when objects are treated as women (in sexual contexts), *in virtue of that very fact* women are made to be objects. The argument offered by Vadas is interesting and striking, and has the great merit of addressing explicitly the question of two solipsisms in pornography, and their connection—the question provoked by MacKinnon's apparently punning remark that in pornography 'the human becomes thing'—and offering the strongest possible interpretation of that connection.

4.4. *There is a causal and constitutive connection*

So far we have considered (briefly) two variants of the claim that there is a *constitutive* connection between the two solipsisms in pornography: the weaker version, defended by myself (elsewhere), and the stronger version defended by Vadas. Let us consider (briefly) the claim that the connection between the two solipsisms in pornography is a *causal* one. One could hold that there is a constitutive connection *and* a causal one (perhaps pornography is an act of subordination, *and* causes subordination); or one could hold that there is simply a causal connection. This latter is, perhaps, the commoner way of understanding the idea that pornography somehow brings about (or 'perpetuates') the subordination of women.

Perhaps there is a causal connection that has to do with human psychology. Perhaps there is be a causal connection between the local solipsisms in general, and not simply in sexual contexts. When we treat things as people, perhaps we teach ourselves how to treat people. When we project human qualities on to the inanimate, perhaps we teach ourselves how to treat human beings. A child's reactive relations with a doll may be rehearsal for relations with people. My habitual rage towards a recalcitrant motor car may nurture habitual rage towards recalcitrant people. Reactive engagement with the fictitious may teach one reactive engagement with the real. And, turning our attention to the sexual solipsisms, perhaps the causal claim is plausible when restricted to pornography of a certain kind. Perhaps there is pornography that celebrates rape, that makes its readers think and experience sexually as Leonard thought and experienced sexually, that makes its reader feel good and powerful and strong and free, by treating an inanimate thing as a human being that is a woman, a defeated enemy, conquered, unable to escape, half terrified, crying 'no', obeying from fear and awe. Perhaps habitual sex with this pornography could teach one how to treat women sexually. This solipsism of treating things as women could lead (causally) to a solipsism of treating women as things. On this understanding the subordination of women arises not from the sexual use of an inanimate thing 'as a woman', *simpliciter*, but from the sexual use of a particular kind of pornographic inanimate thing: one that has a certain (violent) content, and is made to be used in a certain (violent) way. Given that restriction, this would be one of the weaker versions of the causal claims I listed above.

Alternatively, the facts about human psychology might have something to do with the *projection* that is common to the solipsism of treating things as people, and (sometimes) the solipsism of treating people as things. Projection is involved in the activities of animating the inanimate; projection is also involved in some of the objectifying attitudes. Recall that on Haslanger's analysis, one part of the objectifying attitude is an illusory projective belief that women have by nature the properties they are 'seen' to have. Recall too that Leonard moves from the private theatre of fantastic events 'in his head', to a projective conclusion about what Maria is actually like. He finds his thoughts 'irresistably exciting', and he substitutes projection for knowledge of other minds: 'he could not believe she would not be aroused'. Perhaps the projective aspect of one solipsism could lead (causally) to the projective aspect of the other, though to suggest this is to speculate. If habitual projection in pornography use were to lead one to habitual projection with real people, then that would be a strong version of the causal claim: there would be something about the very activity of (sexually) treating things as people that builds habits of projection that can result in (sexually) treating real people as things.

5. Concluding Reflections

Feminists have said that pornography instantiates two solipsisms: somehow, in pornography, things are treated as women, and women are treated as things. Here I have emphasized that it is the latter claim that is central, and distinctive of feminism. I have suggested that the former solipsism is irrelevant to feminist argument, except in so far as it has implications for the latter solipsism. And I have considered some different ways to understand the idea that one solipsism might well have implications for the other: that there may be a causal connection, or a constitutive one.

Recall that there was a possible negative answer to the question about a connection between the two solipsisms in pornography. According to that answer, there is no connection at all, and it is a mere coincidence that pornography happens to instantiate both solipsisms. Suppose (as I do not) that the negative answer were correct. Would that mean that we should ignore the solipsism of treating things as people? I am not sure. Perhaps there can be misgivings about pornography's animation of the inanimate that are not exactly feminist misgivings. Recall the voice in Winterson's novel. 'Why hesitate when you could simulate?' cries the advertiser of a brave new Virtual world, a world of teledildonics and virtual lovers. Winterson's narrator is unimpressed. 'For myself . . . I'd rather hold you in my arms. . . . Luddite? No, I don't want to smash the machines but neither do I want the machines to smash me.' In the world of Virtual sexuality, one treats machines as people—but the narrator does not say that people are thereby treated as machines. Winterson's narrator does not say that women are thereby made things; the concern is not strictly, not distinctively, a feminist concern.

It is something else, surely, a broad concern that has aspects that are both epistemic and moral. It has something in common with the struggles of the meditator, who quietly hopes that the figures in their hats and coats are not, after all, automata in disguise. It has something in common with the unease provoked by the (philosopher's) prospect of life in an experience machine. And it has something in common with Kant's general concern about the life of one who 'must shut himself up in himself', who must remain 'completely alone with his thoughts as in a prison'—a prison from which he says it is our duty, epistemic and moral, to escape.

15

Love and Solipsism

1. Solipsism and Escape

The meditator peers through a window, sees people in their hats and coats, and wonders if they are machines. We pity the solipsist; poor lad, how is he to defeat the goliath of skepticism, armed only with the slings and stones of an all too finite intellect? We admire his willingness to follow the argument wherever it might lead. But spare a thought for the people below, should the meditator leave his stove-heated room unconvinced by his counter-skeptical meditations.[1]

Imagine I were the only person, in a world that looked like our own. I would interact with things, but treat them as people, and laugh at the worries expressed in that old book, attributed (falsely) to Descartes; laugh at the idea that the beings beneath the window, with their coats and hats, were mere machines. Solipsism would be true; I would not believe it; and my world would be, in one way, solipsistic. Imagine now the reverse: imagine the world were crowded with people, but my attitude were solipsistic. I would interact with people, treating them as things. Solipsism would be false; I would believe it true; and my world would be, in a different way, solipsistic. If both worlds are solipsistic, then I am not socially interacting with people in either. Where I am alone, I am not interacting with people, but with things. Surrounded by people, there is nothing social about my interactions, if I act as if I am alone.

Imagine Lois would love to meet Superman. She wins a competition whose lucky winner will meet Superman. She puts on a strange helmet,

[1] This is a revised and shortened version of 'Love and Solipsism', in *Love Analyzed,* ed., Roger Lamb (Boulder, Co.: Westview Press, 1997), 123–52. It has a companion piece, 'Sexual Solipsism', this volume. For the meditator, see René Descartes, *Meditations on First Philosophy* (1641), trans. John Cottingham (Cambridge: Cambridge University Press, 1986).

and a strange glove, and meets Virtual Superman. She returns to work. 'So disappointing!' she says to her colleague. 'Too bad!' replies Clark. Has she met Superman? Yes and no, but mainly (I think) no. To meet Superman, to meet him properly, he has to *be* Superman (not Virtual Superman), and she has to *treat* him as Superman (not as Clark). Likewise, to avoid the solipsistic worlds, some of the beings with whom one interacts must *be* people (not things); and one must *treat* them as people (not as things). That was the suggestion with which this essay's companion piece, 'Sexual Solipsism', began.[2]

'Treat' is here being used as a shorthand for a group of epistemic and practical attitudes which deserve more analysis than I give them here. The solipsist who fails to treat people as people adopts an attitude which has epistemological and moral aspects: it manifests itself in a certain practical orientation, certain ways of acting, towards the beings around him; and if belief is a disposition, there will presumably be a conceptual connection between his person-denying behavior, and his person-denying beliefs. Thus described my attitudinal solipsist is an uncomfortably blurry figure. Is he the metaphysical solipsist, who believes he *is* the only person? The epistemological solipsist, who believes he is the only *knowable* person? The moral solipsist, who believes he is the only person who *matters?* Perhaps each of these in turn. I shall be more interested in the connections than the divisions.

I suggested, too, that there can be smaller, local solipsisms. Sometimes there is a local version of the second world, that of the attitudinal solipsist. Sometimes a person will, in a particular context, *treat some people as things*: perhaps by treating them as if they were a mere cog in the vast machine of nature; a mere body; a potential possession; an item whose value is merely instrumental. Philosophers and feminists condemn this treatment of persons as things, this local solipsism, saying, in Kantian idiom, that it fails to treat the other person as an end in herself, or violates the autonomy of the other person, or objectifies the other person. They say something goes wrong morally, and perhaps epistemologically, when people generally, or women in particular, are treated as less than human.[3]

---

[2] Langton, 'Sexual Solipsism', this volume.

[3] Immanuel Kant, *Groundwork of the Metaphysic of Morals* (1785), trans. H. J. Paton (New York: Harper and Row, 1964); as for feminist applications, there is a vast literature but see e.g. Martha Nussbaum, 'Objectification', *Philosophy and Public Affairs* 24 (1995), 249–91; Barbara Herman, 'Could It

This local treating of *people as things* is to be contrasted, I suggested, with its counterpart, a local treating of *things as people*. A young child sings gently to her doll, sleep my little one sleep; a farmer raises his eyes to streaming thunderclouds, whispers thank you; a mother pleads before a painting of a lady in blue. There is no lady to hear any plea; no one to thank for the rain; a doll cannot sleep, or wake. Each person in these examples is alone; but they believe, or make-believe, they direct their actions towards someone, illustrating the striking capacity human beings have, adults and children alike, to glean joy and comfort from merely imagined relations with merely imagined people. In this essay's companion piece, I considered the possible connection between two sexual solipsisms, the treating of people, women, as things; and the treating of things—pornographic artifacts—as people, women. The present essay leaves aside the solipsism of treating things as people, and takes up one aspect of the treating of people as things.

It will be recalled that Kant said, with extravagant pessimism, that 'sexual love makes of the loved person an object of appetite', and that thereby a 'person becomes a thing and can be treated and used as such'.[4] I considered in 'Sexual Solipsism' an interpretation of Kant's idea proposed by Barbara Herman, who thinks the problem is that sexual love takes a person as its object not *qua* person, but *qua* body. This essay considers the competing proposal from Christine Korsgaard, who thinks the problem is that sexual love takes a person as its object not *qua* body, but *qua* person.[5] The two interpretations are compared in Section 2, and in Section 3 I take up Korsgaard's interpretation, illustrating it with a profoundly solipsistic example drawn from Proust.

Like its companion, this essay also considers a possible escape from solipsism, and what Kant had to say about it; which is where we can begin. My world is solipsistic if I am alone, interacting with things, but treating them as people; and solipsistic if I interact with people, but treating them as things. How one escapes these worlds is a matter of debate; one finds a reply to the skeptic perhaps, or pursues the path of virtue. In practice however,

Be Worth Thinking about Kant on Sex and Marriage?' in *A Mind Of One's Own: Feminist Essays on Reason and Objectivity*, eds., Louise Antony and Charlotte Witt (Boulder, Co.: Westview Press, 1993).

[4] Kant, *Lectures on Ethics* (1775–1780) trans. Louis Infield (London: Methuen, 1930), from the notes made by Brauer, Kutzner and Mrongovius ed., Paul Mentzer, 163.

[5] Barbara Herman, 'Kant on Sex and Marriage'; Christine Korsgaard, 'Creating the Kingdom of Ends: Responsibility and Reciprocity in Personal Relations', *Philosophical Perspectives 6: Ethics,* ed., J. Tomberlin (Atascadero, Ca: Ridgeview, 1992), 305–32.

an effective remedy is in friendship. One cannot believe of a friend that he does not exist, cannot be known, does not matter. True, some functions of a friend may, with luck, be performed by beings that are not people: a doll, a teddy bear, a fictional construct of some religious practice. A hymn may tell us what a friend we have in Jesus, all our sins and griefs to bear. But the need for a hymn points to the slenderness of the friendship; we do not need songs to tell us who our real friends are. The idea that friendship provides escape from solipsism is to be found, I suggested, in Kant; not so much the Kant of the *Groundwork*, but of the *Doctrine of Virtue*, and *Lectures on Ethics*.[6] Kant says friendship provides release from the 'prison' of the self: the man without a friend is the man who is all alone, who 'must shut himself up in himself', who remains 'completely alone with his thoughts as in a prison'. We each have a duty to seek out friendship, and escape from that prison, a duty 'not to isolate ourselves'.[7] Here I want to say a little more about this duty of friendship, briefly looking at its relationship to *self-love*, and to *self-knowledge*, in Kant's view.

Friendship is a duty to ourselves and others which is partly implied by our own self-love: we must love ourselves, but 'self-love cannot be divorced from our need of being loved by others (i.e. of receiving help from them when we are in need)'. In loving ourselves we desire that others will love us, and that they will desire to make our ends theirs. This imposes a duty on us to love others as we love ourselves, and to make their ends ours.[8] The suggestion is that we cannot exercise even the self-regarding virtues unless we are part of a moral community of people, among whom there are some who love us, and are loved by us in return. In friendship, what Kant describes as the 'reciprocity' characteristic of moral relations in general is present with a unique intensity, as Korsgaard spells out so well: friendship is 'the maximum reciprocity of love', an 'intimate union of love and respect', an ideal of 'emotional and practical concern' for another's welfare.[9] It is a matter of doing, feeling, and also knowing, having aspects that are both practical and epistemological. Friends do things together, act in ways that bring joy to each other, something which requires each to

---

[6] Kant, *Doctrine of Virtue* (1797) trans. Mary Gregor (New York: Harper and Row, 1964); *Lectures on Ethics*.

[7] Kant, *Doctrine of Virtue*, 144, 145   [8] Ibid., 53, 118.

[9] Kant, *Lectures on Ethics*, 202; *Doctrine of Virtue*, 140. My understanding of Kant on friendship owes a great deal to Korsgaard.

know the mind of the other. In friendship one exercises an active power of 'sympathy', a capacity that is no sentimental susceptibility to joy or sadness, but a communion practical in its orientation, providing a way to 'participate actively in the fate of others'.[10]

Friendship is a duty to know another person—and also to allow oneself to *be known* by another, which in turn has implications for *knowledge of oneself*. In addition to the desire, arising from self-love, that others make our practical ends theirs, there is a more simple desire to be known, which coincides with the demands of a duty to allow oneself to be known. The need to be known by another, the need to 'unburden our heart', is a basic human need; and in order that this 'release' may be achieved,

each of us needs a friend, one in whom we can confide unreservedly, to whom we can disclose completely all our dispositions and judgments, from whom we can and need hide nothing, to whom we can communicate our whole self.[11]

In friendship at its best, there will be a 'complete confidence of two persons in revealing their secret thoughts and feelings to each other'.[12] In allowing oneself to be known by another, one is thereafter better able to know oneself, and thereby to fulfill the first of the duties to oneself. Kant describes the Socratic injunction to 'know thyself' as the first command (despite the fact one can never fully fathom the 'depths and abyss of one's heart'),[13] his chief interest in self-knowledge being knowledge of one's motives and character. Friends can help one to obey the Socratic injunction by providing scope for communication and correction. The process of putting thoughts into communicative words enables us better to learn what we think and feel and desire. Kant might well have said of the communication of friends what he in fact said of prayer, namely that it is

necessary *for our own sakes*.... To grasp and comprehend his concepts a person must clothe them in words.[14]

One's own thoughts are but dimly grasped and comprehended unless one has the opportunity to clothe them in words, and communicate them to another. Besides communication there is correction. When we 'clothe our concepts in words' in the process of unburdening our heart, our

---

[10] Kant, *Doctrine of Virtue*, 126.   [11] Kant, *Lectures on Ethics*, 205–6.
[12] Kant, *Doctrine of Virtue*, 143.   [13] Ibid., 107.
[14] Kant, *Lectures on Ethics*, 98–9, emphasis added.

judgments about ourselves and our motives are as fallible and in need of correction as our judgments about anything else, and more vulnerable to self-deception. Kant says 'self-revelation' in friendship is 'a human necessity for the correction of our judgments'.

> To have a friend whom we know to be frank and loving, neither false nor spiteful, is to have one who will help us to correct our judgment when it is mistaken.[15]

To have a friend is to have someone who enables one to escape from the prison of the self: someone whom one can know, and to whom one can make oneself known; someone who will share ones ends, help one to know oneself better, and thereby help one on the path of virtue.

A friend thus brings benefits, prudential, moral, and epistemological, but these benefits are not the point of the friendship, whose point is always reciprocity: mutual knowledge, mutual sharing of activity, mutual love and respect. Recall those metaphors of self-surrender and retrieval in Kant's discussion of reciprocity in friendship, to which Korsgaard drew attention.

> If I am to love [my friend] as I love myself, I must be sure that he will love me as he loves himself, in which case he restores to me that with which I part and I come back to myself again . . . . Assume that I choose only friendship, and that I care only for my friend's happiness in the hope that he cares for mine. Our love is mutual; there is complete restoration. I, from generosity, look after his happiness and he similarly looks after mine; I do not throw away my happiness, but surrender it to his keeping, and he in turn surrenders his into my hands.[16]

This is an ideal of friendship, to be approximated rather than encountered in this perfect form, according to Kant, for 'in practical life such things do not occur'.

If friendship can provide an effective escape from solipsism, can sexual love provide the same? In 'Sexual Solipsism' I observed that Kant sometimes gives an affirmative answer: sexual love and friendship are alike in their power to unlock the prison of the self, their power to create an 'intimate union of love and respect'.

> Whether it is for one's spouse or for a friend, love presupposes the same mutual respect for the other's character. [It] wants to communicate itself completely, and

---

[15] Kant, *Lectures on Ethics*, 206.   [16] Ibid., 202–3.

it expects of its respondent a similar sharing of heart, unweakened by distrustful reticence.[17]

So Kant writes in a letter to Maria von Herbert, a young woman abandoned by a 'friend'. The status of the 'friendship' is at first unclear, but Kant says that, for the purpose of his moral advice, 'it makes no significant difference', since the same mutual honesty and mutual respect is characteristic of love, 'whether it is for one's spouse or for a friend'. Elsewhere he uses the same metaphors of self-surrender and retrieval in describing the reciprocity of sexual love, as Korsgaard remarks. If I love my friend 'as I love myself', and he loves me 'as he loves himself', 'he restores to me that with which I part and I come back to myself again'.[18] Of sexual love, 'if I yield myself completely to another and obtain the person of the other in return, I win myself back'.[19] If love and friendship are alike, then love, like friendship, will be a matter of doing, and feeling, and knowing: lovers will show 'emotional and practical concern' for another's welfare; will exercise an active power of sympathy, a communion practical in its orientation, that provides a way to 'participate actively in the fate of others'; will want to know the other, and to allow himself, herself to be known. Love, like friendship, will provide that scope for communication and correction which enables one better to know oneself. It will involve the same trust—the 'complete confidence of two persons in revealing their secret thoughts and feelings to each other'.[20] If Kant is right in his letter to Maria Herbert, then a lover can also be a

friend...in whom we can confide unreservedly, and to whom we can disclose completely all our dispositions and judgments, from whom we can and need hide nothing, to whom we can communicate our whole self.[21]

Kant goes too far when he says that it 'makes no difference' whether a relationship is one of love or friendship. Sexual love brings with it a different constellation of desires and emotions, among which is a sheer delight in the body of another person which sets it apart from friendship.

---

[17] Kant's letter to Maria von Herbert of spring 1792. See *Kant: Philosophical Correspondence*, trans. Arnulf Zweig (Chicago: University of Chicago Press, 1967); *Ak.* XI, 331; Zweig's translation has been adapted. 'Duty and Desolation', this volume, addresses the longer correspondence between Kant and Herbert.

[18] Kant, *Lectures on Ethics*, 202.   [19] Ibid., 167.

[20] Kant, *Doctrine of Virtue*, 126, 143.   [21] Kant, *Lectures on Ethics*, 205–6.

There is little positive acknowledgement of this in Kant's own writings, though it finds a vivid description in a book he admired.

> Thou hast ravished my heart, my spouse,
> how fair is thy love!
> Thy lips, O my spouse, drop as the honeycomb,
> honey and milk are under thy tongue.
> A garden inclosed is my spouse,
> an orchard of pomegranates with pleasant fruits,
> camphire with spikenard, spikenard and saffron,
> calamus and cinnamon, myrrh and aloe,
> a fountain of gardens,
> a well of living waters.
> Awake, O north wind, and come thou south;
> blow upon my garden,
> that the spices thereof may flow out.
> Let my beloved come into his garden,
> and eat his pleasant fruits.
> Drink, yea, drink abundantly,
> O beloved.[22]

A gulf of perhaps three thousand years divides this poem from ourselves, yet there is no mistaking the phenomenon it depicts. (Well, *almost* no mistaking. Coy subtitles in my edition find a different meaning: 'Christ setteth forth the graces of the church', and 'the church prayeth to be made fit for his presence'.) The captive heart, the driving hunger for which ordinary hunger and thirst provide faint metaphors, the delight in the body, all set sexual love apart from the 'intimate union' of friendship of which Kant spoke. (And, incidentally, apart from any theological simulacrum.)

These features of sexual love ground Kant's earlier noted pessimism: for despite the occasional optimism, more characteristic is the thought that any virtues in sexual love exist in spite of, not because of, sexual desire. It is to be expected that a rationalistic Kant will be wary of how love might thwart knowledge, with its delusions, its reckless passions: and so he is, warning against the perils of romantic love, and saying a lover is a wishful thinker,

---

[22] *The Song of Solomon,* ch. 4: 9–16, ch. 5:1, somewhat abridged. The song was supposedly written by Solomon in 1014 BC, but usually dated to the 3rd or 4th century BC. Kant often refers favourably to the Bible, e.g. at *Doctrine of Virtue,* 63, 95, 113, 130; *Lectures on Ethics,* 10, 100, 108, 114 (I don't mean to suggest enthusiasm for this poem).

blind to faults in the beloved.[23] But there is also that more basic worry: 'sexual love makes of the loved person an object of appetite; as soon as that appetite has been stilled, the person is cast aside as one casts away a lemon which has been sucked dry'.[24] Sexual love makes of the beloved an 'object of appetite': the beloved is consumed by it, sucked dry, reduced to an empty rind, cast by the wayside. The lover is, in the end, alone, the appetite stilled, a sour taste in the mouth. Sexual love is not the remedy for solipsism, but the disease. It is hard to see how sexual love is even compatible with the moral relations of friendship, let alone it making 'no significant difference' whether a relationship is one of friendship or sexual love. The danger can admittedly be somewhat softened:

Sexual love can, of course, be combined with human love and so carry with the characteristics of the latter, but taken by itself and for itself, it is nothing more than appetite.[25]

Although sexual love 'really has nothing in common with moral love', it can 'enter into close union with it under the limiting conditions of practical reason'.[26] This uneasy grafting of antagonistic attitudes attempts a solution to the problem, and one which has a familiar and prosaic face: 'the limiting conditions of practical reason' are those of marriage.[27]

Whatever the solution, it is worth thinking more about the problem Kant is trying to identify, in saying sexual love makes of a person 'an object of appetite'. In 'Sexual Solipsism' I distinguished two competing interpretations of the idea, offered by Herman and Korsgaard respectively: the idea that sexual love takes a person as its object not *qua* person, but *qua* body; and the idea that sexual love takes a person as its object *qua* person, but *qua* person to be possessed.

2. The Object of Sexual Love: Two Interpretations

Herman draws attention to apparent common ground between Kant and such feminists as Andrea Dworkin and Catharine MacKinnon. Kant says

---

[23] The wishful thinking of lovers is discussed in Kant, *Doctrine of Virtue*, 94; he warns against the perils of romantic love in a letter to Elizabeth Motherby, 11th February 1793, citing Maria von Herbert as a cautionary example (see 'Duty and Desolation').

[24] Kant, *Lectures on Ethics*, 163.   [25] Ibid., 163.

[26] Kant, *Doctrine of Virtue*, 90.   [27] Kant, *Lectures on Ethics*, 167.

sexual love, when taken by itself, is 'a degradation of human nature; for as soon as a person becomes an object of appetite for another, all motives of moral relationship cease to function, because as an object of appetite for another a person becomes a thing and can be treated and used as such by every one'; and 'that [the woman] is a human being is of no concern to the man; only her sex is the object of his desires. Human nature is thus subordinated.'[28] Herman compares this to Dworkin's view that '[t]here is a deep recognition in culture and in experience that intercourse is both the normal use of a woman . . . and a violative abuse . . . her selfhood changed in a way that is irrevocable' and that in sex the man 'confirms for himself and for her what she is; that she is something, not someone; certainly not someone equal'.[29] These bleak writings suggest that sexual relationships have an inherent tendency to objectify women—that they are, as Herman puts it, 'not compatible with the standing of the partners as equal human beings'. Kant says that when a man desires a woman, the fact 'that she is a human being is of no concern to the man; only her sex is the object of his desires'.[30] She is a human being, a rational creature, with desires and plans of her own, an active capacity for sympathy and friendship, a capacity for grasping the moral law and conforming her actions to it: but none of that is relevant to the man who desires her. Only her sex, only her body, is the object of his desires. Kant perhaps acknowledges a special problem for women, but is not bothered by it (as his insouciance about the solution of marriage in his day illustrates); the human nature of men and women alike is 'sacrificed to sex'.

Herman's interpretation takes up the thought that sexual love is 'written on the body';[31] the Biblical lover is entranced by the body of his beloved, fair as the moon, clear as the sun, terrible as an army with banners; the joints of her thighs as jewels, her belly as wheat set about with lilies, her breasts as clusters of the vine. (It would hardly be the same if he were to find his beloved the most rational of ten thousand, her intellect as the morning sun, and as a jewel her capacity for autonomous choice.) Perhaps Kant is imagining a prospect more reductive than this when he says 'only her sex is the object of his desires': he may suppose sexual desire is entirely

---

[28] Kant, *Lectures on Ethics*, 163–4.
[29] Andrea Dworkin, *Intercourse* (New York: Free Press, 1987), 122–3, 140–1.
[30] Kant, *Lectures on Ethics*, 164.
[31] I borrow Jeanette Winterson's title phrase, in *Written on the Body* (London: Jonathan Cape, 1992).

impersonal, even genital in its interest, of the kind expressed today in some pornography, and some novels, where a woman is described by the narrator as a sexual 'automaton', whose body is gratifyingly 'anonymous', 'marvellously impersonal', a kind of sexual experience machine.[32] But whether the body is viewed as an object of unique aesthetic delight, or as an anonymous instrument, it is on this interpretation a *body* that is the object of desire. Does Kant's concern then come from a puritanical metaphysical fantasy, where bodies are irrelevant to real people, a person being a noumenal being, who somehow exists beyond the messy world of bodies? Not exactly: on Kant's view we human beings are partly *constituted* by our bodies.

[O]ur life is entirely conditioned by our body, so that we cannot conceive of a life not mediated by the body and we cannot make use of our freedom except through the body. It is therefore obvious that the body constitutes a part of ourselves.[33]

The concern is, perhaps, that since a human being is partly constituted by her body, surrender of her body is somehow a surrender of herself.

Korsgaard on the other hand suggests that what Kant finds troubling is that sexual love might be directed towards a person *qua* person: cases where from the outset it takes, not just a body, but a person as its intentional object.

Amongst our inclinations there is one which is directed towards other human beings. *They themselves,* and not their work and services, are its objects of enjoyment.... There is an inclination which we may call an appetite for enjoying another human being. We refer to sexual impulse. Man can, of course, use another human being as an instrument for his service; he can use his hands, his feet, and even all his powers; he can use him for his own purposes with the other's consent. But there is no way in which a human being can be made an object of indulgence for another except through sexual impulse . . . it is an appetite for another human being.[34]

Sexual inclination is . . . not merely a pleasure of the senses . . . . It is rather pleasure from the use of another person . . . [it has] nothing in common with moral love.[35]

Sexual love is directed towards a person in his or her entirety: 'they themselves' are its intentional objects of enjoyment. What troubles Kant is

---

[32] Henry Miller, *Tropic of Capricorn* (New York: Grove Press 1961), 82, 181. See Kate Millett, *Sexual Politics* (Garden City, NY: Doubleday, 1970).

[33] Kant, *Lectures on Ethics*, 147–8.   [34] Ibid., 162–3, emphasis added.

[35] Kant, *Doctrine of Virtue*, 90.

the idea that sexual love demands that the beloved put her entire self at the lover's disposal. As Korsgaard says, it is likely to be 'more of a problem about sexual love than about casual sexual encounters'.[36] Viewed through the eyes of sexual desire, 'another person is seen as something wantable, desirable, and, therefore, inevitably, possessable. To yield to that desire, to the extent it is really that desire you yield to, is to allow yourself to be possessed'.[37] Kant says 'a person cannot be a property': to allow oneself to be possessed would be to allow oneself to become a thing.[38] Korsgaard notes a passage which suggests the competing reading but thinks it 'spoils the interest' of Kant's point.[39]

Surely, however, both interpretations are of interest, and worth exploring. And a first question to consider is whether they do really compete. Perhaps one could bring them closer, or find a compromise, by distinguishing opaque and transparent versions of Kant's claim: the extensional object of sexual desire is in fact a person, and on this (transparent) reading Korsgaard is right; but the desire is for that person *qua body,* and on this (opaque) reading Herman is right: sexual desire is a hunger for a (person's) body. When Kant says, in the passage crucial to Korsgaard's interpretation, that '*human beings . . . themselves,* and not their work and services' are the objects of sexual desire, what he says is ambiguous between the opaque and the transparent readings—and compatible with Herman's interpretation if we take the opaque, keeping in mind the earlier-mentioned point about bodily constitution. Sexual desire takes a body as its intentional object (as Herman suggests), but since the body partly constitutes the person, one cannot surrender one's body without surrendering one's self.

The body is part of the self; in its togetherness with the self it constitutes the person . . . . But the person who surrenders [only for the satisfaction of sexual desire] is used as a thing; the desire is still directed only towards sex and not towards the person as a human being. But it is obvious that to surrender part of oneself is to surrender the whole, because a human being is a unity.[40]

---

[36] What I am taking from Korsgaard is the idea that sexual desire may take as its object a person in his or her entirety. The Proustian interpretation I give, though, goes beyond what Korsgaard says, and may conflict with it. She takes the idea to involve a kind of *aesthetic* appreciation of a person, an idea which I do not take up here, despite its manifest interest. See Korsgaard 'Creating the Kingdom', 310, 327 n. 12. The quotation is from n. 13.

[37] Korsgaard, 'Creating the Kingdom', 310.   [38] Kant, *Lectures on Ethics,* 165.

[39] Korsgaard, 'Creating the Kingdom', 327 n. 11.   [40] Kant, *Lectures on Ethics,* 166.

On this compromise interpretation, Korsgaard is partly right, in saying that, on Kant's view, sexual love demands that the beloved put not simply her body but her entire self at the lover's disposal. But it would be no real compromise, for she is partly wrong: sexual love demands that the beloved put her entire self at the lover's disposal, not because the lover desires the person *qua person* as Korsgaard suggests, but rather because of the *essentially embodied* nature of the person desired. On the suggested interpretation, the problematic demand stems not from the intentional content of the desire, but from the extensional nature of the one desired. Since Korsgaard is aiming to describe the *intentional* content of sexual desire, on Kant's view—that it is a desire for a person *qua person*—this compromise interpretation fails to do her justice.

An alternative is to say Kant may hold both views about the intentional content of sexual desire, and they apply to different kinds of sexual love: it can be a desire for a person *qua* body, a *reductive* desire; and it can be a desire for a person *qua* person, but what I shall call an *invasive* desire. To take this path is to retreat from the universalizing aspect of Kant's remarks, taking them instead as descriptions of certain pathologies. Sexual love can focus sometimes on the body of a person, in a reductive way; and sometimes on a person as a whole, in an invasive way; and each of these two ideas is worth pursuing in its own terms. I find the seeds of the two ideas in Herman and Korsgaard, respectively; and while I address the first idea more fully in 'Sexual Solipsism', I here address the second, the invasive desire discussed by Korsgaard, with the modest and exploratory aim of considering what such a desire might look like, and how it might be considered solipsistic.

3. Invasive Sexual Love

The 'appetite for a human being' might be a desire which takes as its intentional object a person in his or her entirety: and Marcel Proust describes a desire that seems to have just this character. The hero has been watching Albertine, of whom he as yet knows nothing, and with whom he is in love; and he reflects on his desire.

For an instant.... I caught her smiling, sidelong glance, aimed from the centre of that inhuman world...an inaccessible, unknown world.... If she had seen me, what could I have represented to her? From the depths of what universe did she discern me? It would have been as difficult for me to say as it would be, when certain features of a neighbouring planet appear to us thanks to the telescope, to conclude from those that human beings live there, that they can see us, and to guess what ideas the sight of us can have aroused in them.

Albertine is an alien creature, as unknown as the inhabitant of another planet; but although the hero, Marcel, describes her world as an 'inhuman' one, he does not mean it:

If we thought that the eyes of such a girl were merely two glittering sequins of mica, we would not thirst to know her and to unite her life to ours. But we sense that what shines in those reflecting discs is not due solely to their material composition; it is, unknown to us, the dark shadows of the ideas that being cherishes about the people and places she knows. It is she, with her desires, her sympathies, her revulsions, her obscure and incessant will. I knew that I should never possess [her] if I did not possess also what was in her eyes. And it was consequently her whole life that filled me with desire; a painful desire because I felt it was impossible to fulfil, but exhilarating, like the burning thirst of a parched land—a thirst for a life which my soul, because it had never until now received one drop of it, would absorb all the more greedily, in long draughts. (I 851–2/793–5)[41]

He is gripped by a thirst for the life of another human being, which he wants to 'absorb . . . greedily, in long draughts'. The biblical poet likewise uses metaphors of thirst: the beloved is a fountain of gardens, a well of living waters, one calls to the other, 'Drink, yea drink abundantly, o beloved'. Metaphors of thirst and its quenching take on a more sinister cast here; Marcel's desire has a predatory, almost cannibalistic, quality. Could it be this quality of desire that appalled Kant, and led him to speak of it as an 'appetite for another human being'? Marcel's desire for Albertine is not simply a desire for her 'material composition' (quaint phrase), not simply a desire to gaze into her glittering eyes, not simply a desire to unite his body with hers, but a desire to annexe her being: to 'unite her life' to his (or to 'ours' as he in fact says, with a conspiratorial plural). It is a desire to

---

[41] Marcel Proust, *Remembrance of Things Past*, trans. C. K. Scott Moncrieff and Terence Kilmartin (London: Chatto and Windus, 1981); *A la recherche du temps perdu* (Paris: Gallimard, 1954). References are to the page numbers in the translation, followed by the page numbers in the Gallimard edition. The translations given are usually very close to Montcrieff/Kilmartin, although they have occasionally been adapted somewhat (as here).

know those dark shadows of her inner life, 'her desires, her sympathies, her revulsions, her obscure and incessant will'.

Marcel's desire, thus described, looks like a thirst for knowledge, and indeed knowledge of the mind of another human being. That makes it sound like a desire to break out of the 'prison' of the self of which Kant spoke—a desire for an 'intimate union' in which Albertine will satisfy him by 'revealing [her] secret thoughts and feelings'.[42] Kant said a certain kind of lover ignores the humanity of the one he desires: the fact that the one he desires is a human being is 'of no concern'.[43] That would be a false description of Marcel. The fact that she is a human being is precisely his concern: 'it is she, with her desires, her sympathies, her revulsions, her obscure and incessant will'. What Marcel desires is that she will reveal the 'dark shadows' of her inner life, perhaps (in heavier Kantian idiom) 'disclose completely all [her] dispositions and judgments', 'hide nothing', 'communicate [her] whole self'.[44] This is not a desire that reduces persons to things. This desire for knowledge of another person, for revelation of a self, is distinctively associated with friendship, according to Kant. So might it be a desire to *escape* from solipsism, through that sexual love which is also friendship?

To say this would be to ignore the predatory character of Marcel's desire. The arrangement he anticipates is, as Kant would say, 'one-sided'.[45] Kant contrasted the 'appetite for another human being' with that 'human love' which is 'good will, affection, promoting the happiness of others and finding joy in their happiness':[46] and whatever we are to say about Marcel's love, it is not the love that Kant described as 'human', nothing so ordinary as an 'intimate union of love and respect'. Instead there is the driving desire for Albertine, which is also a desire to know her, and a desire to possess her: 'I knew I should never possess her if I did not possess also what was in her eyes'. Knowledge of her thoughts, desires, and sympathies is described as possession of what makes her a human being, what makes her eyes something more than glittering sequins. Possessing this, he can possess her. He describes 'perfect knowledge' as 'the complete absorption of a person' (I 859/802). To know someone is to invade an alien territory, and annexe

---

[42] Kant, *Lectures on Ethics*, 202, *Doctrine of Virtue*, 143.   [43] Ibid., 163.   [44] Ibid., 206.
[45] Kant describes various kinds of sexual relationship as 'one-sided' in his chapter on the topic, ibid., 162–8.
[46] Ibid., 163.

it. To know someone is to absorb and assimilate, which is why eating and drinking provide the metaphors:

Whenever the image of women who are so different from us penetrates our minds...we know no rest until we have converted these aliens into something compatible with ourselves, the mind being in this respect endowed with the same kind of reaction and activity as our physical organism, which cannot abide the infusion of any foreign body into its veins without at once striving to digest and assimilate it. (I 859/802)

This is not a reductive desire to enjoy a person's body, as one might enjoy a fruit, but a desire to swallow up a human life. Inspired by an apparent yearning to escape the prison of the self, it is nonetheless quite as solipsistic in its way as a reductive sexual desire which ignores the person altogether. While in one way Marcel does not (yet) ignore the humanity of the one he desires, in another way he does. There is indeed a yearning to escape from epistemological solipsism—a yearning for knowledge of another mind, another human being with unknown but knowable desires, sympathies; so in this sense he does not ignore the humanity of the one he desires, indeed he treats a person *as a person*. But in another sense he does ignore the humanity of the one he desires, for he treats a person as a thing, in treating a person as something to be possessed. The desire to escape the epistemological solipsism coincides with a desire to create a moral solipsism—or rather, *is* that desire, if, as he thinks, the desire to know *is* a desire to possess and control. Because he thinks of knowledge in terms of possession and control, Marcel tries to make the woman he loves conform to a script.

I carried in my mind...the mental phantom—ever ready to become incarnate—of the woman who was going to fall in love with me, to take up her cues in the amorous comedy which I had had all written out in my mind from my earliest boyhood, and in which every attractive girl seemed to me to be equally desirous of playing, provided that she had also some of the physical qualifications required. In this play, whoever the new star might be whom I invited to create or to revive the leading part, the plot, the incidents, the lines themselves preserved an unalterable form. (I 951/890)

Marcel's desire, the desire to know and possess, is doomed, and the frustration is foreshadowed in that first description: 'It was...her whole life that filled me with desire; a painful desire because I felt it was impossible to fulfil.' Why is the desire impossible to fulfil? Marcel's answer is, in the end, the skeptic's answer: it is because knowledge of another person cannot be had. A different answer is that it is because something else cannot be had, namely knowledge of another person that is possession. The goal of possession is not identical to the goal of knowledge, as Marcel thinks, but inimical to it. To treat Albertine as a potential possession, a puppet whose actions are controlled and scripted, is to doom himself to ignorance of her: to aim for possession and control is to thwart the knowledge that was his goal in the first place. Marcel becomes an epistemological solipsist because he began as a moral solipsist of a certain kind, the kind described by Korsgaard, who desires a person as a person, but as a person to be possessed.

Moral solipsism could lead to the epistemological solipsism in more ways than one. If possession and control are in fact inimical to knowledge, to the extent that Marcel succeeds in possessing and controlling, succeeds in making Albertine play his scripted role, to that extent he fails to know her. That is a first way in which the moral solipsism might lead to the epistemological. Second, if one believes, as Marcel does, that the project of knowledge is a project of possession, then one believes failure to possess is failure to know—so to the extent that Marcel fails to possess and control, he believes that he fails to know, and does fail to know. Hope of knowledge is blocked by the attempt to control and possess, whether the attempt to control succeeds or fails.[47]

If there are connections of this sort between moral and epistemological solipsisms, one might expect an interdependence between moral and epistemological virtues. The morally good life depends on some epistemological virtues: Kant mentions the need for the 'sympathy' which yields that knowledge of other minds which is a condition of sharing others' goals. In the other direction, the epistemologically good life, in so far as it relates to knowledge of people, depends on some moral virtues. The person Kant describes will not reveal his 'secret thoughts and feelings' when he is

[47] Martha Nussbaum comments on Marcel's doomed aspirations, see 'Love's Knowledge', in *Love's Knowledge: Essays on Philosophy and Literature* (Oxford: Oxford University Press, 1990), 271. I have learned much from Nussbaum's essays on Proust, especially the final part of her discussion of Marcel in 'Love's Knowledge'; we share an interest in the connection between the moral and epistemic aspects of Marcel's solipsism. For a different discussion of love and the rejection of skepticism, see Bas van Fraassen, 'The Peculiar Effects of Love and Desire', *Perspectives on Self-Deception*, eds., Brian McLaughlin and Amélie Rorty (Berkeley: University of California Press, 1988).

'hemmed in and cautioned by fear': he will allow himself to be known only when there is 'complete confidence', the kind best achieved in friendship, that intimate union of love and respect.[48] Albertine will not 'reveal her secret thoughts and feelings' when she is 'hemmed in and cautioned' by Marcel's demands.

Believing his desire impossible to fulfil, Marcel abandons his 'thirst' for another life; the character of his love changes accordingly, and he turns inward. Proust gives us one of the most claustrophobic portraits in literature of what it might be like to be the solitary described by Kant, who has 'shut himself up in himself', who remains 'completely alone with his thoughts as in a prison'.[49] Love is no longer a relation between two human beings, and communication with Albertine becomes irrelevant.[50]

I knew now that I was in love with Albertine, but alas! I didn't trouble to let her know it . . . the declaration of my passion to the one I loved no longer seemed to be one of the vital and necessary stages of love. And love itself seemed no longer an external reality, but only a subjective pleasure. (I 987/925)

As love retreats from 'external reality', Albertine's very existence becomes irrelevant:

I realised in the end that . . . my love was not so much a love for her as a love in myself . . . not having the slightest real link with [her], not having the slightest support outside itself. (III 568/557)

When we are in love with a woman we simply project on to her a state of our own soul. (I 891/833)

It is only a clumsy and erroneous form of perception which places everything in the object, when really everything is in the mind . . . love places in a person who is loved what exists only in the person who loves. (III 950–1/912)

A love story is not about two people, but one: the individual is 'irremediably alone', and must find the courage to free himself from 'the *lie* which seeks to make us believe that we are *not* irremediably alone' (I 969/908, emphasis added). The individual lover must perform a kind of sense-datum reduction of any apparent relationship with another existing human being.

---

[48] Kant, *Doctrine of Virtue*, 140, 143.   [49] Ibid., 144.
[50] Nussbaum comments that love becomes 'a rather interesting relation with oneself', 'Love's Knowledge', 272.

Courage was needed...it meant above all to abandon one's dearest illusions, to stop believing in the objectivity of what one had oneself elaborated, and instead of soothing oneself for the hundredth time with the words, 'She was very sweet', to read through that, 'It gave me pleasure to kiss her'. (III 933/896)

Here we have an application of an old risk-avoiding philosophical principle: retreat from ontological commitment, retreat to sense-datum constructions. Electrons and photons become nothing but blips and flashes. Apples and desks and cats become nothing but rather different blips and flashes. It is not always easy, admittedly, to follow the principle where it leads. A cat, for example, seems hungry from time to time, but as Bertrand Russell uneasily remarked, a bundle of sense-data is as incapable of hunger as a triangle is of playing football; and 'the difficulty in the case of the cat is nothing compared to the difficulty in the case of human beings'. Still, whoever wishes to become a philosopher must learn not to be frightened of absurdities.[51] Do not say, 'she was kind'; say instead, 'it gave me pleasure to kiss her'. Do not say, 'she was cruel'; say instead, 'I was filled with grief'.

Solipsism provides the excuse for leaving the character of Albertine a hollow shell, since she need be no more than that for the lover, the narrator, or (let me be naive) the author:

A novelist might...be expressing...another truth if...he *refrained from giving any character to the beloved*.... Our curiosity about the woman we love overleaps the bounds of that woman's character, at which, even if we could stop, we probably never would.... Our intuitive radiography pierces them, and the images which it brings back, far from being those of a particular face, present rather the joyless universality of a skeleton.(I 955/895, emphasis added)

The driving thirst for a life, that 'intuitive radiography' which seeks to invade the depths of her being, defeats itself. The initial 'thirst for a life' did have something in common with the human love of which Kant spoke, a desire to reach beyond the self, whose satisfaction could perhaps have been found in that 'intimate union of love and respect' which is friendship, and which involves those mundane virtues of which Kant wrote, trust and sympathy, communication and respect.

---

[51] Russell's remarks about the cat, human beings, and absurdities, are from *The Problems of Philosophy*, first published in the Home University Library, 1912, reprinted (Oxford: Oxford University Press, 1974), 9, 11.

But Marcel's love has followed a different pattern. First there was the dim awareness of another life. She exists. Then: If she exists, I can know her. I want to know her. Then: If I can know her, I can possess her, since knowing is possessing. I want to possess her. Discovery: I cannot possess her. Marcel performs a gruesome *modus tollens*. I cannot possess her. Therefore I cannot know her. Therefore she does not exist. And he contents himself with this conclusion, instead of treating it as the *reductio* of his strategy, his equation of knowledge and possession.

The strategy applied to Albertine is extended to friends.

The sign of the unreality of others is shown in the impossibility of their satisfying us . . . friendship is a simulation, since . . . the artist who gives up an hour of work for an hour's chat with a friend knows that he sacrifices a reality for something that doesn't exist (friends being friends only in that sweet folly which we lend to ourselves throughout the course of life, but which we know deep down to be the delusion of a fool who chats with chairs and tables, believing them to be alive). (III 909/875)

Albertine fails to satisfy him; so she does not exist. His friends fail to satisfy him; so they do not exist. So too for every other human being:

It is the misfortune of beings to be nothing more for us than useful showcases for the collections of one's own mind. (III 568/558)

Chairs, tables, display cases—not people, but things. Marcel lives in a world that is crowded with people, but his beliefs are solipsistic. He interacts with people, treating them as things. Solipsism is false, but he believes it true. Is he the metaphysical solipsist, who believes he is the only person? The epistemological solipsist, who believes he is the only knowable person? The moral solipsist, who believes he is the only person who matters? He is (at least sometimes) each of these.

This web of solipsisms shifts over time. Marcel becomes an epistemological solipsist because he was a moral solipsist in the first place: one whose attitude to other human beings was predatory, one who matched Korsgaard's description, one who desired a human being as a person ('she, with her desires and sympathies . . . '), but as a person to be possessed. The project of knowing others, understood in terms of possession and control, undermines the possibility of knowledge that was its goal. Then arrives the metaphysical solipsism: Marcel infers that he is irremediably alone, his friends have no more life than a chair, or a table, the only mind is his own.

Note however that other beings have their *uses*. Other beings are *useful showcases* for the collectables of one's mind. Albertine herself has her uses. She begins as an unknown person, a human territory, ripe for invasion; she ends up as a useful tool.

These painful dilemmas which love is constantly putting our way teach us and *reveal to us, layer after layer, the material of which we are made . . . .* By making me waste my time, by causing me grief, Albertine had perhaps been more useful to me, even from a literary point of view, than a secretary who would have sorted my papers. (III 947/909, emphasis added)

The important thing is not the worth of the woman but the profundity of the state; the emotions which a perfectly ordinary girl arouses in us *can enable us to bring to the surface of our consciousness some of the innermost parts of our being,* more personal, more remote, more quintessential than any. (I 891–2/833, emphasis added)

Albertine is more useful to Marcel than a secretary, since she helps him to know the one thing he can know about, the one thing worth knowing about, his own dear self, in its innermost parts, the material of which he himself is made.

Here we have a final twist in the knot of solipsisms, ending as we began with a moral solipsism, but of a different kind. Instead of being a project of control premised on the possibility of knowledge, it is a project of control premised on the impossibility of knowledge: this moral solipsism stems from the metaphysical solipsism which preceded it. If I am the only person, then of course I am the only person who matters. And it is no longer the moral solipsism Korsgaard described, which desires a person *qua* person to be possessed. Albertine is no longer desired as a person *qua* person, a human being with discoverable desires, sympathies, and will, but a useful tool. Desire, to the extent it exists, is no longer invasive in character but reductive. Albertine, like any other being, has the status of a table, a chair, a showcase. This moral solipsism is reductive—but not quite in the way that Herman describes either, in her interpretation of Kant. Marcel's attitude is not quite—not even—the attitude of one who reductively desires someone as a body that is a pleasure-giving sexual automaton. Albertine is reduced not merely to her own physical properties, but to Marcel's own psychological properties: Albertine is a showcase, not for her mind, not even for her body, but for his mind.

A showcase can be very useful, if one's mind is a splendid treasure trove, and Albertine unwittingly helps him to mine the treasure. Marcel fails to know Albertine, fails to possess her in the way he desires, and she, as an independent human being, is no longer an item in his ontology. But she nonetheless helps him obey the Socratic injunction, know thyself. She does not help as a friend helps, since she cannot provide the opportunity for communication and correction of his judgments, which would take human interaction, faith in the perception of another person, and a trust rather foreign to Marcel. Albertine helps in a different way, by providing him with new experiences. She produces in him experiences he would never otherwise have encountered—not (primarily) sexual experiences, but experiences of grief and pain. That is how she helps reveal to him the material of which he is made.

It would all sound oddly familiar to the lonely thinker of Descartes's Second Meditation. My awareness of my own self is 'much truer and more certain' than my awareness of Albertine. If I were to judge that she exists from the fact that I experience profound emotion, clearly this same fact 'would entail much more evidently that I myself also exist'.[52] If I were to judge that, beneath the hat and coat, there exists another thinking being, that would help establish that *I* exist, as a thinking being—but not that she is more than an automaton. Every consideration which contributes to my experience of Albertine cannot but establish even more effectively the nature of my own mind. The more I seem to learn about anything else, the more I learn about me. The more I seem to learn about any*one* else, the more I learn about me. Marcel is a solipsist who has abandoned his stove heated room for something that he calls love, but it leaves him alone with his thoughts, 'as in a prison'.

The connection between a metaphysical solipsism and a reductive moral solipsism is explicit in Marcel's thinking: a passage partly quoted above continues:

I had guessed long ago . . . and had verified since, that when we are in love with a woman we simply project on to her a state of our own soul; con- sequently the important thing is not the worth of the woman but the profundity

---

[52] Descartes, *Meditations*. At this stage the meditator is certain only of his own existence, and considers hypothetically: if he were to take his sense experience to indicate the existence of

of the state; the emotions which a perfectly ordinary girl arouses in us can enable us to bring to the surface of our consciousness some of the innermost parts of our being, more personal, more remote, more quintessential than any. (I 891–2/833)

Love is an experience that happens to be caused by some being, but has 'not the slightest real link with that person': it does not quench one's thirst for knowledge of another life, it is not a love 'for her' but rather a love 'in me'. Any property that we mistakenly attribute to her is really 'a state of our own soul'. 'Consequently', says Marcel, 'the important thing is not the worth of the woman but the profundity of the state'. Albertine is not a person, who is kind or cruel, but that unknown something which causes pleasure or anguish. One entertains futile hypotheses about a human reality behind this appearance, shadows of the ideas she cherishes about people and places she knows, shadows of desire, sympathy, revulsion, obscure and incessant will; but such reality is unknowable, irrelevant to practical life. 'Consequently', the important thing is not the worth of the woman; if Albertine has no more inner life than a piece of furniture, a chair, a table, a display case, she has only the value of a tool. Then indeed she proves useful, as an engine for producing those feelings of love and grief so interesting to the narcissist's pursuit of self-knowledge.

Kant too thinks relations with others can help one to obey that Socratic injunction: know thyself. Friends can help us obey it, and lovers, in so far as love and friendship share a common moral core. Proust apparently agrees: love can help one to obey that injunction, help 'reveal to us, layer after layer, the material of which we are made'. What role does the lover play, though? The epistemological benefits of which Kant spoke, for example of communication and correction of our judgements, are little in evidence. For Kant, the human need for communication, the need to 'clothe our concepts in words', is met by a friend or a lover 'to whom we can communicate our whole self'. Marcel's lover cannot have this role. The need to clothe one's concepts in words, the need to communicate one's whole self, is not met in love, but in solitary writing. Love provides knowledge of oneself, not through communication, interpretation, and

other things (which he at this stage does not), that would entail much more evidently his own existence.

correction, but by providing a sort of experimental test. Proust draws a chemical analogy to describe the moment of self-knowledge provoked by Marcel's discovery of Albertine's departure.[53]

> Our intelligence, however lucid, cannot perceive the elements that compose it and remain unsuspected so long as, from the volatile state in which they generally exist, a phenomenon capable of isolating them has not subjected them to the first stages of solidification. I had been mistaken in thinking that I could see clearly into my own heart. But this knowledge, which the shrewdest perceptions of the mind would not have given me, had now been brought to me, hard, glittering, strange, like a crystallised salt, by the abrupt reaction of pain. (III 426/420)

Albertine has usefully helped Marcel learn something about himself; and she helped, not through her communicative and corrective presence, but through her absence.

On Marcel's way of thinking, love happens to be occasioned by some pleasure-causing, anguish-causing being: love brings suffering, and suffering is a catalyst for self-knowledge. That is how a lover can help one know oneself. This is, to put it mildly, a different conception of what it is to be helped by someone else to learn about oneself. Suppose I do not know the answer to some question about myself: suppose I do not know, for example, whether I am brave. There are two ways a friend could help me find out: he could help me reflect intelligently on the character of my past actions, argue with me, alert me to revealing details I may otherwise miss; or he could push me off a smallish cliff. With the former method, he offers communication, interpretation, correction; with the latter, he gives me an experiment. In both ways I am helped by someone else to learn about myself: but with the former method, it must be *someone* else; with the latter, it could as easily be *something* else (a gust of wind, a loose shoe-lace) that provides the test of courage.[54]

Solipsistic love provides no communication, but only the experiment, a nasty fall, and then not even a shoulder to cry on. The role of the other

---

[53] Nussbaum rightly remarks that the role of the lover is almost incidental, and discusses this moment of 'discovery' in detail in 'Fictions of the Soul', and 'Love's Knowledge' (where the minimal role played by Albertine is described at p. 271).

[54] For an interesting discussion of the role of interpretation in friendship, although not (to me) wholly convincing, see Dean Cocking and Jeanette Kennett, 'Friendship and the Self', *Ethics* 108 (1998), 502–27, where it is argued that reciprocal interpretation, and a reciprocal willingness to be interpreted, are essential features of friendship.

is better played by an absent ex-lover than by a lover or friend. Ordinary love, on the other hand, might well provide both routes to self-knowledge. Perhaps love can be a bit like falling off a cliff. Perhaps it does provide a new experimental setting. Perhaps unexpected aspects of one's self do come to light, and one discovers new layers of the material of which one is made. In addition, though, there is something else. The apparent self-discovery generated by the experiment has the chance to be tested and revised in the fires of communication and mutual interpretation, if a lover can also be a friend 'whom we know to be frank and loving', who will 'help us to correct our judgment', from whom 'we can and need hide nothing'.[55]

But why, in any case, assume the primacy of that first Socratic injunction? *Self*-discovery is hardly the point. Why go back to the prison? Why go back, when the gate is open to a garden, an orchard of fruits where things are growing (calamus and cinnamon, myrrh and aloe), where there are cool breezes, the sound of water—and someone seems to be calling.

[55] Kant, *Lectures on Ethics*, 206.

Bibliography

Alcoff, Linda Martin, 'Is the Feminist Critique of Reason Rational?', Feminist Perspectives on Language, Knowledge and Reality, ed., Sally Haslanger, *Philosophical Topics* 23 (1995), 1–26.

_____ and Elizabeth Potter, eds., *Feminist Epistemologies* (London and New York: Routledge, 1993).

Anscombe, G. E. M., *Intention* (Oxford: Blackwell, 1957).

Antony, Louise M. and Charlotte Witt, eds., *A Mind of One's Own: Feminist Essays on Reason and Objectivity* (Boulder Co.: Westview Press, 1993).

_____ 'Sisters, Please, I'd Rather Do it Myself: A Defense of Individualism in Feminist Epistemology', in Feminist Perspectives on Language, Knowledge, and Reality, ed., Sally Haslanger, *Philosophical Topics* 23 (1995), 59–94.

Aristotle, *Nichomachean Ethics*, trans. David Ross (New York: Oxford University Press, 1998).

Assiter, Alison, 'Autonomy and Pornography', in *Feminist Perspectives in Philosophy*, eds., Morwenna Griffiths and Margaret Whitford (London: Macmillan, 1988).

_____ *Pornography, Feminism and the Individual* (London: Pluto Press, 1989).

Astell, Mary, *Reflections Upon Marriage* (London: John Nutt, 1700), reprinted in *Astell's Political Writings*, ed., Patricia Springborg (Cambridge: Cambridge University Press, 1996).

Atherton, Margaret, 'Cartesian Reason and Gendered Reason', *A Mind of One's Own: Feminist Essays on Reason and Objectivity*, eds., Louise M. Antony and Charlotte Witt (Boulder Co.: Westview Press, 1993).

Austin, J. L., *How to Do Things with Words* (Oxford: Oxford University Press, 1962).

Bahadur, Mahomed Yusoof Khan, *Mahomedan Law,* vol. iii (Calcutta: Thacker, Spink & Co., 1898).

Baier, Annette, 'Hume: The Reflective Women's Epistemologist?', in *A Mind of One's Own: Feminist Essays on Reason and Objectivity*, eds., Louise M. Antony and Charlotte Witt (Boulder, Co.: Westview Press, 1993).

Barron, Michael and Michael S. Kimmel, 'Sexual Violence in Three Pornographic Media: Toward a Sociological Explanation', *The Journal of Sex Research* 37 (2000), 161–8.

Bauer, Nancy, 'How To Do Things With Pornography', in *Reading Cavell*, eds., Sanford Shieh and Alice Crary (New York: Routledge, 2006), 68–97.

_____ *How to Do Things With Pornography*, forthcoming.

Baumeister, Roy, *Evil: Inside Human Violence and Cruelty* (New York, NY: W. H. Freeman, 1997).

de Beauvoir, Simone, *The Second Sex*, trans. H. M. Parshley (1949; reprint, London: Pan, 1988).

Bianchi, Claudia, 'Indexicals, Speech Acts and Pornography', *Analysis* (forthcoming).

Bird, Alexander, 'Illocutionary Silencing', *Pacific Philosophical Quarterly* 83 (2002), 1–15.

Blackburn, Simon, *Lust* (New York, NY: Oxford University Press, 2004).

Braddon-Mitchell, David, with Caroline West, 'What is Free Speech?', *The Journal of Political Philosophy* 12 (2004), 437–460.

Brison, Susan, 'The Autonomy Defense of Free Speech', *Ethics* 108 (1998), 312–39.

Broad, Jacqueline, *Women Philosophers of the Seventeenth Century* (Cambridge: Cambridge University Press, 2003).

Bryant, J. and D. Zillman, 'Pornography and Sexual Callousness, and the Trivialization of Rape', *Journal of Communication* 32 (December 1982), 10–21.

Burgess, Anthony, 'What is Pornography?', in *Perspectives on Pornography,* ed., Douglas A. Hughes (New York: St. Martin's, 1970).

Burgess, A. W., ed., *Rape and Sexual Assault*, vol ii (New York: Garland Publishing Company, 1988).

Burkhart, Barry R. and Annette L. Stanton, 'Sexual Aggression in Acquaintance Relationships', in *Violence in Intimate Relationships*, ed., Gordon Russell (New York: PMA Pub. Corp., 1988).

Burstyn, Varda, ed., *Women Against Censorship* (Vancouver: Douglas and MacIntyre, 1985).

Butler, Judith, *Bodies that Matter* (New York: Routledge, 1993).

—— *Excitable Speech: A Politics of the Performative* (New York and London: Routledge, 1997).

—— *Gender Trouble* (New York: Routledge, 1999).

Caputi, J., *The Age of Sex Crime* (London: The Women's Press Ltd., 1987).

Caruso, David B., 'Internet Fuels Child Porn Trafficking', *Associated Press*, 15 January 2005.

Chester, Gail and Julienne Dickey, eds., *Feminism and Censorship: The Current Debate* (Bridport: Prism Press, 1988).

Cocking, Dean, and Jeanette Kennett, 'Friendship and the Self', *Ethics* 108 (1998), 502–27.

Code, Lorraine, *What Can She Know? Feminist Theory and the Construction of Knowledge* (Ithaca, NY: Cornell University Press, 1991).

—— 'Taking Subjectivity into Account', *Feminist Epistemologies*, eds., Linda Alcoff and Elizabeth Potter, (London and New York: Routledge, 1993), 15–47.

Coggrave, Frank, 'Bugwatch: The Perils of Peer-to-Peer', VNU Business Publications, 31 March 2004.

Cohen, Joshua, 'Freedom of Expression', *Philosophy and Public Affairs* 22 (1993),
207–263.

Cornell, Drucilla, ed., *Feminism and Pornography* (Oxford: Oxford University
Press, 2000).

——'Pornography's Temptation', in Cornell, ed., *Feminism and Pornography*,
(Oxford: Oxford University Press, 2000), 551–67.

Craig, Edward, *Knowledge and the State of Nature: An Essay in Conceptual Synthesis*
(Oxford: Clarendon Press, 1990).

Criminal Justice and Immigration Bill, UK House of Commons, Session 2007–8,
vol. i Part 5 http://services.parliament.uk/bills/2007–08/criminaljusticeand
immigration.html, consulted 26 March 2008.

Curley, E. M., 'Excusing Rape', *Philosophy and Public Affairs* 5 (1976), 325–60.

Currie, Gregory, 'The Moral Psychology of Fiction', *Australasian Journal of Philosophy* 73 (1995), 250–9.

Dalmeyer, Vrinda and Linda Alcoff, 'Are "Old Wives' Tales" Justified?', *Feminist
Epistemologies*, eds., Linda Alcoff and Elizabeth Potter (London and New York:
Routledge, 1993), 217–44.

Davidson, Donald, 'Communication and Convention' (1982) in *Inquiries into Truth
and Interpretation* (Oxford: Oxford University Press, 1984).

——'Deception and Division', in *Actions and Events: Perspectives on the Philosophy
of Donald Davidson,* eds., E. LePore and B. McLaughlin (Oxford: Blackwell
1988).

Descartes, René, *Meditations on First Philosophy* (1641), trans. John Cottingham,
(Cambridge: Cambridge University Press, 1986).

Dickens, Charles, *Hard Times* (1854), ed. Paul Schlicke (Oxford: Oxford University
Press, 1998)

Donnerstein, Edward, Daniel Linz, and Steven Penrod, *The Question of Pornography:
Research Findings and Policy Implications* (New York: Free Press; London: Collier
Macmillan, 1987).

Dworkin, Andrea, *Woman Hating* (New York: E.P. Dutton, 1974).

——*Pornography: Men Possessing Women* (London: The Women's Press, 1981).

——*Intercourse* (New York: Free Press, 1987).

——*Mercy* (London: Secker and Warburg, 1990).

Dworkin, Ronald, *Taking Rights Seriously* (Cambridge, Mass.: Harvard University
Press, 1977).

——*A Matter of Principle* (Cambridge, Mass.: Harvard University Press, 1985).

——'Do We Have a Right to Pornography?', *Oxford Journal of Legal Studies* 1
(1981), 177–212; reprinted in *A Matter of Principle*.

Dworkin, Ronald, 'Reverse Discrimination', in *Taking Rights Seriously*.

———— 'Liberalism', in *A Matter of Principle*.

———— 'What is Equality? Part 3: The Place of Liberty', *Iowa Law Review* 73 (1987).

———— 'Liberty and Pornography', *The New York Review of Books*, 15 August 1991, 12–15; published as 'Two Concepts of Liberty' in *Isaiah Berlin: A Celebration*, eds., Edna and Avishai Margalit (Chicago: University of Chicago Press, 1991), 100–9 and (London: Hogarth Press, 1991); reprinted as 'Liberty and Pornography' in *The Problem of Pornography*, ed., Susan Dwyer (Belmont, CA: Wadsworth, 1995), 113–21.

———— 'Women and Pornography', in *The New York Review of Books*, 21 October 1993.

———— 'A New Map of Censorship', *Index on Censorship* 1/2 (1994).

Dwyer, Susan, ed., *The Problem of Pornography* (Belmont, CA: Wadsworth, 1995).

———— 'Enter Here—At Your Own Risk: The Moral Dangers of Cyberporn', in Robert Cavalier, ed., *The Impact of the Internet on Our Moral Lives* (Albany, NY: SUNY Press, 2005), 69–94.

———— 'Pornography', in *The Routledge Companion to Philosophy and Film*, eds., Paisley Livingstone and Carl Plantinga (London and New York: Routledge, forthcoming.)

Duggan, L., N. Hunter, and C. Vance, 'False Promises: Feminist Anti-Pornography Legislation', in *Caught Looking: Feminism, Pornography, and Censorship*, ed., Feminist Anti-Censorship Taskforce (Seattle: the Real Comet Press, 1986).

Dyzenhaus, David, 'John Stuart Mill and the Harm of Pornography', *Ethics* 102 (1992), 534–51.

Einsiedel, Edna F., 'Social and Behavioural Science Research Analysis', *Report of the Attorney General's Commission on Pornography*, vol. i (Washington, D.C.: United States Government Printing Office, 1986), 901–1033.

Evans, Gareth, *The Varieties of Reference*, ed., J. McDowell (Oxford: Clarendon Press, 1982).

Feinberg, Joel, *Offense to Others* (New York, NY: Oxford University Press, 1985).

Fiss, Owen, 'Freedom and Feminism', *Georgetown Law Review* 80 (1992), 2041–62.

———— *The Irony of Free Speech* (Cambridge, Mass.: Harvard University Press, 1996).

Flax, Jane, 'Political Philosophy and the Patriarchal Unconscious', in *Discovering Reality*, eds., Sandra Harding and Merrill Hintikka (Dordrecht: Reidel, 1983).

van Fraassen, Bas, 'The Peculiar Effects of Love and Desire', in *Perspectives on Self-Deception*, eds., Brian McLaughlin and Amélie Rorty (Berkeley: University of California Press, 1988).

Fricker, Miranda, 'Rational Authority and Social Power: Towards a Truly Social Epistemology', *Proceedings of the Aristotelian Society* (1998), 159–77.

—— *Epistemic Injustice: Power and the Ethics of Knowing* (New York: Oxford University Press, 2007).

Friedan, Betty, *The Feminine Mystique* (New York: Dell, 1964).

Friedman, Marilyn, *Autonomy, Gender, Politics* (Oxford: Oxford University Press, 2003).

Frye, Marilyn, *The Politics of Reality: Essays in Feminist Theory* (Freedom, CA: The Crossing Press, 1983).

—— 'The Possibility of Feminist Theory', reprinted in *Women, Knowledge and Reality*, eds., Ann Garry and Marilyn Pearsall (London and New York: Routledge, 1996), 34–47.

Gettier, Edmund, 'Is Knowledge Justified True Belief?', *Analysis* 23 (1963), 121–3.

Gilbert, Harriet, 'So Long as It's Not Sex and Violence', in Lynne Segal and Mary MacIntosh, eds., *Sex Exposed: Sexuality and the Pornography Debate* (New Brunswick, NJ: Rutgers University Press, 1993).

Gilligan, Carol, 'In a Different Voice: Women's Conceptions of Self and of Morality', in *The Future of Difference*, eds., Hester Eisenstein and Alice Jardine (Boston: G. K. Hall and Co., 1980), 247–317.

—— *In a Different Voice* (Cambridge, Mass.: Harvard University Press, 1982).

Goodchilds, Jacqueline D., Gail Zellman, Paula B. Johnson, and Roseann Giarusso, 'Adolescents and their Perceptions of Sexual Interactions', in A. W. Burgess, ed., *Rape and Sexual Assault*, vol. ii. (New York, NY: Garland Publishing Company, 1988).

Green, Karen, *The Woman of Reason: Feminism, Humanism and Political Thought* (Cambridge: Polity Press, 1995).

Green, Leslie, 'Pornographizing, Subordinating, Silencing', in *Censorship and Silencing: Practices of Cultural Regulation*, ed. Robert Post (Los Angeles: Getty Research Institute for the History of Art and the Humanities, 1998), 285–311.

—— *The Authority of the State* (Oxford: Oxford University Press, 1989).

—— 'Pornographies', *Journal of Political Philosophy* 8 (2000), 27–52.

Greendlinger, Virginia and Donn Byrne, 'Coercive Sexual Fantasies of College Man as Predictors of Self-Reported Likelihood to Rape and Overt Sexual Aggression', *Journal of Sex Research* 23 (1987), 1–11.

Griffiths, Morwenna and Margaret Whitford, eds., *Feminist Perspectives in Philosophy* (London: Macmillan, 1988).

Grosz, Elizabeth, *Sexual Subversions: Three French Feminists* (St. Leonards, NSW: Allen and Unwin, 1989).

Habermas, Jürgen, *The Theory of Communicative Action*, trans. Thomas McCarthy (Boston: Beacon Press, 1984).

Hacking, Ian, 'The Looping Effects of Human Kinds', in *Causal Cognition: A Multidisciplinary Approach*, eds., D. Sperber, D. Premack, and A. J. Premack (Oxford: Clarendon Press, 1994).

Hamilton, William, *Lectures on Metaphysics and Logic*, eds., H. L. Mansel and J. Veitch, vol. ii (Edinburgh and London: Blackwood, 1859).

Harding, Sandra, 'Rethinking Standpoint Epistemology: What is "Strong Objectivity"?', in L. Alcoff and E. Potter, eds., *Feminist Epistemologies* (London and New York: Routledge, 1993).

____ and Merrill Hintikka, eds., *Discovering Reality: Feminist Perspectives on Epistemology, Metaphysics, Methodology, and Philosophy of Science* (Dordrecht: Reidel, 1983).

Hartsock, Nancy, 'The Feminist Standpoint Theory: Developing the Ground for a Specifically Feminist Historical Materialism', in Sandra Harding and Meryl Hintikka, eds., *Discovering Reality* (Dordrecht: Reidel, 1983).

Haslanger, Sally, 'On Being Objective and Being Objectified', in *A Mind of One's Own,* eds., Louise Antony and Charlotte Witt (Boulder Co.: Westview Press, 1993), 85–125.

____ 'Ontology and Social Construction', Feminist Perspectives on Language, Knowledge and Reality, ed., Haslanger, *Philosophical Topics* 23 (1995), 95–125.

____ 'Gender, Race: (What) Are They? (What) Do We Want Them To Be?', *Noûs* 34 (2000), 31–55.

____ 'Feminism in Metaphysics: Negotiating the Natural', in *Cambridge Companion to Feminism in Philosophy*, eds., Miranda Fricker and Jennifer Hornsby (Cambridge: Cambridge University Press, 2000), 107–126.

Hawkins, Gordon and Franklin Zimring, *Pornography in a Free Society* (Cambridge and New York: Cambridge University Press, 1988).

Heilbrun Jr., Alfred B. and Maura P. Loftus, 'The Role of Sadism and Peer Pressure in the Sexual Aggression of Male College Students', *Journal of Sex Research* 22 (1986), 320–32.

Henley, Jon, 'Pornography Forms French Children's Views on Sex', *Guardian*, 25 May, 2002.

Herman, Barbara, 'On the Value of Acting from the Motive of Duty', *Philosophical Review* 90 (1981), 359–82.

____ 'Could It Be Worth Thinking about Kant on Sex and Marriage?' in *A Mind of One's Own,* eds., Louise Antony and Charlotte Witt (Boulder, Co.: Westview Press, 1993).

Hodkinson, Keith, *Muslim Family Law: A Source Book* (London: Croom Helm, 1984).

Holton, Richard, and Rae Langton, 'Empathy in Animal Ethics', in *Singer and his Critics*, ed., Dale Jamieson (Oxford: Basil Blackwell, 1998).

Hornsby, Jennifer, 'Philosophers and Feminists on Language Use', *Cogito* (Autumn 1988), 13–15.

—— 'Speech Acts and Pornography', *Women's Philosophy Review* 10 (1993), 38–45, reprinted in *The Problem of Pornography*, ed., Susan Dwyer (Belmont, CA: Wadsworth 1995).

—— 'Illocution and its Significance', in *Foundations of Speech Act Theory*, ed., S. L. Tsohatzidis (London: Routledge, 1994).

—— 'Disempowered Speech', in Feminist Perspectives on Language, Knowledge and Reality, ed., Sally Haslanger, *Philosophical Topics* 23 (1995), 127–47.

—— and Rae Langton, 'Free Speech and Illocution', *Legal Theory* 4 (1998), 21–37.

Humberstone, Lloyd, 'Wanting, Getting, Having', *Philosophical Papers* 29 (1990), 99–118.

—— 'Direction of Fit', *Mind* 101 (1992), 59–83.

Hume, David, *The Natural History of Religion* (1757), ed., H. E. Root (London: Adam & Charles Black, 1956).

—— *Enquiries Concerning Human Understanding and Concerning the Principles of Morals* (1777), ed., L. A. Selby-Bigge, 3rd edn. revised P. H. Nidditch (Oxford: Clarendon Press, 1975).

—— *A Treatise of Human Nature* (1739–40), ed., L. A. Selby-Bigge, revised P. H. Nidditch (Oxford: Clarendon Press, 1978).

—— *Dialogues and Natural History of Religion*, ed. J. C. A. Gaskin (Oxford: Oxford University Press, 1993).

—— 'On the Immortality of the Soul', from *Essays Moral and Political* (1741–2), reprinted in *David Hume: Selected Essays*, eds., Stephen Copley and Andrew Edgar (Oxford: Oxford University Press, 1998).

Hursthouse, Rosalind, 'Arational Actions', *Journal of Philosophy* 88 (1991), 57–68.

Hyman, John and Helen Steward, eds., *Agency and Action* (Cambridge: Cambridge University Press, 2004).

Irigaray, Luce, *Speculum of the Other Woman*, trans. Gillian Gill (Ithaca: Cornell University Press, 1985).

—— *I love to you* (London: Routledge, 1995).

Itzin, Catherine, ed., *Pornography: Women, Violence, and Civil Liberties* (Oxford: Oxford University Press, 1992).

—— 'Sex and Censorship: The Political Implications', in Gail Chester and Julienne Dickey, eds., *Feminism and Censorship: The Current Debate* (Bridport: Prism Press, 1988).

Jacobson, Daniel, 'Freedom of Speech Acts? A Response to Langton', *Philosophy and Public Affairs* 24 (1995), 64–79.

—— 'Speech and Action: Replies to Hornsby and Langton', *Legal Theory* 7 (2001), 179–201.

Jaggar, Alison, *Feminist Politics and Human Nature* (Totowa, N.J.: Rowman and Allanheld, 1983).

James, William, *The Will to Believe and Other Essays in Popular Philosophy* (London: Longman's, Green and Co., 1891).

—— *The Will to Believe and Other Essays in Popular Philosophy* (Norwood, Mass.: Plimpton Press, 1896).

Johnston, Mark, 'Self Deception and the Nature of Mind', *Perspectives on Self-Deception*, eds., Brian McLaughlin and Amelie Oksenberg Rorty (Berkeley, CA: University of California Press, 1988).

Kail, Peter, 'Projection and Necessity in Hume', *European Journal of Philosophy* 9 (2001), 24–54.

—— *Projection and Realism in Hume's Philosophy* (New York: Oxford University Press, 2007).

Kant, Immanuel, *Gesammelte Schriften*, ed., Königlich Preussischen Akademie der Wissenschaften (Berlin and Leipzig: de Gruyter, 1922).

—— *The Cambridge Edition of the Works of Immanuel Kant in Translation*, eds., Henry Allison, Reinhard Brandt, Paul Guyer, Ralf Meerbote, Charles D. Parsons, Hoke Robinson, J. B. Schneewind, Allen W. Wood (Cambridge: Cambridge University Press, 1997–2007).

—— *Philosophical Correspondence,* trans. Arnulf Zweig (Chicago: University of Chicago Press, 1967).

—— *Immanuel Kant: Correspondence* (Cambridge: Cambridge University Press, 1999).

—— *Lectures on Ethics* (1775–1780) trans. Louis Infield (London: Methuen, 1930), from the notes made by Brauer, Kutzner and Mrongovius, ed., Paul Mentzer.

—— *Lectures on Ethics*, trans. Peter Heath, eds., J. B. Schneewind and Heath (Cambridge: Cambridge University Press, 1997).

—— *Critique of Pure Reason* (1781/1787), trans. Norman Kemp Smith (London and Basingstoke: Macmillan, 1980).

—— *Groundwork of the Metaphysic of Morals* (1785), trans. H. J. Paton (New York: Harper and Row, 1964).

—— *Groundwork of the Metaphysics of Morals* (1785), trans. Mary Gregor (Cambridge: Cambridge University Press, 1997).

—— *Critique of Practical Reason* (1788), trans. L. W. Beck (New York: Macmillan, 1956).

_____ *Doctrine of Virtue* (1797) trans. Mary Gregor (New York: Harper and Row, 1964).

_____ *The Metaphysics of Morals* (1797) trans. Mary Gregor (Cambridge: Cambridge University Press, 1996).

Kennedy, Randall, *Nigger: The Strange Career of a Troublesome Word* (New York, NY: Pantheon Books, 2002).

Kermode, Mark, and Russell Levin, *The Real Linda Lovelace* (film documentary), first broadcast on Channel 4 in the UK, 26 September 2002.

Kittay, Eva Feder, 'The Greater Danger—Pornography, Social Science, and Women's Rights: Reply to Brannigan and Goldenberg', *Social Epistemology* 2 (1988), 117–33.

Koch, Howard, *The Panic Broadcast: Portrait of an Event* (Boston, Mass.: Little, Brown and Co., 1970).

Korsgaard, Christine, 'The Right to Lie: Kant on Dealing with Evil', *Philosophy and Public Affairs* 15 (1986), 325–49.

_____ 'Creating the Kingdom of Ends: Responsibility and Reciprocity in Personal Relations', *Philosophical Perspectives 6: Ethics* (1992), 305–32.

_____ *Creating the Kingdom of Ends* (Cambridge: Cambridge University Press, 1996).

Langton, Rae, 'Whose right? Ronald Dworkin, Women, and Pornographers', *Philosophy and Public Affairs* 19 (1990), 311–59.

_____ 'Beyond a Pragmatic Critique of Reason', *Australasian Journal of Philosophy* 71 (1993), 364–84.

_____ 'Speech Acts and Unspeakable Acts', *Philosophy and Public Affairs* 22 (1993), 305–30.

_____ 'Sexual Solipsism', in Feminist Perspectives on Language, Knowledge and Reality, ed., Sally Haslanger, *Philosophical Topics* 23 (1995), 181–219.

_____ 'Love and Solipsism', in *Love Analyzed,* ed., Roger Lamb (Boulder, Co.: Westview Press, 1997), 123–52.

_____ 'Free Speech and Illocution', co-authored with Jennifer Hornsby, *Legal Theory* 4 (1998), 21–37.

_____ 'Subordination, Silence and Pornography's Authority', in *Censorship and Silencing: Practices of Cultural Regulation*, ed., Robert Post (Los Angeles, Cal.: Getty Research Institute, 1998), 261–83.

_____ 'Scorekeeping in a Pornographic Language Game', co-authored with Caroline West, *Australasian Journal of Philosophy* 77 (1999), 303–19.

_____ 'Pornography: A Liberal's Unfinished Business', *Canadian Journal of Law and Jurisprudence* 12 (1999), 109–33.

_____ 'Feminism in Epistemology: Exclusion and Objectification', in *Cambridge Companion to Feminism in Philosophy,* eds., Jennifer Hornsby and Miranda Fricker (Cambridge: Cambridge University Press, 2000), 127–45.

Langton, Rae, 'Intention as Faith', in *Agency and Action*, eds., John Hyman and Helen Steward (Cambridge: Cambridge University Press, 2004), 243–57.

—— 'Projection and Objectification' in *The Future for Philosophy*, ed., Brian Leiter (Oxford: Oxford University Press, 2004), 285–303.

—— 'Feminism in Philosophy', in *The Oxford Handbook of Contemporary Analytic Philosophy*, eds., Frank Jackson and Michael Smith (Oxford: Oxford University Press 2005), 231–57.

—— 'Feminism in Philosophy', in Frank Jackson and Michael Smith, eds., *The Oxford Handbook of Contemporary Philosophy* (Oxford: Oxford University Press, 2005).

—— 'Disenfranchised Silence', in *Common Minds: Themes from the Philosophy of Philip Pettit*, eds., Geoffrey Brennan, Robert Goodin, Frank Jackson and Michael Smith (Oxford: Oxford University Press, 2006), 199–213.

—— 'Objective and Unconditioned Value', *Philosophical Review* 116 (2007), 157–85.

Lederer, Laura, ed., *Take Back the Night: Women on Pornography* (New York: William Morrow, 1980).

le Doeuff, Michèle, *Hipparchia's Choice*, trans. Trista Selous (Oxford: Blackwell, 1990).

—— *What Can She Know?*, trans. Kathryn Hamer and Lorraine Code (New York: Routledge, 2003).

Lewis, David, 'Truth in Fiction', *Philosophical Papers*, vol. i, 261–80, first published in *American Philosophical Quarterly* 15 (1978), 37–46.

—— 'Scorekeeping in a Language Game', in *Philosophical Papers,* vol. i (Oxford: Oxford University Press, 1983), 233–49, first published in the *Journal of Philosophical Logic* 8 (1979), 339–59.

Livingston, Sonia and Magdalena Bober, 'UK Children Go On-Line: Final Report of Key Project Findings', London School of Economics, April 2005 http://www.children-go-online.net/

Lloyd, Elisabeth, 'Pre-Theoretical Assumptions in Evolutionary Explanations of Female Sexuality', *Philosophical Studies* 69 (1993), 139–53.

—— *The Case of the Female Orgasm: Bias in the Science of Evolution* (Cambridge, Mass.: Harvard University Press, 2005).

Lloyd, Genevieve, *The Man of Reason: 'Male' and 'Female' in Western Philosophy* (London: Methuen, 1984).

Longino, Helen E., 'Pornography, Oppression and Freedom: A Closer Look', in *Take Back the Night: Women on Pornography,* ed., Laura Lederer (New York: William Morrow, 1980).

Lovelace, Linda (with Mike McGrady), *Ordeal* (Secaucus, N.J.: Citadel Press, 1980).

McEwan, Ian, *The Innocent* (London: Picador, 1990).

McGowan, Mary Kate, 'Conversational Exercitives and the Force of Pornography', *Philosophy and Public Affairs* 31 (2003), 155–189.

—— 'Conversational Exercitives: Something Else We Do With Our Words', *Linguistics and Philosophy* 27 (2004) pp. 93–111.

—— 'On Pornography: MacKinnon, Speech Acts, and "False" Construction', *Hypatia* 20 (2005) 23–49.

—— with Ishani Maitra, 'Limits of Free Speech: Pornography and the Question of Coverage', *Legal Theory* 13 (2007) 41–68.

Mackenzie, Catriona and Natalie Stoljar, eds., *Relational Autonomy: Feminist Perspectives on Autonomy, Agency and the Social Self* (Oxford: Oxford University Press, 2000).

Mackie, J. L., *Ethics: Inventing Right and Wrong* (Harmondsworth: Penguin, 1990).

MacKinnon, Catharine, *Feminism Unmodified* (Cambridge, Mass.: Harvard University Press, 1987).

—— *Toward a Feminist Theory of the State* (Cambridge, Mass.: Harvard University Press, 1989).

—— *Only Words* (Cambridge, Mass.: Harvard University Press, 1993).

—— *Are Women Human? And Other International Dialogues* (Cambridge, Mass.: Belnap Press, 2006).

McMillan, Carol, *Women, Reason and Nature* (Princeton, NJ: Princeton University Press, 1982).

Maimonides, Moses, *The Guide for the Perplexed,* trans. M. Friedländer (New York, Pardes Publishing House, 1946).

Mahon, James, 'Kant and Maria von Herbert: Reticence vs. Deception', *Philosophy* 81 (2006), 417–44.

Maines, Rachel, *The Technology of Orgasm: 'Hysteria,' the Vibrator, and Women's Sexual Satisfaction* (Baltimore, Md. and London: Johns Hopkins University Press, 1999).

Maitra, Ishani, 'Silencing Speech', forthcoming.

—— with Mary Kate McGowan, 'Limits of Free Speech: Pornography and the Question of Coverage', *Legal Theory* 13 (2007), 41–68.

Malamuth, Neil M., Tamara Addison and Mary Koss, 'Pornography and Sexual Aggression: Are there Reliable Effects and Can We Understand Them?', *Annual Review of Sex Research* 11 (2000), 26–91.

Martin, Nicole, 'BT Blocks 20,000 Attempts a Day to Access Child Porn', *Daily Telegraph* (London), 21 July, 2004.

Matsuda, Mari, Charles R. Lawrence III, Richard Delgado, and Kimberlè Williams Crenshaw, *Words that Wound: Critical Race Theory, Assaultive Speech and the First Amendment* (Boulder, Co.: Westview Press, 1993).

—— 'Public Response to Racist Speech', in *Words that Wound*, eds., Matsuda et al. (Boulder, Co.: Westview Press, 1993), 17–51.

Meese, Edward (Chair), *Report of the Attorney General's Commission on Pornography* (Washington, D.C.: United States Government Printing Office, 1986).

Michelman, Frank, 'Conceptions of Democracy in American Constitutional Argument: The Case of Pornography Regulation', *Tennessee Law Review* 56 (1989) 291–318.

Mill, J. S., *On Liberty* (1859), in *On Liberty and Other Writings*, ed., Stefan Collini (Cambridge: Cambridge University Press, 1989).

—— 'On Liberty', in *J. S. Mill, Utilitarianism and Other Writings*, ed., Mary Warnock (NY: New American Library, 1962).

Miller, Henry, *Tropic of Capricorn* (New York: Grove Press, 1961).

Millett, Kate, *Sexual Politics* (Garden City, NY: Doubleday, 1970).

Minneapolis City Council, *Pornography and Sexual Violence: Evidence of the Links* (London: Everywoman, 1988), transcript of *Public Hearings on Ordinances to Add Pornography as Discrimination Against Women*, Committee on Government Operations (12–13 Dec., 1983).

Nagel, Thomas, 'Sexual Perversion', in *Mortal Questions* (Cambridge: Cambridge University Press, 1991).

Nelson, Edward C., 'Pornography and Sexual Aggression', in Maurice Yaffé and Edward Nelson, eds., *The Influence of Pornography on Behaviour* (London: Academic Press, 1982).

Nussbaum, Martha, *Love's Knowledge: Essays on Philosophy and Literature* (Oxford: Oxford University Press, 1990).

—— 'Objectification', *Philosophy and Public Affairs* 24 (1995), 249–91.

—— 'The Professor of Parody', *New Republic* 220 (February 1999), 37–45.

Oakley, Justin, 'A Critique of Kantian Arguments against Emotions as Moral Motives', *History of Philosophy Quarterly* 7 (1990), 441–59.

O'Neill, Onora, *Constructions of Reason: Explorations of Kant's Practical Philosophy* (Cambridge: Cambridge University Press, 1989).

Papadaki, Evangelia, 'Sexual Objectification: From Kant to Contemporary Feminism', *Contemporary Political Theory* 6 (2007), 330–48.

Parent, W. A., 'A Second Look at Pornography and the Subordination of Women', *Journal of Philosophy* (1990), 205–11.

Paul, Pamela, *Pornified: How Pornography is Transforming Our Lives, Our Relationships, Our Families* (New York: Henry Holt, 2005).

Perry, Ruth, *The Celebrated Mary Astell: An Early English Feminist* (Chicago: University of Chicago Press, 1986).

Post, Robert, ed., *Censorship and Silencing: Practices of Cultural Regulation* (Los Angeles, Cal.: Getty Research Institute, 1998).

Proust, Marcel, *Remembrance of Things Past*, trans. C. K. Scott Moncrieff and Terence Kilmartin (London: Chatto and Windus, 1981); *A la recherche du temps perdu* (Paris: Gallimard, 1954).

Rachman, S., 'Sexual Fetishism: An Experimental Analogue', *Psychological Record* 16 (1966), 293–6.

Raz, Joseph, *The Morality of Freedom* (Oxford: Oxford University Press, 1986).

Rosenthal, Robert, and Lenore Jakobson, *Pygmalion in the Classroom* (New York: Holt, Rinehart and Winston, 1968).

Royalle, Candida, 'Porn in the USA', in Drucilla Cornell, ed., *Feminism and Pornography* (Oxford: Oxford University Press), 540–9.

Russell, Bertrand, *The Problems of Philosophy* (1912) (Oxford: Oxford University Press, 1974).

——*Human Knowledge: Its Scope and Limits* (New York: Allen and Unwin, 1948).

Russell, Diana, *Rape in Marriage* (Bloomington: Indiana University Press, 1982).

——'Pornography and Rape: A Causal Model', in Drucilla Cornell, ed., *Feminism and Pornography* (Oxford: Oxford University Press, 2000), 48–92.

Sadurski, Wojciech, 'On "Seeing Speech Through an Equality Lens": A Critique of Egalitarian Arguments for the Suppression of Hate Speech and Pornography', *Oxford Journal of Legal Studies* 16 (1996), 713–23.

Sartre, Jean-Paul, *Being and Nothingness* (1943), trans. Hazel Barnes (London: Methuen, 1966).

Saul, Jennifer M., 'On Treating Things as People: Objectification, Pornography, and the History of the Vibrator', *Hypatia* 21 (2006), 45–61.

——'Pornography, Speech Acts and Context', *Proceedings of the Aristotelian Society* (2006), 229–48.

Scanlon, Thomas, 'A Theory of Freedom of Expression', *Philosophy and Public Affairs* 1 (1972).

Schauer, Frederick, 'Speech and "Speech"—Obscenity and "Obscenity": An Exercise in the Interpretation of Constitutional Language', *Georgetown Law Journal* 67 (1979), 899–933.

——*Free Speech: A Philosophical Enquiry* (Cambridge: Cambridge University Press, 1982).

Schauer, Frederick, 'Causation Theory and the Causes of Sexual Violence', *American Bar Foundation Research Journal* 4 (1987), 737–70.

Schauer, Frederick, 'The Ontology of Censorship', in Robert Post, ed., *Censorship and Silencing: Practices of Cultural Regulation* (Los Angeles, Ca.: Getty Research Institute, 1988).

Schwartz, John, 'Leisure Pursuits of Today's Young Man', *New York Times*, 29 March 2004.

Schwartzman, Lisa, 'Hate Speech, Illocution, and Social Context: A Critique of Judith Butler', *Journal of Social Philosophy* 33 (2002), 421–41.

Scoccia, Danny, 'Can Liberals Support a Ban on Violent Pornography?', *Ethics* 106 (1996), 776–99.

Scruton, Roger, *Sexual Desire: A Philosophical Investigation* (London: Weidenfeld and Nicolson, 1986; reprint, London: Phoenix, 1994).

Searle, John R., *Speech Acts: An Essay in the Philosophy of Language* (Cambridge: Cambridge University Press, 1969).

——— *Expression and Meaning* (Cambridge: Cambridge University Press, 1979).

Segal, Lynne and Mary MacIntosh, eds., *Sex Exposed: Sexuality and the Pornography Debate* (New Brunswick, NJ: Rutgers University Press, 1993).

Skipper, Robert. 'Mill and Pornography', *Ethics* 103 (1993), 726–30.

Soble, Alan, 'Bad Apples: Feminist Politics and Feminist Scholarship', *Philosophy of the Social Sciences* 29 (1999), 354–88.

Spender, Dale, *Women of Ideas and What Men Have Done to Them* (London: Routledge and Kegan Paul, 1982).

Sperber, D., D. Premack, and A. J. Premack, (eds.), *Causal Cognition: A Multidisciplinary Approach* (Oxford: Clarendon Press, 1994).

Strawson, P. F., 'Intention and Convention in Speech Acts', *Philosophical Review* 73 (1964), 439–60.

——— 'Freedom and Resentment', in *Freedom and Resentment* (London: Methuen, 1974), 1–25.

Strossen, Nadine, *Defending Pornography: Free Speech, Sex, and the Fight for Women's Rights* (New York: Scribner, 1995).

Sunstein, Cass, 'Pornography and the First Amendment', *Duke Law Journal* (1986), 589–627.

——— Review of *Defending Pornography*, by Nadine Strossen, *The New Republic*, 9 January, 1995.

——— *Democracy and the Problem of Free Speech* (New York: The Free Press 1993; 1995).

Ten, C. L., *Crime, Guilt and Punishment* (Oxford: Oxford University Press, 1987).

Thornton, M. T., 'Rape and Mens Rea', in Kai Nielsen, and Steven C. Patten, eds., New Essays in Ethics and Public Policy, Canadian Journal of Philosophy, suppl. vol. 8 (1982).

Tribe, Laurence H., American Constitutional Law, 2nd edn. (Mineola, NY: Foundation Press, 1988).

Vadas, Melinda, 'A First Look at the Pornography/Civil Rights Ordinance: Could Pornography Be the Subordination of Women?', Journal of Philosophy 84 (1987), 487–511.

_____ 'The Manufacture-for-use of Pornography and Women's Inequality', Journal of Political Philosophy 13 (2005), 174–93.

Vance, Carole, ed., Pleasure and Danger: Exploring Female Sexuality (London: Routledge and Kegan Paul, 1984).

Velleman, David, The Possibility of Practical Reason (Oxford: Clarendon Press, 2000).

Wallis, Claudia, 'Onward Women!', Time, 4 December 1989.

Walton, Kendall, Mimesis as Make-Believe (Cambridge, Mass.: Harvard University Press, 1990).

Warshaw, Robin, I Never Called it Rape: The Ms. Report on Recognizing, Fighting, and Surviving Date and Acquaintance Rape (New York: Harper and Rowe, 1988).

Welles, Orson (director), The War of the Worlds, Mercury Theater of the Air, broadcast on CBS, 30 October 1938.

Wells, H. G., The War of the Worlds (1898), (London and New York: Penguin, 2005).

West, Caroline, 'The Free Speech Argument against Pornography', Canadian Journal of Philosophy 33 (2003), 391–422.

_____ 'Pornography and Censorship', Stanford Encyclopedia of Philosophy, ed., Edward Zalta, http://plato.stanford.edu/

_____ with David Braddon-Mitchell, 'What is Free Speech?', The Journal of Political Philosophy 12 (2004), 437–60.

Wieland, Nellie, 'Linguistic Authority and Convention in a Speech Act Analysis of Pornography', Australasian Journal of Philosophy 85 (2007), 435–56.

Williams, Bernard, 'Deciding to Believe', in Problems of the Self (Cambridge: Cambridge University Press, 1973).

_____ 'Drawing Lines', (review of MacKinnon's Only Words), London Review of Books, 16, no. 9 (1994), 9–10.

_____ (chair), Report of the Committee on Obscenity and Film Censorship. Cmnd. 7772 (London: Her Majesty's Stationery Office, 1979).

Williamson, Timothy, Knowledge and its Limits (Oxford: Oxford University Press, 2000).

Winterson, Jeanette, *Written on the Body* (London: Jonathan Cape, 1992).

Wittgenstein, Ludwig, *Philosophical Investigations*, trans. G. E. M. Anscombe (Oxford: Blackwell, 1958).

Wolf, Naomi, *The Beauty Myth: How Images of Beauty are Used against Women* (London: Vintage, 1991).

Wolf, Susan, 'Moral Saints', *The Journal of Philosophy* 79 (1982), 419–39.

Wollstonecraft, Mary, *A Vindication of the Rights of Woman* (1792), ed., M. B. Kramnick (Harmondsworth: Penguin, 1992).

Wyre, Ray, 'Pornography and Sexual Violence: Working with Sex Offenders', in *Pornography: Women, Violence and Civil Liberties,* ed., Catherine Itzin (Oxford: Oxford University Press, 1992).

Yaffé, Maurice and Edward Nelson, eds., *The Influence of Pornography on Behaviour* (London: Academic Press, 1982).

Index